P9-AQA-436

Human Behaviour and World Politics

Human Behavior and World Politics

RALPH PETTMAN

ST. MARTIN'S PRESS NEW YORK

St. Martin's Press, Inc., 175 Fifth Avenue, New York, N.Y. 10010
Printed in Great Britain
Library of Congress Catalog Card Number: 75-10759
First published in the United States of America in 1975

Contents

Preface

The contemporary academic study of world politics is a very diverse one. I am particularly concerned here with that considerable part of it which in a loose sense represents the 'behaviouralist' school. By 'behaviouralism' I mean the fashion of analysis that flowered in the 1950s and 1960s, principally in the United States, on the strength of three distinct but interconnected ideas: that there should be a scientific, self-consciously theoretical approach to the study of politics; that the study of politics should be founded upon the study of human behaviour; and that the study of politics can be reduced to the study of external, observable phenomena that regularly recur and can be quantitatively assessed. Each of these interests is reflected in recent fashions in the field of 'international relations', and is discussed in turn in what lies below. Despite the current critique of the behaviouralist neglect of matters of value, norms or ends, its preoccupation with 'theory', with the causes and contexts of human action, and with the empirical analysis of patterns of conflict and war, are of perennial concern.

After several years' teaching and research in the field I have come to appreciate the need for a study that combines a sufficient breadth of transdisciplinary concerns with a proper regard for the theoretical and analytical endeavours against which these interests proceed. I have tried to meet that need here, as far at least as a single volume might permit. The work is introductory, but it is not in this sense either elementary or complete. Rather it attempts to organise a wide variety of ideas that these might be brought to bear in a comparatively novel way upon the study of global affairs. It introduces topics seldom considered in works of this kind, and makes a sustained attempt to break down the barriers that continue to prevent the inter-disciplinary understanding of politics at the most comprehensive of levels. It summarises what, at several important points, is a scattered body of literature, difficult to compare because of its ill-coordinated character. I have made an effort to render this material more accessible to the student and specialist alike.

My thanks are due to several people who at one time and another read and commented upon sections of the manuscript: Michael Leifer, William Brugger, Norman Wintrop, Norman Feather, Gina Geffen, and Leon Lack; and to Lin Smyth, who typed the separate drafts. They are not solely responsible for the shortcomings herein. Michael Banks first convinced me that the behaviouralists had useful things to say, and I owe him something for that. I would also like to thank the lady in my life, Jan P., who sat on the children and suffered the curtailment of her own research commitments that this work should appear. I dedicate it, with my love, to her.

RALPH PETTMAN

Research Fellow,
Department of International Relations,
Australian National University

CHAPTER 1

The Academic Heritage

The following study is an attempt to map some of the major features of the modern field of international relations, using not the established historical approach, but drawing instead upon the substantive results of diverse social and natural sciences, and upon the work of contemporary theorists, who have developed new analytic and quantitative ways of describing and explaining important aspects of global affairs. It will soon become apparent how liberally I have interpreted the scope of world political concerns. This is an important feature of what follows and it deserves some scrutiny at the outset. Firstly, however, though it seems far from a novel strategy, I shall begin with the question of academic antecedents and discuss briefly the history of the study of world affairs,* how that study has changed over time, and the sort of direction in which it now seems to be moving. What one talks about this year in the field is not what one would have talked about five, ten or fifteen years ago, and it is certainly not what will be talked about in five, ten or fifteen years time. The rate at which the focus shifts seems to be accelerating too, and a work on theories of human behaviour and world politics like this one already has an antique ring to it as developments in the discipline promise to bypass such preoccupations, at least as they are understood at the moment.

Discussions of interstate relations have venerable antecedents. From the time of Thucydides or Kautilya, through the writings of Machiavelli, Dante, Rousseau, Kant and Clausewitz, among others, we can draw out the threads of a continuing concern with affairs *between* states, rather than those only *within* them. Of course the conception and the reality of just what a state is

* I shall be concerned with only the non-Marxist tradition here.

has also changed over time, and the 'state' each of these individuals talked about is not what we would necessarily recognise today as a collective actor on the world stage.

Given this tradition, why did E. H. Carr write in 1939,[1] just before the 'Second World War',[2] that the science of international politics was still in its infancy? The reasons are historical, it seems, and the 'First World War' is the watershed. Before the First World War the study of international relations was a comparatively marginal affair, and one has to pick over the great middens of classical scholarship to find those serviceable bits and pieces that might muster as a hypothesis or a prescription about world affairs. After the First World War, however, a substantial body of literature on the subject begins to emerge. In a pointed and characteristically chauvinistic statement, F. Neal and B. Hamlett have argued that: 'international relations is an American invention dating from the time after World War I when the American intellectual community discovered the world. Like most American essays in regard to the world, it has been enthusiastic, well-financed, faddist, nationally-oriented, and creating more problems than it solves.'[3]

Before the First World War nearly all ideas about the global system were neatly filed away under the box for international law, or diplomatic history, or the parent discipline of political thought itself. After 1918, however, a generation of scholars and writers, appalled by the horrors of the conflict just past, began to scrutinise interstate politics in systematic terms. They remained for the most part with discussing international law and organisation, or with the currents of contemporary affairs, and they were predominantly utopian about international morality and the chances of maintaining peace. The general effect of their utopian predilections was to reinforce the status quo, to justify, that is, the post-war position in Europe as the best possible disposition of affairs. The League of Nations and the rules of interstate conduct were depicted as the principal means of managing world stability, and it took the Second World War to point out that the utopian morality so generally espoused was that of the haves against the have-nots, and that there was no natural harmony of interests between men that the 'truth' about their affairs could somehow reveal and render acceptable to all.[4]

E. H. Carr's *The Twenty Years' Crisis* was the forerunner of the anti-utopian tide. The years immediately after the Second World War, not surprisingly under the circumstances, came to be dominated by the anti-utopians, by the 'realists' – those who saw the time between the wars as characterised by an 'almost total neglect of the factor of power'.[5] The utopian phase of the study of international politics was over. The intellectual structures that were advanced to prevent another violent struggle of this kind, and which made up the bulk of the kiddytot literature on 'international relations' as such, had been severely undermined by a gross dose of 'realpolitik', by ruthless, dedicated men with armies, economic might, propagandist zeal, and a will to win. They made nonsense of utopian and moral restraints. The academic palm passed to 'power' and to those who saw as their key concern the spelling out of its various components and effects. The main textbook in the field became Hans J. Morgenthau's *Politics among Nations*,[6] subtitled 'the struggle for power and peace', and it survived for many years as a standard reference work. In some respects, and for good reasons, it has never been supplanted. The realist position carried considerable weight – the politics of the cold war, the advent of thermo-nuclear weapons, the vast military and industrial complexes that grew up to service the security of the great nations – each predisposed a power-centred interpretation of international affairs. It was many years before the power-political approach was exposed for the disguised ideology it really was, and its exclusivist and objective aura laid to rest.

Ten years ago, then, a course in 'international relations' would have looked something like this:

1. A historical discussion of the antecedents, the origins and development of the contemporary state system.
2. The elements of international law, of diplomatic practice and international organisation.
3. Power politics – the economic, military and cultural components of state power – and war.
4. Colonialism and the retreat of empire. Perhaps revolutionary insurgency.
5. A run-down of recent diplomatic history, and the foreign policies of the major powers.
6. Political geography and political demography, that is, the way states and their populations are distributed across the face of

the land, and the effect that distribution has upon interstate affairs.

It is instructive to compare this list with economic theories of world politics and with the chapter headings given in the contents list of the present work. And it is interesting to speculate what such a list might look like in ten years' time.

In the late fifties and early sixties a movement gathered strength in the social sciences in general, in the academic field of politics, and the field of American academic politics in particular, that was dedicated to the *scientific* study of the subject. In an age dominated by scientific technology it is no wonder that students of politics eventually looked to the natural sciences – to the methods of physics and chemistry for example – for clues to help them describe and explain political phenomena. The leading shoot of this movement became known as 'behaviouralism', not to be confused with 'behaviourism' and the stimulus–response experiments performed by B. F. Skinner and J. B. Watson in psychology. 'Behaviouralism', the study of political behaviour whether within states or between them, was the attempt to apply many of the techniques and methods of the natural sciences to political phenomena in the hope that increased rigour in the way facts were handled would generate better, more general and more reliable statements about the subject than had heretofore been the case. As 'utopianism' had once given way to 'realism', so 'realism' and its single-factor account of international politics in terms of power gave way to 'behaviouralism' and the search for a science of world affairs.*

The history of the behavioural movement in international relations is most conveniently traced through four articles: the first, by Robert Dahl, appeared in the *American Political*

* This second succession was not as neat or as simple as such a truncated statement might infer. The Idealist/Realist debate centred on the *substantive* issue of 'power' and the predominance of its place in world affairs. The Realist/Scientist debate was somewhat different, however, since it was in considerable part (though not only) a *methodological* one. Thus Realism 'gave way' to Behaviouralism in that the pursuit of a 'scientific' methodology came to predominate in the discipline as a whole; but in substantive terms Realism remained very much alive and Realists could readily be Behaviouralists too, and many students of international politics came to exhibit just such complementary concerns. Further, the subsequent development of a post-behavioural 'utopianism' did not exclude behaviouralist methodological preoccupations as well.

Science Review in 1967;[7] the second, by Hedley Bull, appeared in *World Politics* in 1966;[8] the third, by Michael Banks, was published in the *Yearbook of World Affairs* for the same year, 1966;[9] and the fourth, by David Easton, in the *American Political Science Review* for 1969.[10] The end date clearly sets the ebb point of the behavioural wave, and it simply remains to sort through the wrack and rubbish left behind and to assess what look like the solid gains.

To begin with Dahl, and I quote him: 'Historically speaking the behavioral approach was a protest movement within political science . . . a number of political scientists, mainly Americans . . . shared a strong sense of dissatisfaction with the achievements of conventional political science, particularly through historical, philosophical and the descriptive and intuitional approaches.' They believed that

> additional methods and approaches either existed or could be developed that would help to provide political science with empirical propositions and theories of a systematic sort, tested by closer, more direct and more rigorously controlled observations of political events. At a minimum, then, those who were sometimes called 'Behaviorists' or 'Behavioralists' shared a mood: a mood of skepticism about the current intellectual attainments of political science, a mood of sympathy toward 'scientific' modes of investigation and analysis, a mood of optimism about the possibilities of improving the study of politics.[11]

The result, he concludes, was an attempt to 'improve our understanding of politics by seeking to explain the empirical aspects of political life by means of methods, theories and criteria of proof that are acceptable according to the canons, conventions and assumptions of modern empirical science'.[12] The talk of 'moods' here is instructive – the line between the behaviouralists and the non-behaviouralists separated optimists and pessimists, and this is often the only clear way of identifying which particular camp a scholar belonged to.

What is 'science'? Wherein lies its magic? Why the often uncritical embrace it was accorded here? Perhaps the best way to answer these questions is to press the distinction between science as *substance*, science as *method*, and science as *aim*, that is, the distinction between the intellectual product, the intellectual process, and the intellectual goal.

SCIENCE AS SUBSTANCE

As substance 'science' is a huge success, the most spectacular and conspicuous ornament of man's new brain.[13] The products of science have contributed knowledge relevant to politics, most particularly about the mechanism of mind, and via psychology much of that knowledge is readily available to students of political phenomena though not so often employed by them there. The transdisciplinary focus of the present study is one attempt to rectify this neglect. But it is not so much the empirical findings themselves that have attracted the diffidence and deference of students of political behaviour, but the scope and rigour of those findings over the whole range of natural events, including those that constitute man. And this has led many to enquire about prerequisites, and of course, methods as well.

Success seems assured, Thomas Kuhn asserts, once a field of search acquires what he calls a 'paradigm', once the majority of its searchers cease to scrutinise events at random and take a common body of belief for granted, once they accept as sufficient the status of some particular body of scientific practice – its laws, theories, experiments and instruments – and allow it to guide their own work and furnish them with criteria of relevance for further exploration.[14] Shared paradigms liberate the committed searcher from fundamental speculation about first principles and basic concepts, and permit that rigid, highly directed enquiry into preselected phenomena which explains much about scientific progress and its cumulative quality. They are universally recognised scientific achievements, Kuhn says, that provide for a while model problems and convincing solutions to a community of practitioners.*

There is something circular in this, with success waiting upon manifest success. However, the circularity is apparent not real. The emergence of a paradigm with the cumulative power it can confer, the crucial index here of scientific maturity, depends upon

* T. Kuhn, *The Structure of Scientific Revolution*, 2nd ed. (University of Chicago Press, 1970) ch. 2. Kuhn's use of his own concept is not as consistent as one would like. Margaret Masterman identifies twenty-one

the agreement of practitioners, and this, at least in the beginning, must be conferred, it cannot be assumed. Old intractable problems must seem to be solved, precision must be enhanced, new predictive capacities must be demonstrated to the satisfaction of most if not all the practitioners in the field, and non-logical and aesthetic criteria such as 'simplicity' and 'elegance' must be satisfied as well. Once established such ideas promise immediate progress, but at a tyrannical price. They are the framework upon which further research is hung; their validity is established and scientific failure is apt to rebound on the scientist rather than the paradigm. The construction of this first order, consistent within itself and with the experimental or observed facts known at the time, may well come too early, selecting subsequent observations and obscuring more important truths which are then never revealed or remain hidden much longer than they might have been. But science knows no other way. Only in those critical and revolutionary periods when anomalies have become acute, the paradigm is breaking down, and another is taking its place, is enquiry likely to return to matters of first principle.

'In its normal state . . . a scientific community is an immensely efficient instrument for solving the problems or puzzles that its paradigms define. Furthermore, the result of solving those problems must inevitably be progress . . .',[15] at least of a kind, though the relative nature of these paradigms precludes a definition of such progress in terms of the forward projection of any one of them. Progress is also evident in the abnormal state of theoretical turmoil and paradigm change. Thus one can argue that despite the difficulties involved in comparing the new with the old, cumulation carries across the Gestalt divide of paradigm change, where practitioners can either 'see' the alternative or

different sense in which it is used, and hints at more. She compresses these into three main types – metaphysical or meta-paradigms, sociological paradigms, and artefacts or construct paradigms. The last type is the fundamental one, she argues, for with it one can solve the puzzles of normal science, and so practise it. This practical aspect of Kuhn's basic idea usefully counter-balances the 'current philosophic bias . . . towards examining what is conceptual', at the expense of considering what scientists actually do. M. Masterman, 'The Nature of a Paradigm', in *Criticism and the Growth of Knowledge*, ed. I. Lakatos and A. Musgrave (London: Cambridge University Press, 1970).

they cannot, and what becomes accepted *after* the process of paradigm replacement is complete is better than, not just different from, what was known before. However, this does not support any absolutist notion of ultimate truth that science is inevitably drawn towards.

Kuhn has been roundly assailed for his conclusions.[16] Most noticeably Paul Feyerabend has seen in his analysis of the way science is done an implicit methodological prescription of an unsavoury sort. Those who would have a social science, for example, are encouraged to cease their debate about first principles and to make the leap to a 'normal science' by collapsing the field of competing theories into one and accepting this as the paradigm for all subsequent study. The effect, however, would be to stifle speculation and to create a conformist body of practitioners who work on detail and no longer on design. We can recognise here something of the behaviouralist recommendations. The effect would probably be pernicious since Feyerabend concludes that knowledge grows not by the 'puzzle-solving activity' of Kuhn, but by 'the active interplay of various tenaciously held views',[17] that only occurs for Kuhn during scientific revolutions. Rather than foreclose the opportunity to generate new views and advance them in a continuous fashion, we should encourage this process, and find the happiness and the fulfilment of the individual therein: '. . . we want a methodology and a set of institutions which enable us to lose as little as possible of what we are capable of doing . . .',[18] and Kuhn's idea of science is not it.

While we may agree that Feyerabend has revealed an anti-humanitarian feature about Kuhn's view, it seems to me that Kuhn has the edge when it comes to depicting realistically how science proceeds. There is a constant tension between the creativity Feyerabend exalts and the constrictions any disciplinary paradigm imposes. The very word 'discipline' implies restraint, and it is, as Kuhn argues, restraint to a purpose. We can and should aspire to Feyerabend's ideal, but in the actual conduct of science we will never realise it because of the foreclosure effect that Kuhn so clearly outlines.

The question that flows from this discussion is: why has the discipline of politics remained so stunted in its scientific growth?

Why has its plethora of competing theoretical assumptions and its multitude of concepts and generalisations failed to converge upon one total paradigm and upon one habit-tradition of puzzle-solving? A number of scholars have in fact attempted to demonstrate that shared assumptions, models and solutions of this kind do exist for the study of politics generally and for world politics in particular – structural-functionalism in comparative government, for example, and power theories in interstate relations – but they seriously over-estimate to my mind the professional acceptance such 'paradigms' have enjoyed. Again, one should not forget the separate tradition of Marxist analysis, and in world politics, the comprehensive theories of imperialism. Here analysts do lay claim to a general explanation or set of explanations with predictive power. To all intents and purposes they share a paradigm, but this paradigm, too, enjoys substantially less than universal acceptance. Why this is so is a question of the nature of the subject-matter as such. The study of physical reality is a different realm of discourse from that of social reality – Marxists and non-Marxists alike can agree on the first principles of the structure of the atom, but not on the condition of man and the workings of society. The one can be externalised with some success; the other proceeds immediately from the social reality one is part of, and simultaneously attempts to define. The 'paradigm' is already an ideology.

The study of politics has remained at the level Masterman calls multi-paradigmatic, that is

> . . . far from there being no paradigm, there are on the contrary too many. (This is the present overall situation in the psychological, social and information sciences.) Here, within the subfield defined by each paradigmatic technique, technology can sometimes become quite advanced, and normal research puzzle-solving can progress. But each subfield as defined by its technique is so obviously more trivial and narrow than the field as defined by intuition, and also the various operational definitions given by the techniques are so grossly discordant with one another, that discussion on fundamentals remains, and long-run progress (as opposed to local progress) fails to occur.[19]

No comprehensive paradigm has emerged capable of encompassing them all; no single insight has solved the puzzles with which politics abounds; and those put forward as performing this function have failed to bring about the collapse of its competitors, and failed to contribute fundamental insights that most practitioners would accept as necessary and sufficient to guide and inform their subsequent research.

SCIENCE AS METHOD

Why then the limited science of political, and hence world political affairs? The answer has been sought in two different directions, and from this point the so-called 'classical' and 'behavioural' positions, the 'philosophic' and 'scientific' stances diverge. The 'behaviouralist' has sought in the exacting methods of the natural sciences the key to their impressive scope. Substantive success, it is said, is the result of a strict and logical process of enquiry, of analytical rather than intuitive techniques, of ethical neutrality, of public and empirical knowledge, and emulating the features of this process in a studied and self-conscious way ought also to ensure more comprehensive and powerful explanations for politics. 'Scientific' use of evidence promises, it is claimed, to cut away the confusion that has characterised political debate for so long, and ought in time to generate the first accepted principles of a successful, paradigmatic 'science'. Questions about the subject-matter of the enquiry and any intrinsic limitations its complexity or its value-laden character may place upon the utility of scientific methods are treated as irrelevant. Such methods are neutral as to intellectual aim, neutral as to whether, that is, we treat of atoms or men for good or ill, and any limitations in practice can only be realised in practice and not pre-determined before we begin.

The 'classicists' have replied that there is nothing new here, that though they have often been to blame for much loose and ill-supported argument, the methods of scientific enquiry are a child of their own. However, the heart of the matter they tend to say lies in the complex, contingent and normative nature of political behaviour. The metaphysical and non-logical assumptions scientists make about the uniform and predictable, or at least probable, quality of the phenomena they study, are inadmissible when we come to explain the performance of human beings.

The behavioural case merits closer consideration. At a minimum, it recommends the application of scientific methods to the subject matter of social science, and it conceives of such methods in an unequivocal way. Independent and dependent variables must be clearly differentiated, their relationship and forms of variance must be specified in precise hypotheses that are empirical, that is, formulated in potentially falsifiable ways and not just as precise statements about the real world. Evidence must be generated, careful observations made, and strict canons of proof applied to all those insights with which analyses of political affairs abound, culling out the ill-conceived to locate a hard core of substantiated theory. At least that is the hope, and to say that the more precise the techniques that are applied the more trivial the findings are likely to be hardly deters the enterprising from their optimistic end.

Ultimately, however, rules of search are not enough. Even if one admits no logical distinction between the phenomena of political science and the phenomena of natural science, methods that are theoretically applicable to politics involve in practice difficulties so great as to impose real limits on truly 'scientific' exploration in the discipline. If one argues a fundamental distinction in subject matter as well, the difficulties are compounded. The behaviouralist, then, cannot rest upon the minimal position of method and most of them do not. The inability of methodological measures to uncover unique and generalised substantive conclusions of themselves soon becomes apparent in social enquiry. But then 'science' is not just a search for systematic and organised knowledge, it is a desire for explanations, a perspective as well as a process, a generalising mood, an attempt to outline in the end general theories applicable to all phenomena. This is the last of the three categories introduced above, science as *goal* and purpose, and in reality it comes first.

SCIENCE AS AIM

This purpose – the desire to describe the universe in an orderly language that enables us to cast forward with some measure of confidence as to what we might expect – is one which most classicists would share. They are equally prone to ask, whatever their prescriptive dispositions might be, of what larger pattern any example of human behaviour is simply one particular instance, and they likewise seek propositions about recurrent phenomena that survive under empirical test over time. They are much less confident, however, that truly generalised propositions will have more than marginal relevance, or that human phenomena are ultimately reducible to a strictly limited number of precise theorems with precise predictive power. They will still look for regularities, and they will still make meaningful generalisations, with explicitly stated premises, but they are unlikely to subscribe to the idea that some fundamental simple order or pattern or set of orders or patterns underlines social behaviour. Such patterns as do exist they expect to be of a less elevated kind. This is not to depict social behaviour as random, impulsive, occurring for no reason and therefore unknowable. It is usually either a more modest assessment of the explanatory potential of the subject-matter, or plain pessimism, or a specific attack on the moral desirability of a generalising imperative at all.[20]

The debate about the relevance to social research of a generalising scientific consciousness leads back to the debate over the propriety of method. Again, though the classicist might accept the wisdom in specifying units of analysis, identifying relevant variables, framing testable propositions and subjecting them to an unambiguous test, he might well question the precision with which key concepts can be made measurable, the precision with which data is quantified, the precision with which categories are defined and models are constructed, or the desirability of any or all such operations. He would contest *a priori* the claim that universal theory is a conceivable, practical or good end, and he would point up the impossibility of measuring all the relevant variables, or ultimately of rendering findings independent of the observer and the judgements he has had to make.

Why is this so? Why can natural science assume a close correspondence between regularity, 'significance', and precise method, and social science cannot? Why, if we confine ourselves to strict standards of verification, can very little of theoretical rigour be said about human society, as has so far been the case? The answer has already been introduced above. The important questions in world politics for example, such as the causes of war, or the attributes of the international system and their effects, respond badly to scientific treatment. The ladder of generalisation, the rungs of theory that one can ascend to encompass and explain more and more, does not reach very far. The pervasiveness of complexity and change, the difficulties of controlled experiment, of separating subject and object from cause and effect, of rendering significant variables in quantitative terms – all undermine the possibility of 'scientific' precision.

There is nevertheless a behavioural defence on every point. For experiment one substitutes careful simulation. Quantification can be hedged about and qualified to approximate reality. The process by which analysis itself can intrude upon the events being analysed becomes in turn a fit object for dispassionate scrutiny. The complex and fortuitous quality of events is a challenge, not a source of despair, an opportunity and a motivating force. None of these defences, however, holds the discussion to matters of method alone, and stops the limitations implicit in a subject matter leaking back into the debate. Simulation does not confront it. Qualified quantification has so far failed to measure it. Rigorous methodology is an elaborate ambush set to surround social phenomena but unable in the end to capture their essential characteristics.

Where does this leave Dahl? The appeal to 'science', as he depicted it, was a reaction against a tradition of enquiry couched in descriptive, historical, institutional and discursive terms. It sought to build the generalising aims and the rigorous methods of science into the body of social research, that is, to develop empirical propositions and systematic theories about social phenomena subject to direct and strictly controlled observation and test. The generalising aims and the rigorous methods were meant to initiate a political science of substantive success. There were, however, immediate and obvious problems. At the level of group behaviour it became very difficult to know what to exclude, when and where to eliminate intervening variables in favour of ones that always apply. And, at the individual level, the uniqueness of each human unit and the way that 'anticipated consequences are major causes of action' made scientific analysis, as Quincy Wright early observed, 'peculiarly difficult'.[21]

The further question occurs: are scientific methods and aims, developed to explain and peculiarly successful in dealing with less animated phenomena, wholly *in*appropriate to the study of social events? The answer is clearly: no. The spirit of scientific enquiry – explicit and self-sustaining – is just as applicable to social and normative questions as to atoms or animal cells. And science-as-substance, as a set of tested observations, has much to contribute to normative judgements and political debate. Values may choose and interpret fact, but fact informs value, and scientific facts can contribute a good deal to the quality of any political argument's empirical justifications. It is not unrealistic to posit a 'normative political philosophy, basing its mode of thought on the criteria of science so far as it can and taking its content from the corpus of scientific knowledge where that is possible'. Further:

> It is the function of political science to state the terms of the political world man has built and the goal of the political philosopher to criticize that world in terms of another 'world' that is an intellectual construct. Science can help establish the necessary properties of that world against the contingent, and this is important since necessity is beyond criticism, and it can contribute substantially to our total conception of what the human condition might be.[22]

There is one other feature of behaviouralism, apart from its preoccupations with science, which I have already introduced but would like to reiterate briefly here. This feature is particularly important in international relations because it represents a shift in focus away from the assumptions implicit in that disciplinary label, away from the traditional unit of analysis – the state – to the levels of analysis above and below it. Under the influence of behaviouralism attention has been moved upwards to the whole system, to the globe, and to politics as global politics and only in part as interstate politics. And at the same time attention has been moved downwards to the individual and the way he or she behaves, individually or in groups. States and the groups within them, world organisations of every kind, are made up, after all, of thinking, believing, acting human beings, and one way of describing such organisations is to look upon them as behaviour systems, that is, as individuals related in certain regular ways. These patterns of behaviour can readily be made the focus of enquiry, allowing the formal structure of the group-body itself to emerge therefrom. This is not to deny the reality of institutions, but merely to assert what is self-evident – that they do not exist apart from the persons who inhabit them and whose expectations define social roles.

This change in focus reflects a change in the definition of politics, away from the *nouns* like government, power, policy, and influence, towards the *verbs* and the acts of governing, bargaining, obeying, oppressing, fighting and fearing. Politics is seen as 'transactionalism',[23] where the basic unit of analysis is some social atom of an on-going relational sort within its environmental context. There is a frivolous parallel here with theology, where god has suffered a similar transition from noun to verb. I god, you god, we all god. 'Godness' becomes a quality of moral conduct, a pattern of behaviour, something toward which human beings aspire, rather than a formative and powerful influence from which they and the universe derive.

On the level of the individual, political behaviour is only one aspect of total behaviour. Our political acts are usually inextricable from what we do out of social, economic or cultural motives. Each aspect of our lives affects the others, and therefore differences in political behaviour should be sought in the whole human being, and the whole explanation leads as already discussed to diverse other disciplines.

The best-known classical attack on the behavioural pursuit of a 'science' of world politics came from Hedley Bull,[24] and so trenchant was it that two leading American academics, Klaus Knorr and James Rosenau,[25] felt obliged to assemble a book of articles by those prepared to discuss and confound it. Bull's criticisms were not from the 'realist' tradition that the behavioural revolt supplanted,* but from the historico-philosophical-legal tradition that came before realism and lives on still in a defiant fashion. In essence Bull argued, along lines already pursued, that rigorous proof of general statements about world politics can only be achieved if those statements are insignificant or deal in trivia. Scientific purity is attained only by avoiding the

* Or, rather, ran beside.

profound questions that we really ought to ask. And when we do ask such questions, our use of evidence is necessarily less than scientific or strict.

In particular, Bull has made a number of charges against behaviouralism, all but one of which can be dismissed as misplaced. For example, he has argued that where international-relations 'scientists' have been successful they have in fact employed the traditional approach, rather than their own exalted methods. To accept the validity of this criticism one has to accept Bull's own criteria of success and significance, and these are at best debatable. Further, Bull has argued that political 'scientists' are unlikely to make cumulative progress of the sort to which they aspire. This can readily be construed as an empirical question, and though Bull may well be correct, it is not likely to stop behaviouralists from making the attempt. Here lies the line already alluded to between optimism and pessimism. Bull goes on to attack model-building as a positive disservice to the subject. His particular points, however, are those familiar to most practitioners in the field and are usually taken into consideration there. He also takes to task those 'scientific' works he sees as distorted by a 'fetish for measurement', a fair complaint in itself but one behaviouralists are also well aware of and which they actively negate, where appropriate, in their own defence.

Despite such ready replies, a critical point persists in the paradoxical relationship between strict procedures for verification and the ability of an analyst to come to grips with questions of political and moral substance, and on this Bull is not easily deterred.

The best and most modest statement of the behavioural approach still remains that by Michael Banks, and he replies with conviction to the 'classicist' assault. The behavioural approach, he argues, was both wider and narrower than traditional analyses. It was *narrower* in that it sought regularities and patterns of behaviour – it was not so concerned with the unique and the novel. He refers here to what I have already called the generalising imperative, the reflex response that asks of what general proposition is any particular phenomenon just a single case.[26] Only from general propositions was it felt that useful explanations with some predictive power would flow. The behavioural approach was also *broader*, however, in that it pursued a 'powerful, if undefined vision' of a 'general theory' applicable to all human behaviour, including the political.[27] This almost metaphysical ideal it pursued 'without reference to the existing division of labour between the various sub-disciplines of the social sciences . . .';[28] it was non- or trans-disciplinary rather than inter-disciplinary, and it encompassed whatever it saw as necessary to the furtherance of political explanation. As a result, a most diverse body of information came to be applied in behavioural analysis. It did not replace the traditional approach, Banks argues, but sought to challenge old assumptions and introduce new ideas and new techniques into political research. It was exploratory, though for all its academic verve it failed to uncover much that was truly new. Where it was precise it was very small-scale. Where it was broad, it dissolved into conceptual frameworks, ways of looking, and it contributed no more than pre-scientific approaches had done to the on-going fund of insight and evidence. Despite its conspicuous inadequacies, however, the vision persists, and it is a very powerful one.

In 1969 David Easton declared the end of the behavioural revolution and the beginning of a new era in the study of politics. He outlined in his presidential address to the American Political Science Association the substance of an overwhelming attack on the behavioural movement. To return briefly to Dahl, we find him concluding eight years before that the attempt to increase the scientific quality of political studies would inevitably be judged by results. I quote him again:

> If closer attention to methodological niceties, to problems of observation and verification, to the task of giving operational meaning to political concepts, to quantification and testing, to eliminating unproductive intervening variables, to sources of data, hypotheses, and theory in the other social sciences; if all of these activities do not yield explanations of some important aspects of politics that are more thoroughly verified, less open to methodological objections, richer in implications for further explanation, and more useful in meeting the perennial problems of political life than the explanations they are intended to replace; . . . then we may confidently expect that the attempt to build an empirical science of politics will lose all the impetus in the next generation that it gained in the last.[29]

The generational reassessment did indeed take place, and in Kuhnian terms we can readily understand why. Those practitioners who blithely followed academic fashion without clearly examining the paradigmatic premises they chose to accept built a 'normal science' upon a bed of sand. 'In the end phoney scientific normal-research lines collapse, or fail to yield any results, or topple, or evaporate – or so one hopes; and so in the past . . . it has finally proved.'[30]

The *post*-behavioural revolution gained further impetus, however, from the felt need for scholastic relevance and social action. Whereas Bull's traditionalist response was to deny the very possibility of a science of politics, the post-behavioural revolution has depicted even the attempt at such a study as an academic obscenity – spurious science, disguised politics, with repugnant moral sensibilities. The motivating force was again war, this time in Vietnam. From 'utopianism', through 'realism' and 'scientism', we come now to 'consciencism'. The horrors of that conflict recalled the discipline to its moral obligations and reasserted the primacy of the conscientious imperative over the generalising one, namely, that substance must precede technique. We should not avoid vital political issues simply because they do not suit our sophisticated tools of analysis. It is better to be vague and well meaning, the post-behaviouralists have argued, than irrelevant, even pernicious, and precise.

To this Easton appended a number of specific charges:

1. That behavioural science conceals an ideology of *empirical conservatism*. By concentrating on description and factual analysis it has conspicuously failed to explain and to understand what is going on in the world, and it has failed thereby, to participate in the drive for needed socio-political change. Quincy Wright much earlier made a similar point:

   Social science . . . assuming the continuity of most human and social relations, makes generalisations which will be valid in the future only so far as fundamental customs and traditions continue. Social scientists, therefore, are likely to have a conservative influence on society because their professional distortion makes them propagandists for the assumptions on which the validity of their work depends.[31]

2. That behavioural research, by dealing so much in abstrac-

tions, must miss many of the brute facts and harsh realities of politics. Its dry technical jargon builds barriers of silence around social needs and human issues that cry out for articulation. Indeed such language may serve merely to disguise under a neutral terminology a value stance of a positively odious sort. Thus, for example, 'adaptation' becomes a pallid synonym for 'pogrom', and talk of 'equilibrium' serves to replace that of 'tyranny'.

3. That any attempt to value freedom as espoused by many behaviouralists must be a deception, and a dangerous one, whatever the integrity of their intent.
4. That academics have a special role to play in protecting the humane values that are the very definition of civilisation, and this duty the behaviouralists conspicuously fail to perform.[32]
5. That to know is to bear the responsibility for action, and the universities, as seats of higher learning, must become part of the political struggle for a better world.

So the circle is closed. From the ethical prescriptions of the legalists and the institutional utopians, we return to the moral imperatives of the post-behavioural world. The detour through 'science' has simply led us back to the starting place. Or has it? Not quite, for cycles never repeat themselves exactly in human affairs, rather spirals ascend, or descend, or dissipate for lack of consequence. Certainly as Easton indicates in his recantation, mankind today is working under the pressure of time – nuclear weapons, population, pollution, resources – all inspire profound fears for the future of homo sapiens, and the label man has given himself may in the end prove to be the final irony. The post-behavioural 'conscience' requires every political scientist to accept the impelling need for relevant knowledge whatever this may mean, and to eschew the received nature of his particular social reality for a more objective statement as to the play of the world. It reaffirms, in fact, very traditional scholastic values.

There is no doubt that American political science spectacularly failed to anticipate the problems it faces today. In a much-quoted statistic, Easton pointed out that of the hundreds of articles in the *American Political Science Review* for the ten years from 1958 to 1968, there were only three on the urban crisis in the United States, only four on its racial conflicts, only one on poverty, and only two on violence. The study of American foreign politics suffered a similar fate. Something was rotten in the state of the union, and the question persists: why?

Firstly, it is argued that the very attempt at science skewed academic vision away from the mud monster of social and global crisis rising before it. This is the gist of Easton's remarks above, and on the whole it is true, I think, though it need not have been. Scientific method, and the results of scientific research conducted in other disciplines, could well have been applied to important and relevant issues. Indeed, it hardly seems too much to say that: 'Science is the only mode of cognition known to man that can produce an appreciation of the objective world . . . [and] a politics based on a scientific appreciation of the objective world is clearly in a better position to change it.'[33] We need all the information we can get, the more accurate and the more generalised the better. But we also need active civilised purposes to which such information can be put, and here science is not enough. To appreciate this *subjective* world we must extend the debate elsewhere, and we must look beyond the methodological imperatives and the intrinsic conservatism of the scientific ethos of its American practitioners, to the scientists themselves and the structure of their profession. Here we find the second explanation for the failure of relevance.

Whose interests, one must ask, did the behavioural movement serve? And who sustained or helped to sustain that behavioural movement?

Given what seems to have been a spontaneous re-direction of academic concerns within the politics discipline, one does not have to cry conspiracy to recognise the selective financial support that led to behaviouralism's predominance. In this way American political science was successfully sidetracked for several crucial years from systematic analysis of many critical issues averse to the American government and to American corporations, and their activities at home and overseas. Those outside the legitimised umbrella suffered mostly maverick status. R. Dahl has been quoted as saying: 'If the foundations had been hostile to the behavioral approach, there can be no doubt that it would have had very rough sledding indeed.'[34] In the same article David Horowitz goes on:

> The emphasis on observable behavior, and the acceptance of the given socio-economic framework as the basis of analysis, together with a scientistic bias against the kind of theoretical probing which calls into question the basis of the status quo order itself, were naturally congenial to the men who put up the millions...[35]

a fact that has led to a system in which the

> prostitution of intellect has become so pervasive and profound that all but a small minority mistake it for academic virtue. The foundations, with their practical monopoly on substantial discretionary funds, have purchased control over the fundamental direction of research and academic energies on a national scale. . . . Even if individual researchers and ideologues are not corrupted – though plenty of them are – the *system* of academic research and ideology formation is. Most academics no more perceive the ideological basis of their work than we smell air or taste water. The politically inoffensive (not neutral) is seen as unbiased, objective, value-free science; a radical orientation stands out as prejudiced, inappropriate and, gravest of all, unprofessional.[36]

This is pungent stuff. The main problem is that its substantiating evidence relies heavily upon innuendo and rhetoric. But then the channels of influence which Horowitz discusses are hegemonic and informal, and far less open to the demonstrable proofs one would like to see. There is still a marked lack, despite recent attempts to make this lack good, of research about the men and the corporate institutions who control the American economy, plan its foreign policy and seek to define its socio-political reality. Such research has global ramifications, for it is the great engine of American scholarship that sets the style for much of the rest of the academic world. It is not unfair, I feel to indict kept minds in this way.

In conclusion, what has 'behaviouralism' left to offer? Two things, if the foregoing argument is correct. One is its transdisciplinary interest in sociology, anthropology, biology and psychology, an interest pursued further here. While assembling such a range of interests may militate against mastering any one of them, at this point 'behaviouralism' and 'consciencism' clearly come together.

The other offering is on the scholarship side of the radical scholarship coin. One may readily allow a radical conscience to ask relevant or important questions, but one should also admit scientific imperatives to the pursuit of their answers. The behavioural approach has fruitfully emphasised the importance of method and the need to build 'theories'. The best radical studies will not abandon science, they will simply put it to better use. And they will not neglect what the exact sciences have to offer in the way of substance and understanding. 'In a field so largely made up of conflicting emotions and symbols, appreciation of the scientific virtues can prevent hasty opinions, ill-considered decisions, and the application of methods unlikely to achieve the ends desired',[37] which is not to deny the need to define and pursue desirable ends, to engage in the endless dialogue which such definition involves, and to pursue the good so defined with due reference to moral debate.

CHAPTER 2

On Method and Against It: The Decision-making Process, 'Linkage' and 'Theories' of Foreign Policy

In the first chapter I argued that one of the beneficial consequences of the 'behavioural' movement that captured the social sciences in the 1950s and 1960s was the expansion in those topics felt to be relevant to the study of political affairs. The lateral grab into other disciplines has been somewhat ungainly, if not downright clumsy in parts, but it has netted none the less a most interesting bag of far from random or merely eclectic material. These horizontal expeditions out into the adjoining territory have now moved beyond the local annexation espoused by the behaviouralists, though the fundamental quest for general explanations of a comprehensive sort was a necessary antecedent to such an expansion, and made it almost inevitable that the traditional boundaries would be increasingly ignored.

Along with the inter-disciplinary urge common to political science as a whole, there has been a trend more peculiar to its sub-branch of 'international relations'. One is much less tardy these days in appealing to a number of levels of analysis in explaining political phenomena on a global scale. In a way there is nothing new in this, and Kenneth Waltz[1] early drew our attention to the practice in political philosophy of selecting the particular level of analysis best calculated to sustain a protagonist's argument about the causes of war. What does seem to be new, however, is the conscious inclusion of a number of levels at once and the earnest attempt to combine them in comprehensive patterns of much greater explanatory power, drawing not only upon the configuration of the global system as a whole, but upon the characteristics of selected sub-systems, their strategic human units, and selected human sub-units as well. There is no longer the 'shortage of systematic attempts to relate the behavioral sciences to the problems of international politics',[2] that Waltz complained of in 1959. The growth of inter-disciplinary interest has substantially enhanced the number of levels that can be related to a political explanation of world affairs, with the horizontal expansion into other disciplines further encouraging the number of vertical levels brought to bear. The contemporary study of world politics now ranges from the evolutionary ascent of humankind to his possible ecological demise, from Betelguese to the man in the street, from the machinery and social performance of the brain to the group behaviour of baboons. It moves with more or less ease on the horizontal plane from biology to cosmology, from psychology to physiology, and from ethology to anthropology, and on the vertical plane from the gene through multiform man to his world systems and societies.

In this way international relations is beginning to realise its logical commitment to a 'world politics' in the inclusive sense of a politics of the whole. It promises in the end to subsume the discipline from which it derives, though the professional structure of the field is likely to resist this conclusion for some time and to continue to reflect in its teaching and research outmoded concerns of an anachronistic kind.

Such an approach, such an expansion of perspective both horizontally and vertically, is anathema to those who view politics as affairs of state, and world politics as simply affairs of inter-state intercourse. Certainly there is a core definition that will continue to direct us to that pervasive and indiscrete process of bargaining about social values, along with the civilly disguised use of force, that invariably comes to characterise relations between men whatever the size and disposition of the human group happens to be, and which is most commonly called 'politics'. But one can and should go beyond this definition, and it is no reply to complain that a greater breadth of concern renders a global focus so diffuse as to be meaningless. The question is one of application, keeping the spinning knives in the air, not losing the conceptual edge of the whole bright construct before it has solicited its fair share of illumination and applause. And further, it is no excuse to adopt a limited definition of politics and to wait upon politically relevant pronouncements from related disciplines before incorporating such findings into the main body of substantive concerns. Trans-disciplinary information should be solicited as a matter of course.

This is still to beg objections, however. The marginal utility of post-behavioural research about the brain, the environment, animals and the universe; the abstract nature of the behavioural approach itself – of systems, General Systems, cybernetics, and theorising about foreign policy, integration and conflict: are these not in part or whole trivial evasions of what most reasonable men would consider to be politics? Are such foci not evasions of pressing human problems – who are the top dogs in the world, and who are the under-dogs, who are the oppressors and the oppressed, what are the mechanisms of oppression and how might they be subverted, and how might social justice be achieved and at what cost to world or local or personal order? Should one be allowed to chronicle the analysis of 'non-problems' while such vital issues are thereby ignored? Is it not an academic duty to exploit one's privileged position to combat the evils that abound in world politics, evils, that is, construed in humanistic, non-dogmatic terms?

There are two answers here, I think, and both are to do with provincialism. Firstly, while there is moral force and admitted relevance to questions like those above being asked and answered at every opportunity, there is in fact a large body of literature, a whole realm of political scholarship, which does not subscribe so directly to such concerns, but lurks none the less like some contemporary version of Darkest Africa – a large often unexplored region with a bad name. Unless some attempt is made to come to terms with the main organising devices of both the behavioural and post-behavioural literature, much of value comes to be ignored. I would take the point of urgency, but would counter it with one of perspective.

What does such a stance leave out? The contemporary concern with theories of imperialism is a particularly interesting aspect of the academic field today, which is not considered here. The resurgence of critical discussion about the economic determinants of global patterns of influence and power, reborn in a devious line of scholastic descent from Marx to Engels, Hobson and Lenin, have brought new and committed insights into the understanding of our times. A growing list of contributors have sought to answer pertinent questions about neo-colonialism, sovereignty, aid and trade, about national and multi-national corporations, about development and retro-development, in an attempt to uncover afresh the substructural economic foundations of world affairs. Paul Baran and Paul Sweezy, André Gunder Frank, Harry Magdoff, Pierre Jalee,[3] and others, have contributed to this forceful and critical body of knowledge. Any review of such literature, however, would require a volume of its own. It also lies very much in the mainstream of world political concerns; and my endeavour here, while happily admitting the admonitory counsel such authors provide, lies in redressing the balance elsewhere.

The second answer can be stated thus. What precisely one knows will depend on what one seeks to do, which will hinge in turn on an image of the world and the perspectives and instruments that image predisposes (though such an image is not static but sits in symbiotic concourse with the process of perception, selecting and modifying but being modified in turn). One way out of the dilemmas the self-fulfilling nature of human knowledge presents is to opt, as some of the behaviouralists have, for the largest possible view, concentrating upon particular concerns only after the whole picture has been sketched in. As already indicated, the behavioural approach sought in part some set of grand metaphysical explanations that might tell us why people behave as they do, and how that behaviour might be predicted and changed. Political phenomena constitute only one component of the much more general human enterprise, and to talk about politics (as normally defined) alone, even the economic determinants of politics alone, excludes the rest of our activities, some of which at least we may need to understand if our politics are to make sense as well.

It is not enough then to know about bargaining and authority, legitimacy, administration and control, imperialism and racialism, and the traditional concepts included in the usual definitions of the subject, for these are necessarily part-topics in the study of human beings; the knowledge they generate is inevitably always fragmentary and does violence, however fruitful, to our understanding of human affairs. The knowledge of politics we seek must take its proper place as only one aspect of human behaviour, divorceable in theory from other aspects but never so divorceable in practice. How, for example, can we talk about war, a central question in the study of world politics, without talking about conflict in general of which war is a particular, albeit especially violent, form? How can we talk about conflict in general and war in particular without talking about aggression or self-transcendence, loyalty, obedience or the urge to survive? And how, in all humility, can we pronounce on drives, needs, and capacities like these without some associated knowledge of psychology, biology, ethology (comparative animal behaviour) and brain physiology? To do less would be to abuse the real scope of the problem in the interests either of analytical precision, misplaced academic modesty, activist fashion, or some such defence of a provincial status quo. Likewise, can we talk about imperialism and the profit mechanics of the market economy without discussing dishonesty and greed? And these in turn may well have to be seen as human attributes of a biological or cultural-anthropological kind, or as psychological or sociological processes, before their full *political* implications become clear.

Even more important, perhaps, is the fact that holding our discussion down to just those topics considered politically relevant usually excludes what may be the most interesting and important facets of the question from the point of view of bringing about political change to some more just or humane way of life.

So I think we are justified in following where the links lead as far as we can. Of course this makes things immensely more complex, and there is always the chance of ever more diminishing returns the further one strays from the core character of politics as usually espoused. But the attempt is well made I feel, and this work is a self-conscious step in that direction. Knowledge is not only the 'clear definition of differences',[4] it is something more – it is the intuitive reach for some fundamental unitarian principle, some completed construct that will inform particular distinctions or parts. Substantive findings on human behaviour emerge from a wide variety of disciplines. It seems quite legitimate therefore to assume that natural scientists, social scientists, philosophers of history and so on all have distinct contributions to make, and we are required to study these contributions in combination with each other if a thorough-going comprehension is to be attained. Some of these findings rarely find their way into works on world politics, even works of a behaviouralistic kind. This is a pity because I think we need to recognise now that a knowledge of the social sciences is by itself no longer a wholly adequate foundation for understanding world politics, regardless of how broadly the social sciences are themselves defined.

There are two more questions to be discussed before the work can proceed. The first has to do with the sociology of knowledge, and consists of the simple reminder of the perpetual necessity to ask questions about how social reality is defined, how the institutions of communication and education are used in that process, and in whose interests such definitions are made and propagated. Any interest described here as 'meaningful' is an interest defended; likewise close attention should always be paid to what a society or its elite defines as unreal or meaning*less* and to the motives behind that pejorative definition. Within this there is the question of the identity of the author, and what effect known. Though the art was never lost, it seems to be a particularly his training and predilections might have upon what is given as widespread academic practice these days to assess the knower before one considers what exactly is being said. Curricula vitae are scrutinised with care; shrewd readers busily solicit *ad hominem* insights, hold them in store with all the diligence of hibernating rodents, and have been known to impute the gist of a volume simply from the selection of facts garnered in this way. And the practice pays. A general paucity of ideas, the predictable nature of much intellectual performance which results from this, professional pressures to publish none the less, and certain clear, though often unconscious, ideological commitments that arise from the way research is financed, all these factors share part blame for producing that air of sad familiarity so characteristic of much analysis of world affairs. I offer no biography here, however, because I do not think it could be used to foreguess what follows, and I do not wish to give compulsive categorists such an easy means of foreclosing on what I have to say. Suffice to admit that my justification for attempting this work is two-fold – a certain curiosity on my part to see what strange beasts could be brought back to my home pasture of world politics from the forests and the factories of modern knowledge before their colours began to fade; and a certain conviction, already expressed above, that the expedition is relevant and intrinsically interesting in itself. It is an ongoing enterprise, and one's field notes have a habit of changing markedly from day to day. This is incidental evidence of the vitality of the quest.

The second preliminary question is the felt need on my part for some introductory statement about methodology, at least as far as this impinges upon the discussion of the approaches and 'theories' to come. Much of what follows raises issues of a methodological kind, and there is point therefore in preparing some of the ground for these debates. If the trouble was always taken to consider some of the underlying methodological premises, many misdirected criticisms in political science would never need to be made, and many a speculative fancy would very quickly be revealed as the charlatan construct it really was.

Despite this disclaimer, it may still seem somewhat perverse in times as critical as our own to continue asking questions about methodology. 'Thinking about how to think' evades many real problems, and in this sense it is a retreat from the world, and a rather reactionary one to boot. James Rosenau speaks at one point of the malady of 'methodologism', and we might well condemn as he does all such efforts for substituting the 'form of language for the substance of thought'.[5] However, the issues are not so readily dispatched. No body of coherent thought is without its assumptions about the most desirable or most useful way to arrive at conclusions, and though these may be implicit or unrecognised rather than on view from the beginning, canons of empirical adequacy, of appropriate technique, of acceptable sorts of analysis, are all party to the first-minted fact. Indeed, methodological devices are inevitable if one is to lift from the infinite congress of human events bounded collectivities of any kind. The important point is that such assumptions, while arising from a prior conviction about the scope and rigour of the knowledge the subject-matter will allow, determine in turn the range of facts sought, and the range of conclusions themselves.

It may be possible to ignore questions of methodology but their consequences cannot be escaped. And if one set of methods disposes one sort of answer, while another set disposes something else again, the theorist is under some obligation to seek those modes of analysis and those epistemological imperatives most appropriate for him, his subject-matter, and the purpose of his enquiry. The debates are never-ending. There is a constant tug-of-war between the positivists who would have a science of method itself and a systematic body of rules for determining with some precision the status of any analytic statement, and the epistemological relativists, even anarchists,[6] who see such attempts not only as unnecessarily constricting but also as neglectful of the social contexts in which explanations grow, of the assumptions of practitioners, and of the purposes they serve.

The most important but the least common of the explanatory structures in social science is the *theory*, though this term is used loosely by the disciplines involved. Theory and the theorising process gather together general statements in some 'significant' array, though criteria of significance are not easy to come by. They are man-made constructs that are self-consciously held apart from 'reality', though they define in turn the way the world and reality itself are perceived. The attempt can be made, and usually is, to wind such affairs empirically down to earth, but there are no fast guarantees when ground has been reached, and moving off can be an act of predictive faith in the uniformity of nature, and the faculties of man, a mental step quite as hazardous and tentative as a first five-toed foot on the moon.

Like more limited forms of explanation, theories consist of general statements which they connect in certain ways. The rigour and breadth of the constituent statements will depend, as we have already seen, on the nature of the subject under consideration, and will impinge in turn on the power of the theory. Broad axiomatic statements appear in economics for example, and comprehensive deductive theories, though widely criticised, have been used there. In politics, however, the theories we possess cannot be structured deductively since we lack explanations that can be universally maintained.* Our general statements are, on the whole, tendency statements; our knowledge is a non-cumulative

* This is a very strict view of the possibilities open to us. In practice, hypothetico-deductive constructs abound.

on-going debate of a most thorough-going kind. Political theories, where they exist, are weak and insubstantial, if they are strictly theories at all, and their weakness must be recognised explicitly as such. This is not, however, a counsel of despair.[7]

The criteria by which theories are judged will depend on many non-technical factors, but questions as to whether they connect general statements deductively or not, and as to the nature of the subject-matter, will clearly intrude here. If the subject-matter is amenable to generalised analysis then explanatory power becomes one key criterion, that is, the scope of the data which the theory can encompass with the least number of variables. 'The ideal scientific theory' Levy has observed 'would be a general proposition applying to all empirical phenomena containing only two variables from which all other general propositions about all empirical phenomena could be rigorously deduced.'[8] However, if the subject-matter is difficult to grasp in a generalised way, theories will have a tentative quality and will depend largely upon their usefulness in posing questions (or in avoiding them), or in answering those of prediction-hungry policy-makers.

Besides the *theory*, there is a group of explanatory devices used in political science that clearly lack a strict deductive form. These are the methodological stock-in-trade of students of politics, though the problem remains, as Meehan has put it, 'to find theories that will relate general statements in some meaningful and useful pattern without recourse to strict logical inference . . . what is needed is a theoretical structure that will link tendency statements; [and] since the tendency statements are not universal in form the linkage cannot be deductive'.[9]

The only obvious candidate here is theory built around the selection of *factors*, the selection, that is, of 'strategic' general statements, and the rules that outline how they interact. This is the sort of construct toward which James Rosenau builds in his so-called 'pre-theory' of foreign policy formation,[10] and I shall look in more detail at this study later in the chapter.

This leaves us with the *approaches* and *models* that make up the bulk of the analytical work in world politics. So-called 'systems theory', 'cybernetic theory', and any extant 'theory of foreign policy', are good examples of such structures. The key feature of approaches and models is their inability to explain anything of themselves, though this generalisation often breaks down in practice, and anyway does not deny their usefulness in guiding research and generating concepts and hypotheses.

An *approach* is implicit in any analytical activity and stems from the process of human perception, that is, the existence of images that screen and select in-coming stimuli. Through such devices the mind orients itself and comprehends its environment. 'Systems theory', for example, is not an explanation but a recommendation, a way of approaching the study of society. It is a tip on where the subject should be opened up to get the best possible results, though to the extent that it provides a preview of how the subject might look it represents an explanation and a theory of an incipient sort. Generally, given its somewhat more modest standing, there is something misplaced in the entrenched defence or uncritical advocacy of any one approach, since such a defence can only be an act of faith about the likely advantage of its use. Substantive applications of an approach either realise its benefits independent of prior debate or they do not, and its explanatory potential is evident as a result.

Models likewise have less of an explanatory capacity, but they are distinct and powerful devices and are widely used in scientific enquiry. A model is a replica of the form of the system under scrutiny; it is a structural simulation that is held to correspond in some way to that system. Thus a relationship seen to exist between two parts of the model is also seen to exist between the corresponding parts of the system it represents, though this inference has no automatic validity and must be independently verified. By nature and function any model is, then, a simplification, and if there is any point to its use it should be easier to manipulate than the system or real phenomena that it stands for. There is a close connection here with 'theory' in that theories also abstract and simplify, and the two indeed run together. The best we can do is agree that while '. . . The theory *states* that the subject-matter has a certain structure, . . . the theory does not therefore necessarily *exhibit* that structure itself',[11] as a model does. Herein lies the difference, though in *exhibiting* such a structure models often implicitly or explicitly *state* it, which is what a theory does.

Strictly constructed, models are *isomorphs*, bearing a known homologous correspondence to the original system, a correspondence that is often mathematically expressed. Loosely constructed, however, models are merely metaphors, similar in some significant way to the subject system but open to all the problems of analogical argument. It is this loose sense which Max Black terms 'archetypes', that is, '. . . a systematic repertoire of ideas by means of which a given thinker describes, by *analogical extension*, some domain to which those ideas do not immediately and literally apply'.[12] Analogies are fruitful and heuristic, and without them human thought would largely be impossible, but they are informal devices and prone to an imprecision which can be beneficial or abused. They are common in political thought and the repertoire to date includes images from pottery, spinning, weaving, building and the stage, from pyramids, wheels, beam balances, mechanical devices, living organisms of different kinds (trees, the human body) and electronics. A history of political science could readily be written to trace the evolution of dominant metaphors as they first describe, then explain, and then justify and prescribe some state of affairs for a world that in the end they have helped to create. Policy-makers, imbued with an analogy of world states in critical 'balance', act in such a way as to realise that idea whether it actually existed in the first place or not. Thus an analogy can fulfil itself and become an ideology, sometimes of extraordinary power.

The analysis of foreign policy is a central and conventional concern of the student of world affairs. Various 'theories' and quasi-theories now claim to offer comparatively conclusive explanations, part explanations or suggested ways of proceeding to an explanation of foreign policy. The character of the behavioural revolt discussed in Chapter 1, as well as the methodological points I have just made, can be better expressed by discussing some of these offerings in greater detail.

One of the most familiar of such contemporary approaches is that centred on 'decision-making', and persistent attention to the decisional contexts of foreign policy is a particularly useful one, long established in the field. First formulated in 1954 by Richard Snyder and associates,[13] it was in its day a comparatively novel idea to adopt, and an unambiguous blow in the behavioural revolt against the externally orientated, deterministic and reified approach to state performance still prevalent at the time. With the advent of Snyder's scheme, and the general trend that followed it, those preoccupied with the process of foreign-policy formulation sought to delineate more the variety of choice open to the politicians and diplomats involved and less the inexorable nature of the geographic, historical, technological and political 'realities' that press upon them; they sought to describe the domestic concomitants of foreign policy and how internally engendered priorities interlock with external ones; it was no longer enough to review the contextual imperatives that prompt state response without discussing how such responses might be subjectively perceived. There was less talk, in other words, of France doing this and China doing that, and more attempts to understand the individuals who act in the name of the countries concerned and why they act in the ways they do.

A *decision* in this context is simply the choice of one of several perceived alternatives with a view to a particular and expected consequence. The focus of *decision-making* analytically isolates the choosers, since in some form or other such a process is germane to all the important actions that occur in world politics and most of the unimportant ones too, and the point where the decisions that bear upon foreign policy are made is likely to be one where many relevant influences converge and where concrete policies can be seen to be generated. Decisional foci can also be located with some precision, in official terms at least, and what goes on at them can be seen to animate the state itself.

Policy-making is profitably construed in personal terms, since as the behaviouralists have pointed out, no state has independent status apart from the conduct of the individuals who inhabit it and who relate its organisational parts by behaving toward each other in regular and characteristic ways. A state exists and acts as it does only in so far as the people composing it act as they do, and state behaviour is determined 'by the way in which a situation is defined subjectively by those charged with the responsibility for making choices'.[14] Far from a concept of governmental leaders as 'merely decision sub-routines which weigh "national interest" and "national power" against the opportunity for "national gain"',[15] interest, power, and the definition of gain proceed in large part from the individual decision-maker's conception of them, and a substantial plank of idiosyncratic factors must be built into the analysis of foreign-policy formulation to explain the decision-maker's own view of what is happening and what policy-making is about. This is not to deny the impact of systemic and role constraints for few decision-makers are able to sustain a foreign policy on purely to deny the impact of systemic and role constraints, for few from the inside, as it were, as the practitioners themselves perceive them.

Snyder, Bruck and Sapin set out to construct a conceptual framework, a field of reference and a list of 'significant' factors relevant to the making of decisions about foreign policy. Data solicited and disciplined in the ways they have suggested cannot be arraigned in any explanatory or theoretical order other than that implicit in the choice of the concepts and categories themselves, because they do not present one. Explanation and theory are meant to arise only from the repeated application of the framework itself, and the comparable results adduced by such an activity.

The features of their approach are many and diverse, summarised in part in a cryptic diagram.[16] A brief and somewhat more comprehensible formulation was used, however, to preface Snyder's sole empirical application of his work, an analysis of the American decision to resist aggression (*sic*) in Korea,[17] and it is this formulation I shall follow most closely here.

Snyder argued that four sets of factors determine the behaviour of official foreign-policy-makers and shape what they will do. These stem from the organisational–institutional setting in which they act, from the internal setting of the state itself, from the external setting of the state, and from the various properties of the particular situation, event or problem to hand including the decisional event itself and the variables perceived by the policy-maker in the three settings above. Thus foreign-policy-makers must take into account firstly 'the reservoir of persons, roles, rules, agencies and functions from which a particular decisional unit is formed and within which it operates';[18] secondly, 'the society and culture; resources, technology, groups, elites, public opinion, mass media; the political climate; cultural values; social wants and needs'[19] of the state; thirdly 'the international system: friends, allies, neutrals, enemies; international organisation; diplomatic rules; bilateral and multi-lateral relationships; relevant internal factors in other nations; policies of other states' that impinge upon them;[20] and finally the situation itself. This defines the field in which a policy-maker will see his decisional solutions and out of which he builds his perceptual world, the same world the analyst attempts to reconstruct.

From the external viewpoint of any observer, however, a 'related but different' approach is necessary to describe and explain how policy-makers deal with these four groups of factors and what determines how they behave. Here Snyder distinguishes *spheres of competence*, *communication and information*, and *motivation*. Thus to understand the process of decision-making we must first understand the decisional system as a 'sphere of competence', by which Snyder means the set of explicitly prescribed as well as conventionalised rules and relations which constrain the decision-maker and influence in turn the way decisions are made, and more important, the actual content of the policies that emerge. These formal regulations and informal habits or precedents define the way in which the 'state' responds to a situation, and in the process they shape the nature of the response itself. Such rules and behavioural norms, such 'competences', do not have an independent life but are perceived and practised by their human bearers, whose interpretations of what their individual competence might be is a further factor to be considered.

'Communication and information' refer to the cybernetic insight that any social system is built upon the process of communication. The way information flows through the channels of the decisional system – which is in effect a form of learning net – will help to establish patterns of authority and will outline, for example, how information is lost, and will help to decide the viability and objective capacity of the decisional system as a whole. It will prompt important questions about sources of information, about the way in which information enters the system and is brought to the attention of the decision-makers and is considered by them.

Finally, by 'motivation' Snyder indicates that if we wish to describe and explain the nature of foreign-policy objectives, the multiplicity of those objectives and the relative priority accorded them, the conflict between objectives, the scarcity and the appropriateness of the techniques and strategies that are seen to express the gratification of national wants and needs, some discussion will be necessary of motives, as well as of 'personality, perception, values, learning and attitudes'.[21]

The Korean case-study of Snyder and Paige is the only fully articulated application of this framework since it was first put forward, and it hardly inspires confidence in the explanatory potential of the concepts and categories outlined above. The reason advanced by this case-study for an American decision at all at the time is the fact that the decision-makers who were 'authorised to act, motivated to act, and prepared to act were present'.[22] Why the decision favoured intervention specifically was due to the threat to basic values the North Korean policy represented, the probability that limited commitment could contain their advance, the favourable estimation of the risks and costs involved, the desire not to 'lose' South Korea, and the ready availability of the means not to do so. The decision-makers involved, it seems, perceived intervention as necessary and felt that they could sustain such a move, a conclusion which would hardly seem to advance our understanding of that particular American action very far.

Generally it is agreed that the decision-making framework, while performing a useful service in redirecting attention to the decision-making *process*, has wafted aloft without the sustained support of an adequate *theory* about how foreign policy is formed. Snyder identified a pertinent list of relevant variables, but failed to say how they might be related and what hypotheses they predisposed – when, for example, and under what specified conditions, a factor from the internal setting might have a given effect upon policy formulation compared to a factor from the external setting. 'As the proposal now stands it includes few propositions which refer to the actual *content* of decision-making in international affairs, but has mainly to do with the *kinds* of data one would collect *if* one were to do research using the decision-making device.'[23] We are told what to gather, but not what to do with what we might assemble in the recommended ways. Furthermore, so many variables are specified in fact that any attempt to apply Snyder's framework would involve saying something about everything, or at least, failing in the attempt to do so. This latter point has been clearly made by James Rosenau:

> Theories of political decision-making . . . can never be exclusively comprised of propositions about the officials who make choices. . . . To reconstruct the world from the perspective of the decision-maker, the researcher must examine the world itself in order to comprehend the dynamics and limits of the decision-maker's perspective. . . . A unified theory of political decision-making would be nothing less than a theory of the entire political process.[24]

Whatever is gained by concentrating on a single framework is dissipated in the attempt to accommodate every variable that might significantly influence a decisional outcome.

Time has been the real test of the decision-making approach to foreign-policy formulation. The term itself and a vague idea of what its strict use implies have passed into the general repertoire of analytic ideas, but that is all. Criticisms of it have only proliferated with the years. The decision-making approach has, it is argued, an implicit bias toward a detached attitude of efficiency, and away from any debate about values and the moral worth of the policy objectives that decisions convey. It is hard pressed to cope with the *quantity* of decisions that foreign policy entails, and when it attempts to distinguish comparatively significant decisions from the comparatively routine ones in order to concentrate on those felt to matter most, the criteria of significance often leave considerable room for debate. The Korean case-study was chosen because President Truman regarded it as his most important decision, and by 'almost any measure' it was a major policy event.[25] Whether it was the most important of the sequence of events that led to the American intervention is not made clear, and it might be argued that this particular decision was the near-inevitable result of a sequence of previous acts and an emerging commitment to a group of value predispositions to which Snyder's framework and his use of it does less than justice.[26]

The decision-making approach also neglects the existence of 'non-decisions', of policies arrived at by a process of bureaucratic drift or as a result of their co-option by groups outside government such as the military and corporate commercial organisations, and of a 'good deal of activity . . . not decisional in any precise sense'.[27] Marc Pilisuk, in a brief study of the U.S.

State Department and its foreign-policy-making potential, concludes that the most frequent goal of this body is that of 'organisational accommodation'. The informal culture of the department 'is essentially inhospitable to any efforts other than those designed to meet immediate problems'.[28] Soliciting a State Department decision means contending with an organisational context that positively avoids decisional activity and the creative process this implies, that prefers instead more predictable, familiar, and unobtrusive routines and the tasks of policy justification after the fact. The Snyder framework does subsume a factor of this kind under 'internal setting' and 'spheres of competence', but the central focus upon concrete decisions readily leads to its neglect.

This same point has been made with considerable conceptual clarity by Graham Allison. The decision-making approach slides very easily into the assumption 'that events in international politics consist of the more or less purposive acts of unified national governments and that governmental behaviour can be understood by analogy with the intelligent, co-ordinated acts of individual human beings'.[29] To understand a particular foreign policy from this perspective we need only explain how the decision-makers could reasonably have done what they did at the time in the light of the various ways the national interest could have been secured and as each alternative was carefully assessed for its potential losses and gains. This leads to the neglect of two other processes of consequence for the study of foreign policy: (1) the output of big organisations like the State Department that function according to their own particular and regular behavioural habits. In this view a ' "government" consists of a conglomerate of semi-feudal loosely allied organisations, each with a substantial life of its own. . . . Governments act as these organisations enact routines';[30] (2) the outcome of the conflict between such organisations or at least the individuals at the top of them, who disagree about what policy should be pursued and who bargain for some compromise result that meets part way their several and competing conceptions of the national interest abroad and their political, organisational and personal commitments at home.

Allison has also produced a very suggestive list of commonsense propositions[31] that alert us to many familiar and not so familiar facets of foreign policy and interstate interaction. For example, he observes that '. . . strong advocates of . . . [a] war effort, whose careers are closely identified with the war, rarely come to the conclusion that costs outweigh benefits';[32] that the 'larger the number of players who can act independently on an issue, the less the government's action will reflect decisions of the government on that issue';[33] and that the

> actions of nation A that appear to an outside observer to be designed to influence the actions of nation B will in fact be a combination of: (a) routine patterns of behaviour; (b) maneuvers in decision games that are incidentally visible to other nations or deliberately visible, since to be effective they must appear to be a 'signal'; (c) actions by players in the absence of decisions; (d) actions following a decision game not related to influencing nation B; as well as (e) actions following a decision game related to influencing nation B.[34]

Such observations are reminiscent of handbooks on statesmanship and the sort of advice liberally bequeathed to the nation in the memoirs of retired world leaders or diplomats. They fall considerably short of theory. They do point us to particular aspects of the foreign-policy process, but we have to enlighten ourselves as to the effect of these phenomena in any individual case.[35]

At whatever level of analysis we seek to understand its formulation, and regardless of the units or the foci we choose to discuss, somewhere out of the general area sketched above comes foreign policy. There is, inevitably, some dispute about just what the concept of foreign policy should entail, though the definitional problem is not a serious one. At one extreme we might envisage the pursuit of high policy, the implementation of an implicit or explicit plan of how the state or system should be represented to the world, and should act there, that determines in any specific instance which particular external stance the decision-makers will adopt. At the other extreme is the *ad hoc* response to scattered external stimuli which taken together yield a political pattern. In this latter sense the policy of one country towards another is, at best a

> poor makeshift. It is conceived in the heat and urgency of pressing affairs, and, from the nature of the case, must be grounded upon ignorance, irrelevance and misunderstanding. Directed to the attainment of advantage and the securing of interest . . . a policy which survives through the years, which generations of statesmen and diplomats practise and modify, gradually begins to live and fascinate: little by little it takes on the aspect of a dogma, and becomes independent of the purposes for which it was first devised, ruling the thoughts and actions of men.[36]

Between the grand designs of a De Gaulle, and the day-to-day reaction of diverse policy-makers to foreign events in the light of their habits of response, lies the range of practice that we call 'foreign policy'.

The main question such a definitional dichotomy fails to answer, however, is where we should locate the line between foreign policy and domestic policy. This boundary problem is now acute, and has given rise to its own comprehensive analytic focus, that of 'linkage'. The study of what the international relations theorists concerned have labelled 'linkage politics' is one attempt to conceptualise more clearly and to structure analytically the interconnected nature of state and interstate systems: 'identifying points at which the two types of systems overlap and . . . precipitating thought about the nature and scope of the phenomena that fall within the area of overlap'.[37] It is born of an understudied but widespread awareness that the level of state interdependence, at least in the minimal sense of states having to take account of each other's actions, has over the last two decades shown a dramatic rise.

Analysts now seek signs of an increasingly conspicuous coalescence of intra-state and interstate political affairs; evidence has been gathered to demonstrate how more and more the conduct of domestic policy involves external considerations, and how internal factors directly affect politics between states as well as affairs within them. Separating the sources from which such policies are derived has become increasingly difficult, and as the behavioural boundary (as opposed to the territorial line) where nation or state ends and where a distinct external environment seems to begin has become a matter of heightened confusion and debate, the conviction has grown that state and interstate systems, and domestic and foreign politics, can only be treated apart by making more or less vital omissions from their respective subject matters. Analysts are now prone to ask whether, and if so under what circumstances, foreign policy can be viewed as domestic policy writ large; and conversely whether and when domestic policy may be simply foreign policy writ small.[38] Identifying the origins of political action may mean a search back and forth across state boundaries in a sequential way that can easily be obscured by the existence of such boundaries. The 'linkage' metaphor itself depicts any particular causal factor as only one part of a chain of events extending into a state and out of it again wherever these links might lead.

There is nothing new in the fact that any state exists, as do other human organisations, within larger contexts that condition it and to which it responds. Likewise the literature on foreign-policy formulation, colonialism and neo-colonialism, foreign aid and trade, and the evolution of international organisations, bears witness to a continuing concern with the domestically engendered aspects of global affairs. The 'linkage' theorists, however, argue that the results of the contemporary increase in interstate interdependence deserve a 'sustained, systematic and comparative inquiry'[39] that they have not had before, and they herald 'no less than the emergence of a new field of inquiry in the discipline of political science'.[40]

The phenomenon of interdependence itself I have not the space to consider here.[41] Clearly it exists, but it is a more complex process than might at first appear. Rosenau goes only so far as to claim that: 'Modern science and technology have collapsed space and time in the physical world and thereby heightened interdependence in the political world',[42] which tells us little about what is actually involved. The general fact remains, though, that the world system has evolved, and in surprising ways, such that prior notions of invulnerability, of power-balancing and bloc politics, are insufficient to describe new forms of interstate interaction. Formal, and particularly informal techniques, can now be used to reach into another country to bring about changes and even to implement control there.[43] Advances in weapons technology and in communications, and developments in the forms of economic and psychological influence, have made colanders rather than canopies of territorial boundaries, a trend reinforced by the inability of leaders and elites themselves to distinguish meaningfully on many counts between foreign and domestic policy. Decision-makers have become increasingly aware, something Snyder sought to confront, of the growing variety of actors that can indirectly and directly affect the political bargains they strike, the distribution of resources they can make, and the patterns of authority they can assert within their own institutional structures – areas that traditional theories of sovereignty hold sacrosanct. And this is so not only for new states in the throes of consolidation, but also for established industrial ones of much longer standing.

Attempting a comprehensive account of the policy results of interstate interdependence runs into the same problem that undermined the decision-making focus. While the effects are real enough, they are also all-inclusive, raising

> some of the largest questions about the nature of political processes. . . . Hardly any important topic of inquiry, empirical or normative, is not somehow connected with the constant ebb and flow of interactions between a political actor and the scenario of the environment. To talk about the connection between internal and external politics means to talk about all the major elements that form the patterns of power and purpose in the domestic as well as the international system.[44]

Complexity is once again the stumbling-block. The integrated analysis that linkage recommends must treat both the 'input' from a state into the environmental system, the 'input' from the environment, that is, from the states and non-state organisations that make it up into the state, both with their 'feedback' resultants as well as the simultaneous analysis of what is happening inside the state and separately at the level of the whole system. An analogous study of the inter-relationships between the individual and his environment forms the subject matter of social psychology. As Johan Galtung points out: 'at the level of the study of nations there is no such discipline . . . the trouble is . . . that when this effort is made . . . theory formation becomes virtually impossible and the net result is enlightened [or unenlightened] essayism'.[45] We are back with a traditional approach that attempts to say, with more or less success, everything at once.

Only Rosenau has attempted to confront analytically chains of linked domestic and foreign events in a direct fashion, and in doing so, as I have argued above, he confronts nothing less than the reactive traffic between countries that is a key feature of world politics. In his essay, 'Toward the Study of National–International Linkages', he posits a state, any state, in its environment. He depicts such a state by twenty-four of its internal features ('policy subcategories') that sustain political behaviour 'at different levels (actors, attitudes, institutions and processes) and . . . unfold in different settings (the government, the polity and the society)',[46] and he differentiates the environment in terms of six sub-environments variously characterised by contiguity, geographic region (variously defined), bloc alliance, racial or ethnic group relations (experimental), activities that result in the use of goods and services, and international organisations with a structure and personnel apart from the states belonging to them. He hints at others of a legal, technological and military kind. The former dimension is then listed directly against the latter. The resulting framework can be reproduced three times over to take account of three sorts of interaction process: the 'penetrative', when 'members of one polity serve as participants in the political processes of another', the 'reactive', that is the existence of 'recurrent and similar boundary-crossing reaction rather than . . . the sharing of authority', and the 'emulative', which corresponds to the so-called ' "diffusion" or "demonstration" effect whereby political activities in one country are perceived and emulated in another'.[47] These three frameworks are reproducible in turn a number of times to accommodate varying combinations of purpose, from direct intentional policies to indirect informal influence.

A possible 3800 combinations result. This is patently unworkable, and Rosenau admits that the categories are 'imprecise, incomplete, impressionistic and overlapping'.[48] His task, he says, is to be suggestive, not exhaustive, which is realistic since an exhaustive list would approach infinity. What he provides is a check-list that compares in one place all the general variables internal to a state that Rosenau can think of with a number of external environments that he assumes may exist as operational entities in the minds of decision-makers. No attempt is made to rank factors by relative causal potency. No set of hypotheses links the factors in explanatory array, apart from the design implicit in Rosenau's selection of sub-environments and of internal state features that he finds significant. It is simply a starting tool, a matrix, and by definition that is only a place in which something is developed; by geological analogy a 'mass of rock etc. enclosing gems'.[49] Here to be found by good fortune rather than science.

Rosenau himself concludes by asking, somewhat rhetorically, whether it is 'self-defeating to propose research based on impressionistic and overlapping categories that have not been derived from a theoretical model and that may thus prove more misleading than helpful'.[50] His reply is to call for the arbitration of the discipline, its approval or disapproval, its interest or lack of it. Like the Snyder framework, it is probably decisive that so little use had been made of the matrix by other analysts,* and those analysts who have used it, have served to fragment rather than consolidate the original scheme.

Further, Rosenau retreats from coming to terms with an interstate traffic that is anything more than two-step, recurrent and one-way. Outputs and inputs that continuously reinforce each other to form a reciprocal relationship, sequences in which an output from one system results in an input into another that in turn results in an output elsewhere, are what he calls 'fused' linkages that 'cannot meaningfully be analysed separately'.[51] This is an important admission, for if outputs and inputs of this mutually animating sort are at all as common as they seem in fact, then it amounts to a surrender to complexity and a bland

* It should be noted that more empirical studies have considered from time to time specific pieces of linkage analysis, at least as that analysis has been construed here. This would include the specialised studies done by Rudolph Rummel and Raymond Tanter, who attempt to assess with a battery of sophisticated statistical techniques the precise relationship between certain structural and behavioural attitudes of states and their domestic and foreign-conflict behaviour. Certain studies overlap linkage analysis by examining what are in essence linkage phenomena, for example, Rosenau's study on 'Internal War as an International Event', ch. 2 of Rosenau (ed.), *International Aspects of Civil Strife* (New Jersey: Princeton University Press, 1964). See also J. Rosenau 'Theorizing across Systems: Linkage Politics Revisited', in *Conflict Behavior and Linkage Politics*, ed. J. Wilkenfeld (New York: David McKay, 1973) esp. pp. 46–53.

declaration of the irrelevance of 'linkage' to most of world politics. One is left either to make somewhat more impressionistic stabs at explaining particular sets of interactions as has been done before, more or less well, and unaided by Rosenau's construct – an approach certainly not meaning*less* – or to focus only upon the differentiable two-step one-way state actions which may repeat themselves but originate in one state and reach into another with no further interactive or feedback effects. Non-'fused' linkages in which a sequence of behaviour terminates with the secondary reaction and does not have repercussions beyond it are those to which the matrix is limited by definition. There must be very few such linkages in world affairs.

This critique is smudged, however, by the fact that in the questions Rosenau formulates as a result of his scheme he uses 'linkage' in a much more general and less limited sense to mean the general relationship between a sub-environment such as the 'contiguous' or 'cold war' and a particular feature of the state political system such as its parties. Now any relationship of the kind will conceivably consist of complex interactions that are more than just two-step, state to state, recurrent or cease. It will be 'fused', and thus by Rosenau's admission impossible to break down into its constituent analytical units. There is a distinct if unwitting evasion here. At the most specific level Rosenau recognises the difficulties of intruding upon the flow of events, but at the more exalted and stimulating level of general questions and propositions he simply ignores these difficulties to talk of broader issues in the hope that their complex and intractable core will be forgotten or simply go away.

What can we conclude about the addition of the linkage concept to the literature on foreign policy? To the extent that descriptions of interstate relations have been distorted by undue regard for boundaries; to the extent that these boundaries are of diminishing significance in the present-day world; to the extent that the range of sources of state action has been artificially delimited thereby; to each such extent the idea of linkage may act as a reminder and a corrective. To the extent that an emphasis upon a lack of interest in changed circumstances is to accuse a false neglect and only erects into contemporary debates an analytically tactical but strategically irrelevant straw man, then the idea of linkage is spurious. To the extent that the idea of linkage, as currently defined, only leads others directly into the most marshy tracts of foreign-policy theory and analysis no better equipped to traverse them than before, it is a positive impediment. The most critical response in this case would seem to be the most valid one. Rosenau himself has now condemned his framework as loosely designed, atheoretical, and a failure as a research strategy. Without going so far as to agree with those who called the matrix 'irresponsible' and a 'scandal', he has now publicly asserted the desirability of burying it forever. The concept-hungry academicians of the North American market will exhume the body with fair regularity, however, and even Rosenau himself, despite his disclaimers, has attempted to give it another lease of life.[52]

Except for Rosenau's matrix outlined above, linkage theorists have generally forgone their logical concern with the simultaneous study of state and interstate systems and the interactions between them, and concentrated instead upon those analytic areas which they feel have suffered most neglect. Here they include the study of the external sources of and influences on internal-state policy and political behaviour; and the study of the internal sources of and influences on foreign-state policy and political behaviour.

Karl Deutsch has built a 'linkage group' model[53] that traces the former, that is, the external influences on the internal behaviour of states. Very briefly, Deutsch locates a state (labelled S) in its environment (E), and traces the communication channels that run between the two via 'linkage sub-systems' (L), which are physically located within the state but are linked directly to the environment, or at least, are more weakly bounded against it than the rest of the state will be. The model is meant to map the flow of messages and other transactions within each of the systems – the state, its linkage groups and the environment – and between them, in order to enable Deutsch to suggest ways in which a government might reduce or enhance any given environmental input and how it might regulate the impact of external forces upon its domestic affairs. My main criticism here concerns the central feature of the model – the idea of 'linkage groups'. The role of such groups, and they certainly exist, could be important, but not exclusively so. Traffic between the state and the environment does not pass through distinct linkage groups alone, unless this key concept is so defined that any external influence must, by definition, be piped through one to get into the country, and any new influence thereby automatically calls up its own 'linkage group' from potential to actual status to carry it. And, so defined, the 'linkage-groups' concept loses the discrete meaning Deutsch seems to reserve for it. If transactions occur beside those that pass through linkage groups, then control mechanisms other than those which Deutsch gives will be necessary as well.

At least two attempts have been made to apply the 'linkage-group' idea – one highly impressionistic and the other unfortunately brief.

D. A. Chalmers[54] has attempted to outline the linkage-group characteristics of Latin American states by identifying four major foci: one, the character of the international system; two, *external* linkage groups, that is, political groups or organisations with whom the state in question has most direct relations, and the relationship itself of the state to those groups; three, *internal* linkage groups, that is, the political groups or organisations within a state most directly responsive to external events and which are related to the external linkage groups, as well as the relationship of these groups to the state itself; and four, the character of the particular state under review.[55] The linkage pattern that emerges is summarised for selected historical periods from the colonial to the contemporary. This pattern is employed in a general way to discuss the foreign influences that have built or influenced aspects of the Latin American infrastructure, such as its authoritarian tradition, the 'demonstration effects' that flourish there, and the distribution of power within the various states. Interstate linkages include the contemporary ideological conflict between communists and non-communists, which have spilled over into domestic Latin American politics. Foreign solutions to internal problems have often been imported to incongruous and sometimes disastrous effect. Further, the presence of domestic sub-systems with firm links to the outside, such as groups of foreign businessmen, diplomats, military missions, and various revolutionary organisations, have all affected the stability of Latin American states and the sorts of political institutions they have developed. The historical establishment of representative institutions owes much to the impositions of external linkage groups, and their continued weakness is directly related to the continued existence of internal ones.

There are drawbacks to the Chalmers scheme. Firstly, it does not differentiate, as he is well aware, between the different Latin American countries. Generalising about a continent, despite disclaimers, is not as easy as he would have it appear. Secondly, it is not clear that the recognition of linkage groups as such adds to the analysis of Latin American affairs anything it did not have before. Specialists in this area have been well aware of the sort of international environment in which the various states have had to operate historically, of the varying external groups, business corporations, religious and revolutionary bodies that have tried at one time or another to penetrate and link up with groups within them, and of the varying domestic sub-systems which have impinged on state politics because of their foreign connections or their externally derived ideological stances. The Latin American linkage pattern seems to have been widely recognised already in all but name only, though to the extent that Chalmers feels that it merits special attention he quite rightly affords it his particular concern.

Secondly, Martin Meadows[56] has attempted to fit his view of the impact of Indonesia's 'confrontation' of Malaysia upon Philippine politics into the pigeon-holes of the Deutsch diagram. In this way he hopes to clarify the nature of the Philippine reaction to the external pressures presented at that time.

To elucidate the attempts by the Filipinos to regulate traffic and information between their state and its environment Meadows looks at the Philippine press. This, he says, was a 'sensitive spot' and one where the government made efforts to exercise control. Further, he isolates Deutsch's prediction that under certain circumstances the activities of 'linkage groups' may be circumscribed, and places under this heading Philippine actions against illegal immigration from Indonesia, and Philippine demands for the return of unassimilated Indonesians already in the country. The integrationary pressures that arose as a result he sees as confirmation of Deutsch's prediction of the trend toward 'partial destruction, alienation, expulsion, or . . . absorption of many such groups'.[57] Finally he outlines several cases of Philippine attempts to control their external environment. Thus Macapagal's claim to North Borneo, the setting up of Maphilindo, and the rapprochement with Indonesia in 1962–3, arose he suggests from apprehension about the proposed formation of the Federation of Malaysia and the likelihood that it would be dominated by the Chinese. More obscurely, he attributes the early prospects and eventual failure of Raul Manglapus's Party for Philippine Progress in 1965 to its emphasis on the communist threat, 'a policy amounting to attempted environment control'. This party collapsed after the anti-communist uprising in Indonesia, shortly before the Philippine election day.

Despite his assertion that the usefulness of the Deutsch model is self-evident, this is far from being the case. Indeed Meadows's own analysis would suggest that it is superfluous. His discussion of Philippine–Indonesian relations, which makes up more than half the article, while open to more specific criticism on matters of fact and interpretation, is quite self-sufficient as it stands, and organising parts of it in line with Deutsch's analysis explains nothing that his generalisations about the political interchange of the time do not already make clear. It does draw attention to particular Philippine policies, but much more detail would need to be given to show that the organising scheme has brought to light the most significant of these with respect to the confrontation's effects upon the Philippines, and that it has suggested the most convincing explanations for them. Until Meadows does this, criticism must remain as marginal as his use of the model itself. However, it seems significant that the group of insurgent Indonesians that Meadows picks out as 'the only important linkage group directly involved'[58] was peripheral to, rather than instrumental in, the subsequent 'semi-confrontation,[59] of the Philippines, a fact that fails to support the prominence Deutsch gives such groups in his scheme, and one substantiating the general criticism that the most important influences may by-pass specifically defined linkage groups altogether. These may still be important, but by no means exclusively so.

Considerably more attention has been given over the last few years to the second analytic area of 'linkage' concern felt to have suffered neglect, that is, the place of internal influences on external state behaviour. Single-cause explanations of world politics are too simplistic and deterministic these days, and are out of fashion. Thus, accepting the obvious influence of external factors upon foreign policy, a long list of tangible and intangible domestic factors are seen now as cause or condition of any particular external stance. Since everything from the state of the weather to the dyspepsia of the policy-maker's mother could be cited in an explanation of why a policy emerged as it did, some selection is usually made of particular strategic or significant factors felt to matter most, and that depends in turn upon the purpose of the inquiry, on the level of generality, and on the pre-conceptions of the analyst.

A typical example here is that given by K. W. Thompson and R. Macridis in their introduction to *Foreign Policy in World Politics.*[60] Firstly, they identify the relatively permanent material elements of a state such as its geography, natural resources, minerals, food and energy. They then list the less permanent material elements such as industrial and military capacity and how these change, the human elements of a quantitative kind like population, and of a qualitative kind like ideology, information, and the role of policy-makers. These factors, they say, are processed by governmental and non-governmental agencies and are subject there to the influence of national purposes like peace and security, to the effects of diplomacy, to the effects of the nature of the political system, that is, whether it is democratic or totalitarian, and to the impact of the 'cold war'.

A list of descriptive labels like this one provides headings similar to those used in a filing cabinet. They represent one specific organisation of facts, one particular classification of categories and concepts which are thought to have some general importance or usefulness. Ideally all foreign policies should be covered by the list, and information about any one of them should not overlap from one category to the next. Though general principles about world politics are implicit in the criteria of significance that inform those factors chosen to map out the problem and indicate key areas of search, the list does not explain anything as it stands. The categories have to be linked in specific ways to do that, a state's geographic position, for example, being held more important in determining its external stance than its material resources, and if not in general, then in known particular cases. Then we would have an explicit hypothesis that would articulate the underlying theoretical premises.

To identify factors is not to trace their influence. To uncover processes that affect external behavior is not to explain how and why they are operative under certain circumstances and not under others. To recognise that foreign policy is shaped by internal as well as external factors is not to comprehend how the two intermix or to indicate the conditions under which one predominates over the other.[61]

J. N. Rosenau's 'Pre-Theories and Theories of Foreign Policy' is a notable step toward formulating causal propositions about the components of external state behaviour. The schema he presents in this essay is a complex one, but it is worth outlining its main features despite the risk of distorting them.

Firstly, he constructs a traditional check-list of factors, though compressed into five sets of variables, that he claims can cover all the elements proposed so far by analysts like Thompson and Macridis as determining foreign policy. They are (1) the idiosyncratic nature of the decision-maker with his values, talents and experiences; (2) the role behaviour that any official in a particular office may be expected to display irrespective of his idiosyncrasies; (3) any respect of a government's structure that limits, enhances or otherwise conditions a decision-maker's choice; (4) major non-governmental societal variables like the degree of national unity, the extent of industrialisation, the communal value preferences and so on, and (5) the systemic limitations that influence a leader's choice, like geographical position or the existence of some external threat.

Secondly, he ranks these five sets of variables in their order of potency under different sorts of states – whether they are large or small, open or closed, and economically developed or underdeveloped. These differences in state class, that is, in size, governmental ethos, and development, cause he claims significant differences in foreign policy, the result in turn of the different comparative influence of the five sets of factors that emerge in each.

Thirdly, since an '. . . almost unlimited number [of theories] can be fashioned out of similarly processed data . . . appropriate concepts for compiling them into meaningful patterns'[62] must also be agreed upon as well. To this end Rosenau proposes the idea of a 'penetrated system' and the idea of 'issue-areas'. A *penetrated* system is one that has been taken over by another system, a state but not a state, in which 'non-members of a national society participate directly and authoritatively, through actions taken jointly with the society's members, in either the allocation of its values or the mobilisation of support on behalf of its goals'.[63] For example, as a result of American policy in their region, centralised South Vietnamese institutions became totally penetrated by the United States in a war against insurrection and infiltration, and a curious sort of sovereign-yet-subject state system was evolved. As the issue palled the Americans sought to intervene less and to allow the system to stand more on its own, though not unassisted, feet. The picture of a country like South Vietnam with another country's troops and advisers physically on the premises and involved in its government is an obvious case of penetration, though illustrative instances of authoritative interference are not always so clear-cut. The concept of an *issue-area* refers to the way in which different issues can involve completely different parts of a state political system. A study of world trade, for example, may lead to quite a different set of personnel and political priorities within a state than, say, the study of defence strategy. Thus Rosenau identifies the development and allocation of 'non-human resources', such as foreign aid, housing and agriculture, as one possible cluster of values which lead the people involved in administering and winning support for them to form a distinct group with distinct characteristics regardless of the government level at which they are found – local, state or interstate. A state may thus be penetrated to differing degrees depending not only upon the sphere of activity involved – political, economic or whatever – but on the particular 'issue area' involved. Depending on the circumstances a state may be 'penetrated' with respect to its 'non-human resources', but not, say, with respect to the 'territorial, status or human resources' issue-areas.[64]

Finally, Rosenau expands his matrix to include these additional concepts. Another dichotomy, 'penetrated' versus 'unpenetrated', is added as a major class of states, and the five sets of variables are also ranked as to their comparative strength for each class under each of three types of issue area ('status, non-human resource, and other').

Rosenau's scheme is certainly an improvement on the sort of

static list Thompson and Macridis provide. Here is someone prepared to say, for example, that if a state is small, underdeveloped, open and penetrated, and the issue it is dealing with is one that falls within its 'status' arena, then the causes of its consequent foreign policy can be ranked in order of importance from more to less, thus: systemic, idiosyncratic, societal, role and governmental. He provides an interesting idea of how he would have 'facts' solicited and arranged. Any one state would ideally fit the generalised categories and its type could therefore be fixed. Issues would come in recognisably different bundles. The appropriate ranking of variables could therefore be applied and its foreign policy rendered predictable in some elementary sense at least. As an essay in deductive exploration it is both ingenious and interesting. As an indication of the difficulties facing systematic study in this field it is admirably clear.

But there are serious problems: firstly, with the five sets of variables – idiosyncratic, role, governmental, societal and systemic. There is no indication as to how these might be measured, whether they mutually exclude each other, or whether they can be justified on grounds more substantial than Rosenau's own personal sense of where cause is located in world affairs.[65] There is also no discussion of how much more or less potent one set of factors is compared to the others. They are ranked in a relative way, but never more precisely than this. The field, Rosenau argues, is too 'underdeveloped' for greater precision, but I wonder if it will ever be 'developed' enough, given the complex nature of the subject-matter, to allow the order he seeks.

The five sets of factors, even if an agreed use were found for each of the labels used, which is in itself doubtful, can logically be listed 120 different ways together thus providing 120 quite different pre-theories as to relative causal effect on foreign policy. This is nearly as many pre-theories as there are states, so that selecting only five sets still provides enough variation to see nearly every state as unique. Rosenau asserts that: 'Ultimately, of course, the number of pre-theories will dwindle.'[66] But will it? Could not more systematic and comprehensive knowledge about the sources of foreign policy lead rather to the appreciation that all are somewhat different at different times in different ways? Will any single ranking prove so 'unreal' as to be irrevocably abandoned for ever and all state situations, leaving a select number of more 'real' ones? The diversity of foreign-policy formulation would argue against this.

Further, so would the dichotomous sorts of states: large, small; open, closed; developed, underdeveloped; penetrated, unpenetrated. Rosenau does not attempt to justify these dichotomies, except to say that it is impossible to avoid having such a framework and positing alternatives of some kind, whether one is aware of the fact or not. 'Even the most historical-minded analyst makes the initial assumption', he says, 'that events derive from an underlying order, that every external behavior of every society stems from some source and is therefore, at least theoretically, explicable.'[67] The sorts of states and issues he selects give rise in the end to forty-eight of the 120 possible ranked lists. Again, this is nearly one-third of the number of states in the world, and the complexity of the whole is not noticeably diminished thereby. Given the fact that any look at Rosenau's definitions, either of sets of variables, sorts of states, or types of issue (and here the 'other' category is uncomfortably conspicuous) must lead to their expansion and sophistication and hence to the expansion and sophistication of the scheme they represent, the whole could conceivably lapse again into the confusion of empirical complexity. Different issue-areas readily suggest themselves, proliferating to the point where their pursuit can become a 'retreat from analysis', the 'bit-by-bit application of government and politics to specific issues as they occur. This, in present terms, comes precariously close to foreign policy as practice'.[68]

The idea of discrete issue-areas will also depend to some extent on the sort of state in question, since a diverse and complex bureaucratic one such as Britain or the United States will be much more appropriate for issue-area analysis than more rudimentary systems in which a few men play several policy roles and many more sorts of issues are processed in the same place. The distinctions are ultimately a matter of degree; it is not always clear, for instance, where mere inter-connectedness ends and 'penetration' begins, or where the precise boundaries of an 'issue-area' should be. They focus enquiry, but can they bear the weight of more positivist concerns?

The fundamental point is that Rosenau seeks an order of events in world affairs that probably does not exist, or is far less general than he thinks it is if it does. We may still seek regularities, but we should expect them to be of a less elevated, fundamental and simple kind than Rosenau leads us to expect. It is no accident that there are many histories of specific foreign policies but no generally accepted theories of foreign policy.

Rosenau's reply to such criticism is once again to ask all concerned to suspend judgement, to use his scheme, and to see what happens. If we make explicit our unavoidable and usually implicit pre-theories and assumptions, by some sort of dialectical leap we may be able to give the theoretician the data he needs 'to fashion if–then propositions and to move to even higher levels of generalisation'.[69] It cannot be shown that this optimistic evolution would not come about, but on past experience the chances are against it. Mutual revelation is not mutual agreement. Rosenau espouses hope rather than any real prospect of success, since it is unlikely that the subject matter will ever be so accommodating.

There is a further fundamental flaw in the framework too. Rosenau claims merely to have identified and amplified 'the materials out of which any theory of foreign policy must be fashioned',[70] and thus that he has not dictated or limited the kind of theory that can be built. However, in the explicit choice of variables, dichotomies, issues and rankings, the schema clearly reflects Rosenau's own conception of what causes foreign policy, and as an analytical means it will inevitably condition any theoretical end. Rather than an objective working of essential factors, it is a prejudgement on what the final hypotheses might be.

Rosenau's intellectual modesty makes it more difficult to assess these consequences of his work. His 'pre-theory', he claims, is 'not much more than an orientation, and is not at present subject to verification. . . . The point is not to demonstrate the validity of the rankings but rather to indicate what the construction of a pre-theory of foreign policy involves and why it is a necessary prerequisite to the development of theory.'[71] For a theoretician Rosenau has been too coy. He is well aware that if the rankings are wrong then the long-run results will be 'less productive and enlightening than those based on pre-theories which more closely approximate empirical reality'.[72] Patently unwilling to labour in empirical vineyards, he is forced into humility, into the diffident assertion that we only have the author's way of organising materials for closer inspection and not the inspections themselves, despite the distinctly misleading consequences this organisation could have for the end product.

In the end, too, we really are dealing only in pre-theory, and not theory itself. Nowhere does Rosenau distinguish different sorts of foreign policy as such – exploitative or submissive, expansive or retractionist or consolidative and so on – which he links to his lists of ranked factors in a general way. Given the difficulties apparent in constructing even a pre-theory, if this is a necessary prerequisite to theory itself then the latter endeavour is undermined from the outset as well. Signposts are offered aplenty, but is there a road?

Initial applications of Rosenau's framework, and extensions of it, have centred around the concepts of the 'issue-area' and the 'penetrated system'. Parts 2 and 3 of R. Barry Farrell's book in which this schema was first published do discuss the relationship of the open and closed, developed and undeveloped dichotomies to international politics, but not with respect to Rosenau's use of them.

With regard to 'issue-areas', Rosenau himself has pursued and refined the idea as contributor to another symposium that steadfastly proceeded to ignore it.[73] He argues in this study that 'In terms of the motives, roles, and interaction sequences they activate, foreign and domestic issues do seem to differ in significant ways',[74] though with major exceptions. In the case of the abnormal issues that cross the boundaries between the two, he concludes that: 'The more an issue encompasses a society's resources and relationships, the more will it be drawn into the society's domestic political system and the less will it be processed through the society's foreign political system.'[75] In other words, some foreign policies impinge more on internal politics, precisely because for varying reasons they have far-reaching internal effects.

It is difficult to know how much reliance can be placed on such a speculative study, self-avowedly 'distinguished not by its validity, but by its effort to be systematic'.[76] However, Rosenau's analysis is certainly limited in the one sense that he does not differentiate within either the domestic- or foreign-policy issue-areas but attempts only to distinguish a total one from a whole other. The nature of issue-areas is much more complex than this, at least if Rosenau's own analysis of pre-theory, which at one point distinguishes at least four issue-areas as pertaining to foreign policy, is to be believed.[77] And domestic studies would suggest the same for internal policy as well.[78] The picture clearly needs sophisticating, but is such sophistication possible without jeopardising to some extent the strength of more general propositions? Clearly not, and we are back to the dilemma of complexity.

As for the concept of a 'penetrated system', Wolfram Hanrieder for one has fastened upon it and has broadened it considerably in the process. Rosenau confines the label to a sort of third level-of-analysis, penetrated states having political processes functionally distinct from those of the state or the interstate system. Hanrieder, however, finds this definition too limited, stressing as it does the authoritative participation in a state's decision-making machinery of people not belonging to the state, and the sharing of control in a 'face-to-face' fashion. He expands it to include the ideal of 'permeability', that is, those penetrative processes that take place without direct, personal and authoritative intervention. This would include, for example, a decision-maker's perception of external events such as changes in weapons technology, and the consequent effect of this perception on a particular allocation of values. For Hanrieder

> a political system is penetrated: 1. if its decision-making process regarding the allocation of values or the mobilisation of support on behalf of its goals is strongly affected by external events, and 2. if it can command wide consensus among the relevant elements of the decision-making process in accommodating to these events.[79]

It is difficult to guess just what Hanrieder means by a penetrated state being one 'strongly affected' by external events. Just how strong must this be? And why must there be any acquiescence to the intrusion?

Rosenau has criticised the weakening of his concept from an absolute and distinct type of political system into a relative form of any state. This obscures, he claims, more than it delimits, by substituting influence for penetration and equating politics with interaction. All systems today, he argues, are 'strongly affected' by external events, and therefore all national systems are now of this 'permeated–penetrated' type. None the less, he expands his own definition in his 'linkage' matrix to include 'reactive' and 'emulative' processes along the lines of 'permeability' Hanrieder has suggested.[80] There has been much nit-picking about terminology as a result.[81]

Only one significant attempt has been made so far to apply Rosenau's framework as it stands to a particular state situation.[82] Martin Meadows, after organising his case-study on Philippine–Indonesian relations during confronation under the Deutsch rubric, goes on to do the same for Rosenau's scheme. First he determines what type of society the Philippines is, given the four dichotomies, and decrees it small, underdeveloped, open and penetrated. Secondly, he decides that two foreign-policy issue-areas were operative for the period under study – 'status' and 'territorial' (the latter presumably included in the final Rosenau framework under 'other') – and discards 'non-human' and 'human resources' considerations. Status goals,[83] Meadows decides, were characteristic of the period 1962–3 when Macapagal sought, despite the security argument attached to the Sabah claim, to build up Philippine prestige internationally, especially as the dispute between Indonesia and Malaysia began to unfold. Territorial goals,[84] however, were characteristic of the administrative attitude to Indonesia for 1964–5 as the external challenge from that quarter began to assume a more determined air.

For the 'status' issue-area of a small, underdeveloped, open, and penetrated state, Rosenau ranks his five sets of variables from most to least important thus: systemic, idiosyncratic, societal, role, governmental. Meadows verifies this ranking for Philippine–Indonesian relations in 1962–3. The systemic 'imperative of geography' and the 'ideological challenges from potential aggressors'[85] were most important of all, he claims, followed by Macapagal's idiosyncratic 'anti-American' posture, his 'flirtation' with Sukarno, the Maphilindo proposal and the North Borneo claim.[86] Next in influence came societal values, grounded in the basic Philippine paradox of an occidental history and an oriental location, and the generalised quest by the Filipinos for a more Asian identity. This had particular, if tertiary, effects at the time. Then came the negligible constraints upon Macapagal of his presidential role, followed finally by the almost complete lack of control the government has had over any Philippine president in the field of international affairs.

For the 'territorial' issue-area Rosenau ranks his variables by relative potency: systemic, idiosyncratic, role, societal, governmental. Meadows verifies this placement for 1964–5. Indonesia's proximity and 'ideological challenge' confirmed the continued primacy of systemic factors. And idiosyncratically Macapagal altered his stand and returned to a more 'pro-American' position. Role factors became more important while societal pressures decreased, but they did not outstrip the idiosyncratic variable.[87] Any president may have reacted by reason of his office as Macapagal did, but voluntarism prevailed. Finally congressional leverage remained very small, and was relegated to the bottom, with societal factors by default one above.

It is possible to argue that Rosenau's schema does usefully draw attention to certain questions – such as the necessity to judge openly, where conclusions can be criticised and refined, the potency of one set of policy-determining factors over another – as Meadows has done for developments in Philippine–Indonesian relations. It is not clear, though, that the result is 'more satisfactory explanations of those developments than have yet been advanced',[88] as Meadows believes. What he has done is to take Rosenau's categories on trust, as Rosenau would have us do, and see if the rankings apply. The specific analysis brings immediate questions to mind which Meadows, however, begs altogether. It is somewhat optimistic to assume that all Asian specialists will agree on the classification of the Philippines as small, underdeveloped (does an average annual per-capita income of under $200 say enough?), open and penetrated by the United States. And as soon as any attempt is made to sophisticate the dichotomies as more or less so, possible combinations of the variables are multiplied as well. To highlight the 'status' and 'territorial' issue-areas, Meadows has to work back from the conclusions of his case-study, a selection that predetermines which set of rankings he will use. But is 'status' sufficient to explain the period 1962–3? One can argue that security considerations, for example, played a far greater part at this time than Meadows will allow. And if so at least one other set of rankings should be brought into the study for comparison and contrast. Equally provisional is the characterisation of the period 1964–5 as dominated by 'territorial' issues. The artificial selection of areas of single-cause can only be justified if it does not exclude information as important as the explanations they themselves suggest. Simplicity has been achieved here where complex events prevailed, but it is a deceptive simplicity, that offers part-analysis for the whole. Such simplicity is attractive, but in the study of politics it is a fair indication of lack of depth.

If all this is ignored to look at the body of the work, it soon becomes obvious that even Meadows's assessment of relative potency is open to debate and with it his more specific verification of Rosenau's rankings. Though he attempts to answer in advance some possible ojections to his ordering of causes, they are less than convincing. It is too easy, for example, to place a deterministic set of systemic imperatives at the head of each column. It says no more, in fact, than that external as opposed to domestic influences were more important in some identified way, and it is possible to argue at the very least that the personality of Macapagal was the crucial factor in Philippine initiatives and responses for the whole period 1962–5.

No new insights into the politics of the period emerge. In fact, with respect to Macapagal's role as one example only, it may have obscured some old ones. Weakness in defining the content of categories precludes convincing explanation, though the very coherence of the framework gives it a false air of authority. Rigorous and productive organisation of knowledge does not occur so easily. A scheme that begins by being self-defining becomes, through Meadows, self-serving and self-justifying as well.

The thrust of the criticisms above is based upon my earlier argument that a *general* theory of foreign policy in the study of world affairs is probably not feasible. The idea of imperialism offers the closest approximation to such a theory, but I shall not elaborate upon the political economics of global affairs here. Instead I want to underline this point by looking at an early work by George Modelski, *A Theory of Foreign Policy*,[89] which lays claim to such a status and clearly demonstrates the shortcomings of this most demanding analytic mode.

The focus of Modelski's framework of ideas is the 'policy-makers', who mediate in a market-place way between the public to whom they sell policy products and the processes whereby they manufacture their wares. There are state ends, state means for carrying these out, and a state context, which is the foreign policies of other states. There are four basic elements to any foreign policy: the formulation of interests, the procurement of power-input, the definition of objectives, and the allocation of power-output. Each is defined and discussed – for example, 'power-input' can be derived internally or externally, from human or non-human sources, from the current services of organisation personnel, or from the advantageous results of past or future action. Each sub-heading is further developed to provide 'not an inventory of the power-input of any one state, but a number of rubrics under which the components of the power-input of a state may be entered and thus summed up more easily'.[90] There is more in this vein, and although a very crude sketch of Modelski's 'theory', this will do to illustrate the argument in hand.

What Modelski has done is to apply economic terminology to the political sphere in the hope that it will systematise and subdue the subject matter. His 'theory' on the level at which it was consciously or unconsciously conceived, is really an extended metaphor. Thus 'power' is discussed as if it were in units of some international currency; there is 'power investment' and 'power liability'; there must always be a formal equality between power-input and output, with any discrepancy traceable to a growth or decline in 'power resources', that is, to the state's stock of its power assets and liabilities; a state must balance its power budget for it cannot live beyond its power means for ever, as it cannot live indefinitely beyond its economic ones either; and the 'costs' of policy must continually be reckoned up, and a balance sheet in the form of an annual state power budget should be outlined and acted upon along with the financial one.

How does this fare as an organising device in the field? Firstly, the key concepts are not made operational for their application to empirical events. How are we to measure, for example, 'power resources' unit for unit, one element against another, as they are earned or lost or depreciated? Indeed Modelski empties 'power' of any independent meaning at all, equating it for practical purposes with foreign policy. And 'If foreign policy is power, power, however finely categorised, cannot explain foreign policy'.[91] Secondly, while offering a set of headings by which a policy-maker might organise his world view, little in the way of concrete rules of action or 'if–then' hypotheses for further test are offered as guidelines to policy formulation. There is, in other words, little useful theoretical fall-out. What can be made of generalisations of the order of the following: '. . . it is a condition of the internal stability of a foreign policy that a change in one of its policy elements should be followed by positive or negative internal adjustment processes'?[92] Or, 'external equilibrium has been reached when the offensive actions of a state have been met by the defensive reactions of other states and when the offensive actions of other states have been successfully countered by the ego-state's own defensive reactions'?[93] Their vacuous natures are symptoms of a third and most fundamental weakness.

The framework itself is one example of those 'elaborated systems of mental constructs of wider significance' which Modelski sees as constituting theory.[94] However, the schema is far too general and all inclusive to make any more sense of previously known and accessible facts than was possible before. Though I am well aware that one man's sense is another man's nonsense, it would still seem possible to judge theory on criteria of illumination. Without this property, without the positively simplifying effect such that from a few variables further-reaching implications and hypotheses can be drawn, mountains of pre-established ideas will remain of marginal value and minimal explanatory power. At best such approaches provide novel ways to group facts and ideas, and from them relevant conjecture flows, though there are logically as many ways of organising data as there are people thinking about it. Some will seem more important and useful than others, but Modelski's contribution here describes relationships which observation, unstructured in the way he suggests, has arrived at already. It is, therefore, largely irrelevant. Such frameworks quickly become abstracted esotericisms that lose all sight of the political realities they attempt to contain. Empirical research tends to obliterate them altogether by the diverse addition of qualifying factors from a comparison with real events. Modelski's attempt to lead the mercurial flow of events and motives into channels of cause rather than mere categorisation does not work. No particular problem of foreign policy is illuminated by it. No group of such problems is simplified by it. Its hypotheses are sustained only at the most summary and tentative level since there is much debatable order but little and uninteresting theory. There is an important lesson here, I feel, for all who would give us generalised principles about foreign policy in world affairs, and the level at which these might be derived.

CHAPTER 3

Perspectives on World Politics: The Contemporary Human Location

Behaviouralists have emphasised the importance of method and the desirability of building theories, but they have also argued, along the lines already introduced, the relevance of trans-disciplinary perspectives upon international affairs. The question is: where should one begin? The choice is very wide and when one stops to consider the point many subjects have something to say that might be of interest to those who study and practise in the discipline. In order to structure the discussion a little more clearly, I shall begin with the more remote and less familiar analytical and interdisciplinary areas, and work in toward the comparatively more usual and immediate ones from there.

I shall attempt, first, to place the subject matter of world politics in the distancing contexts of time and space, at least as these are presently perceived. If we are concerned with world societies, the individual human beings who make them up and the global implications of their political behaviour, we should glance, however briefly, at the human enterprise as a whole – at the development of society, culture and technology in recent times and the relationship between these three. We should also consider how such relationships have developed, and the manner in which contemporary groups and their attendant cultures and technologies reflect the changing ways we think and act, and in the end the ways in which we conduct our world politics. Nor should we limit ourselves to the consideration of strictly recent concerns. We may be able to glean from the history of man's earthly endeavours illustrative examples, or alternative models of political organisation, or indeed a whole range of political possibilities we might emulate or seek to transcend in the practice of world affairs. We seek most of all, in our somewhat precarious age, evidence of historical 'forces' that might predispose one sort of future rather than another. The *historical* perspective has the most immediate relevance for the study of international behaviour, and I shall dip mainly into this, the nether end of the time-stream. But we could well glance, however briefly, beyond this perspective to consider the prehistorical *evolutionary* context and the all-embracing *galactic* one as well. I would like to consider initially something of these two springs or head-waters which feel the descendant historical delta and from which it ultimately derives.

By the *evolutionary* perspective I mean nothing less than the biological ascent of man. Pushing beyond the historical record, we quickly enter a realm of which only the faintest echoes remain in myth and dream, though fortunately more coherent noises now emerge from the findings of contemporary palaeontology and anthropology. One can hardly begin to discuss politics without reference to the perennial philosophical question 'What is man?', and these two disciplines have discovered much that bears upon the answer there. A great deal in the way of limits and potentialities hangs upon the reply, and no treatment of the human enterprise should ignore the biological parameters of life itself, or some consideration of the fruitful workings of those chance mechanisms by which we seem to have arisen and from which we still stem.

Life is not one of the basic phenomena of the universe like time, space, energy or matter, though it may finally be found, despite all our strictures against teleology, to be implicit in such phenomena and practically inevitable from the beginning. It is the characteristic manifestation of certain molecular combinations,[1] the complex flow of a contingent process that at any one instant demonstrates a multi-dimensional structure which is the living thing. Living things reproduce themselves, and over time mutate, and those mutations may in turn be reproduced to provide for evolutionary change. And throughout the astonishing variety of life on earth runs one wide line, the 'continuous yet almost inconceivably intricate molecular flow of matter and energy'[2] that unites and animates the whole.

The substances that make up living things – the salts, organic compounds and the water – have not always existed, and the elements of which these substances consist in turn had their own origins, which must pre-date that of life itself. The earth is calculated to have formed about five thousand million years ago. The beginnings of life on earth have been put at about four thousand million years ago, give or take half a thousand million years – somewhere, that is, between the date of the earth's formation and that of the first known microfossils. The conjectural mechanism here usually describes the gradual concentration of chemical components in some potent pre-Cambrian brew, their assembly somehow into crude organisms, the development of photosynthetic, prokaryotic (not truly nucleated) autotrophs (organisms that can make their organic food out of inorganic materials) which diversify and give rise to the cell-built forms that teem about and within us today. 'The extraordinary variety', Elso Barghoorn points out, 'of plant and animal life that has arisen on the earth over the past 600 million years is due entirely to the invention of the eukaryotic cell, with its potential for genetic diversity.'[3] Barghoorn's own research into bacterial and algal fossils, taken in conjunction with the well-known experiments by Stanley Miller, Cyril Ponnamperuma, and Sidney Fox on pre-biotic chemical evolution, demonstrate that some such progression came about. Indeed, the pre-Cambrian conditions of change, in play with the laws of chemistry and physics, may have made it difficult for the critical breakthroughs *not* to have occurred.[4]

The pattern of Cambraic consequences is much clearer. Compared with the distant origins of life some four thousand million years or so ago, fossil evidence of living things in abundance is found only some six or seven hundred million years ago. They were sea creatures. Animal life on land was an even more recent innovation which took place about three hundred million years ago, vertebrate amphibia giving rise to terrestrial reptiles, and these reptiles eventually spawning a progeny that joined the insects in the air. With the disappearance of the great dinosaurs, mammals began their long move to global preponderance. About seventy million years ago the small tree-dwelling primates appeared which became the common ancestors of apes, monkeys and men. Five million years ago the stock that led to mankind as we know it diverged from what was to become chimpanzees and gorillas, man's closest collateral relatives. As the Pleistocene ice came and went and the descent continued – from ape-man to man-ape, Australopithecus, Pithecanthropus and on* – the palaeontological record finally begins to show signs of conceptual industry. There are chipped tools, the domestication of fire, and burial of the dead. With the fourth and most recent retreat of the glacial sheets just ten thousand years ago homo sapiens clearly emerges as the dominant living force in the world at large. His characteristic attributes are quickly listed, '. . . his brain is large in relation to the body size, his hands are fit for tool manipulation, toolmaking, and for carrying objects. He engages in play, is capable of abstract thought, laughter, formation and use of symbols, of learning and using symbolic language, of learning to distinguish between good and evil . . .',[5] and of defining these last two in elaborate and contradictory ways.

What does an *evolutionary* perspective contribute to studies of world politics? Two things, I believe, the first to do with the question of human limits, and the second to do with our ideas about man's potentialities. As T. L. Thorson argues: 'Whatever deserves the name political science must start with a conception of the human animal in nature.'[6] Viewed in the full context of evolutionary time we realise how recent our natural advent has been. By virtue of his freak brain, homo sapiens has transcended the process that brought him about. Though derived and constituted in biological terms, human affairs cannot be reduced to biology – the emergent properties of the living human being are qualitatively different from any simplistic sum of that being's constituent elements. Nevertheless we are still subject to the operation of fundamental biological principles, every one of the 10^{14} cells that makes up a human individual clearly resembles the first known units of this kind, and genetic and evolutionary forces assail us still. We are indeed 'an appalling mixture of excellence and weakness'.[7] Human choice operates within the parameters laid down when life began, and as I come to discuss the findings of contemporary brain research and their relevance to world affairs I hope to outline more precisely what some of

* This descent was probably far from the simple, linear series of stages of evolution implied by the sentence as it stands. Instead of a single straight progression there seems to have been one main branch, with many experimental side branches which failed to make the grade. See L. Leakey, 'Development of Aggression as a Factor in Early Human and Pre-human Evolution', in *Aggression and Defense*, ed. C. Clemente and D. Lindsley (Berkeley and Los Angeles: University of California Press, 1967) p. 1.

the important parameters imposed by our evolutionary descent might be.

What then of the potentialities? The knowledge we have acquired about the origins and development of life on earth is very recent even by human historical standards. It is extraordinary how little the radical insights which this knowledge provides have penetrated the common consciousness of most human beings. Philosophy has not yet come to terms with it; it is arguable, I suppose, whether the practitioners of world politics ever will. But many authors have attempted to articulate the striking awareness that comes with the scientific ideas we have so recently derived. Julian Huxley has called the human phenomenon one of evolution become conscious and aware.[8] George Wald has described mankind as matter so organised as to contemplate itself.[9] Dobzhansky has talked, as I have done already above, of a fundamental 'transcendence'.[10] Though still explicable in terms of adaptation – the way we have organised and integrated our physical and mental capacities and the means by which we have learned to control the environment – human self-awareness is an absolute advance over any level of animal consciousness that has come before it as far as we know. Teilhard de Chardin captures best the thrust of the evolutionary perspective and the way it can convincingly subsume all the valid and important but essentially prosaic verities about such things as exploitation and economic oppression that normally co-opt the world politician's view. We have now some real idea of what the human enterprise means in universal terms, and what an appalling loss it would be should it fail by cosmic accident, or through human mismanagement of planetary resources or through war. World politics gains, I feel, a new and impelling dimension seen in this light. Thorson puts the point:

> Twentieth-century man . . . can see the vastness of time and its overriding significance, man's connection with the natural world through evolution, and the fact of modern culture. . . . The recognition of these factors – all of them together – provides a standard, a perspective, utterly unique in human history in terms of which man can decide what he *ought* to do. . . . What arises from this perspective is a new understanding of recommendation and justification. . . .[11]

We have apprehended our cosmic significance, and the fortuitous nature of the transcendent process we represent only heightens the extraordinary character of that realisation. World politics, then, becomes part of our self-conscious duty to maximise the human potential, to nurture each individual, to encourage his or her development, and now that we know what mankind means, to discover just how far it can proceed. 'We can envisage a world', Teilhard de Chardin declares, 'whose . . . heightened interest would find their vital issue in fathoming everything, trying everything, extending everything; . . . a world in which, as happens already, one gives one's life to be and to know, rather than to possess.'[12] Presumably some such vision informs the logic of justification that Thorson recommends.*

The real measure of mankind's advance lies in the development of human culture. Culture has become our chief adaptive mechanism; our instincts, and anything less than the most comprehensive social conditioning, are no longer enough to shape our behaviour in any effective fashion. Conversely, we no longer need to await the development of a new limb for example, or a pre-coded behaviour trait, to exploit a change in the environment or to survive some sudden discontinuity there. Further, we can now define our own ends, moral ones like the building of a welfare state and material ones like reaching the moon, and we can set about, technologically at least, achieving them. We have a consummate talent for self-steering and self-actualisation that we share with no other earthly living thing. We are, in sum, 'incomplete or unfinished animals who complete or finish ourselves', and this by the 'apprehension and application of specific systems of symbolic meaning'.[13]

The human modes of social communication – of language and its written representation, and the ability so conferred to fix the symbols that man devises – have become ever more important thereby. Social communication is the plastic medium on which the transmission of culture depends. All that man knows must be re-learned by every generation, and what must be re-learned

* This attitude was foreshadowed even before the evolutionary perspective became scientific fact. See J. Needham, *The Grand Titration* (London: Allen & Unwin, 1969) p. 158: 'One might say that the Taoists felt in their bones, as it were, that until humankind knew more about Nature it would never be possible even to organise human society as it should be organised.'

is not only the technical accomplishments and the instrumental formulae that serve our material needs, but also the whole cultural apparatus itself with its political ways of thinking, feeling and acting which determine what we define our individual and group needs to be, and how we might pursue them. Political change is limited only by the speed at which people can change their ideas of the world they live in, and '*government* is our major instrument of adaptation'.[14]

Many have examined the phenomenon of culture and tried to see in its constant change a mechanism at work analogous to the evolutionary ones of adaptation, mutation and selection.[15] This neglects the human talent for setting its own goals, often maladaptive ones in biological terms. Certainly, however, it is culture that has been the vehicle for the contemporary transcendent advance. Mankind can now listen to the galaxies turn, but it did not have to depend upon genetic evolution to build its receivers. The human gene pool had sufficient potential for us to build such instruments directly. The interesting thing is that this potential has existed for some hundred thousand years. The fact that instruments like these have indeed been constructed reflects a change in human culture, not one in our genes. The abolition of technological ignorance was a cultural victory, the produce of modern modes of social, economic and philosophical thought and organisation. The abolition of war may also lie in the same realm of achievement.

The evolutionary perspective primarily highlights the rise of life in earth-time. The *galactic* perspective places the human enterprise in space-time, in the ultimate (as far as science knows) context of universal distance and cosmic descent. The earth, as already indicated, is thought to have formed from interstellar dust and gas about five thousand million years ago, part of the system that produced our local sun and its attendant planets. Our galaxy, the Milky Way, probably predates this gravitational condensation by about ten thousand million years. Modern calculations[16] give the age of the universe as eighteen thousand million years, but if one subscribes to the hypothesis that the universe is pulsating, expanding now but destined to collapse again in the grand alternation between energy and matter, then this might be only one instant of a cosmic flux of infinitesimal duration. Asimov gives a figure of twenty-six thousand million light years as a contemporary judgement on the diameter of the whole universe.[17] This is a far cry from flat earth and a fixed canopy of heavenly lights, but it is hardly likely to be the ultimate view of the size of space. 'Size' is a four-dimensional phenomenon anyway in the curved universe that Einstein depicted and astronomers largely accept, and nothing much like the regular and cluttered cube that most of us three-dimensional creatures naturally construe. Man stands as one, albeit the predominant component, of a thin organic film that envelops the third planet of a very ordinary second-hand dwarf star on the main sequence of the Hertzsprung–Russell diagram[18] – this star being one insignificant member of a galaxy of total mass some 200 thousand million times that of itself; this galaxy being one insignificant member of a universe of at least 10^9 more.

It is difficult in these bald terms to elicit any conception of the enormities which such a simple description involves. The progress of the Copernican revolution has reduced mankind from its self-centred, self-appointed and once exalted status in the universe to a very relative position as the inhabitant of one of many planets, some of which might well be inhabited too. Though the prospect of interplanetary politics is extremely remote, it does now exist, and presumably as mankind spreads itself in space, will become a reality. There is also the interesting idea that we may turn out to be far inferior, physically, mentally and spiritually, to more highly evolved beings that live elsewhere.[19] We need not be demeaned by the thought. John Platt has affirmed the human presence in the most striking terms:

> We begin to realize that our brains are the most complex and self-determining things in the known universe. . . . If this property of complexity could somehow be transformed into visible brightness so that it would stand forth more clearly to our senses, the biological world would become a walking field of light. . . . The sun with its great eruptions would fade to a pale simplicity compared to a rosebush. An earthworm would be a beacon, a dog would be a city of light. . . . We would hurt each other's eyes. Look at the haloed heads of your rare and complex companions. Is it not so?[20]

No political project, it seems to me, could have a finer objective than the sustenance and furtherance of any and all such beings.

I would like to turn now to the main concern of this chapter, that is, to the use of history in contemporary studies of world politics. How do we find the *historical* perspective on the human enterprise applied to world politics today? Before discussing its transdisciplinary potential, however, I want to point out the technical use of historical material in building broad propositions, even 'theories' about global affairs.

The central imperative of the scientific study of world politics is: *generalise*. A war, foreign policy, or crisis decision can most profitably be seen, it is argued, as a particular instance of a more general phenomenon that analysts seek to formulate as explicitly as possible and put to some sort of empirical test. This generalise-or-bust imperative has been cogently attacked as one that fatally misleads socio-political enquiry.[21] T. L. Thorson[22] has further put the point, and he is not alone, that the generalising imperative accepts uncritically the classical Newtonian approach to what happens in the socio-political process; it posits a mechanical, universal, predictable model of events that is steeped, unlike reality, in static order, and produces explanatory statements which, because of the nature of the subject-matter, are empty and meaningless. What we should attempt to employ, he says, is more the evolutionary, developmental, probabilistic model of modern biology and modern physics that does not enshrine any-time any-place laws as the necessary end of research, and is therefore much more appropriate to the study of the complex and contingent affairs of human society. As Jacques Monod has explained:

> . . . a universal theory, however successful in other domains, could never encompass the biosphere, its structure, and its evolution as phenomena *deducible* from first principles. . . . In a general manner the theory would anticipate the existence, the properties, the interrelations of certain *classes* of objects or events, but would obviously not be able to foresee the existence or the distinctive characteristics of any *particular* object or event . . . the biosphere . . . is a particular event.

It is, he concludes, compatible with first principles, and explicable in these terms, but not predicted by them.[23] Such a statement applies equally well, if not more so, to the sociosphere and its political components.

One can readily admit criticism of this kind, and still see some point, however, to comprehensive general statements, universal *descriptive* generalisations rather than universal explanatory ones, if they be modestly advanced and carefully documented. The difference is essentially that between the 'idiographic' and 'nomothetic' approaches to the study of world affairs. If we were to proceed in traditional ways we would tend to select a geographical locale like that of the 'Soviet Union', and a temporal span like that of the twentieth century, and construct a chronological narrative about its foreign policy – how the leaders of this contiguous area over some continuous period of time have moved about the rest of the world initiating a policy here and responding there. The analysis would centre upon the story so told, and any explanations advanced would point to the reasons why the Soviet position has come to be what it is over eighty or so preceding years. This is the *idiographic* method, and any more general statement, such as that foreign aid has no effect on the governmental structure of the recipient state, would be tested in this way by case-study, by the detailed elaboration of one or two situations of the hypothetical kind on a country by country basis. All this is quite acceptable by Thorson's standards.

The trouble begins with the *nomothetic* method, the one most characteristic of the behavioural and post-behavioural approaches, which tends to reflect a different and less exclusive mood. Nomothetes prefer to select some specific issue or problem, make a guess as to why the problem exists and what its possible causes might be, and test the propositions so asserted in many different places and at a number of points in time. Logically there are two intervening alternatives – a contiguous geographic area examined at many points in time, and a number of different areas compared for the same and one period of time[24] – but the nomothetic method demonstrates most clearly the eclectic nature of the generalising imperative. This brings me finally to the use of history, since the nomothetic approach uses historical examples in a much more comparative way, assembling a systematic assortment of case studies to justify or discredit a suggested explanation or to flesh out a conceptual framework. Kalevi Holsti, for example, in his textbook on *International Politics*,[25] spells out five categories that describe an international system, and in his illustrative evidence ranges from the Chinese state system under the Chou dynasty (1122 B.C.–221 B.C.) to the Greek system of city states (800 B.C.–322 B.C.) to the international politics of Renaissance Italy in the fifteenth century A.D. He does not advance any explanation of world politics which he thinks is valid for all three historical systems, but he does point up certain typical patterns of behaviour that seem to recur in each once the obfuscating detail has been stripped away. This does not contravene Thorson's strictures against general *explanations*, that is, statements of more than descriptive import, though one would like to see Holsti articulate the common causes that permit such a recurrence despite one's misgivings about such a universalistic attempt.

Another behavioural device has been to experiment with a number of factors that depict certain political attributes of states, combining them statistically in different ways to see what correlations might result. Rudolf Rummel, for example, reports the findings of the Dimensions of Nations (DON) project, which set out in 1962 to determine by factor analysis 'the major dimensions of variation among all nations for the mid-50's and the grouping of nations on these dimensions',[26] and then to define 'the dimensions of interaction *between* nations for separate periods of time'. According to the results obtained so far national characteristics clump together, it is claimed, along seven major unrelated dimensions that include the level of a state's economic development, its size, density, political orientation, Catholic population, and foreign- and domestic-conflict behaviour, as decided in each case by the project workers. Among the most interesting findings are the negative correlations between a state's 'national characteristics' and its foreign-conflict behaviour so defined. Negative correlations also exist between the level of internal instability and conflict within a state and its foreign-conflict behaviour. And between the foreign-conflict behaviour of a state on the one hand and its level of inter-state communications or transactions, its level of co-operation with other states, its power and military capabilities, its 'modal psychological variables', its 'values', its government's totalitarian proclivities, and its number of borders with other states, on the other. Clearly this technique could be applied in nomothetic fashion at other points in time to the sorts of interstate system that Holsti identifies – though obvious limitations upon the basic information available would soon present themselves. Longitudinal patterns might emerge which could be extended into the future to sustain probabilistic statements about how a state might behave in years to come under certain very broad circumstances at least.

This smacks of historicism and, as Mackenzie points out, the constraints that emerge arise 'not from history as something "out there" in the past but from history as it exists now, in the minds of men. That sort of history (unlike the "real past") can be changed; but cautiously and with a sense of its power as myth'.[27] The conservative lesson that Mackenzie presents is not one we need necessarily accept, though the determinism implicit in many historical studies is a phenomenon that has drawn its fair share of critical objections. Historicist or not, the search for regularities in the historical record goes on. The real problem is not just its effect upon human action, but that what gets deleted as irrelevant detail in the process may rob the emergent pattern of anything that resembles a produce of human endeavour. While it is 'probably fundamental to all knowledge processes that we gain knowledge by the orderly loss of information',[28] this is to risk the imposition of the logic of some previously abstracted system of interrelated concepts and categories. This is the old dilemma of all who seek to cut into the intricate matrix of human affairs for explanatory purposes. The order one finds is at least in part the order one applies; the knower confronts not only the external reality he seeks to comprehend, but must also discover himself. It is inescapably so.[29]

Beyond these somewhat technical uses of selected historical material in building up general descriptive or explanatory propositions, there is a distancing imperative of much greater power. This proclaims the necessity of keeping in mind, regardless of the contemporary nature of the problem under review, the whole sweep of man's affairs, or at least those that the written and archaeological record give us access to. We ought not to build thereby some static memorial sarcophagus to weigh upon the mind and obscure what is truly unique about contemporary affairs. What we should do is to stay alive to the fact that the breadth of human experience is not coterminous with ourselves, but reaches back into autonomous living worlds whose passing should give us pause. The social and political heritage of mankind is barely perceptible by geo-astronomical standards. By more subjective standards, however, it is a long and fascinating one. It should be not only a source of empirical observations, of theoretical models and constant connections, but a place of bewilderment, delight and disgust. Bad science though it may be, we do indeed 'read about the past seeking a myth to support us as we venture into the future',[30] and this reading has its rewards.

The political globe we live in is a very recent invention and in many important ways it is the product of only the last thirty years. It is as well to remember that fact, for the future bids fair to move even faster. In other ways, however, it has been millennia in the making. Unreliable though the record may be, however open it must remain to endless re-interpretation and however closed to conclusive test, some grasp of world history is an important prerequisite to a study of world politics.

I cannot present such material here, but it is important to realise that 'People think about, and act upon, each day's events only in terms of what they know about past events and about the things the events remind them of . . . each bit of experience is meaningful only in relationship to other bits of experience. . . .'[31] If people only think of terms of personal experience then enlarge that experience, expand their terms of reference, world politics will assume its extensive and most subtle dimensions.

It is interesting to see this outlook re-emerge in the post-behavioural era, first in W. J. M. Mackenzie's *Politics and Social Science*, published in 1967, and in recent texts like that of George Modelski and his *Principles of World Politics*.[32] Mackenzie develops a tentative distinction between the empires, cities and invaders that preceded the Roman Empire and the Christian age. Empires, he says, brought to the central political tradition their peasantry, priests and god-Kings. By cities he means something smaller, more plastic and commercial, which evolved for their part 'sailors, free workers, merchants, demagogues', and petty dictators. The invaders, the unrelentant levellers of empire and city alike, introduced 'the free warriors . . . the tribal chiefs . . . the leaders of war coalitions . . . the train of thralls and bondmen' to the pool of political potentialities.[33] The three types came together in the Roman Empire, built upon a fundamental triad of government, arms and law, and buttressed in time by Christianity and a spiritual dominion of considerable longevity and strength. The eventual development of states and then nations has given us the curious global subsystems we see in such numbers about us today.

Unlike Mackenzie, who uses the historical context simply to introduce a discussion about the tradition of political science, Modelski reads specific lessons from the historical record. He defines the study of world politics as the study of the politics of world society. The present world society, he argues, is unique in that it is the first *global* society – the result of a process of European expansion begun in the fifteenth century that continues today and is built upon a growing sense of shared consciousness, a raised level of interaction, and a body of common values now sufficiently widely spread to justify the appellation he seeks to confer. The global society can also be viewed, however, as one member of a historic class of world societies, not global admittedly, but 'large-scale, complex and relatively self-sufficient'.[34] The study of such systems is important, Modelski maintains, 'because their weaknesses make it possible to understand certain important problems of contemporary world society . . . .'.[35] Further: 'small-scale societies can afford lessons about the problems of managing total (that is "world") societies that cannot easily be perceived in other ways'.[36]

Here is a twofold historical context; firstly the process of globalisation that has led to the predominant feature of the emergent socio-political system of the present day, and secondly, the lessons that can be learned from the scrutiny of past world orders, both big and small. To Modelski the historical perspective presents both a deeper understanding of the crucial properties of the contemporary world system, and a store-house of salutary examples of how such a system might be controlled. 'In a broad sense', he concludes, 'world society is therefore life on this planet. Its politics is fundamentally concerned with the survival and enhancement of all life on earth.'[37] It is difficult to think of a focus of concern more comprehensive than this. Unfortunately Modelski shirks his self-assumed task, and of the three major segments of the earth's story that he later delineates he elects to deal only with the last of them – 'civilisation', and its three successive sub-components, the 'agrarian world societies', 'globalisation', and the evolution of the modern nation-state system.[38] With no more than a nod he turns his back upon the question of the origins of the earth and of life itself, and the question of the evolution of man, and most important, the effect that answers to such questions have had upon man and his politics. Concerns of this kind deserve more than cursory treatment, and something of the supplementary view has been presented here.

Modelski is not afraid, however, to draw unambiguous conclusions from his squint down the historical line. From a brief consideration of 'primitive' pre-agrarian society he concludes that: 'Settled or civilised societies might be violence-prone because of the survival, outside their effective borders, of unassimilated, and perhaps unassimilable, "barbarians". In this sense, equality and inclusiveness could be regarded as requisites for the well-being of world society.'[39] He goes on: 'a rigid and monopolistic derivation of sexual roles [men rather than women being the more aggressive, and mostly dominant in positions of political leadership] might also contribute to shaping the character of world politics'.[40] Here we have, he implies, two clear lessons we might well learn for future reference.

Further, in his discussion of 'agrarian world societies', Modelski draws a fundamental distinction between *empires* and *autonomy* systems, the former being centralised world orders built upon monopolistic power like that of the Roman, Byzantine, Incan, Persian, Alexandrian, and early Islamic empires, and the Ch'in Dynasty of China, and the latter being comparatively decentralised, more competitive, manifesting above all common religious, intellectual, and aesthetic resources, and a penchant for trade. His examples here include the fifteenth-century system of Italian city-states, the Greek and Sumerian city-state systems, the civilisation of the Maya and the later Moslem world after the devolution of the earlier empire there. 'The chief product of the empirical political structure was order', Modelski asserts, though 'the price of order was the depreciation and destruction of autonomy . . . the discouragement of innovation and a general decline in creativity and imagination.'[41] *Empires* provided the stability and continuity that agricultural societies required, but in imposing such stability they thwarted diverse freedoms and the just distribution of ensuing benefits, sowing the seeds of their own eventual decline and disarray. *Autonomy* systems avoided the self-defeating consequences of monopoly power, and culturally and politically were much richer as a result. Here in this one sharp contrast lies the real relevance of the past to Modelski's present concerns, and his central recommendation for the future. The benefits of imperial world orders are, he concludes, illusory. 'None offere solutions for organising global societies; none have developed successful political techniques that combine order with a range of freedoms allowing for creativity and change. They offer little else but the false ideal of a society that is ruled from one center by absolute power.'[42] However unique the future might be, Modelski feels it is not likely to escape the fundamental dilemma identified here. The preferred system lies, one assumes, with the sort of world John Burton[43] has consistently depicted over the last few years, a world of independent, competitive, non-aligned states, mutually self-regulating, autonomous, adaptive and free. It is an attractive picture, anti-totalitarian, with more than a hint of the laissez-faire. Given contemporary levels of global interdependence, however, it is not a convincing one.

The lessons of the globalisation process of the last five hundred years Modelski finds much more ambiguous. This process 'helped to consolidate the system of independent states for Europe, and ultimately for the world',[44] but it has also been 'profoundly divisive and the effects of this divisiveness are yet to be fully experienced'.[45] Big systems can be bad systems that lead away from that close sense of community mankind seems to find most congenial. And more and more the burden of adjustment will probably fall, at least *ought* to fall, upon those Western nations who made the running so successfully in the last century. The evidence amassed by contemporary theorists of imperialism breeds less than optimism here. As Modelski argues:

> Most of the time globalisation was a process of incorporating external parts into the ongoing fabric of Western-

> centred world politics. Those governments, societies, individuals that proved adept and adaptable enough were brought within the mainstream by means of co-optation. The great majority were either dominated, controlled, ignored or isolated. An alternative mode of adaptation – that of adjusting Western-type life patterns to the requirements of the rest of the world – has not been adequately considered. . . . The work of globalisation could yet be carried to completion in unsuspected ways.[46]

Though the argument that such a reversal might come to pass is a powerful one in terms of long-run self-interest, the question remains: how is one to achieve something like justice when, as Modelski himself is aware, such a value breeds best in a culture of equality?[47] The process of globalisation has run close to producing power monopolisers of the sort he abhors. It is to be expected that they will continue to frustrate the process of adjustment he recommends and no wonder that his alternative mode of adjustment has not heretofore been 'adequately considered'. Is it enough to await with historic optimism the ultimate demise of the West? Should we not begin now to expose the iniquitous nature of the profound inequalities which Modelski among many others points to? Given the historical perspective with which he chooses to view this process, Modelski misses a splendid opportunity here to elaborate upon some of the exploitive realities of world politics, and to come out himself for the competitive, creative, adaptive and just values he seems to prefer. How else are 'unsuspected processes' to become, at least in the short run, the realised mechanisms they ought to be? If the historical record is unanimous on what such power differentials mean there seems no reason for not giving their ultimate devolution a nudge along the way. But Modelski does not pursue the point, and the opportunity is irretrievably lost.

As I observed at the beginning of the chapter, the most urgent scrutiny of history seeks to locate 'forces' that might predispose one sort of future rather than another. These 'forces' will not be 'out there', they will work through the minds of men, but they will evidence some larger pattern to human affairs that might bear modest extrapolation into the future. Here one meets, among others, the cyclical systematisers – Toynbee and Spengler – and the largest unit of socio-political import, the 'civilisation'. It will serve to introduce a brief discussion of these two analysts to ask what the historical perspective, or more precisely, what prehistoric archaeology has to say about the break-through to 'civilisation' so-called.

A number of different criteria have been developed by which we might identify such a system. The most obvious, from the archaeological record, is the existence of an urban centre that can be shown to have accommodated some reasonably large number of people. Where evidence is uncovered of a sizable city it seems permissible to assume that there must have been a sufficient surplus of food available from the surrounding countryside to sustain a large number of agriculturally unproductive beings, and this in turn, one can conclude, was predisposed by some take-off level of technological expertise that permitted fewer men to produce the necessary extra whether those men were free, at least in a nominal sense, or slaves. The development of agriculture alone, however, critical though food control seems to have been, is not enough to identify a 'civilisation' since 'pre-civilised' peoples herded beasts and grew grain, producing their food around them rather than gathering it in some more transient way. Often they were technologically accomplished. Literacy, too, is a paradoxical indicator since it well defines the first civilisations, but is not a feature of later ones, like that of the Incas. The sole common distinguishing feature lies in the growth of an urban centre. But why should such a centre develop in this way? What was the cause, of which the populous conurbations that sprang up in many parts of the world with their complex social groupings, ceremonial religious rites and rich cultures were the conspicuous consequence?

The first such evolution occurred in southern Mesopotamia, in the Tigris–Euphrates plain. Upon the already considerable achievements of the Semitic and Ubaidian peoples who dwelt there, those who came to call themselves the Sumerians built rivalrous 'synoecisms',[48] city-states that is, of wealth, power and multi-form cultural achievement. The process was a long and continuous one without perceivable purpose beyond the creative drive of the people who brought it about. As farms grew almost imperceptibly into villages, villages into towns, and towns into a major urban mass, the complexities of the causal chain become more and more evident. Spiritual fervour was manifest in elaborate shrines, and shrines both resulted from and reinforced communal values. Religious rites were served by a priesthood that fostered learning. Priesthoods were sustained by the surplus crops of an irrigated agriculture that flourished in a reciprocal way with the support of a secular administration. Codes of law were developed, and were written down for the first time. Each interrelated feature developed out of a proto-predecessor, and each proto-predecessor grew from a web of living and changing cultural forms before that.

However difficult it may be to unravel these interdependent threads, and however carefully we guard against a retrospective determinism, the evolutionary changes were obviously real ones and about 3200 B.C., at the site of Uruk, level IV, we find unmistakably a city, and hence by the definition here, a 'civilisation'. There were other events of the same sort – in Egypt, the Indus Valley, the Yellow River in China, in Mexico, the Yucatan and Peru – and to considerable but much debated degrees they were each original and unique. Sumer was the earliest. A 'stimulus-diffusion' effect seems to have worked from there upon the similar but independent process already present along the Nile and the Indus. A lesser 'contact-and-borrowing' effect can be discerned for the similarly independent rise of civilisation in China. The pre-Columbian American cities of the Olmecs, Zapotecs and Mayas, however, seem to have arisen without benefit of significant Old World influence.[49] These seven sites were the first, and they were followed later in other parts of the world, in Crete, Assyria, Mycenae, Greece and Japan, along what were by then well-established lines. 'We should now think', argues Glyn Daniel, 'in terms of multi-linear evolution leading inevitably . . . for some societies with geographical and ecological and cultural possibilities, to synoecism – one of the finite number of social and historical processes behind the events of history.'[50] Depending upon certain favourable environmental circumstances some such evolution does seem, given the human potential, to have been well-nigh inexorable.

Though a far cry from the traumatic and rapid business of human birth, the protracted beginnings touched upon above are often depicted in natal terms, and the biological analogy is then carried through its predestined round of growth, senescence and death. From the historical record, at least as interpreted today, it does seem that a number of 'civilisations' have come into being over specific periods of time, that they have had conspicuous eras of scientific, cultural or religious success, and that they were eventually transformed into something else, or succumbed, for both internal and external reasons, to near-complete decay. The crude metaphor of an organismic life-cycle applied to the vagaries of civilisation is the simplest of the 'forces' felt to govern the historical process. Oswald Spengler[51] wove a theme of juggernaut status with it. Arnold Toynbee explicitly attacked Spengler for doing so, arguing that 'civilisations are entities of a kind that is not subject to the laws of biology',[52] which did not prevent him from developing for great societies like these a very life-like cycle of genesis, growth, breakdown and disintegration, and adding to it the Darwinian analogy of environmental challenge and critical response. Both analysts, however, have offered the most broad and adventurous general statements upon man's historical affairs and deserve at least token consideration here. Both directly espoused the generalising mood reformulated by the behaviouralist school.

Toynbee saw the 'intelligible unit of historical study'[53] as neither the nation-state nor mankind as a whole, but as that grouping of humanity he called a *society*, by which he meant the most comprehensive of man's cultural systems. He was well aware that there are an insufficient number of such groupings on record to warrant the application of statistical or scientific techniques and the elucidation of 'laws'. But in the spirit of optimism that best characterises the social scientist, he hazarded the attempt none the less. The result turned out to be theology in disguise, shot through with historical inaccuracies, and culminating in the sort of empty and meaningless general statements that Thorson and many others warn against. It is little wonder that his monumental work is almost totally neglected, except as a historiographical curiosity.

The environmental challenges that result in civilised society, Toynbee decided, are of five basic kinds. They include the stimulus that results from 'hard countries', 'new ground', 'blows', 'pressures', and 'penalisations'. Each of these adverse situations, within certain limits, rouses the society so confronted to 'hitherto unprecedented effort', and in certain notable cases, to 'civilisation'. This dialectic revolutionary process is not easily reconciled with the slow development ascent outlined earlier, and accords much less well with the archaeological facts now known. Only under duress can Toynbee conceive of men giving their best.

Once across the threshold, however, the civilisation might still turn out to be stunted. Over-extended by the particular challenge that brought it into being, it could simply sit – static, specialised, caste-ridden, ant-like – too exhausted to initiate that self-sustaining growth that 'normal' societies display as they build toward even greater achievements. It is here one catches a glimpse of Toynbee's own vision, and the felt purpose that informs the whole:

> . . . the variety manifested in human life and institutions is a superficial phenomenon which masks an underlying unity without impairing it. . . . The seeds sown are separate seeds, and each seed has its own destiny. Yet the seeds are of one kind; and they are all sown by one Sower in the hope of obtaining one harvest.[54]

Here is Toynbee's historical 'force'. No matter how complex the socio-cultural reality might be God moves all – which is teleology closed to all empirical contravention, and hence beyond debate from a social scientist's point of view.

Of the twenty-eight civilisations Toynbee identified in this way only the Western one has not yet broken down, died or come to the end of its time of growth. The power of its 'creative minority' has not yet failed; the majority still ape the inspiration of their leaders and give their allegiance to them; Western Civilisation is still socially unified as a result. The remaining twenty-seven, Toynbee argued, present a contrasting but uniform picture. Once 'breakdown' occurs, any one such society seems to be heading either for complete disintegration, or for petrification. It splits into three main groups – a leading minority, now simply 'dominant', rallying to establish a 'universal state', an 'internal proletariat', the exploited and dispossessed living in but not really of the society, who turn to religion, and an 'external proletariat', the barbarian primitives on the periphery who harass and eventually destroy the contracted heartland. Under such conditions human behaviour, social sensibilities, whole ways of life become decadent and impoverished, vulgar and debased. The past becomes Golden; the future Millennial. The militant would maintain the 'universal state' by might alone; the philosophers would have contemplation king; Toynbee opts for Jesus of Nazareth: 'And now, as we stand and gaze with our eyes fixed upon the farther shore, a single figure rises from the flood and straight away fills the whole horizon. There is the Saviour; "and the pleasure of the Lord shall prosper in his hand. . . ." '[55]

Toynbee's Darwinian proclivities reinforced the divine pattern that he saw in the diversity of human action and intent. Like organisms, societies could adapt too well to their environment and find themselves in a dead end – long-lasting perhaps, but robbed of creative power and the possibility of that further innovation that might lead to 'civilised' status. Thus:

> The primitive mammals were weak and puny creatures who unexpectedly inherited the Earth because the heritage had been left derelict by the magnificent reptiles who were the previous lords of creation; and the Mesozoic reptiles – like the Eskimos and the Nomads [two of his arrested civilisations] – were conquerors who forfeited their conquests by straying into the blind alley of over-specialisation.[56]

Toynbee is one of a continuing tradition of social scientists who have found metaphysical insight in the findings of modern biology. Through the General Systems Theorists to the contemporary field of bio-politics, this tradition has remained very much alive. However clearly we are warned about well-rehearsed dangers, analysts do not seem to be able to resist the images and conceptual devices that have been developed by that discipline. Indeed, as I have already argued, far from ignoring such things we ought actively to solicit the insights offered by many of its substantive rather than its analogical findings. Toynbee, however, holds to the latter alone.

Spengler presents a much less erudite and more intuitive progression. His diagnosis is full of dark judgements and evocative imagery. His tale, we are told, is one of 'word-sounds and pictures',[57] of moments of fate and of inner weight and of deep necessities. He was a romantic categoriser of the first order.

Firstly, he felt, the great cultures of Egypt, Babylon, India, Arabia, China, Greece, Rome, and the West could be divided into four *spiritual* epochs: these were *spring* ('Rural-intuitive. Great creations of the newly awakened dream-heavy Soul . . .'), *summer* ('Ripening consciousness. Earliest urban and critical stirrings'), *autumn* ('intelligence of the City. Zenith of strict intellectual creativeness'), and *winter* ('dawn of Megalopolitan Civilisation. Extinction of spiritual creative force. Life itself becomes problematical . . .'). Classical Culture, for example, begins about 1100 B.C. with Homer and the birth of a new 'god-feeling', moves next into a time of reformation and internal opposition to the emergent forms, and then to a phase of enlightenment, of 'rationality' and great systems of thought. Finally it enters an era of materialism, with its attendant cults of science, utility and prosperity, and one witnesses the 'degradation of abstract thinking into professional lecture-room philosophy' and 'compendium literature' of which both Spengler's own and the present work would presumably be examples.[58]

Secondly, there was a contemporaneous cycle of *cultural* epochs: a pre-cultural period of mystical symbolism and primitive chaos; an early cultural period that conveys the 'elementary expression of the young world-feeling'; a late cultural period, urban, mature and self-conscious; and finally 'civilisation', a term Spengler reserved to denote decadence, 'existence without inner form', a time of rapidly changing fashions, of revivals and borrowings and mere 'nerve-excitement' – the titillation of the senses rather than sustenance for the soul. This last stage slid finally into vacuous pretension, with imperial displays and a return to provincial craft-art.[59]

Thirdly there was a similar succession of *political* epochs: pre-cultural pre-state tribalism; an early-cultural feudalism that gave way to the aristocratic state; a late-cultural maturation of the state form, accompanied by the rise of the bourgeoisie, the differentiation of urban and rural sectors, and the eventual victory of the city over the countryside; and 'civilisation' as above, the inevitable winter-time where 'the body of the people, now essentially urban in constitution, dissolves into formless mass',[60] where economics comes to dominate politics and is usurped in turn by brute despotic force, to persist finally under a private Imperium that is doomed to enfeeblement and decay.

The whole cumbrous set of cycles pointed for Spengler to one abiding phenomenon, however – the decline of the West – and it is not unfair to argue that he merely imposed retrospectively upon other culture categories that he constructed primarily to depict this decline:

> . . . at the peak of many a Civilisation, in its great cities, there arrives finally the moment when technical critique becomes tired of being life's servant and makes itself tyrant. The Western Culture is even now experiencing an orgy of this unbridled thought, and on a tragic scale. . . . Man has listened in to the march of Nature and made note of its indices. He begins to imitate it by means and methods that utilize the laws of the cosmic pulse. He is emboldened to play the part of God. . . .[61]

We live in an age, Spengler concluded, of 'Faustian Technics' when men confront Nature with great machines in order to overpower it, conjuring up 'fabulous forces pressed together to a focus to obey the hand of a child . . .'.[62] Unlike the classical contemplative approach to the earth's gifts and mysteries, he now bends the world to his will and feels it as beneath him. He is unique in this respect. 'Our whole Culture has a discoverer's soul' Spengler declared, '. . . To *dis*cover that which is not seen, to draw it into the light-world of the inner eye so as to master it . . .',[63] to construct cunning devices that we might control them, to run the Faustian gauntlet of the Devil to pay.

Human life has become precious thereby, and *work* is the 'great word of ethical thinking'.[64] There has followed and follows still a great burst of human activity, an 'outward- and upward-straining life-feeling . . . the intoxicated soul wills to fly above space and Time. An ineffable longing tempts him to indefinable horizons. Man would free himself from the earth, rise into the infinite, leave the bonds of the body, and circle in the universe of space amongst the stars.'[65]

There is hubris here, an arrogance and unseeing logic that tempts fate, whatever that might be, and Spengler almost gleefully called down what he saw as history's repeated retribution.

Machines become in their forms 'less and ever less human, more ascetic, mystic, esoteric. They weave the earth over with an infinite web of subtle forces, currents and tensions. Their bodies become ever more and more immaterial, ever less noisy'.[66] One thinks immediately of the master banks of a third-generation computer. And despite the extraordinary nature of the final achievement and the fact that 'little life-units' by the 'sheer force of their intellect' should make the 'unliving dependent upon themselves',[67] the masters end by enslaving mankind. The whole process is in thrall to the organismic necessity of its own extinction. All cultures, all civilisations die, and 'civilisation' as such is the dying process. Spengler specifically set himself to chronicle the end.

What can be made of these two comprehensive attempts to plumb the patterns held to be implicit in man's history? Both schemes build toward a diagnosis of the contemporary human condition, though Toynbee's in a conspicuously more voluntaristic fashion than Spengler's, and I shall next turn explicitly to a consideration of what this condition might be. As far as the historical record goes, however, despite the common cyclical principles they espouse, a closer reading shows no such clearly directed sequence to the process of cultural change. Certainly societies evolve, and civilisations have developed complex contents of a political, social and cultural kind that then cease to exist, at least in the fashion that identifies a particular civilisation with its characteristic stamp. But human affairs are, to repeat, complex and contingent. Foreguessing on what is to come can only work when we allow those guesses to foreclose on the possible range of our alternative futures. No one can say conclusively what the limits of that range might be. One does not have to be a technological determinist,[68] for example, to acknowledge the enormous effect of technology upon social and cultural systems, even as they bring particular technologies into being. And modern technology is something profoundly new in the world, as Spengler well understood. We are in the midst of the changes that result from it, and we can adopt no distancing perspective here, since we *are* this history and must come to terms with it as best we can as it occurs. The trap which both Toynbee and Spengler conceal is the truly novel opportunity that contemporary technological advances present us with. As the advent of 'agriculture' led ultimately to 'civilisation', then the advent of 'industry' could well lead to a wholly new set of comprehensive cultural systems of a quite different and transcendental kind. At the very least we should keep our options open.

CHAPTER 4

Perspectives on World Politics: The Contemporary Human Condition

'History', says Herbert Marcuse, 'is the realm of chance in the realm of necessity.'[1] If we reject the determinism implicit in the grand cycles of a Spengler or Toynbee, as I argued above that we should, does this release us entirely from the grip of past events? What options are open to us as we might perceive such options to be? To what extent are we bound to a wheel of events that might roll us down regardless, before we decide to take charge of them or learn how to do so? In what does the quality of historical 'necessity' reside? How much of world politics is 'given' at any one time, and less susceptible to change thereby?

One answer is given in the set of negative attributes which Robert Heilbroner calls 'inertia', that is, the 'viscosity which is imparted to history because people tend to repeat and continue their ways of life as long as it is possible for them to do so',[2] protecting and nourishing what they have in the familiar ways that they hope will work for ever. While 'inertia' fails to explain those discontinuous periods when new direction and new momentum is self-consciously given to human affairs, the constant tradition that mankind finds congenial is still a hard brake riding perpetually upon social change.

Perhaps, however, 'necessity' simply means that there are material and intellectual *limits* that favour the success of some opportunities for social engineering rather than others. The idea of limits is germane to that of *direction*, and rather than cyclical constructs perhaps we should be looking for spirals and an absolute progress to human affairs, where time's arrow moves in one direction only and does not double back. Though change in this sense means no more than a journey from, and not towards anything in particular, it is wholly understandable that this movement has been construed in goal-directed terms, and a most powerful set of ideologies has grown up around the idea, the logical obverse of Spengler's predictive end, of socio-political development towards impending utopia rather than social old-age and an ultimate civilised decay. The most prominent of these ideologies have been derived from the writings of Karl Marx.

Marx had no need of organismic analogies for his interpretation of man's historical ascent and of what moved it. Social structures, he argued, grow out from the modes of agricultural and industrial production prevailing at any one time. These essentially economic mechanisms predispose certain socio-political relationships between men, usually of an exploitative nature, that typify the method of production whatever it happens to be and endure as long as it does. From slave societies, through feudalism to capitalism, the mechanism has remained the same. As long as men are unconscious of this, the real cause of their condition, they will remain subject, he claimed, to a profound but hidden evolution they cannot transcend. Once aware of the nature of their plight, however, they can guide the historical process unerringly to its ideal conclusion. Awareness alone can bring about the ultimate state of human liberation. Friedrich Engels amplified this idea in an optimistic if somewhat simplistic way that is worth quoting at length:

> The forces operating in society work exactly like the forces operating in Nature: blindly, violently, destructively, so long as we do not understand them and fail to take them into account. But when once we have recognised them and understood how they work, their direction and their effects, the gradual subjection of them to our will and the use of them for the attainment of our aims depends entirely upon ourselves. And this is quite especially true of the mighty productive forces of the present day . . . . The seizure of the means of production by society puts an end to commodity production and therewith to the domination of the product over the producer. Anarchy in social production is replaced by conscious organisation on a planned basis. The struggle for

individual existence comes to an end. . . . The conditions of existence forming man's environment, which up to now have dominated man, at this point pass under the dominion and control of man, who now for the first time becomes the real conscious master of Nature, because and in so far as he has become master of his own social organisation. . . . Men's own social organisation which has hitherto stood in opposition to them as if arbitrarily decreed by Nature and history, will then become the voluntary act of men themselves. The objective, external forces which have hitherto dominated history, will then pass under the control of men themselves. It is only from this point that men, with full consciousness, will fashion their own history; it is only from this point that the social causes set in motion by men will have, predominantly and in constantly increasing measure, the effects willed by men. It is humanity's leap from the realm of necessity into the realm of freedom.[3]

Western society has changed since Engels wrote, and our understanding of it has varied too in diverse and often incompatible directions. But the desire to understand and to control human history remains the same. And here, neatly encapsulated, are the three interlinked and overlapping preoccupations that I would see as central to philosophic circumstances today: (1) the question of 'necessity', of history's man-borne urgings; (2) the question of 'consciousness' and 'self-awareness', the capacity, that is, to recognise what these urgings are by a process of critical analysis and introspection, and to discern our place in them; and (3) the fundamental question of human 'freedom', that is, what truly liberated men or women would look like, how they would behave, and the conditions under which they might be liberated and encouraged to remain so. This is no more than a caricature of the question of course; it is crude, but recognisable none the less. Certainly such preoccupations condition world affairs at many key points, and to subtle and powerful effect.

These three issues are neither perennial nor universal. They reflect a particular conjunction of historical and philosophical events peculiar in the main to so-called Western industrial societies and their immediate derivatives. To the extent, however, that the process of globalisation is one of Westernisation too, such concerns have gained a wider currency than they might otherwise have done. They are major features of those who, from the world political viewpoint, count most – at least for the moment.

I am adopting a self-consciously constricted view here. The most prevalent human condition is not one of philosophical anxiety, for example, but of sheer physical need.[4] To be a Peruvian peasant, a Chinese commune-worker, an African compound-dweller, or an American slum-dweller for that matter, is to live in ways radically different from those that I shall mention. Blithe generalisations like this one should not blind us to man's capacity to accommodate habitual circumstances and remain optimistic despite their severity, but the conditions of human existence are, on the whole, very far from ideal or even adequate. However, man is also known to languish in the most advantageous of material environments, and this is much closer to the dilemma I wish to discuss now. World politics is not explicable in terms of 'Western culture' alone, though 'Western culture' will be implicated at most key points of such an explanation. I am particularly concerned here with contemporary interdisciplinary perspectives upon world politics, and such perspectives are overwhelmingly the published product of Western societies, and bear the stamp of their present philosophic predicament.

What is that predicament, Let me narrow the field even further. Its most important feature, I would suggest, resides in the second of the preoccupations posited above, the growth, that is, of a secular *self-awareness* of a novel and pervasive sort. 'Three great events stand at the threshold of the modern age and determine its character', Hannah Arendt argues,

> the discovery of America and the ensuing exploration of the whole earth; the Reformation which by expropriating ecclesiastical and monastic possession started the twofold process of individual expropriation and the accumulation of social wealth; the invention of the telescope and the development of a new science that considers the nature of the earth from the view point of the universe.[5]

Two of these three were perspective-setting enterprises, and the last was the most important by far. For the first time mankind, or some section of it at least, can perceive something like a total view of the enterprise in which it is located. Keen human minds have unravelled the logic of many fundamental natural processes, and what is most astonishing, made some sense of them.

The result of these discoveries has been to raise the level of human awareness to exciting and unprecedented heights; to promise a most thorough-going liberation of humankind from both material and mental bondage. It has also brought, however, a new and unexpected set of inhibitory dilemmas. 'Instead of the old dichotomy between earth and sky we have a new one between man and the universe or between the capacities of the human mind for understanding and the universal laws which man can discover and handle without true comprehension.'[6] With the growth of our mental grasp many have also come to doubt the reality of what they think they know, and to face the possibility that the sharper our insights, the more likely it seems that we observe merely the play of the mind itself. Most people are happy at least to assume that what is known is in some sense extrinsic to them and hence liable to yield external truths of at least conditional validity, but the general process has indeed had a most debilitating effect with a paradoxical potential to impoverish experience rather than to enrich it: thus ' . . . we look and live in this society as though we were as far removed from our own human existence as we are from the infinitely small and the immensely large.'[7] The result has been *alienation*. We have only recently grown aware of the cosmic gulfs about us, and we tend to shrink before an indifferent universe that moves to no apparent purpose. We are thrown back therefore upon the slender base of our own self assertions. 'We would like to think ourselves necessary, inevitable, ordained from all eternity. All religions, nearly all philosophies, and even a part of science testify to the unwearying, heroic effort of mankind desperately denying its own contingency.'[8] We have not notably succeeded in our most recent attempts, and to that extent we remain unfree.

The phenomenon of alienation is a complex one, and is far from exhausted by an analysis of science and its effects upon our self-confidence. Its philosophical roots lie in the precarious extension of perceptions and awareness touched upon above, but it has clear social roots as well which are usually traced to the advent of the 'mass society', or to the de-humanising effects upon the individual of the modern means of industrial manufacture and the attendant, culturally imbued values, that exalt production and consumption. Melvin Seeman separates the concept into distinct sub-categories, an alienated person suffering from all, or some, or one of (1) a sense of individual impotence in the face of external forces, (2) a sense of the meaninglessness and the absurdity of his own, or his society's situation, (3) a sense of cynicism toward the norms of behavioural conduct in force around him, (4) a sense of estrangement from the society's goals and values such as artists and revolutionaries are supposed to feel, (5) a sense of self-estrangement derived from the need to perform unrewarding work or the failure to fulfil some ideal self-image, and (6) a sense of social isolation or exclusion or rejection for one or more of a number of reasons.[9] Any one of these might be a socially rather than philosophically engendered condition. Indeed, it is more likely to be so. The fundamental result, however, is an individual less than he might be, and diminished by the distance that has come between himself and his society or some aspect of his life situation. It is assumed that there is a human condition of a more fulfilling and emotionally sustaining kind that is being denied him or that he somehow denies himself.

What evidence do we have for such assertions about the alienated condition of Western man? It is no accident, perhaps, that we can readily turn to contemporary psychiatrists for documentation of this predicament and for discussions of 'normalcy' and its pathological causes and consequences. R. D. Laing, for example, points to the fact that in the last fifty years human beings have killed close on one hundred million of their own species. This is more important to him than the number saved in that time. 'No one can begin to think, feel or act now except from the starting point of his or her own alienation . . . alienation as our present destiny is achieved only by outrageous violence perpetrated by human beings on human beings.'[10] The exact figure is immaterial; whatever it is, it is very large, and is mostly attributable to the wars and repressions of the West. We are all, he says, caught in the hell of frenetic passivity. He argues the need for humane action, and for the necessity of experiencing as a personally immediate fact the enormities that men perpetrate daily upon their fellow beings. We must assume individual responsibility for what happens in the world and awaken to the terrifying reality of its terrible plight. Our common condition, one of 'being asleep, of being unconscious, of being out of one's mind, is the condition of the normal man', he says. 'Society highly values its normal man. It educates children to lose themselves and to become absurd. . . .'[11] The mechanism of this estrangement is subtle, and to maintain the orthodoxy of our inside-out world the attribute of value-unconsciousness is construed as a positive awareness and insane conduct is passed off as sane and purposive behaviour. Indeed the purveyors of this orthodoxy, Laing concludes, are really very concerned. Thus 'they will try to cure us. They may succeed. But there is still hope that they will fail.'[12]

Viktor Frankl,[13] another psychiatrist, argues that many members of Western societies suffer from a profound sense of inner emptiness, and present themselves for psycho-analytic help in this state. Since they are no longer programmed by instinct, nor held fast by a matrix of traditionally practised and internally consistent principles, nor aware often of what they would want to do even if they had the means to do it, most just conform to what others expect of them or seem to be doing, or succumb to totalitarian directives. Alienation, or as he calls it, 'noogenic neurosis', is the result. Beside Freud's pleasure principle and Adler's drive to power, Frankl posits a 'will to meaning' that under present-day circumstances is continually frustrated and accounts for much of the contemporary mental malaise.

As well as assertions by people like Laing and Frankl about the non-experiential nature of contemporary life in Western communities, one can also see in critical questions about how social reality is defined, and the neo-Marxist proposition that the dominant ideas and values of a society are the ideas and values of its dominant class, further evidence of human alienation. Analysts of this stamp also support the socio-economic contentions made earlier as to *cause*. Contemporary industrial technology is considered as prompting a political system that in industrialised states at least is often felt to have robbed the majority of people of their potentialities, both by pre-empting the ground for radical change and by constructing exploitative structures in the name of material advancement for all. Oppression is thus masked as social welfare, and tolerance becomes, as Marcuse has claimed, a mere disguise for thorough-going control. The individual learns to love his tailored chains, and to thrive upon a 'false' awareness inured against its own falsity.[14] Political, economic and intellectual freedom can only be derived from a psychological awareness of our life circumstances and of our 'real' needs and aspirations. Our goals should not be conditioned on our behalf, as they are in the main today, but chosen without constraints upon our choice. This choice should be a broad one and not the deceitful selection of a favoured end where all are administered by the state or its dominant class, where every ideology more or less unconsciously censors itself. The Marcusean utopia is 'a yet unchartered realm of freedom beyond necessity',[15] where each individual is no longer forced to prove himself on the market but is '. . . free to exert autonomy over a life that would be his own'. In this way

> . . . economic freedom would mean freedom *from* the economy – from being controlled by economic forces and relationships; freedom from the daily struggle for existence, from earning a living. Political freedom would mean liberation of individuals *from* politics over which they have no effective control. Similarly, intellectual freedom would mean the restoration of individual thought now absorbed by mass communication and indoctrination, abolition of 'public opinion' together with its makers.[16]

A similar body of evidence is drawn, most notably by psychoanalyst Eric Fromm, from a reading of the mental-health statistics of those who live in modern industrial cultures. There are difficulties with the informative value of mental-health statistics for non-Western countries, but if we ignore these a pertinent question is immediately evident. Why do the inhabitants of the most prosperous states suffer the most prevalent incidence of mental stress? What has gone wrong where one would have expected, for reasons of material and medical success, much to have come right? Firstly, Fromm concludes, mankind's situation is unique. He has evolved beyond his original and natural state of animal simplicity, but is still in many ways subject to his animal and physiological needs and drives. He is in a state of transition, and this is a source of much unresolved tension. The issue is a contentious one that I shall discuss separately in a later chapter. Suffice to say that it is much more uncertain than Fromm seems to suppose. Secondly, he argues, 'mental health' can only be characterised 'by a sense of identity based on one's experience of self as the subject and agent of one's powers, by the grasp of reality inside and outside of ourselves, that is, by the development of objectivity and reason'.[17] Thirdly, he argues, 'mental health' 'cannot be defined in terms of the "adjustment" of the individual to his society, but on the contrary . . . must be defined in terms of the adjustment of society to the needs of man'.[18] The healthy, that is, the good society furthers love, creative work, the development of reason and a sense of self based upon the personal experience of one's own productive powers. All these, he claims, are attributes of an integrating kind. Each would work to dispel alienation as it is presently conceived. Conversely the sick society is one of fear, suspicion and distrust, and of men exploited as things for use. If a high proportion of mentally sick people in a society reflects its unhealthy condition, then Western industrial culture must logically be in a pathological state. Finally, Fromm asserts, the sickness of modern industrial society arises in turn from the economic structures upon which it is built, to wit, the consumer-directed capitalistic enterprises that sustain and condition it. These enterprises require, if they are to function effectively, a certain sort of human unit which will co-operate, produce and consume in a bland and conformist way. These human units must feel free, but must still feed the socio-economic machine with a minimum of friction; they must make up their own minds but within restricted, manipulated and anticipated limits. The fundamental imperatives that direct them render such a society's members abstract, quantified, and divorced from any truly *human* qualities they might otherwise possess. Western man thereby 'does not experience himself as the active bearer of his own powers and richness, but as an impoverished "thing" dependent on power outside of himself unto whom he has projected his living substance . . . an investment to be manipulated by himself and by others'.[19] Alienation, then, is socio-economically induced.

Stated in this way, the remedy for our predicament is clear. Freedom can only be won by asserting our 'essential' humanity, that is, by stepping outside the inhibiting constraints of social role and function to affirm such vital human experiences as love or fear. We should remember, however, that such an affirmation can cut several ways. Though it is certainly not what Fromm means by the concept,[20] love, for example, may liberate but also enslave, and devotion is the binding spell at the heart of self-transcendent political philosophies that have cured the alienation of their adherents only at the expense of considerable human harm. There is no guarantee that the good society will proceed from love alone in its instrumental rather than substantive sense, unless we posit an essentialist definition of the good in axiomatic terms. There is one test, though, that Fromm does recommend which goes part way to such an axiomatic standard. 'Free man is by necessity insecure', he declares, and thinking man is ' . . . by necessity uncertain'.[21] The necessity here is that of relativism over and against absolutism, and it depends in the end upon the favourable correlation between humane ideals and a non-authoritarian personality.

In Spenglerian fashion Fromm has chronicled Western man's growing mastery over nature and the parallel subordination of his social and psychological life to the web of machines he has so cunningly contrived. Managerial industrialism is served by vacuous puppets, he argues, by men and women made a hollow mockery of what they might be. We are sleepwalking and must awake to the robotic realities of our common lot before it is too late. We must construct anew the meaning of our lives that has been lost, with due regard to human 'needs' and the critical parameters of reason and love. Each individual must affirm his personal existence, and pursue the social and political consequences of that affirmation.

He is not necessarily out of the wood even then, however, since in any thoroughgoing process of 'liberation' he must cast aside what values he has received from the society in which he grew up, and he must attempt to evolve his norms and values anew and with as little pre-direction as possible. This in itself is one of the most characteristic bases of alienation and anguish, which is 'not so much the fear of any precise danger, as the lively sentiment of having been placed here without having wished it, and of being forced to make choices whose consequence we cannot foresee, and which cannot be justified; a sentiment at once painful and noble, for it places us once more in authentic existence'.[22] Man can attempt to be himself, but what 'himself' might be is not given in any obvious or self-evident way except by the cultural context, he is under these circumstances, trying to deny.

There is a deeper despair that lurks beneath this detachment, for not only, as Seneca said, must we learn to live, but there is a coincident process whereby we are condemned to death. In a culture like that predominant in the West where notions about cyclical re-birth or apocalyptic resurrection have a comparatively limited acceptance, the concept of death, of personal extinction, is not one to which many individuals find they can be readily reconciled. Frankl suggests that the neurotic preoccupation with mortality can be circumvented by 'dereflection', that is, by paradoxically encouraging it and by allowing it to dissipate in irony and ridicule. This will only be a temporary strategy, however, if it merely serves to restore the individual to his bored and frustrated social vacuum.

If we accept the summary evidence above and the arguments as to cause as correct, and posit the central feature of the Western condition as one of incipient awareness and manifest alienation, then where does this afflicted yet influential body of mankind go from here? How might we alleviate our present plight?

On the one hand the social consequences might be dealt with by support for any politico-economic revolution that would free individuals from the debilitating effects of conformist autocracies and democracies, and of capitalistic consumerism. Freeing people from one set of inhibitions, however, unless one is an optimistic proponent of anarchism or of chiliastic communism, requires substituting others that would preserve the freedom won in this way for both the short and long run. There is no ready agreement upon what such a set might be, and proposing and justifying a preferred version of it would take us beyond the immediate task here, which is merely to pose the problems involved. Frankl offers his 'logotherapy' as a means of enlightening people as to their mental impasse and helping them out of it. Not surprisingly, however, he slides away from positing an ultimate meaning to human existence, sufficient such that people might be fulfilled thereby, asserting that the meaning of life differs from individual to individual and from moment to moment, and is not something to be generalised in a way that might be relevant in personal terms. He has a few suggestions to make, however, the first of which is the familiar existentialist proposition about assuming individual responsibility for what happens in the world. Secondly, he claims, life's meaning can be discovered through achievement, human encounter or through suffering. Thirdly, a sense of meaninglessness or alienation may itself be simply the result of stunted perspectives. It may be illusory, a mirage, perhaps never to be dispelled, but whose chimeric quality can be accepted as an article of faith. 'What is demanded of man is not, as some existential philosophers teach, to endure the meaninglessness of life; but rather to bear his incapacity to grasp its unconditional meaningfulness in rational terms.'[23]

Others have sought the solution to the apparent lack of meaning in much of Western social life in the use of our capacity for 'significant dreams'.[24] This confronts our *philosophical*, rather than social predicament. We may think we have sketched out the limits of our temporal and spatial environment, but these are a direct function of an ever-changing history and culture and a subject to the same flux as the societies that sketch these limits for us. Contemporary ideas about the cosmos and about our place in it are more comprehensive, but no more final than those of our hunting and gathering forebears.

Far from feeling demeaned by our insignificance we might also seek solace and sustenance in the fact that it is the 'physical universe that is insignificant until man emerges from it and takes possession of it and interprets it in terms of his own past and future'.[25] Mankind can thus be seen as a sort of cosmic hyphen, gradually growing cognisant of the whole, and with a potential for self-development still largely unrealised. Though we are born into a universe not of our making, we can, to an increasing extent, rebuild that universe within the confines of each human intellect. There are limits most probably, but even these can be turned to philosophical advantage. The constraints upon what man knows and perhaps can know might be the paradoxical core of meaning: 'The ultimate gift of conscious life' could be 'a sense of the mystery that encompasses it'.[26] At this point we may return to the open-ended nature of the human endowment and underscore it heavily. We have come thus far because we are 'relatively imperfect, unspecialized, uncommitted, self-willed, and even mal-adjusted . . .'.[27] We are nature's delinquents and have transcended our biological heritage to the point where, as discussed already, we largely direct ourselves. We have had to endure a heightened awareness of the status of life and the character of death, but the intellectual exchange has been the added immediacy and urgency we are given in what we do. The most potent features of this transcendence have been the development of language, and of imagination, by which I mean in particular those intrinsic ways we allay our anxieties and compensate for what we do not have. To sustain ourselves under contemporary circumstances, it is urged, we ought assiduously to cultivate this inner life and allow its untrammelled exercise.

Finally, while remaining aware of their potentially disastrous results, we might look to the same sciences that have served to secure our alienation for help in alleviating it. To establish, as George Steiner says, some 'personal *rapport* with the sciences is, very probably, to be in contact with that which has most force of life and comeliness in our reduced condition'.[28] Only here, he concludes, can we recapture some sense of the intellectual force of the human enterprise, some sense of its moral venture and of its delights as well. We ought not to be uncritical, however, of what such a stance portends, since radical questions can be asked about the consequences of such a prescription. The ideology and the substantive results of modern science and technology have proved themselves to be in many ways environmentally, socially and culturally deleterious. They depend upon a number of deep and value-bound convictions, 'centrally woven into the Western temper, at least since Athens, that mental inquiry must move forward, that such motion is natural and meritorious in itself . . . that man and truth are companions, that their roads lie forward and are dialectically cognate'.[29] All such propositions may well be wrong.

Central assumptions like these and the recommendations that flow from them, bear closer scrutiny. In particular we should ask whether there are realms of research we should consciously forgo. 'It may be – and the mere possibility presents dilemmas beyond any which have arisen in history – that the coming door opens on to realities ontologically opposed to our sanity and limited moral reserves.'[30] It is not clear that we can afford the detrimental effects of the advance of knowledge to date, let alone what may be loosed upon us tomorrow. Steiner argues that we shall not turn back because it is not in our nature to do so, but we need not, on the evidence we have, subscribe to such a narrow and unavoidable conclusion. Our self-awareness extends to this process too. We could well learn to subvert the undesirable consequences of what we might come to know or indeed know already, though there is a question of time lags, and of forecasting all the results of our actions before they run beyond our manipulative range. We might well demonstrate the restraint that Steiner denies, and affirm our capacity to desist where it seems that we should.

I have talked briefly of necessity, of self-awareness and its paradoxically alienating effects, and of the social quality of the central predicament. The third philosophical preoccupation mentioned at the beginning of the chapter, the question of human freedom, lies in this area of analysis and debate. Its conditions depend upon the mitigating prescriptions outlined above. Once freedom has been won from the more obvious kinds of poverty and repression, what can we see as a definition of it, not *from* but in and of itself? What quality would a free individual possess that he or she might be recognised as such? One direction in which we might proceed is furnished by Murchland's view of 'the centred self. This is what must essentially underlie social systems and ideologies and serve as the ultimate point of reference. . . . To know truly who one is and the reasons why one acts is the good life.'[31] This Socratic stance is an individualistic, rather than a collectivist one, where knowledge of the self is the starting point for the measure of all other things. It is not an irresponsible one because of that. At the grave of Nikos Kazantzakis is written the legend: 'I hope for nothing. I fear nothing. I am free.' He is also, significantly enough, dead. The idea of the centred self does not subscribe to detachment of a non-moral and value-neutral sort. It denotes engagement and the constant reassessment of the level of awareness one can presently espouse. Nihilism ill befits the living, though life alone is often insufficient to explain man to himself.

In conclusion, we might ask what the implications of such a context are for world politics. Can we on the one hand describe and explain American foreign policy, for example, or French, German or Soviet foreign policy, or the actions of a multi-national corporation, as the behaviour of 'alienated' men in global systems whose members and leaders are afflicted by the malaise I have briefly discussed and who act on the world stage in 'unliberated' ways? The exercise would be a somewhat rarefied one, and would probably degenerate into definition and counter-definition. Nevertheless if there is, as I believe, a philosophical condition of the sort described, then it characterises some of the most important actors in world politics, and its influence should be detectable conditioning policy stances, limiting perceived options, and permeating such political phenomena as legitimacy, loyalty and resolve in subtle but evident ways. However subterranean the process, the way we think and feel conditions how we behave in general, and our world political behaviour in particular. As human beings grow more aware of their ephemeral status in the universe, we might expect that instead of affirming the beneficial attributes of their common humanity they might grasp at surrogate significance of some religio-mystical sort, with unforeseen political consequences. Instead of humanising science, for example, they may seek to dispel it as a disastrous myth, though a world in which this happened would be somewhat, though perhaps not very, different from our own. Analyses of contemporary human conditions also convey recommendations for a different sort of world. How these might contribute to a programme of global politics will depend upon the predispositions of state and extra-state decision-makers, and whether they accept the generalisations as valid or not. A world without the debilitating effects of 'alienation' might be better or worse than the one we have today, but the mitigating suggestions made above would predispose the more optimistic alternative.

CHAPTER 5

Futurology and the Ecological Context

Having located the study of world politics in its historical context and very briefly in its contemporary philosophical one; having fed in what substantive insights we might glean from such an enterprise, I would like to consider world politics not in terms of what has gone before or where it is now, but explicitly in terms of where it is going from here.

Policy-making is a futuristic enterprise. Policy is built out of a more or less perceptive view of past and present circumstances in the specific attempt to realise one set of consequences rather than another. Assessments are made of what the future will probably produce given a minimum of further intervention, given, that is, a policy of drift. Some other destiny is designed and steps taken to construct it. The ground shifts continually, however, the chosen means do not seem to accomplish the intended ends, and the policy-maker goes back to his site plans and his crystal ball. It is not an idle question to ask what today he thinks he sees there, and in particular what students of world politics now declaim as the shadowy shade of the global predicaments to come.

'Futurology', prognostics, futuristics, these are the terms used to describe the contemporary study of future affairs. Political conjecture is so inevitable a policy reflex, in fact, that we can merely attempt to do it better or worse, and can safely assume that since foresight is one of mankind's most conspicuous attributes, we will never live in a world where it is not done at all. B. de Jouvenal has argued that perspicacious prevision is *the* defining characteristic of political science, since he holds that predictive power, even of a modest and probabilistic kind, is the ultimate test of the validity of any science worthy of the name. Predictive power is a stringent criterion to apply, however, and it presupposes considerable explanatory capacity as well.

De Jouvenal asserts a universalistic, generalising standard that in recent years has suffered some decline. Nevertheless, those who must make a political decision now about how to cope with what will not happen until later, or who wish to implement goals that they want effectively realised in the future, seek answers, and convincing ones, to their questions about the likely state of political affairs. The political scientist, de Jouvenal argues, should be able to provide such answers with a consistently greater degree of success than the average politician or citizen. As he points out, 'this is not a great deal to ask, and whoever denies that it can be achieved, thereby denies any practical value to political research'.[1]

This is an unnecessarily restrictive definition of what is useful, I feel. We could argue with equal force that a coherent set of moral values, ranked with articulate precision, would serve a policy-maker just as well as a policy guide as some *ad hoc* voyage from predictive point to predictive point. The two indeed run together:

> . . . no creative political theorist . . . has failed to recommend those political systems which he considered best, i.e. which, if adopted, are likely to yield those results which, according to his system of values, are most positive. Thus implied, and at times explicit, conjecture forms an essential part of any political theory, philosophy, or ideology ever conceived. . . .[2]

Prognostics in their present sense are best seen as an academic tool in the service of a concept of what the future should be.* On these grounds de Jouvenal seeks to establish futurology as a discrete field for analytic endeavour. He argues the need for improved prognostications for the use of political decision-makers, and adds some precautionary prescriptions for budding futurists. They will, he says, attempt to anticipate the many consequences of technological, economic, and social as well as political change,

* This definition is a means-directed one that excludes the end-centred doctrines of a millenarian kind and like beliefs in the coming of happiness and benign government. It also excludes their prognostic obverse – the prophecies of doom.

and co-ordinate them in some sort of 'Surmising Forum' that ranks their instrumental priorities, compares the rankings, and judges the rational utility of current as well as projected policy thereby. They will try to warn against mistakes, or at least regard it as part of their job to offer constructive advice, to predict the pitfalls and discontinuities as well as the linear projections that lie along the way. They will not neglect the study of individuals and the whims of leaders – the idiosyncratic, affective traits that influence political affairs – since personalities always matter in politics, and 'never have they counted for more than in our century, which has, at one and the same time, tended to collectivize the individual and to individualize collective power'.[3] They will strive for objectivity but will not eschew their intuitions nor exclude such vital data as the changing state of people's passions, their feelings, wants, aspirations, judgements and moods.[4] They will foresee the need for institutional change and recommend the nature of the changes they consider necessary to accommodate impending demands. But they will not, one should add, forgo a concern for moral philosophy, without which we can have 'nothing but sentiments'.[5] This is an unexceptional list to which any good policy adviser would subscribe. It would still seem desirable, however, to have a specific look, at very least, at contemporary habits of forethought, if only to retard the process by which ill-defined and implicit conjectures tend to fulfil themselves or be falsified by the process of their pronouncement. Every general statement about political affairs has an import for the future, and that submerged component might well be given explicit scrutiny from the beginning.

Benjamin Akzin has given one list of political generalisations that could be, and in some cases already have been, tested for varying degrees of probability, which might serve to support more reliable forms of prevision. These include the 'socialist theory of mankind's social and moral perfectibility', which given greater credence could more firmly support the conjectural likelihood of a 'co-operative society for all time'; the theory of Aristotle, Montesquieu, and Rousseau concerning the correlation between a state's size and its regime; the familiar observation about external war as a diversionary displacement for domestic strife, or as the inevitable consequence of capitalism; the 'iron law' of bureaucracy; and other such linkages.[6] The list could be lengthened with ease. Any regularity of this sort, shown to have held in the past, that continues to hold for the present, could well be assumed, with the necessary reservations about the idiosyncratic behaviour of individual actors and the contingent quality of human affairs, to hold for the future. The more secure the hypothesis, the more likely its continued relevance and the more likely it is that it will be taken into account by policy-makers. The less reliable that an explanation of past and present events seems to be, the less likely it is that it will be used to foreclose upon our alternative futures. It is no accident that the rise of 'futurology' as a specific focus followed fast upon that of 'behaviouralism', with its generalising imperative and its desire to establish tested hypotheses about politics that might permit of modest and probabilistic, but still enhanced, predictive power. In the end debates about the likely advantages of futurology are conducted in the same terms, with the same propositions, as debates about the merits and demerits of a behaviouralist approach: except, that is, for the case where the analyst elects to deal with everything at once, and places in print his impressionistic views on what will happen and how we might mitigate or successfully realise the fate in store for us. Here disputes about methodology are no longer relevant; it is left to the future to prove him either right or wrong.

What do the futurologists give us to expect for world politics? What substantive results do they offer as relevant to international affairs? Firstly, there are a number of models that specifically set out to show how the world system and world society is likely to evolve, either in realistic detail or in some more abstracted way. Secondly, there are those who anticipate problems that they feel will either flow directly out of present socio-economic and technological trends, or will follow the exhaustion of those trends under grossly discontinuous conditions such as breakthrough, collapse or the advent of intervening limits. These problems will bear upon world politics in a profound but more substructural way. I would like to examine some examples of the two overlapping areas of analysis in turn.

Probably the best-known of the former category – those who prognosticate directly about world affairs – is Herman Kahn, whose synthesis of the views of the Hudson Institute can be found in *The Year 2000*, and more recently in *Things to Come*.[7] In the first book, after discussions on methodology, the nature of historical change, and present technological, economic, demographic and cultural trends, he considers 'The International System in the Very Long Run'. He argues here that large-scale catastrophic change is unlikely for some time. The arms race between the big powers will probably slow to a stroll rather than end in nuclear war, and even if it does result none the less in violent conflict, there are signs that such a mishap would be more limited than is popularly supposed. The diffusion of nuclear weapons to other states, however, will present new problems. Global disparities in economic development will grow worse, though the difference in resources, military ones in particular, would seem to preclude for the immediate future the likelihood of a development-war of the rich states against the rest.

Given basic continuity in the present global structure for the rest of this century, Kahn goes on to conjecture about some features of the twenty-first century. He suggests the possibility of one or more large-scale or limited nuclear conflicts, either by a strong and developed state against a weak and underdeveloped one, or within the small or poor state arena. This possibility will not countermand, however, a general eschewal of all-out war, but rather it will instance the increased use of instrumental conflict to specific and restrained ends. Moves toward the growing institutionalisation of those security congeries like Western Europe, where war seems no longer to be an accepted option in settling disputes, will further reinforce the evolutionary course of global stability.

For good measure he includes some consideration of what more radical changes might bring. Here he discusses:

1. The likelihood of some partial interstate coalescence, that is, the growth of a number of large and lasting political blocs, each with enough resources to be invincible, each with a central government, each with inter-bloc boundaries clearly drawn and perhaps adjudicated by a common world forum.
2. The possibility of a 'condominium' between two or more major powers to enforce certain agreed principles upon the world at large.
3. The possibility of a similar, more comprehensive, but less formal big-power hegemony.

4. The remote possibility of a small-power concert developing out of the U.N. General Assembly.
5. The equally distant likelihood of world federalism or world empire.
6. The extraordinary possibility of an unofficial system that uses anonymous missiles to punish disturbers of the peace.
7. The ultimate nemesis of major war, the collapse of contemporary civilisations as we know them, and the disappearance of nuclear weapons altogether.

No firm opinions are offered on whether one version rather than another is more likely to come to pass. They are alternative constructs meant to expand our political vision, not co-opt it.

One review of this work dismissed it as a 'non-book',[8] and for a good reason. Any thoughtful attempt at political prevision soon demonstrates the imaginative poverty of Kahn's conjectures. For example, there are enormous potential consequences in the fact that 'as interdependency rises as a function of modernisation, there are no domestic policies without international implications, and vice versa. . . . As interdependency in highly modernised situations goes up, the possible catastrophic implications of any error also go up.'[9] Here, if anywhere, we need more knowledge and we need to be able to forecast with much greater precision. Kahn has little to say on the subject. The impending ability to determine the sex of offspring could see 'revolutions in social structure beyond the wildest dreams in the ideological clichés of the present'.[10] What will be the foreseeable results of the developing conflict between the 'direct allocation that must come with increases of centralization' and the 'increasing generalisation of media of exchange'?[11] Will highly modernised societies be able to survive on a self-indulgent or narcissistic basis instead of on the 'this-worldly asceticism' and the strive-motivation that has animated the most dynamic societies heretofore? How will the contemporary reliance upon rationality, specialisation, and emotional disengagement continue to marry with the human strain toward the non-rational, the personal, and the diffuse? Are there limits to the rate of change that mankind can withstand? How should we socialise for such futures as we can conceive when they remain unrealised and yet are so immediate? Kahn cannot say.

But there is more to the problem than the poverty of Kahn's

predictive imagination. Ultimately he offers nothing that informs the multiform attributes of the whole. There is, in fact, 'no theory. . . . All the predictions are *ad hoc* predictions . . . we are given no rhyme or reason for their beginning or end'.[12] Except for those attempts to forecast the truly novel and accidental things to come, conjectural pronouncements are only as good as the hypotheses about contemporary affairs and the nature of historical change that underpin them. Here the work is at its weakest.

In the later book Kahn lowers his sights from the nature of long-range systemic change to consider the short and middle-placed prospects for mankind. On the whole we are offered the same fare, bordering at best upon Spenglerian baroque. Thus the Westernistic post-industrial society of the year 2000 is likely to be characterised by a 'widespread sense of its civilization being the culmination of history, by a sense of decadence . . . by great works projects (e.g. great transport systems, space exploration), which will be an exciting fulfilment of modern technology but will probably be viewed by the most highly cultured elites with a sense of ennui or even contempt'.[13] His Atlantico-centric perspective on world affairs is even more evident, and his prolific categories equally unhelpful. What does one make of '. . . many new hostile emotions' as a source of instability in the basic political environment; of '. . . shocked, hysterical, or irrational behavior' as a 'classical' reason why major violence may still occur;[14] and of 'bizarre issues' as a likely cause of special technological dangers by 1985?

The possible number of *ad hoc* projections about world affairs is enormous. Kahn selects a few that he feels represent the range of likelihood, and pushes the rest into catch-all categories like that of 'bizarre issues'. 'Bizarre' and unlikely with respect to what, we may ask? An aberrant departure from a social theory that was thought would hold for the future, perhaps? But there is no such theory apart from that which can be inferred from Kahn's rules of selection. Instead of the tested general statements of the sort that Akzin recommends, Kahn offers metaphor, historical analogy, models and maxims[15] which, however heuristic they may be, are limp forms of argument indeed. All this would be quite inoffensive if Kahn did not commit himself explicity to arguing major issues[16] and offering alternative policy 'packages' based upon his assertions. In one particularly elliptical exposition Kahn lists 'twenty-one themes' which he suggests should cover the important political features of the next two decades. These range from continued containment and confrontation, through a resurgent communism on the march, various challenges from Europe, Japan, China, Latin America, new super powers, and technology generally, to possible modes of arms control, types of nuclear war, and the inevitable 'other' category to co-opt what has been neglected.[17] Far from stimulating and stretching a policy-maker's stock of perceived possibilities, Kahn serves simply to impoverish it. At best he can confirm ideological half-truths already widely accepted.

This is not an argument against future studies as such, but against the Hudson Institute's stunted version of what they can encompass, and the foreclosure effect this presumably has upon the individuals whom the Institute advises. The not-so-hidden prescription is a gradualist ascent from status quo to status quo. The Standard World' which Kahn constructs, where all the basic trends for population growth, for economic growth, for energy use and resource depletion continue unabated, is posited unquestioned. It is not a radical place, and there is no discussion of the morality of the distribution patterns involved nor of the nature of exploitation or of global neglect. At best the cloak of objectivity is used to conceal the dearth of explicitly derived and humane goals against which we might measure the alternative futures he presents and their manifest policy implications. At worst the supposedly non-moral and realistic character of such studies is a thin disguise for moralising imperatives of their own, often of a repugnant kind. 'Prognostics is policy by other means' and should be recognised as such. The decisions of politicians will influence our global future as much as the technical processes that move society at large. Those who would inform the decision-makers and review the crises and choices to come have a special duty to scrutinise the moral values which they implicitly recommend.

Any attempt at a more detailed and specific form of political forecasting clearly demonstrates the futility of the enterprise. 'Major fighting in Vietnam', Ithiel de Sola Pool wrote in 1965, 'will peter out about 1967; and most objective observers will regard it as a substantial American victory.' In 1968, he argued, Johnson would be returned as President for another term. And in the open-ended fashion reminiscent of *Old Moore's Almanack*, we find that for Africa by 1970 'there will have been sporadic famines, general chaos, and predominantly military dictatorships'.[18] As the level of analysis ascends, the useful content of the general statements that result is reduced to vanishing point. One is hardly led to feel optimistic about the value of Pool's prognostications for the periods 1970–2000, and 2000–15, and one readily agrees with Johan Galtung that he who would *predict* rather than conjecture 'should lock up his findings rather than publish them'.[19]

Galtung, better known as a contributor to the field of peace research, has also turned his hand to futurology, but unlike Kahn he has been careful to place his remarks in an explicit conceptual and theoretical framework, and not to ignore the morality of what he does. He is primarily concerned with the likelihood of war in the years to come, and he develops a detailed analysis of the structure of the world system upon which to build his pre-visionary views. Peace is made, he argues. through *associative* rather than *dissociative* strategies and there are three basic formulae by which it might be achieved :

1. global sub-systems must develop a mutually co-operative yet egalitarian interdependence,
2. the whole and its components must avoid abrupt discontinuities between, for example, race and race ('high entropy'),
3. the number of supra-group organisations both inter-governmental and international non-governmental in form must be large.

Structural changes to the world system will develop, he feels, from the disjunction between state and society. More developed societies will tend to outgrow their nation-state carapaces as their disenchanted members extend their loyalties or transfer them completely either to subnational groups or to complementary groups in other nations, to international non-governmental or to international supra-governmental organisations of one sort or another. Less developed societies, on the other hand, will grow into their nation-statehood, their rural sectors combining with their urban market economies, and their newly built industries spawning a powerful class of technocrats. As nationalism declines in the more developed nations, then, it will be matched by a parallel growth in nationalism in the less developed areas. The effect of the former, of retro-nationalism, Galtung feels will be to fulfil the three peace-making formulae mentioned above, and to herald the rise of peaceful coexistence among more developed states: 'East and West will rapidly disappear as meaningful contradictions . . . because of de-ideologization and technification of the economies and a relatively complete mutual interdependence. . . .'[20] Barring accidents or collapse before a significant level of integration of this sort is achieved, there will be in this region 'no major war'.[21] The effect of the latter, of ascendant nationalism, will be to fail the same three formulae, and for the less developed states to suffer a time of domestic strife within each as well as war among themselves.

But what of relations between the two sorts of societies – between North and South? Galtung discusses a number of such relationships and is prepared to predict that except for 'adopted' states like Puerto Rico the less developed nations will come to resent their exploitation as a source of intellectual talent, or cheap labour for the more developed block. As they perceive their common predicament they too will tend to integrate, but along 'trade union' lines for the purposes of collective bargaining. They will seek in a group way both higher prices for the raw materials they supply to the North, and some form of world welfare-state provisions to slow the rate at which the development gap is growing. If the developed nations do not respond constructively, Galtung concludes, the only alternatives are world class-war, which like Kahn he considers unlikely because of the weakness of the poor states and the organisational power of the rich ones, or intervention by the more developed sector in the affairs of the less developed states to keep them divided, quiescent, and amenable to the desired levels of assistance and exploitation.

There are difficulties with Galtung's arguments. He overestimates to my mind the role that might be played by the United Nations or its like of the future, and he overestimates too the likelihood that some 'strong ideology', charismatic national example, or 'discontinuous event' will weld the poor sector of world states into a cohesive and formidable whole. But the picture is well-grounded, it carries a set of policy implications that decision-makers could well consider closely, and his value premises are well-known. Some idea of the moral quality of the human society that underpins Galtung's view can be gleaned from another article of his: 'On the Future of Human Society'.[22] He espouses there an egalitarian, individualistic ideal of a communist utopia where self-realisation is the right of each and all – a familiar aspiration perhaps, but no less worthy because of that. The comparison with Kahn is instructive.

At this point I would like to re-introduce the second of the futurological approaches mentioned above – the tracing of substructural socio-economic and technological trends, the elucidation of the relationship between the political system and its changing social and physical environment,[23] the *ecology* of world politics as this bears upon its future.

The concern with war overrides much else in the modern world. With the advent of modern weapons no state is invincible and all look to their anticipated defence with what means they can muster. But war most likely will be only part of the major question that will face mankind in the future. It is quickly becoming apparent that there are ecological limits – important problems of over-population, pollution, and the accretion and exhaustion of the earth's natural and non-renewable resources – which may also result in war, and even if they do not, could cause civil life to collapse altogether or persist in some more diminished condition. The realm of man and all his activities, the cultural sociosphere discussed in the previous chapter, is only one of the world's systems. It now directly endangers or depletes the other great global arenas – the rocks and minerals of the lithosphere, the waters of the hydrosphere, the vapours of the atmosphere, and the biosphere of all other living things. The obvious fact is that exponential processes like, for example, population growth, cannot continue indefinitely within a finite living space like the earth, which must provide most of the vital support resources from its own and ultimately limited reserves. We do not know where the objective ceiling lies, which all these human heads will finally encounter, but presumably it is well short of the apocryphal Friday, 13 November 2026 when the population density will be such as to squash us to death.[24] Surely man's propensity for cultural adaptation will arrive at a variety of self-imposed control mechanisms before then :

> the question whether population growth will bring disaster to the human race turns not on the numbers, nor even on the speed at which they grow; but on a sober assessment of the likelihood that societies which have somehow managed to survive for the best part of two million years will at this stage in their history exhaust their capacity for taking prudent steps for their own survival.[25]

Nevertheless, ecological crisis would seem to loom large in all our alternative world futures, and the political repercussions of what may come to pass have hardly been conjectured. The implications of proposed solutions to the impending collapse are revolutionary, and at very least, the world politics of global support systems will be a growing point in the discipline.

Just what the dimensions of the ecological crisis will turn out to be is a much disputed question. One clearly formulated picture of what these limits might look like is contained in the Club of Rome–M.I.T. computer-simulation World Model 3. The study traces the complex interactions that occur between population growth, the depletion of non-renewable resources, levels of pollution, levels of industrialisation and capital accumulation, levels of food production, and attempts to assess their multiple and interlinked effects.[26] Here Dennis Meadows and his colleagues confront what they see as the world's 'great challenge – negotiating some form of orderly transition from world-wide growth in population and capital accumulation to an equilibrium in those two elements' so that they might be 'very much more in balance with the globe's finite resources'.[27] The time delays that accompany social change due to the inertia of complex socio-economic systems; the time delays between the emission of a pollutant and its appearance elsewhere in the ecosystem; and the long period that can often elapse between exposure to a pollutant and the manifestation of its deleterious effects[28] – all further erode the room for manoeuvre that we, as environmental engineers, might have.

Meadows's preliminary forecasts for the next fifty years are clear:

1. that population growth will slow dramatically as numbers rapidly approach the level that technological progress can sustain,
2. that most of those living in poor states will not be able to achieve the standard of living common in the rich,
3. that the rich states could well see a deterioration in their own living standards,
4. that 'there is no unique, optimal long-term population level. Rather there is an entire set of tradeoffs between personal freedom, material and social standard of living, and the population level . . .',[29]
5. that 'there is, in theory, no fundamental human value which could not be better achieved through a substantial lowering of the global population base',[30]
6. that the global achievement of an eco-responsible equilibrium could well be an uncontrolled and cataclysmic affair, and to subvert that possibility, strategies for orderly change that will keep the alternative options open must be implemented as soon as possible.

Generally, he concludes, the limits to growth on earth will be reached within the next one hundred years. 'The basic behavior mode of the world system is exponential growth of population and capital, followed by collapse.'[31]

The World Model 3 that Meadows constructs may turn out to be fundamentally misleading on its own terms, however, and has been taken to task for several alleged inadequacies. It has been assailed, for example, for its non-explicit character and the failure of its designers to understand that 'logical mathematical analysis *by itself* – i.e. without any empirical content – is quite unable to tell us anything about the behaviour of the real world . . .'. Tautological equations and propositions about the nature of exponential growth may conceal the occurrence, in fact, of levelling-off effects, and they tell us nothing in strict terms about the responses to its growing at any particular rate for any length of time.[32] Further, despite the allowances for error that Meadows includes, there is, for example, 'no *absolute* standard, independent of empirical evidence, of what is an "optimistic" or a "pessimistic" assumption to make about the rate at which the pollution content per unit of output could be reduced, or the rate at which food output can be increased. In the same way there is no absolute standard of what is a "small" or a "large" change in one of the equations . . .'.[33] The model subsumes statistical and econometric solutions that it does not substantiate, it seriously understates the amount of our planetary resource reserves, and it neglects the exploration, recycling and substitution processes that will come into play as such resources are depleted. Fundamentally, population collapse and resource depletion cannot be aggregated in the way that Meadows seems to assume. Population will not rise and fall simultaneously, but differentially, and shortages will occur not suddenly together but at different times and speeds.

Further force is given to such arguments in a set of detailed critiques by the Science Policy Research Unit at Sussex University.[34] Several members of this group have attempted to assess the worth of the model's assumptions about the present world and its likely development, on the understanding that computer models in particular are only as good as what goes into them. The M.I.T. approach is, in general, a neo-Malthusian one that overrates, they argue, the physical limits to growth and underrates the human potential for changing its values and for revising the social and political perspectives that bear directly upon the physical parameters that ultimately constrict what we shall do. 'In our view', one summary asserts, 'the Growth versus No Growth debate has become a rather sterile one . . . it tends to ignore the really important issues of the *composition* of growth in output, and the *distribution* of the fruits of growth. Some types of growth are quite consistent not merely with the conservation of the environment, but with its enhancement. The problem . . . is a socio-political one of stimulating this type of growth and of more equitable distribution both between countries and within them.'[35] In this respect the Sussex group has adopted the standard neo-Marxist response to the nay-saying tradition of Malthusian gloom.

The M.I.T. approach also underrates, they claim, the human capacity for technical progress, and the inclusion of this capacity is sufficient to postpone any drastic global collapse. Indeed, by building in 'technical progress in natural resources, pollution and agriculture . . . at rates that have been achieved historically for large parts of the world, all modes of "collapse" are avoided'.[36] The model is self-delusory, and hence 'inherently dangerous'.

World 3 is then broken down into its component sub-systems for closer scrutiny, and these are criticised in turn. The relative cost of 'non-renewable resources' is not increasing, they assert, and the discovery of new reserves continually adds to what is now available. Sustained exploration, recycling, and the more economic use of what we have already, should ensure that catastrophic depletion is avoided. The population component, it seems, is built upon wholly inadequate information, and ignores the possibility for population control by policy rather than by more brutal and physical means. Technical advances and a well-planned approach to agricultural production should ensure that most of us will be fed. Energy resources cannot be measured with any accuracy, and the use of figures in this regard tends to mislead rather than enlighten. Forecasts of future supplies must also attempt to predict the advent of new techniques that will affect such forecasts profoundly.

There are serious implications here. To what extent does a pessimistic model like the World 3 one constitute a subtle assault on poor states, who are thereby told by rich ones that they and everyone else are better off under the status quo? 'Adam Smith's benevolent "hidden hand" has been replaced by a malevolent "hidden boot"',[37] and it is the under-privileged who are most likely to find this leather instrument about their teeth and nostrils.[38]

The M.I.T. group has replied in vigorous terms to the Sussex assault. Optimism is a meagre retreat, they say, when 'exponential growth, physical limits, long adaptive delays, and inherent instability are obvious, general attributes of the present global system'.[39] There are, furthermore, numerous technical errors in the critique, the most important being 'the choice of perfection as the standard used in evaluating the World models'.[40] This choice has led to the spurious concentration of those opposed to the work upon secondary aspects of it, upon the numerical assumptions and the mechanics of the sub-systems involved, rather than the primary causal relationships that are the 'real substance' of the M.I.T. results. They defend their view of the aggregate character of the eco-crisis, and the possibility that a number of problems will come together at the same time, and not, as might be expected, over some protracted period. The most important part of their case is the delineation of the long feedback delays that are the 'main source of instability' in their model systems. This is the 'overshoot' effect they fear most. 'When rapid growth is coupled with a long delay between cause and effect, the growth may proceed far beyond sustainable limits before the effects that can stop it come into play.'[41] They find no reason to mediate their concern in this respect, despite such possible mechanisms as economic price adjustment (compare Beckerman's opinion that the 'problem of environmental pollution is a simple matter of correcting a minor resource misallocation by means of pollution charges'[42]), and factors of technical change and the revision of human values. They conclude that problems of physical growth cannot be viewed independently of the composition and distribution of the margins involved. Further, technology is no panacea that will negate the inexorable effect of physical limits, and to place upon the future the burden of eco-salvage by scientific means as yet unknown is to pursue a policy of maximum risk. Finally, they support their model as the best available example of its kind to date, and only fit for refutation by some superior alternative.

The World Model 3 has been criticised most fundamentally, then, for its elitism and its technocratic exclusion of social factors. The greatest cause for ecological optimism lies in the latter direction. Social and value concerns are very difficult to quantify, to assess or predict, and Meadows has explicitly admitted his failure to deal with them.[43] All the results can only be seen in this light and that of previous comments about man's transcendant reliance upon social and cultural evolution in coping with environmental stress.

Nevertheless, few now consider that the dimensions of the eco-crisis will substantially diminish in the normal course of events. What sparks academic conflict are the different interpretations placed upon assessments of their significance. Population growth is probably the least ambiguous factor in current eco-equations and its phenomenal rise has been seen as the 'most significant terrestrial event of the past million millennia'.[44] This betrays some rather odd criteria of import, but with at least 3·5 thousand million people now on earth, a number that will nearly double in thirty-five years or so, it is perhaps no surprise that contemporary commentators often talk in apocalyptic terms about the consequences. Under such populous conditions whatever indispensable resource or whatever polluted subsystem gives out first will spell the collapse of the whole. The complex interlocked chains are only as strong as their weakest link, and there is much debate about what that link might be and where it lies. The single burden of population growth is only part of the problem, but it is here that the radical character of the ecological perspective emerges most clearly.

The statistics on population density, that is, the number of people per square unit of land, show that Atlantico-European countries like the United States, England, France and Holland are far more crowded than their former colonies in the underdeveloped world. And yet those who live in them are comparatively much better off and the population growth rates are consequently much lower. This would suggest that levels of development and industrialisation, rather than population or population growth *per se*, are of primary concern. Certainly rich states are not considered drastically overpopulated by the contemporary critics of procreation, in the same way that poor states are. To support its members in relative affluence, however, an agriculturally and industrially developed nation like the United States must draw heavily upon the resources of the rest of the world. Limiting the numbers of the rich, then, may alleviate economic problems more effectively than limiting the numbers of the poor. 'We use roughly one half of all the raw materials consumed on the face of the Earth each year', Ehrlich admits. 'We need the ferroalloys, tin, bauxite, petroleum, rubber, food and other materials we import. We, one fifteenth the population, grab one half as our share.'[45] Why does the United States need such vast resources? It could clearly nourish its populace at the recommended levels compatible with health and vitality on much less. We have the extraordinary example in recent times of the People's Republic of China, of one quarter of mankind, reaching just such a 'recommended' status out of a history of recurrent famine and a more recent base-line of deprivation, revolution, widespread poverty and war.

This lends considerable force to the socialist argument that the pressing problem, for the present at least, lies in the realm of distribution and the inegalitarian mode of parcelling out goods that typifies even the welfare capitalism of the West. It is here that the mechanics of reform should probably turn first, which leads directly back to debates about the relative merits of freedom from want as opposed to freedom from distributive controls. It also restates the question of *over*-development, and whether the inordinate proportion of world materials appropriated by rich states does not in fact betray an elitist and self-aggrandising form of political and economic dominance, and further, a level of production and consumption which is unrealistc in the long term and exploitative in the short. 'Over-development may . . . be defined as taking more than a fair share of the world's scarce resources, and thus denying to other countries (the underdeveloped or rather over-exploited) the possibility of attaining equivalent levels of living standards as measured by conventional indices.'[46] It denotes a concept of life-satisfaction that is wasteful, extravagant and wilfully blind to the implications of the eco-bind we may or will be in.

Inadequate nutritional levels result, in this view, more from the market-system of food grown for profit than from any absolute lack of arable lands, ignorance of agricultural technique, or any absolute surfeit of mouths to fill. Dishonesty and greed are deftly substituted for the rational satisfaction of basic human wants. To attack overpopulation alone, then, is to misconstrue the interconnected, international and truly ecological nature of the questions involved, and it may well constitute a cynical defence of entrenched and privileged interests. 'The same elites and institutions which made America the world's policeman have long been eager to serve as the world's prophylactic and agricultural provisioner, and they are damned grateful to the academics for creating a new humanitarian justification for the age-old game of empire.'[47] Perhaps the process is not so cynically engendered, but there is a more important point. Where there is 'greater economic security, political participation, elimination of gross class division, liberation of women, and respected leadership, humane and successful population programs are at least possible'.[48] Without such conditions, without the attempt to achieve such conditions at the same time, programmes of this sort can all too readily be construed as the cheapest defence of a favoured status quo.

The threat of neo-Malthusian apocalypse, then, is readily depicted as a rich-state class-based attack upon the poor. And yet if development and distribution are the primary concerns, the control of population is an important secondary one. The regulation of birth rates is now an accepted practice in nearly all socialist states, despite neo-Marxist orthodoxy, though this fact should not distract us from the most critical aspect of the problem and its socio-economic underpinnings. It is possible to accept the ultimate need to limit population growth without either endorsing the export of forced controls, or endorsing foreign policies of indifference or exploitation.

Projections of population growth have been used to support assertions about interstate conflict. Thus R. C. North has argued that '. . . *differential* rates of population growth in combination with *differential* rates of technological growth contribute to conflict insofar as individual human beings and nation-states have *differential – grossly unequal* – access to food, housing, health, education, work, justice, and general influence or control over their environments'.[49] Population and technology denote state power; any decrease in the power gap between two states causes apprehension among the leaders of the stronger, and the likelihood of conflict, he claims, is thereby increased.

Elsewhere he and Nazli Choucri spell out in greater detail this rather inconclusive formulation. Thus, developing technology and a growing population create growing demands on resources; the larger the number of people, and the more advanced the level of technology, the greater and more various their needs and demands will be; specialised capacities develop that produce in turn an ill-defined set of internally generated 'lateral pressures'; the greater these pressures, the greater the likelihood that in the search for raw materials, markets and investment opportunities a society will extend its activities outside its territorial domain, acquiring influence and control over people of lesser strength.

> To the extent that two or more countries with high capability and high pressure tendencies extend their interest and psycho-political borders outward, there is a strong possibility that eventually the two opposing spheres of interest will intersect. The more intense the *intersections*, the greater will be the likelihood that competition will assume *military* dimensions.

When this happens, we may expect competition to become transformed into conflict...'.[50]

There may be an arms race, cold war or a colonial competition that leads to a crisis and thence to hot war. Between the pressuring and the pressured states the familiar features of imperialism will prevail. To gain and hold the order most favourable to its state and commercial interests the pressuring country may seek to crush the pressured group, either directly or by proxy with the help of indigenous sectors who stand to gain from the imperial presence. Though Choucri and North claim for their concept of 'lateral pressure' something beyond the meaning more traditional notions of imperialism and colonialism are meant to convey, in a world of grossly unequal capabilities their alternative use of the term to cover theories of a functional, integratory and federalist character makes very little empirical sense. It obscures in fact two processes that are best kept conceptually discrete. In practice they mean the former imperial notion, and seldom refer to the latter integratory aspect at all.

Choucri and Bennett, on the other hand, find

> no evidence that population densities per se [as opposed to Choucri and North's propositions about differential population *growth*] lead to instabilities. Those correlations that do exist are spurious and do not hold cross-culturally. Many densely populated areas of the world have been highly stable, and many of the most unstable areas . . . have low population densities.[51]

This holds both domestically and as a factor between states. The link between population and violence has to deal in complex ways with intervening variables, with the nature and extent of a country's resource base and of its technological expertise, and any direct connection must answer the negative findings of 'two large-scale empirical studies of conflict and warfare'[52] to the contrary.

The global pattern of resource use certainly suggests that as the industrialised states are forced to rely more and more upon external regions to provide for home needs, there will be political repercussions of some sort – though just what sort is not clear. Big states can protect their vital supplies to a significant degree by diversifying the external sources from which they are obtained, and they are more likely to have the technology to invent, recycle and substitute for what they do not have. They are still vulnerable, however, and their apprehension could well lead to the use of pre-emptive force in a direct or subversive way. In this sense the issue is

> not whether the major powers are exploiting or assisting developing countries . . . but that rapid industrialization in low-income countries, coupled with growing populations, will place additional burdens upon national governments and upon the existing resource base. Their national governments in turn . . . will undoubtedly express dissatisfaction with the industrialized-power–host-state relationship and demand readjustments. To the extent that major powers are willing to modify patterns of interaction and relationships the imbalances may be resolved by peaceful means. If the costs of readjustments are perceived as being too high . . . probabilities are high that the industrialized-powers will exert additional pressure, and non-military means of control might give way before direct military coercion.[53]

The ecological squeeze could see a fairer distribution of the world's goods, but more likely it will reinforce the developed states in the defence of their preferred position. The futurological findings discussed earlier support a similar conclusion.

In the long term, of course, the consequences may not be those most apparent to us now. Industrialised technological states may not only fail to resolve the contradictions to which they give rise, but the social orders they sustain may come to suffer much more in the end than less advanced ones should environmental collapse finally occur. The less organised, less specialised and less integrated character of an underdeveloped country that is already the victim of eco-crisis may inure it to some extent to the worst features of any future collapse. Those who have nothing, that is, have little to lose. Ironically enough it may well be the hungry who inherit the earth. The densely populated, urban-industrial societies with their ever-expanding economies may not, as it turns out, be successfully 'developed' in quite essential ways, indeed they may be lethal to humankind as a whole. By the time we fully appreciate this fact, however, it will be irrelevant.[54] 'You must listen whiteman', said the Amerindian sage, 'you are sitting on short grasses covered with human shit. In all four directions the arrows are broken, the land – barren.'

CHAPTER 6

Systems and Cybernetics

Having located the study of man and his global affairs in the distancing perspectives of space and spent time, having glanced at the future and the study of the future and what some see as being in store there, and having elaborated the propositions I find of relevance in these enveloping concerns, I would like to proceed to the more immediate (non-economic) foci and frameworks applied to world affairs – to 'systems' and cybernetics first, to the findings of brain research, ethology (social biology) and social psychology second, and to the various analytical and substantive studies that have been made of regional and global integration and conflict third. In this way I hope, rather than confronting it directly in the conventional manner, to proceed with the task I have already begun, of surrounding the traditional subject-matter of world affairs, trapping it in a transdisciplinary crossfire, and attempting to capture its most important characteristics in analytic and quantitative terms.

If one concept could be said to have dominated the behavioural approach to world politics it is that of 'system'. Though the steam has gone out of 'systems theory' now, and the chroniclers of disciplinary trend can only comment nostalgically upon what might have been, the malady lingers on. Not all the residual legacies, however, can be ignored. 'Systems analysis', at its simplest, is the *systematic* study of structure and process in world politics,

> the more formalised version of clear thinking about complicated problems which education teaches us to use daily: we divide a large problem into sections, concentrate our attention separately and singly on each section in turn or on a group

> of sections, and we explain each part to ourselves, rebuild the whole piece by piece in order to reconstruct the phenomenon mentally in a form in which we feel we can understand it.[1]

There is nothing particularly novel in this, except that as we move from the incomprehensible totality to scrutinise the parts, we are continually encouraged to keep in mind that the final purpose of the enquiry is not just the collation of piece-meal detail about analytically separable sections but a re-assimilated view of the whole. We move from whole to part, and from part back to whole, and in both directions we hopefully enhance what we want to know.

Thus, in the behavioural literature on world politics, attention was diverted from current affairs and diplomatic history and one-state studies of foreign policy to the *global* process of political transactions. In retrospect:

> The principal merit of the systems approach was to establish a viable characterization for phenomena of global interdependence, and to signal the need for a greater understanding of particular interdependencies. For to say that the world now forms an international system is at the same time to assert that various parts of that system not only interact but also cohere, that changes in one part of the system inevitably set in motion changes in other parts. This serves as a corrective to the unsubstantiated images of chaos, if not anarchy, that were frequently associated with perceptions of international politics. . . .[2]

Close attention is paid to levels of analysis, to the problems involved in combining conclusions drawn at one level with those drawn from another, and to the possibility of ignoring the complex details of one part of the system in order to understand better the generalised interactions of that part with others. There are obvious difficulties at each point, but the underlying purpose persists, the desire, that is, not to lose a good view of the forest as one busily strips the trees. To describe how the global system works one looks for sub-systemic components that seem comparatively autonomous – states, perhaps, or parts of states, or non-state collectivities that bear little relationship to territorial or national boundaries; these are scrutinised and then packed together like analytical Chinese boxes to give a more comprehensive outline, and, depending on the question being asked, to give a more comprehensive answer.

The most inclusive of all the frameworks to be applied to world politics has been General Systems Theory. Little agreement exists over what this is in detail, and a glance at the annual *General Systems Yearbook* will demonstrate just how diverse a set of interests the parent approach can encompass. The *Yearbook* has acquired a cabalistic aura over the years, and it remains a strange place where esoteric formulae abound. It bears continuous witness, however, to a recurrent trend in Western science, that is, the urge to unify all contemporary knowledge, and though dissipated once again in diffuse and diverse practice the metaphysic lure is still very much alive. Though the unification of all science might more realistically be expected to emerge in an empirical fashion, from below as it were, as concrete hypotheses are derived that are seen to explain more and more phenomena with fewer and fewer fundamental axioms, this has not prevented attempts to impose such a coherent schema from above.

General Systems Theory was evolved and elaborated by a biologist, Ludwig von Bertalanffy. For fifty years, or so he tells us, Bertalanffy has been much concerned with the ever-increasing specialisation of modern science and the ever-diverging paths of human knowledge. At the same time he has observed the coincidental yet complementary development of a convergent strain that has grown up beside this divergent one; the development of similar general viewpoints and parallel conceptions in divers scientific fields. In the 1950s he finally set forth his basic idea that models, principles and laws exist which apply to generalised systems and their components, irrespective of what the system is or what its component parts might be. General Systems Theory advances a set of principles valid for any 'system', including of course the international and world ones. Its central postulate asserts that systems resemble each other in fundamental ways, or more formally, that they are isomorphic, and upon this assertion Bertalanffy has built a pyramid of specialised concepts that he intends will achieve nothing less than the far-reaching analytic fusion of all science. He is not just looking for suggestive analogies between paramecia, for example, and world politics. He seeks an abstract, general model that can be applied to paramecia and global affairs alike. As Newton's law of gravitation might equally apply to the descent of a falling apple or the orbit of the planet Earth, though the only resemblance between the two objects be their relative motion, so Bertalanffy seeks laws of 'systems' that might equally apply wherever a 'system' as he defines it can be found. 'Where systems analysis, then, is a tool or a methodology, and is neither wholly novel nor particularly difficult, general systems theory is a set of substantive hypotheses. The hypotheses describe political reality and although they are cast in extremely general terms they can be regarded as forming a skeletal general theory of world politics.'[3]

For years, however, General Systems Theory offered little in the way of 'theory', that is, the hypothetical principles and propositions of exploratory and predictive power applicable to all systems, which were its maximum promise. It offered only a language, a terminology, a set of concepts into which politics might be translated. In 1965, however, J. G. Miller outlined no less than 165 'cross-level hypotheses'[4] which applied, he felt, to all 'living systems', by which he meant that subset of the 'real' or 'concrete' systems as opposed to the 'abstracted' or 'conceptual' ones that are made up of plants and animals, including man.[5] Allowing for the 'dis-analogies' that might emerge when they are applied at any particular level, Miller considers these propositions to be 'more than propositions of systems theory; they are *general* systems theoretical hypotheses',[6] applicable to systems at two or more levels, from one-celled organisms to the political globe, and open to empirical and experimental test. The usefulness of general systems behaviour theory, Miller claims, will only be determined after many such tests have been done. They are difficult, inter-disciplinary enterprises, but their findings alone will determine if a general theory of living systems is practicable or not.

The hypotheses begin with the assertion that '. . . In general, the more numbers or components a system has, the more echelons[7] it has',[8] and end with the observation that 'If a system's negative feedback discontinues and is not restored by that system or by another on which it becomes parasitic or symbiotic, it decomposes into multiple components and its suprasystem assumes control of them'.[9]

From the examples that Miller gives he clearly considers that many of these hypotheses can be applied to world politics. This is problematic, since in a list that he has compiled elsewhere of the attributes that characterise a 'living system' he has specified the presence of a 'decider', that is, an 'essential critical subsystem which controls the entire system, causing its subsystems and components to coact, without which there is no system'.[10] The world political 'system', unlike a state or interstate organisation, has no such decider, and so defined does not exist as a system to which the hypotheses advanced might apply. Nevertheless when Miller maintains that if there are '. . . heterogeneous components in a system, they adjust to being together best if they group together into two or more partially autonomous components on the basis of similarity of their templates, functions or values',[11] he offers as an illustration Amitai Etzioni's argument that 'supranational systems are more stable if they subdivide into blocs and subblocs, with some autonomy, each representing a specific set of common interests'.[12] Further, he asserts that 'The larger the number of subsystems or components in conflict, the more difficult will be resolution of the conflict',[13] and advances both this hypothesis and its logical opposite as current stances in the study of international affairs.

Miller clearly considers the international system to be a 'living system' and one of the levels to which many of the cross-level hypotheses conceivably apply, despite his own definitional criterion to the contrary. He would seem to have disqualified world politics at the outset and then smuggled it back later on, not the most consistent of analytic practices. More important, perhaps, his whole-hearted devotion to the generalising imperative leads him to neglect the likely possibility of hypotheses, theories and laws that might be unique to only one particular level or sort of system.

The question of definitions is a vexed one for General Systems Theory. Firstly, what is a 'system', and what are the properties by which a system might be identified? Following Bertalanffy's lead, a system is seen here as a set of units that interact, that have relationships amongst themselves. The units must be sufficiently alike to form a set, and sufficiently inter-dependent for a change in the state of one unit to cause repercussions for others. These units operate within a *boundary*, which marks the major discontinuities in transactions, in traffic and response, between the set and its environment. A closed system is one where the pattern of interactions falls entirely within this boundary. Few such systems are known to exist. Most are open and to survive must interact with their environments, which involves notions of 'growth' and 'adaptation'. Thirdly, a system will have a structure that depicts the pattern of relationships between the component units, a structure that will usually be in a constant process of readjustment as a result of the changing state of inter-unit transactions. Lastly, a system will have goals, be they only the maintenance of its own stability. The maintenance of stability need not be a static affair and may involve not only conflict resolution and the preservation of some status quo, but the active cognisance of conflict *stimulation* – the attempt to shape, guide and even encourage the destabilising contradictions that infest any system and particularly those of a human kind.[14]

General Systems Theory points to the tendency for all systems to sustain their internal structures despite the upsetting influence of constant change, and calls the mechanism by which this is done 'homeostasis' – dynamic equilibrium – the same term that is used to describe the way the human body corrects within itself for external changes in heat and cold, or for the incursions of injury and disease. A condition of homeostasis, like the other system goals, can be reached in various ways, and this involves another descriptive concept called 'equifinality'.

As the language it uses might suggest, General Systems Theory owes much to biology, and in fact it has often been dismissed as merely an extended biological metaphor. Bertalanffy's desire to formulate abstract statements about all complex systems based upon their fundamental similarities was no isolated phenomenon, and he has come in for criticisms made elsewhere about generalising biologists.[15] Bertalanffy's assertion that the cross-level systemic similarities he seeks are not simply analogous but homologous has been attacked for claiming distinctions of kind where they are rightly considered only by degree, for claiming, that is, a precision and clarity of correspondence that does not in fact exist. Biological principles, and concepts like growth and evolution and those briefly mentioned above, suggest structural likenesses from level to level that are more apparent than real, and those similarities of structure or process that do exist are not necessarily useful or significant thereby. Only Miller has attempted to present isomorphic propositions amenable to test. He does not claim that general statements from one discipline can be directly transposed into another, that the immune reactions of the human body, for example, can tell us anything about the judicial operations of a state police force. But immune reactions and the coincidental nature of police work might be explained by an underlying hypothesis built out of a basic body of principles that applies to them both. This was the underlying hope of General Systems Theory, and it is perhaps significant that no-one, to my knowledge, has attempted the interdisciplinary empirical validation of the hypotheses that Miller recommends. The reason probably lies in the generality of the concepts involved, and the diversity of ideas that the approach would contain. 'Thus, what is true of all systems, even though it may be relevant to the international system, is most often not sufficiently specific to add greatly to our appreciation of a much more narrowly defined, yet promising field.'[16] The more abstract the statement, the more irrelevant or trivial it usually has to be.

There are two other systemic approaches that share many of the features of General Systems Theory. The first of these is *functionalism*, a physiological–anthropological doctrine applied by students of politics to suggest that there are certain functions any political system must perform to survive, and that wherever one finds a political system structures will exist to perform those functions. The best-known structural–functional framework in political science is that of Gabriel Almond,[17] and there has been one attempt, though an unproductive and ultimately unsatisfactory one, to use Almond's functional categories of interest articulation, interest aggregation, and so on, to explain the structural characteristics of world politics.[18] The critique of this doctrine is a well-developed one and I shall not go into it here.[19] Suffice to say that structures and functions may not correspond in any easily identified fashion, since structures may live on, for example, in a redundant fashion long after their specific function has finished, and any one function may be represented by a number of different structures. Ultimately, anyway, parts and process are one, and institutions represent simply the spatial mode of sets of human transactions patterned in discernible ways over time.

The second of these subsidiary systemic approaches is the *input–output analysis* associated with David Easton.[20] This is the political processing-plant idea that the discipline adored for a decade. The only trouble is that Easton, like Miller, defines the political system as that system of interactions in a society which makes binding or authoritative allocations there, and implements them. The global society has no such authoritative unit,[21] and so Eastonian analysis, like Miller's hypotheses, is inappropriate to world politics whatever its merits in use elsewhere.[22]

Apart from Miller's General Systems work, how has the idea of 'systems' been applied to global affairs? There are two main applications, the one a direct descendant of traditional approaches to world politics, with the same *real-politik* results, and the other, in its time, a novel perspective with far more interesting implications.

Firstly, if the world system is simply seen as an *international* system made up of the nation-states plus institutional–corporational units like the United Nations or Standard Oil of New Jersey, then 'system' and 'systems theory' simply rephrases more familiar verities about the 'balance-of-power' in a new and probably less useful way. The balance-of-power approach views state action as a response to a perceived change in the power potential of another state. Crises and wars arise when the balance is upset altogether, or a close equivalence loses its delicate counterpoise. The systems approach translates mechanistic equilibrium into the systems idiom of an interdependent set of units in a steady state that strives to damp down disruptive inputs and to maintain the homeostatic stability that is preferred. This resembles the imperviously bounded, billiard-ball model of states in the world that a more traditional approach would employ: 'On the face of it, the chief characteristic of such an interpretation or explanation of international politics is the removal of volition from the participants. But what systems theory actually does is merely to shift the level of analysis from the conscious policy-making of the units . . . to the interaction at the systemic level.'[23]

Raising the level of analysis, then, serves to justify a very deterministic stance, and one that fell out of fashion after the Vietnam conflict – the first and hopefully the last of the 'systems' wars. The actions of individual state leaders, questions of ideology and will, are ignored in favour of the study of the patterns of relations that arise between global actors. The focus becomes the overall structure of the international system and the effect of that structure upon systemic behaviour. It leads to debates like that between Kenneth Waltz, J. D. Singer and Richard Rosecrance,[24] about the likelihood of stability in a bipolar as opposed to a multi-polar world. In its abstracted way the literature on *international* systems avoids what may well be a critical point. Its remote and restricted perspective can only be justified if the general explanations that result confer greater predictive power than a less rarified one. If these enhanced explanations are forthcoming then the approach is pitched, limited though it may seem, at the right level. So far, however, there is no indication in the literature that such has been the case. As this failure is further confirmed, it becomes necessary to include some consideration of world sub-systems in detail; the question is, how should this be done? Here we come to the second and more interesting use of 'systems' in global affairs.

If the international system is *not* seen as a state system primarily but as a single group of three and a half or so thousand million human beings, organised for some purposes into nation-states but for others into interrelated economic, scientific, cultural, ideological and religious sets that are less apparent but no less 'real', then quite a different picture emerges. The idea of 'systems' used in this way avoids the tendency for what is obvious to dominate what we see, merely because this has been the case to date. Less evident regularities and less formalised *non*-state collectivities come into view. If their constituent units interact, they can be considered world systems as readily as the more traditional state-based sort. A global network of such systems emerges that is concentrated into territorial and administrative areas, but is also dispersed beyond them.

This is a much more interesting use of the idea since it highlights the existence of sets of relationships that the contemporary fact of nation-states tends to obscure. One major exponent of this viewpoint has been J. W. Burton. States, he says, are 'clusters of systems and parts of systems within geographical areas, controlled and integrated in some degree by politically created administrative systems'.[25] Their presence, he continues, tends to 'draw attention to the way in which boundaries disturb transaction flows and prejudices in advance an analysis of the role of States in world society'. By this it is 'not intended to imply that States are no longer significant; on the contrary, their role and range of activities has increased, but it is a role in relation to systems. World society is perhaps best analysed by considering systems first, and then the role of States, which is the reverse of a traditional approach.'[26]

World society is made up in this view of universal networks that cover many parts of it, of regional networks centred on territorial areas, and of local networks down to the level of the family. Analytically each set of relationships, each system that is, can be abstracted from the human whole, though some of the persons involved in one set may, in another capacity, be involved in others. An oil magnate for example, member of a sectional trading and resource network, may also belong to a regional set of an ethnic or cultural kind. Separating out a system becomes less the concrete operation of identifying just those people that interact in it, but more an analytical procedure of abstracting for the purpose of the enquiry the set of relevant roles certain people play under specified circumstances. Boundaries occur where interactions become transactions, and not necessarily along a demarcated line but over a porous zone. In this view world society appears 'like millions of cobwebs superimposed one upon another, covering the whole globe. . . . Each separate cobweb would represent a separate system – trade flows, letters exchanged, tourist movements, aircraft flights, population movements and transactions in ideas, cultures, languages and religions, traffic flows within towns and social interactions within village communities.'[27] Systems are often linked, sharing units or values, and linked systems cluster in geographic areas to constitute societies and states. Administrative units develop that control the interactions of other systems, thus limiting the consequences of change.

The particular use of 'systems' to describe world affairs outlined above has been widely criticised. W. J. M. Mackenzie, for example, argues that

> one could take Politics without States as the norm of politics, and develop an argument leading to these special cases in which politics is state politics. This is attractive intellectually: but the practical arguments against it seem decisive. We are in fact living with a specified number of legally constituted states, each with an individual history, in part fortuitous. It is not feasible to derive the present system of states from general theory; the most one can hope is to place them in a conceptual perspective.[28]

He opts in other words for the traditional view of world politics as primarily an *international* system though he admits the absurdity of that system today and specifically identifies some major sorts of secondary non-state sets – businesses that span the globe, world movements that transmit doctrines and ways of life, and science, the world system of knowledge that is inseparable from the world system of politics. These all cross state boundaries in a very untraditional way and threaten to burst the familiar analytical frameworks asunder, but, at least for Mackenzie, not yet.

At this point it might be useful to look at specific examples of the two basic 'systems' applications just outlined: firstly, the more traditional sort that simply rephrases in systems terminology a view of the world as a set of state units. The best known application here is that of Morton Kaplan and his *System and Process in International Politics*.[29] Even the most cursory glance at the behavioural literature will turn up multiple references to Kaplan and his mechanistic toys, and paraphrasing this book has become a minor academic industry of its own.

Kaplan sets out six abstract models of hypothetical interstate systems that resemble in their simplified fashion six possible sets of interstate relationships. It is these that have prompted such interest. They are:

1. the balance-of-power system,
2. the loose bipolar system,
3. the tight bipolar system,
4. the universal–international system,

5. the hierarchical system, and
6. the unit veto system.

Kaplan is a 'power' theorist and in deterministic fashion he sees systems behaviour as a direct result of systems structure, that is, of patterns of interstate relationships. 'If the number, type, and behavior of nations differ over time, and if their military capabilities, their economic assets, and their information also vary over time, then there is some likely inter-connection between these elements such that different structural and behavioral systems can be discerned to operate in different periods of history.'[30] Out of his six models Kaplan constructs a number of hypotheses that are, he claims, open to empirical test and that elucidate these connections. The purpose of the inquiry that leads him to select the features he does, and to neglect any others, is ostensibly his concern with how interstate systems stay stable over time and how they change from one sort of set to another.

The *balance-of-power* model is the one Kaplan elaborates most. Such a system needs, he feels, at least five countries and preferably more for it to work, and he gives as an example the pre-First World War Atlantic system of England, France, Germany, Italy, Austria–Hungary and the United States. His list of essential rules that each state must observe for the system to survive is a concise summary of traditional balance-of-power ideas – each state, for example, must act to increase its power, fight rather than forgo an opportunity to do so (though it must negotiate first rather than fight), stop fighting before it eliminates another essential state, and act to oppose any coalition or single state that seeks a preponderance of power. In Kaplan's model world the system is maintained quite informally, by mutual self-interest. There is no need for a world government or the like because if one state tries to dominate the others it will be confronted by them, and it in turn joins alliances to defeat those who would attempt to do likewise. This automatic situation should last as long as no alliance emerges that can corner the market.

One can see the attractions of such a device, the balancing out of any attempt at preponderance, self-concerned states swapping allegiance and leaping from one side of the systemic scales to the other. The device is thoroughly misleading as a guide to the real world, however, and has had dangerous ideological consequences when applied there. A simplistic image like this one contributed to American attempts to contain China and the Soviet Union after the Second World War, and the equilibrial imperative, instead of redressing any perceived imbalance, served to excuse a spate of defensive interventions.

The most likely transformation for a balance-of-power model, Kaplan argues, would be into a *bipolar* one where two state actors and their allied coteries form predominant blocs. The *loose* bipolar system most resembles the post-Second World War world – two major alliance organisations like NATO and the Warsaw Pact, oriented to a leading country within each, a third uncommitted clutch of states that lie between the dominant poles, and a global actor like the United Nations. If the blocs are highly organised, only non-bloc countries can change the pattern and the system tends to the tight bipolar or hierarchial forms. If they are loosely organised it works much like the balance-of-power one, though there is less chance to change sides, and the system in Kaplan's view is an inherently unstable one. The *tight* bipolar system is similar to the loose variant, but there are fewer sorts of participant units. Its stability depends again upon the organisation of the blocs – the more organised they are, the more stable the whole becomes. The *universal–international* system is the Grotian image of global order – a community of states living harmoniously together under agreed principles. The use of power would be at a minimum in such a world, and international lawyers would be much in demand as conflict managers. Unlike the systems above in which the sub-systems, that is the state units and other world organisations, are dominant, here the whole system itself would be a super-state that encompassed the rest. This is the utopian view of global federation, and one that under present conditions would break down into the bipolar, balance-of-power or hierarchical alternatives. The *hierarchical–international* system is that of world empire. States as such would recede in importance, and one would dominate the rest. They would become merely administrative territories in a global structure where interest-groups, rather than nations, were the main actors. In the *unit veto* system there are no dominant states since each has the capacity totally to destroy any other. This is the wishful model of an all-nuclear world, a mutual stand-off where each state, regardless of its population or resources, is equal under technology. The common policy device would be blackmail, and this would most likely lead to world war or world empire. Needless to say, by Kaplan's reckoning, this system would be very unstable.

In attempting to abstract the essential features from a number of historical, actual or potential international systems, Kaplan assumes a high degree of repetition there and a regularity of affairs sufficient to formulate general structures and rules: 'by shifting the focus of analysis from the particular event to the pattern of events, seemingly unique or accidental occurrences become part of a meaningful pattern of occurrences. In this way the historical loses its quality of uniqueness and is translated into the universal language of science.'[31] One recognises the generalising imperative of the dedicated behaviouralist. The question is, however, whether such an order obtains in fact or whether it has been imposed upon diverse events from without and rather misrepresents the order of complexity involved. The simplified character of the models outlined is formal rather than real. They are crisp, clear statements of the traditional power-centred view of international relations, and they share the limited perspectives of that view. As to explanation, Kaplan has little explicit to offer. What his models do predispose are explanations of an antiquated sort, which is not to say that in a few years' time we shall not see them restored to fashion on a determined tide of academic nostalgia, prompted, no doubt, by another war. Kaplan has done very little in the way of applying his ideas to the real world, largely one suspects because they lose their analytical purity there and become qualified out of sight. They have contributed neither to the 'meaningful ordering of data' nor to the building of any general theory that was not current before.[32] They would be a fitting inscription on any epitaph for a monument to a failed science.

The traditional use of the systems idea has largely been to ignore what goes on *within* the units that make up the systemic set. Richard Rosecrance, however, in his *Action and Reaction in World Politics*[33] has made some attempt to redress this neglect. Rosecrance selects from the West European record nine systems which existed between 1740 and 1960 that stand apart from each other in discrete ways. Like Kaplan he is interested in the factors that enhance and undermine international stability, and he sorts his nine historical systems into five that were stable and four that were not. He concludes that the *stable* systems remained so because interstate regulator mechanisms existed, like the Concert of Europe or the United Nations, that could damp down any conflict, and the elites of the system were happy with affairs as they were both within states and between them. Diplomatic bargaining was at a premium and national objectives were kept within mutually acceptable limits. *Unstable* systems exhibited exactly the opposite characteristics – much conflict with little systemic capacity for coping with it, insecure elites far readier to appeal to nationalism and ideology and with much less of a prospect for success through negotiation or diplomacy.

On the whole, Rosecrance's argument appears to be built upon retrospective wisdom rather than his own systemic models. Though suitably modest about what his abstracted variables portend for the future, he does advance as an historically demonstrable fact, a direct link between the level of international stability and the felt domestic security or lack of security of national elites. Demonstrable it may be, but it is the selective use of historical evidence rather than any intrinsic advantage in the concept of 'system' that confers the explanatory power.

Having cleared the ground of the Kaplan and Rosecrance contributions I shall reconsider the second and more novel application of the 'systems' idea, in particular that of John Burton in his *Systems, States, Diplomacy and Rules.*[34] After developing the complex 'cobweb' view of world society described above, Burton goes on to construct a more detailed approach to global politics itself. The first and most important part of this approach is his concept of an ideal world system and how it would proceed. when faced with the fact of change a state must either modify the environment from which a stimulus comes or revise its own behaviour (or be revised). Change and the resistance to change are what Burton considers the 'important' cause of conflict.[35] 'The ideal type of world society is one which is fully permissive of change and never requires adjustment by a State or its systems other than that which is slow-moving and continuous.'[36] To this end he builds upon the General Systems concept of 'adaptation' and response. If the protagonists to a conflict, for example, can reperceive their interest rather than confront each other over diplomatic tables or worse, then the chances that they will adjust and that the conflict will be resolved are greatly enhanced. He draws a clear line between 'reciprocal and co-ordinated behaviour which is systemic and functional, and power behaviour, which is non-systemic and hence dysfunctional'.[37] Systemic behaviour he sees as adaptive, healthy and 'normal', while much of world politics today is maladaptive and abnormal. The interstate system, in his view, is a pathological one.

The concept of 'adaptation' is difficult to apply since the detailed measure of a state or system's adaptability is complex and diverse, the result of many of the most important processes by which it is sustained. How well or rapidly it learns or forgets; how likely it is to be able to change permanently in some way should need arise; how likely it is to be able to modify its form temporarily until an internal or external strain subsides: all of these are adaptive considerations. The fundamental problem with the idea of systemic 'adaptation', however, is that we have very little ability to predict even generalised classes of events in world politics. So it is really very difficult to know just what policy or form of behaviour will prove successful in the short, middle or long run. Neither change nor the resistance to change is necessarily 'adaptive'. Slow change of Burton's ideal type may be adaptive for one sub-system but not for another, or adaptive for certain sub-systems in the short run but maladaptive for the larger system in the middle or long run, and so forth. Further, to adapt means to modify to suit changed conditions; it says nothing about the moral nature or the ends and goals of that modification. The biological sense of adaptation implies survival as the goal; human communities, however, do not necessarily subscribe to an end as simple as that. Systems and their decision-makers may choose consciously maladaptive practices to fulfil some greater 'adaptive' vision of their own. Values and interests are often held higher than the desirability of system maintenance for its own sake: 'the pages of diplomatic history are strewn with the wreckage of subsystems whose leaders turned out to be poor judges of adaptiveness',[38] or who judged only too well how to sustain their principles or interests in the face of environmental opposition, or who willingly, sometimes rightfully, usually righteously, carried them into the larger system as criteria for change.[39]

Nevertheless, to talk as Burton does in terms of 'adaptation' is not just an attempt to clothe the stuff of politics in a neutral and evasive terminology, though it may do that. It is an attempt to change the outlook of those who shape world affairs. It is to talk in terms of co-operation and consensus, rather than conflict and counterposed power. If ideas are self-fulfilling in the way that many analysts describe, then if enough people hear and act upon alternative ideas an alternative world system might well be brought about. The world system, in Burton's view, is what it is because people expect it to be that way and for no other reason. Change people's perceptions and we change their expectations and the way global affairs come about. At this point the theory becomes patently optimistic and utopian, and joins the ranks of a whole host of similar appeals to reason or goodness such as Christianity, Communism or Science. The impact of any one of these, however, can hardly be said to have been negligible.

Burton's concept of state and systemic adaptiveness underlies the special and particular emphasis he gives to *decision-making*. 'International relations', he says, 'is essentially the study of the decision-making processes of States and the consequences of failings in these processes. . . . The efficiency – in a policy-achievement rather than in a mechanical sense – of the decision-making process of each State is the vital point in the chain of events that determines peace or conflict.'[40] Decision-making mediates the adjustment of internal to external systems. The process of mediation is the part of world politics most accessible to those who would revise state elites, and in this sense Burton's state-based voluntarism is the direct opposite of Kaplan's systemic determinism.

It is also firmly fixed upon 'low politics' not high policy. Rather than the traditional concern for diplomatic and nuclear strategy and the general business of departments of foreign affairs, Burton prefers to consider first the nature of non-governmental relationships and informal political activity of all kinds. Rather than state structures of a formal sort, he elects to study state symbols and the way these symbols are seized and manipulated by groups of people for particular purposes. He decries the backward-facing behaviour of most contemporary statesmen and the self-confirming consequences of what they see and do. He looks beyond the mechanics of large and remote controls to detail the living systems that animate his cobweb model of the whole. He is more concerned with inter-personal relationships and the possibility of perceptual change at the human level, rather than more formal studies of the authoritative centres that play deadly games at other people's expense. His interdisciplinary referents are psychology and sociology rather than history and law. He may overdo the deliberate attempt to underrate the state as a concrete system and a formal unit of analysis, but in doing so he refocuses our vision upon the human beings who are, after all, the main protagnonists and the final victims.

The policy implications of Burton's approach are equally at variance with traditional ideas and provide an alternative system of thought and practice that deserves further consideration.[41] The conventional view holds sovereignty and nationalism to be bad, the spread of nuclear weapons likewise, and would see the advent of an international governmental power of some kind as a good thing. Collective security and alliances are considered important means of containing conflict. Burton's systemic approach, however, would predispose the opposite – the spread of nuclear weapons is not undesirable, disarmament would be bad and so would world government. Collective security and alliances prevent change, preserve an existing order of things, and hence are potential sources of conflict rather than the main means of containing them. According to Burton conflicts arise from the failure of states, or more precisely their leaders, to adjust to altered conditions and to base their decision-making on the flexible goal-changing processes of cybernetics. A concern for power balances, for the role played by the most powerful states, for the rule of law and the role of international institutions, is replaced by a preoccupation with the national capacity to change aims, to adopt alternative ways of getting what it wants and to make adjustments to external events. Depending upon the frame of reference we accept, quite different answers can be given to the same problem in world affairs. Thus to the question: 'Should relations be broken off between states as a means of coercion?' a traditional approach would tend to reply 'yes' and Burton would say 'no'. Is the personality of a leader an important influence on foreign policy? Is neutralism or non-alignment a desirable international stance? Are the domestic sources of interstate conflict important? The traditional approach would tend to answer 'no', Burton would say 'yes'.

If the advantage of a novel perspective is to suggest new ways of looking at world society, Burton and those like him have undoubtedly succeeded. The second application of the 'systems' idea anticipated the transnationalist post-behavioural school by several years. Its proponents pointed to corporations, diverse movements, a host of important non-state systems in world politics that deserve consideration as world political events. The main problem, however, was that they did not examine them in any more direct fashion, and one of the most important contributions of the post-behavioural critique was to point out that political scientists are morally obliged to labour themselves in the empirical mansions they do so readily map out for other people.

The biological analogy is not the only metaphorical device to be affixed to world politics. For the last twenty years the language and concepts of modern biology have been rivalled for generalised relevance by those of another field, namely electronics, and in particular electrical engineering and computer technology. This *cybernetic* approach to social systems is far less ambitious than General Systems Theory, which set out to build a skeleton for all science, the social sciences included, and probably for that reason it has been more useful. Analogies crop up continually in world politics and they reflect in roundabout ways the dominant styles of thought and the most striking technological achievements of their age. In Western political theory the dominant metaphor is now an electronic one, and a cybernetic conception of global affairs has replaced the much cruder idea of a mechanistic balance.

Cybernetics is the systematic study of communication and control. It is concerned, basically, with the regulation of open systems. We might notice that 'system' has slipped back in again, and indeed von Bertalanffy has made a specific attempt to place cybernetics within General Systems Theory as just a part of his grand scheme.[42] Cybernetic systems, he maintains, are simply a special case of those systems that show self-regulation. We do not need to go into the question of which came first to notice that the systems approach and the cybernetic approach share a number of key concepts such as 'feedback' and 'homeostasis' for example, and in fact the two approaches have developed together, with a good deal of borrowing by biology of cybernetic ideas like 'information' that then ended up in the General Systems sphere.

Cybernetics posits a powerful anology between the computer, individual man and society; it seeks to build one model, one set of principles to describe and explain them all, and the central common phenomenon it dwells upon is the process of communication, that is, the ability to transmit messages, quantities of information, and to react to them. 'It now seems possible', Karl Deutsch argues

> to analyse and describe the *common patterns* of behavior of self-modifying communications network in general terms, apart from the question whether their messages are transmitted and their functions carried out by circuits of electric current in an electronic device, by chemical and neural processes inside a living body, or by spoken, written or other communications between individuals in an organisation, group, nation, or society.[43]

The process of communication is directly related to that of 'steering' and control: 'cybernetics suggests that steering or governing is one of the most interesting and significant processes in the world, and that a study of steering in self-steering machines, in biological organisms, in human minds, and in societies will increase our understanding of problems in all these fields.'[44] W. Ross Ashby's law of Requisite Variety[45] points out that a system's capacity for regulation cannot exceed its capacity for communication. Any organisation, be it a factory, a family, an army, a state or the world, exists within the limits set by its network of communications, by the transmission and processing of the information upon which it depends.

Deutsch has gone on to apply the cybernetic model to politics. Instead of describing the laws and institutions of the state, its skeleton that is, or dissecting its muscles and its diverse sources of power, he seeks to expose the channels of communication, the 'nerves of government', and that is what his book is called. If one views a country's foreign policy as neither exclusively externally determined nor exclusively internally determined, but as a mixture of the two as they emerge from the self-steering mechanisms of that state, one has the sort of process Deutsch seeks to depict.

The language borders at points upon electronic parody, with much talk of 'background noise', 'fidelity', 'lead', 'lag', and 'gain', but the similarities that exist between component units of self-steering systems as compared analogously in the light of cybernetic processes can be very suggestive. A state's *receptors* for example, gather their 'bits' of information and pass them through various *screens.* These receptors can be radio monitoring stations, press agencies, spies, or any of the devices the state uses for gathering intelligence. What they report will be anything that is seen as important or significant, depending upon what they have been directed to scan for, and the nature of the scanning rules and of the reception quality are important factors any successful state must consider all the time. Inefficient spies who report once a year instead of once a week, and then inform the 'screens' from a position of trust within the enemy's ranks that the weather is fine, neglecting to mention that an armed offensive is imminent, are worse than useless. The 'screens' that receive such data (ministers, intelligence departments and the like) sieve and assess what has been collected in accordance with a set of largely intuitive rules, and combine it with items stored in the state's *memory* – its cumulative banks of files. The screening rules are based upon a set of values about relative preference and priority, and spelling out these 'switchboard' directives can tell us much about a state's behaviour. At this point reports are labelled and sorted under key headings and a glance at the filing cabinet tabs in the central office of an external affairs department can tell us much of interest about the implicit way incoming information is processed, and what the values are that determine how and where it is finally directed. Further:

> Any network whose operating rules can be modified by feedback processes is subject to *internal conflict* between its established working preferences and the impact of new information. The simpler the network, the more readily internal conflicts can be resolved by automatically assigning a clear

> preponderance to one or another of two competing 'channels' or 'reflexes' at any particular moment. . . . The more complex, relatively, the switchboards and networks involved, the richer the possibilities of choice, the more prolonged may be the periods of indecision or internal conflict. Since the net acquires its preferences through a process of history, its 'values' need not all be consistent with each other. They may form circular configurations of preference, which later may trap some of the impulses of the net in circular pathways of frustration. Since the human nervous network is complex, it remains subject to the possibilities of conflicts, indecision, jamming, and circular frustration[46]

and so, by anology, remains a political network like the state.

The decision-makers arrive at work, and onto their desks come not vast amounts of intelligence in its original form but brief reports, description sheets, summaries and project requests, plus material from the memory files felt to be relevant. Knowledge is comprehended only in terms of other knowledge. A Chinese decision-maker in Peking, observing events in Vietnam in the mid-1960s, might have considered it a national revolution and part of a protracted struggle for self-determination. American receptors, screening personnel, and decision-makers may have felt the same way, but many also preferred to interpret events as evidence of a communist takeover and part of the communist commitment to global domination. One imagines that much information came through to the decision-makers in this form, accompanied by such files from the memory banks as: U.S. military capability in South-east Asia, a historical brief on the shift in the focus of power since the Second World War away from Europe, and the U.S. industrial capacity for manufacturing armaments.

From the decision-makers, who are not dissected in detail in the cybernetic model, comes the policy *output*, which in the case above included the decision to bomb the North. The most savage sorts of war and human violence are often more effective as acts of communication than instrumental initiatives in their own right.[47] Thus the policy directive has its intended and unintended effects, and *feedback* responses assess the consequences and review what was achieved.

Feedback and *learning* are critical components of the cybernetic model. While positive feedback reinforces what was done, negative feedback acts against it, at least within the limits set by the system's ability to respond and learn. A floating mine, for example, is simply moved about by its environmental medium, the sea; likewise, passive acquiescence and a policy of drift can be adopted by a state as the main feature of its foreign policy responses. A torpedo which moves only in the direction in which it is aimed has no feedback mechanism to allow it to change its course; likewise one could take any particularly single-minded state performance and compare it with such a blind and persistent device. An automatic pilot is a much subtler machine, constantly checking its course, measuring the flight path, and correcting for deviations in a continuous way. This is more like what states are supposed to do and one is alerted to the cybernetic component of John Burton's decision-making propositions discussed above. Institutions are built by human beings; they do not 'naturally' have feedback mechanisms; these have to be put there. They have to be well-designed so that mistakes, when they occur, diminish and are not reinforced. If the network begins to 'hunt', if it begins to oscillate over a widening range of errors and wrong responses, then it is in danger of breaking down. It is interesting to speculate on such a process at work in political systems like the state.

Feedback and learning are always with respect of some purpose or *goal*, whether that be the destruction of a ship, as in the case of a torpedo, or the preservation of a social group, as is the case with politics. For human and animal systems there is also the additional question of *will*, which is essentially the conscious decision not to learn in the future. Governments implement their will by enforcing a host of cultural or legal prohibitions upon messages that might change their pre-determined patterns of behaviour, and censorship, propaganda, indoctrination, socialisation and legislation can all be seen in this light.

What are the implications of the cybernetic model for international relations? Firstly, as the 'systems' model opened up the whole question of world systems other than those of the state, the cybernetic model opens up the whole question of communications and information and the processing of data in contemporary politics – state and global. 'Human societies, with their enduring but changing cultures, are inconceivable except as communication networks.'[48] Sending and receiving information is a major feature of the flow of transactions in the world system. From a communications standpoint international relations is a continuous contest between information and uncertainty.[49] A state system will survive and flourish in the world according to the effectiveness with which its governing personnel can process, interpret, and act on the information in the global flow. The capacity of its communication channels and its ability to scan, screen and learn can vitally affect state response. The Japanese bombing of Pearl Harbor and the inability of the Americans to use the information they had already received of the impending attack to warn those in danger, is a familiar case in point. The channels of communication ended in this case with a boy on a bicycle.

Secondly, the cybernetic model can be used to help to define the concept of the 'national interest', since somewhere in the files of the memory and the way these files are retrieved, in the screening principles and scanning directives, may lie a more precise construction of this important idea.

Thirdly, the cybernetic model points up the importance of psychological and value factors in political activity. It suggests that priority be given to outlining the operating assumptions that are applied to incoming information, that determine what gets through, who it gets through to, how it is identified and classified, what weight is placed upon its input, analysis, storage or output, how feedback is elicited and screened, how memory files are stored and retrieved, how decisions are synthesised and supported – all of which depend upon mental images, value predispositions and cognitive maps of many kinds.

In the end it must be admitted that models of machines, even complex electronic ones, are inadequate as analogues of human behaviour. There is a significant gap still between the performance of inanimate learning networks and organisations of men, despite the fact that communication and control processes are common to both. The problem of value neutrality also remains. Power, Deutsch has said, is 'the capacity to preserve negative entropy in a limited part of the universe by increasing positive entropy elsewhere'.[50] This is a pallid euphemism for the sickening slaughter that has characterised many interstate interactions of the twentieth century. The attempt to generalise meaningfully about the political process is an admirable one; any result, however, that emasculates our outrage over inhuman conduct by its use of a neutral and vapid terminology is morally obscene. If such provisos are kept in mind, however, the exploratory insights that Deutsch offers are substantial. They deserve more than the passing sentence which traditional approaches afford them.

CHAPTER 7

Biopolitics: The Human Brain

Biological models and metaphors have often been used to describe and explain political phenomena. The study of the subject is replete with biological systems of many kinds – living cells, trees, wild beasts and human bodies. The General Systems approach is the most comprehensive such application to date, though as indicated in the last chapter this approach, indeed theoretical biology itself, has been influenced in turn by concepts that were developed in cybernetics to outline the fundamental processes of communication and control. From this source came important ideas about self-regulation and self-maintenance and the mechanics of survival and change.

Recently, as a result of the interdisciplinary awareness of post-behavioural concerns, political scientists have also begun to take account once again of biology's *substantive* findings, thereby introducing a new field now dubbed 'biopolitics'.[1] Rather than translating biological language and concepts into the political idiom for some simply heuristic purpose, as the systems theorists have done, we can now cite concrete findings that seem to have direct relevance for the study of political behaviour. Instead of resting content with the mere analogical extension to politics of concepts, hypotheses and theories developed in biology and at the biological end of psychology, students of political phenomena are coming to consider contemporary scientific findings that have arisen in these fields that are of testable worth and of much more than passing interest. These findings are often very recent, and their transfer as items of political relevance is a new departure that bears consideration in itself. They promise to be of lasting importance.*

* One should not take too seriously Somit's warning that '"new" approaches and constructs in political science have a life expectancy of

Two research areas have contributed most in this substantive fashion to political understanding. The first consists of studies of the human brain and the light which these studies throw upon human nature and its possible modification. More than just 'biology' is involved here, but 'biopolitics' has been used to discuss such research. The second consists of studies of animal behaviour, though the results of this latter area are mostly used in an analogical fashion when applied to human beings. Those who employ ethological (social-biological) findings to describe or explain human affairs inevitably distort what they seek to analyse, since they must ignore man's transcendental qualities to illuminate what they see as our essential and animal selves. But by rephrasing questions about the evolutionary origins and genetic bases of human behaviour[2] they have refocused our attention upon the more unconscious and deterministic side of why we act as we do, and consequently there has been much re-working of the defences of the cultural voluntarists who would oppose such a view. The debate has immediate implications for the study of world politics, and in particular, for the study of the causes and control of war.

I shall consider biopolitical findings in the order raised above – research on the human brain, and then animal behaviour. Firstly, however, it seems an appropriate place to reintroduce the methodological problem of levels of analysis.[3]

It used to be self-evident to say that we deal, in the study of world politics, with three key levels of analysis – in ascending order: man, the state, and the interstate system. Systems analysis has pointed out how misleading this picture can be, and that in reality there are several other levels – sub-state entities, extra-state organisations of a non-state kind, and regional and alliance groupings. There have also been contemporary changes in the nature of statehood that analysts have repeatedly described in recent years. And yet the three-part distinction is useful still, and the levels indicated have a discrete and continuing relevance.

---

perhaps a decade'. A. Somit, 'Biopolitics', *British Journal of Political Science*, vol. 2 (1972) pp. 231–2. Biopolitics will flourish as the substantive psycho-physiological and ethological findings warrant its development. If such findings are not forthcoming, and this is a very pessimistic expectation, then the field will disappear or persist in a purely peripheral way.

When treated with considerable reservation, so do the explanations they provide, and the formulation of the levels question by Kenneth Waltz[4] is still a good introduction to the problems involved. Does war, for example, which is the question that preoccupies Waltz, arise from some changeable or fixed attribute of human nature? Or does the final cause lie in the way the whole state is organised? Does a structural logic which leads men under good government, whatever that might be in economic, political or social terms, into peace, under bad government lead men the other way? Or is it the whole world of states and the uncertainties of the interstate system which are at fault, the precarious circumstances in which all states exist today imposing upon them security-centred requirements that cannot be escaped and that lead inevitably to war?

J. D. Singer[5] has spelled out in general terms the comparative advantages and limitations involved in selecting one level to describe, explain or prescribe for world politics rather than another. Though he is concerned only with the interstate and national state levels, his analysis can easily be extended to take in the level of the individual human actors who animate the state. For descriptive purposes, he argues, the global approach is the most comprehensive, but the state or personal picture provides more depth, detail and vividness. From an explanatory point of view, however, the global approach has so far proved very unsatisfactory, while the state or personal levels, because of the more complete insight they give into the processes by which foreign policies are made, has been of much more practical use. Any of the three levels has predictive value depending upon what one wants to predict, whether, for example, one wants to know if Thailand's leaders will opt for non-alignment next week, for which the state or personal perspective is probably more appropriate, or whether all democracies become aggressive and war-like as they garner the economic means to be so, for which the whole systemic approach might do. The ideal course is to use all three levels at once, and more, but this is no easy task and requires us to keep continually before us all the different ways of approaching the subject. The same empirical phenomenon has several facets and one is drawn several analytical ways at once. To use one of Singer's examples, at the global level we might conclude that when power is dispersed, more equitably distributed between states or blocs of states, the whole system seems more stable. Moving down to the next level of analysis, however, we find under the same dispersed conditions that 'states' seem to be satisfied with the particular distribution of power as it is, and describing and explaining why they should be so is surely part of the complete picture we seek. At the third level we find in the same dispersed power situation individual decision-makers concluding that this is the best disposition of affairs, and refraining from idiosyncratic or ideological behaviour that might jeopardise the general stability they have attained.

The last is the personal behavioural component that brings the 'state' to life, and it deserves equal attention if the final analysis is not to leave questions about human motivation unanswered. At which level should we begin? Does it matter? Restricting the focus to the political behaviour of individuals runs the risk of missing the patterns that emerge as larger systems bring together and arbitrate the demands of millions of people. On the other hand to become preoccupied with the totality is to overlook the individual interests, needs, demands and perceived duties that are the raw stuff of politics, and bring it about. The trees or the forest, detailed composition or aggregate, emergent works: it will depend in the end upon the explanatory power of the propositions we produce, and this rests in turn upon the purpose of the enquiry and the predilections of the enquirer. One man's answer is another man's critical question, and the pursuit of a comprehensive view can send us leaping and sliding from conceptual level to conceptual level, and back again, in the continuous attempt to resolve the one into the other.

The severest risk we run is that of *reductionism*, or over-simplification, of depicting complex and synergistic phenomena as nothing but some other thing; which they may well be, of course, though the human tendency to simplify any set of inter-related processes in order to understand it is so strong that we may be forgiven the prima facie urge to resist this drive regardless. The reduction or simplification may in fact serve to describe and explain, but it must be shown to do so at all levels; it cannot be assumed that this will occur. To talk, as I shall in a moment, about brain physiology is not to say that world politics is nothing but brain physiology, or that it can be explained satisfactorily in these terms alone. At each level of human society emergent patterns may modify the way in which such reduced conclusions can be applied. At each level one particular sum of the parts may be more than any other conjunction of them. The pieces of a clock held loosely in the hand represent the original machine in its simplified condition, but organised in a complex and particular way and the assembled system will perform a set of integrated movements that tells the time. A similar transformation applies to the physical elements of which we are all composed, and the exquisite conjunction of them that is the living being. This also applies to world society and world politics, and the summation these represent of their constituent human units.

On the other hand, however, in understanding a whole system we seek, of analytic necessity, to understand the parts and their multiple interconnections. This requires us to probe as far as we think relevant to the purpose. Initially much is lost but then much is gained and in the end, if we *are* able to describe the parts and explain the detailed ways these interact, we do in fact describe and explain the emergent whole. A facetious question might be posed in reply: Why stop at the level of the structure and function of the human brain? Why not push beyond that? The readiest answer is to build up to the individual human starting-point from below. I quote Roger Sperry:

> There exists within the cranium a whole world of diverse causal forces; what is more, there are forces within forces within forces, as in no other cubic half-foot of universe that we know. At the lower-most levels in this system, we have local aggregates of some sixty or more types of sub-nuclear particles interacting with great energy, all within the neutrons and protons of their respective atomic nuclei. These chaps, of course, do not have very much to say about what goes on in the affairs of the brain. We can pretty well forget them, because they are all firmly trapped and kept in line by their atomic nuclei. The atomic nuclei and associated electrons are also, of course, firmly controlled in turn. The various atomic elements are 'molecule-bound' – that is, they are hauled and pushed around by the larger spatial and configurational forces of their encompassing molecules.
>
> Similarly, the molecules of the brain are themselves pretty well bound up and ordered around by their respective cells

> and tissues. Along with all of their internal atomic and sub-nuclear parts and their neighbouring molecular partners, the brain molecules are obliged to submit to a course of activity in time and space that is very largely determined, for the life-time of any given cell, by the over-all dynamic and spatial properties of the whole cell as an entity. Even the brain cells, however, with their long fibers and impulse-conducting properties, do not have very much to say about when they are going to fire their messages, for example, or in what time pattern they will fire them. The firing orders for the day come from a higher command.
>
> In other words, the flow and the timing of impulse traffic through any brain cell, or even a nucleus of cells in the brain, are governed largely by the over-all encompassing properties of the whole cerebral circuit system, within which the given cells and fibers are incorporated, and also by the relationship of this circuit system to other circuit systems.[6]

Thus we arrive at the 'circuit properties of the whole brain', and the patterns of mental excitation that mean hunger or thirst, pleasure or pain, lust or anger, hate or love or indifference to us. Here the study of politics can begin, with the single mind at the top of the organismic ladder and at the bottom of the socio-cultural one; at the point of intersection of the individual intellect, and the family, tribe, city and state. At this level we can begin to explain human behaviour, which is the real purpose of our enquiry, and seek to understand how it is derived. Below this level the analytic return is minimal. Thus the emergent behaviour of a watch is its ability to tell the time. The detailed analysis of its parts and their relationships will explain why it moves as it does by the minute and the hour, but an understanding of the molecular properties of the balance wheel will be less relevant to this purpose, unless, for example, it fails from metal fatigue. By analogy, human behaviour is most likely to emerge as a function of the circuit properties of the integrated whole. We will only be concerned about sub-systemic performance, cell structure and so on, as these are directly implicated in the behavioural patterns we seek to explain.

Why extend the criteria of political relevance to include studies of the human brain? There are two reasons that come most readily to mind. Firstly, contemporary findings in this field contribute to the better understanding of human nature, a familiar reference point for political philosophers and a fundamental place of departure for any kind of political recommendation. There is a direct link between one's view of man and one's view of his political potentialities. Contemporary findings promise to provide scientific evidence for an explicit and testable definition of human nature which heretofore has had to rely upon axiomatic philosophic observation alone. Whatever these findings may turn out to be, important policy prescriptions will hang upon them. Humankind seems to have arrived at something of a critical point in its progress, and its structures and social aims are ever more subject to radical reappraisal. Any prescription for change, any solution to the far-reaching problems posed by population growth, modern technology, global poverty and war, rests upon assumptions about basic human attributes, and for the first time we are getting generalised non-speculative knowledge to that end. Scientific debates about human motivation are probably central to the future success of our species,[7] political or otherwise, and information about the brain will permit a more complete assessment of social phenomena in terms of individual initiation and response. What is world politics, the discipline asks, that human beings may understand and manipulate it? What is a human being, I would add, that he or she may know such things? The two questions are at bottom the same, though the second at the moment suffers grievous neglect.

The second reason for discussing the human brain is more direct. Certain electrical treatments, certain surgical treatments, and particular drugs are known to have specific and powerful effects upon it and hence upon human behaviour, including political behaviour. They have considerable potential for misuse both as techniques of political control *within* a state and as weapons of war, and we should seek to understand them because of the political relevance of their possible consequences.

The human brain is a singularly unprepossessing object. Convoluted like some great grey walnut, it weighs on average a little less than the second edition of James Rosenau's *International Politics and Foreign Policy*.[8] Composed of neurons and glial cells, these microscopic building blocks comprise the communication channels and the sub-systems that make up most of the brain's bulk. The crowning component, however, is the outermost layer – the cerebral cortex – which enfolds the two hemispheres and correlates the whole. The brain is an electrical machine that runs in its usual state upon an energy input of about twenty watts; it is also a chemical machine that derives most of this energy by oxidising glucose; and yet it is more than any machine we can yet construct, its self-conscious quality betraying the great complexity of its integrated function.

Let me look more closely at the two areas of interest and concern introduced above, beginning with the initial and more general question of attributes. One well-known and controversial attempt to explain *human nature* is that implied in the physiological model of the brain outlined by Paul Maclean, and strongly amplified and supported by Arthur Koestler. 'Perhaps the most revealing thing about the study of man's brain', Maclean argues,

> is that he has inherited the structure and organisation of three basic cerebral types which for purposes of discussion I label reptilian, old mammalian, and new mammalian. . . . Man's brain of oldest heritage is basically reptilian. It forms the matrix of the brain stem and comprises much of the reticular system, mid-brain and basal ganglia. . . . [It] programmes stereotyped behaviors according to instructions based on ancestral learning and ancestral memories.[9]

Blood pressure, respiration, and other such functions basic to life are carried on by these basement mechanisms. Maclean also hints that they might well be implicated in mankind's compulsive observance of ceremonial, legal, political and religious tradition,[10] and in our selection of and obedience to political leaders.[11] Hitler, one assumes, elicited a 'reptilian' response in his followers. The evolutionary development of a palaeocortex, however – the old mammalian brain – freed its possessors somewhat from such stereotyped behaviour, which was an important advance because automatic responses, under certain circumstances, could prove inappropriate and hence maladaptive. This second component structure Maclean identifies as the 'limbic system'. It plays an important part, he says, in emotional, viscero-somatic and endocrine function, and continues to work at an animalistic level in man. It is a 'functionally as well as an anatomically integrated system . . . implicated in the generation of affective states',[12] and the fundamental drives and emotions of hunger, sex, pleasure and fear are derived here. Maclean contrasts the old cortex with the new, for the latter not only controls movement and the senses but correlates human experience in terms of abstract thought. The neo-cortex has conferred upon man an extraordinary ability to learn and improvise, to develop new skills and to govern his fundamental drives. The result, however, is 'schizophysiology', a dichotomy of function and a lack of co-ordination between the old brain and the new:

> The limbic brain has many connections in series with the reptilian brain, but the indications are that its channels of communication with the neomammalian brain are largely indirect. This applies both to the horizontal lines of communication at the cortical level and the vertical lines of communication with the brain stem . . . the opportunity exists in the antero-medial thalamus for reciprocity of action between the third subdivision of the limbic system and the pre-frontal neo-cortex. Through these various vertical lines of communication, there is presumably the machinery for affects to arouse thoughts and for thoughts to generate affects. But whatever the mechanism, it may be inferred that the limbic cortex is too primitive in structure to allow communication in verbal terms.[13]

Hence, Maclean concludes, the 'paranoid streak' in man. And as others have conjectured, a fundamental explanation for the general emotional 'immaturity' of human beings[14] and their capacity for terrible wars and inhumane conduct of the most extreme sort. The new brain has to interpret and domesticate the feelings of the old, though the inarticulate outcries of this palaeo-mammalian construct often remain unclear. An unpleasant side-effect is generated – fear. 'Conditions existing in Europe before World War II illustrate what can happen when there are widespread, uneasy feelings among whole nations. . . . The lesson here seems to be that if a deranged leader rubs hard enough on the "paranoid streak" of his followers, it will flare into a pseudo-psychosis."[15]

Koestler spells out more clearly the implications of the Maclean model.[16] The brain seems to be its own worst foe. The enemy is of evolution's making and it lies deep within; man is a biological freak, the result of some remarkable mis-step in the adaptive line. Evolution is a process that proceeds by trial and error and species do disappear down dead-ends as they fail to adapt, or persist in some more deadlocked condition. There is Maclean's model to suggest that man is one of these mistakes. In evolutionary terms the expansion of the neo-cortex occurred at great speed, and it is perhaps no surprise that insufficient co-ordination was developed between the old sections and the new specifically human areas that were so hastily built on to what was there before. Hence the split physiology that plagues us all. The old part of the brain, the limbic system, is very much involved with man's emotional responses. Studies of epileptics with lesions in or near their limbic circuits show that irritation in such regions gives rise to basic survival-directed feelings of hunger, thirst, nausea, suffocation, cold and warmth, and general emotional states of paranoia, familiarity, strangeness, the desire to be alone, sadness and terror. Perhaps it is possible to place the inchoate and exaggerated aversion to communism that many individuals seem to feel in this region of the brain; here breeds the sense of foreboding that cannot be clearly identified and for which our newer analytical faculties invent plausible explanations. The newest part of the brain on the other hand is the site of our transcendent awareness, the place of our rational capacity for detached thought which is man's most conspicuous ability. It has no clear-cut hierarchic control over the older limbic subsystems which, when aroused, tend to dominate our behaviour, including our political behaviour. Indeed Koestler uses stronger terms than this. Emotive belief-systems actually compel the neocortex to provide spurious rationalisations for such beliefs.[17]

Thus the classical philosophical dichotomy of subjective emotions versus rational thought is given a specific physiological foundation; a two-part picture of the brain's structure and function can be drawn to match it. Instinct and intellect, affect and reason, the two are counterposed and it is anatomically so. Adaptive limbic feelings of aggression and anger, for example, adaptive under earlier environmental conditions, could prove maladaptive under our own, and the miscombination of the neo-cortex, and the old and reptilian components, could well turn out to be a deadly one.

Koestler is wary of oversimplification here and he does take pains to point out that the old brain is not *merely* the seat of human emotions; it also, he says, 'perceives, remembers and "thinks" in its own quasi-independent [though illiterate] ways . . . '.[18] He quotes Maclean to the effect that cognitive and memory functions are performed there, albeit of a primitive kind, and the old brain seems quite capable of learning simple lessons. Indeed each of the three basic brain units has its own 'subjective, gnostic, time-measuring, memory, motor and other functions'.[19] Between the analytical faculties of the new and the visceral assertions of the old there are also several levels of intermediate interaction, though what these might be is far from clear. Despite such provisos Koestler soon slips back into dicho-tomous clarity, counter-posing the two fundamental and in-adequately co-ordinated cerebral components, 'the old brain getting in the way of the new; the passionate neighing of affect-based beliefs preventing us from listening to the voice of reason. Hence the mess we [have] made of our social history . . . '.[20]

Thus Koestler argues that all the members of mankind are mentally sick. Their normal condition is a pathological one – a conclusion that might allow us to characterise Koestler as a physiological existentialist. Man's paranoia, his misplaced urge to self-transcendence, his fear and hysteria, his affective capacity itself ought to be controlled. Because of the ambiguous nature of the brain's own construction we should invent and distribute a mind-pill, some chemotherapeutic agent that would restore the harmonious and hierarchic state of thought over feeling. Reason can then dominate our wayward emotions, freed from confusion and the passionate importunities of the palaeo-cortex. The pervasive evolutionary mistake that now threatens our extinc-tion might yet be put right; we might still be 'normalised' by a 'supreme effort of self-repair'.[21] No totalitarian compulsion would be needed to administer such a drug since example alone would suffice. The cure would recommend itself.

Koestler's optimism is not contagious. Even if a rational search were instituted to find the unifying compound, the search would be a random one until much more is known about the neurophysiology and neurochemistry of the disjunction Maclean has outlined. Even with certain knowledge of the psycho-behavioural functions to be controlled there is little likelihood at the moment that a deliberate attempt to synthesise the formula with the desired effects would succeed.[22]

How valid is the psycho-physiology upon which Koestler's recommendation is based? One contemporary critic has dismissed it out of hand as a gross misrepresentation of the complexity of both our minds and our motives.[23] 'Although the limbic system . . . is undoubtedly an engine of emotion,' Calder says, 'the new cortex amplifies the intensity and effects of emotion, using the very connections that Maclean minimises.'[24] Furthermore the absolute and hierarchic control that Koestler claims we lack may in fact already exist, and to a far greater extent than we usually realise. Recent studies have demonstrated something of the potential which the new brain has to steer, not only our palaeo-mammalian emotions but the autonomic functioning of the reptilian centres as well. The conscious intervention of voluntary thought is enough, it seems, to dominate and regulate some of the most involuntary and unconscious of our brain centres, the ones that direct many glands and organs in the dynamic preservation of our most basic bodily processes. If it is possible to learn to direct the autonomic nervous system, at least to some extent – our blood pressure, heart rate and so on – then presumably it is possible to direct the primitive pits of passion that lie, according to Maclean, in the next region of the mind up the evolutionary scale. Koestler would presumably reply, however, and one might come back on his behalf, that this need not necessarily be so, and anyway it does not cover those cases when the old brain is aroused. Such contemplative control is conducted in tranquillity when it clearly is possible to assert the hierarchic pre-eminence of the neo-cortex. But disturb this tranquillity, through sickness perhaps, or the arousing effects of some environmental stimulus like cultural difference or war, and Koestler would maintain that the old brain will then tend to assert its non-rational presence.

The question of complexity is more difficult to dismiss. The famous case of Phineas Gage, a construction worker who blew a four-foot tamping rod, over an inch thick, through his head, is instructive here. He lived for another twelve years, not noticeably retarded by the experience in intellectual terms we are told but grown, hardly surprisingly, 'fitful and irreverent, indulging frequently in gross profanity and manifesting little consideration for others'.[25] Before the accident it seems that he had been quite the opposite. The neo-cortex then is not just a place of 'learning' or 'intelligence'[26] since damage to its front part at least may cause large changes in personality while leaving the rational faculties intact. This would tend to undermine the Koestler–Maclean dichotomy to some extent, though Maclean might still seek to explain the effect in terms of the 'reciprocity of action' that he notes between the 'third subdivision of the limbic system [the antero-medial thalamus] and the prefrontal neocortex'.[27]

Wilder Penfield has outlined a map of co-ordinating pathways in the brain that at first sight conflicts with Maclean's ill-met layers. Instead of drawing lines along the horizontal strata of evolutionary acquisition in the way Maclean does, emphasising the disassociation and the discontinuities that developed along the way, Penfield directs his attention to the linkages that exist between the brain's hemispheres and to the vertical connections between the brain-stem and the cerebral cortex, that is, between the evolutionarily oldest component and the outermost convoluted layer, only a fraction of an inch thick, which organises our most complex behaviour. Far from being a competitor for behavioural control Penfield depicts the brain-stem, or more accurately the higher brain-stem, as the site of a *centrencephalic* system that connects the two hemispheres, as a hive of neuronal activity 'which co-ordinates and integrates brain action and makes conscious thought possible . . .'.[28] Secondly, he constructs a fountain-like model of cranial communication to depict the 'probable functional interaction of the areas of cortex with the corresponding portions of the diencephalon [part of Maclean's reptilian brain] from which each area of cortex is a developmental projection.'[29] Sensory linkages, for example, extend from the underlying brain-stem into the cortex and then back again: 'The high road of elaborative sensory conduction goes to the cortex and then returns directly to the thalamic centres . . . .' Subsequent electrical instructions to the voluntary muscles flow out to the motor gyrus of the cortex on both sides and only then on to the muscles themselves.[30]

Maclean's palaeo-mammalian or old brain, however, is not a discrete feature of Penfield's model, so he does not confront the earlier scema directly. The evidence 'partly hypothesis and partly proven' that Penfield gives of a very significant amount of reptilian and neo-cortical interconnection does not counter Maclean's view. Maclean claims that linkages between the limbic system and the neo-cortex are 'largely indirect . . . as in the case of our business and governmental organisation, transactions between the new and old cortex depend largely on the relatively slow vertical lines of communication'.[31] Where they do exist, because of the primitive character of the limbic structures, the traffic cannot be 'verbal',[32] and at this point Maclean begins to draw the conclusions already outlined above. Penfield does not specifically confront or confound the picture upon which such conclusions are based.

There is another, more philosophical objection to the schizophysiology hypothesis. A pervasive tradition in the West tends to posit that reason is good and emotions bad, and though there is much scope here for playing with definitions, Koestler for one does seem to ignore the status of his dichotomy in this light. The most 'rational' as well as the most 'emotional' of men could still ring down the cataclysmic nuclear curtain. 'The confusion arises', Calder declares, 'because we say "reason" when we mean "reasonableness" – which implies a lot of love and altruism as well as logic – while we talk of emotion as if it were all blind rage [or as Koestler would have it, blind self-transcendence].'[33] But Koestler is not so concerned with the fact that the present balance of intellect and affect have seen their successes in the past, he is preoccupied with the failures, with the question of where do we go from here, and with the new need for a success rate of close on 100 per cent. Cultural and social conditioning are to little avail if, under crisis conditions, the brain's imbalance largely determines how we behave, and certainly it would be nonsense to claim that mankind is physiologically 'perfect' in any absolute way. The most cursory review of our historical and contemporary doings ought to dispel that idea.

The Koestler–Maclean construct is a deterministic one, an

unpopular notion in an age that has grown very aware of the potential good as well as evil to be had in the exercise of a liberated will. Evolution marches on, either through us or over us, we like to think we have a choice. 'Schizophysiology' amounts to a sobering reminder of what the limits upon that choice might turn out to be. If the view is anywhere near valid, the policy implications are immediate. This way an end to war, for example, lies not in constructing more perfect political institutions, nor in redistributing the world's economic and nutritional and technological resources, the downfall of capitalism, the universal victory of democracy or socialism, or some less hazardously structured global conflict system. All these solutions would finally, perhaps fatally, miss the point. It lies in the better co-ordination of human brains within themselves, all of them, or at least those that politically matter most.

Much remains to be done, however, before a final answer is possible. Destroying or stimulating certain brain areas, for example, can alter aggressive responses of a general kind, but the control of aggression is still far beyond our reach – the neurophysiology involved is too complex, too little understood, and too much research has yet to be conducted. The same applies to all other politically relevant responses.

The discussion of the physiological substrates of human behaviour remains a technical and inconclusive affair from the social scientist's point of view, though the consequences of such research promise to be very important indeed. Many findings already extant bear upon political questions despite the fact that we do not at the moment draw the connections that would explicate their relevance. We must rely largely upon neurophysiologists who have an interest in politics to spell out any implications of their work that they think might have more than an indirect application to social science. It is not until students of politics equip themselves with more than a passing expertise in what most see as a field quite remote from their own that the potential significance of what is being learned there will be fully revealed.

Moving away from these questions about human nature in general, I want now to discuss the second of the foci on the brain introduced above – the specific findings and scientific techniques that have made possible the manipulation, limited though it may be at the moment, of political behaviour. Their most effective use would almost certainly be a combined one, but for the purpose of analytical clarity I shall consider them separately here.

Firstly, there is surgical intervention of an irreversible kind. Various permanent effects have been achieved over the years by psycho-surgical incision and excision, though this is an extreme measure and any repercussions for specifically political behaviour would usually be part of a much more general modification in personal performance. Monkeys of a dominating or savage temperament, parts of whose limbic system are then removed, lose much of their self-assertive drive, indeed may even lose the instinctive responses they need to survive at all. Similar ablation in man can cause a host of aberrant effects, and prefrontal leucotomy, the severing of nerve pathways in the frontal lobes, though now too crude a 'cure' in the light of later developments, certainly succeeds in pacifying its human recipients. More recent techniques employ electrodes implanted directly into the amygdala, for example, or the temporal lobe, which are then used to probe for pathological bodies of cells and to destroy them with an electrical discharge.

Surgical intervention as a major and non-selective form of control over political behaviour, particularly in world politics, is science fiction still and likely to remain so. One can conceive of an 'ablatarchy' and an end to world war by the electrical excision of precisely mapped regions of fear, rage or anxiety in the heads of key decision-makers or in whole populations, but the conception is decidedly far-fetched. How these decision-makers might be convinced to submit, and where one would find the facilities to treat several thousand million people in this way, are the most obvious technical objections. Many pertinent questions, however, present themselves before this. A world that even contemplated such a resort would be a world radically different from our own and the result of political trends largely unforeseen today. Nevertheless, the psycho-surgical assault on the mind has begun, and few dare say with certainty what ramparts will never fall.

Secondly, there is surgical intervention of a less drastic though scarcely less effective sort – either the induction of chemical substances into specific areas of the brain by means of micro-pipettes, or the precise implantation of a coated needle that permits the covering substance to dissolve, or the electrical stimulation of the brain with fine wires that prompt but do not destroy. The location of centres of pleasure and pain has already been used to modify behaviour by such means, and Herman Kahn has given a satirical picture of the potential moral repercussions that might arise from more widespread use of the last device:

> Imagine a human being with his pleasure centers wired to a console fitted on his chest. . . . Would it be necessary to be married to play the console of a member of the opposite sex? . . . Perhaps society would agree that any two consenting adults could play each other's consoles, but this might risk perversion: 'Have you ever tried one and five together?' If you were really 'square', you might be disgusted by the idea of playing your own console.[34]

Jose Delgado concludes from analysis of rat brains that while 60 per cent of the whole brain is neutral on a pleasure–pain continuum, 35 per cent is rewarding and only 5 per cent punishing. If anything like the same ratio obtains in man then there is much support for the expectation that man's predominant potential for pleasurable sensations rather than painful ones could have significant implications for behaviour control.[35]

The main areas implicated in the output of human *aggression* are believed to lie deep within the temporal lobes and in the subcortical structures of the limbic system, the hypothalamus, for example.[36] Electrodes have been used to modify or elicit aggressive responses there. In all, it seems, the individual has no defence against the direct manipulation of his brain. Experimenters have found that electrical stimulation of the appropriate kind always prevails over 'free will'. The technique is sufficiently discriminating in fact to 'delay a heartbeat, move a finger, bring a word to memory, or set a determined behavioral tone'.[37] And yet electrical treatment is not likely to solve the problem of war, for example, either by inhibiting aggression or prompting fear, at least not yet. The futuristic vision of a 'telemetarchy' – the world citizenry with its implanted electrodes being monitored by radio telemetry; central boards of control tuning down the attack desires of a nation, filling others with foreboding, sending every second person to sleep or wake, or causing whole continents to down tools and dance about together – is a nonsense. Emotional reactions can be and have been altered, but the manipulation cannot make us performing automatons in the way that is suggested above. The telemetered electrode does not enter a neutral psychophysiology but a place replete with esoteric life experiences and genetic inheritants. Factors of social and cultural upbringing are part of one's personality and cannot be replaced simply by a swift kick in the brain circuits. Any stimulated response relates to an individual universe that will condition and confine that response in turn. A telemetarch might intensify mass aggression, but his electrical treatment could not create that emotion where it had never been before, nor determine the target for that aggression, nor could he direct the sequence of aggressive behaviour. Eliciting anxiety or fear, for example, is not to elicit anxiety or fear for any particular object. Fear involves an intra-cranial assessment of the environment and is built out of a host of cultural factors and life-experiences that have their own logical and non-logical concomitants. The same applies to any other electrically induced change in affective tone.

I would not like to foreclose upon alternative visions of our more distant future, however. Delgado's success in modifying the social behaviour of groups of monkeys[38] certainly suggests possible parallel effects in men. Monkeys low on the hierarchical rungs of their social group can learn to modify the status-building aggression of their telemetered peers by pushing the right button, and analogous mechanisms are conceivable, though hardly probable, for human society. In a less automatic way this is how the democratic vote is meant to work. But again a world that even contemplated such measures for other than psychotherapeutic reasons would be quite different from our own. Definitions of psycho-therapy, however, as Laing and others point out, are to an important extent political definitions, and wide open thereby to political abuse. Electrical stimulation of the brain is similarly open to political abuse, but any world that actually acquiesced en masse in treatment of this kind is one we would hardly subscribe to today. All the same we should keep in mind that the resistance to this form of manipulation, as to any other, is a 'manipulative tool for modifying human behaviour in its own right'.[39] The fundamental questions remain: in whose interests is behaviour controlled, to what end, and with what results?

Thirdly, we have the chemical assault upon the mind, an assault that not only has possible consequences for political control but has further implications as a means of waging war.

It is hardly new to suggest that human behaviour is modified by the ingestion of psychoactive substances. Opium, cannabis, alcohol and many other such substances are a familiar feature of most historic cultures. Hormones, too, are known to have pervasive effects upon human performance. What distinguishes the present, however, from any other period in this respect is, firstly, the range of modern drugs, secondly, their superior synthetic potency, and, thirdly, their potential for discrete specificity in use. Psycho-pharmacology represents the most subtle of all the techniques of mind and mood control; drugs act directly upon the brain chemistry without the need for physical intervention of any kind.[40] It is no accident that it is to this area that Koestler turned for the possible manufacture of a super-evolutionary cure for what he has depicted as our ill-coordinated mental condition.

I do not wish to exaggerate these qualities. Certainly as political instruments they are still not specific enough to be of much use except in the gross sense that by rendering a whole society or parts of it unconscious or otherwise incapacitated[41] one could command it absolutely for a limited period of time. Indeed it is the prevention of unwanted behaviour that is likely to be the main contribution of this technique. Eliciting particular responses and more select and relative displays of any kind are much harder to achieve, and in 'normal' people especially there is much evidence that the physical and psychological differences between human beings, the individual's expectations, the cues provided by the immediate environment, and the attitudes of the therapist may significantly alter the effectiveness of any compound.[42] It is this question of idiosyncratic response that most undermines the possibility of elite or mass 'somatarchy', or rule by drugs. As an example of the confused nature of expert opinion in this field I would like to quote David Krech's three 'laws' of psychopharmacology and, though formulated several years ago, they still seem to hold. He says (1) 'there are no generalisations concerning the biochemical control of the complex mind that can now be made'; (2) 'there are many exceptions to the generalisations set down by the first law'; and (3) 'the first and second laws hold only for extreme cases of pathology, except where they do not hold'.[43]

Beside this critique, however, one should place the rapidly growing body of knowledge about the receptive properties of cellular membranes, the chemical character of inter-neural synaptic transfers in the brain, and the precise molecular structure and active affinities of synthetic chemical compounds. Aggression, for example, may yet turn out to be subject to drug control, particularly that of hormonal compounds, even if a single pill alone could not be expected to cover the broad class of behavioural repertoires involved.

> A drug whose primary function is to reduce hyperactivity may also be an effective inhibitor of aggression in one person, while a drug which primarily reduces anxiety may have the same effect on another. The aggregate of such drugs may provide an aggregate of control over aggression, even though a single pill, usable with a singular lack of specificity for preventing aggression in anyone, cannot be envisioned.[44]

The most relevant and critical discovery in this field from a political scientist's point of view would probably be a drug that uniformly and predictably increased the human response to external demands, since such a substance could be used to modify moral values or political convictions and alliances, in the short run at least. Holger Hyden has reported that 'the administration of tricyano-aminopropene is followed by an increased suggestibility in man'.[45] Indeed, any substance that induces changes in biologically important molecules in the neurons and the glia and affecting the mental state in a negative direction could be used for socio-political conditioning. 'It is not difficult to imagine the possible uses to which a government in a police-controlled state could put this substance. For a time they would subject the population to hard conditions. Suddenly the hardship would be removed, and at the same time, the substance would be added to the tap water and the mass communications media turned on.'[46] On the other hand, Hyden adds, 'a counter-measure against the effect of a substance such as tricyano-aminopropene is not difficult to imagine either',[47] though who would have access to countermeasures in a police-state would presumably reflect the political structure too. The implications for a country like South Africa are obvious. Fortunately Hyden's results have not been borne out by that of other researchers in the field.

In addition to chemo-suggestibility, one can easily imagine hallucinogens, tranquillisers or the like sprayed into the air and used to pacify militant demonstrators or civil dissent in much the same way that CS gas has already been used in the United States – provided, that is, the wind blows aright.

In contrast to the authoritarian applications above, where social consent or pressure may not be considered, one can also conceive of a society whose members happily and voluntarily assault their minds and emotions, as many do already, with psycho-specific compounds. Tranquillised or hallucinated, they would be much less likely to question their social conditions and political circumstances. Drugged conformity and acquiescence, already the neglected plight of many coca-fed Andean Indians, could well be induced in a burgeoning body of the world's poor so that they might suffer in silence.

In one of the few self-conscious attempts to examine political behaviour in the light of biochemical intervention, Dean Jaros[48] has reported an experiment designed to test whether a depressant drug (pentobarbital) might modify political choice. Specifically, he set out to discover if the ability of this compound to impair one's powers of discrimination could lead one to favour more obvious and extreme political alternatives. He also sought to discover (1) if depressants, by temporarily suspending one's social inhibitions and one's aversion to overt dependency, lead to an increase in the quantity of political responses (whether, that is, one participates more); (2) if 'drugs induce dependency which results in the increased probability of manipulation of political acts';[49] and (3) if depressants lead to lack of consensus particularly over the permissible limits of conflict, and hence to more conflict. His findings, while subject to methodological criticism, purport to show that American college-going recipients of a chemical depressant are more likely to support a demagogic candidate in an imaginary election, and the less politicised participants most of all. However, the second effect to do with the level of individual participation was not realised, a fact readily explained by the experimental situation; the third effect also showed no pattern, that is, there appeared to be no change either way in subject manipulability under chemo-depressed conditions; and the fourth effect was likewise limited and inconclusive. All this is far short of a result that would enable a uniform and predictable increase in human response to external demands.

Much of the above is cast in the future and certainly that is where the most radical psycho-chemical discoveries still seem to lie. However, given that the brain is not an undifferentiated and amorphous mass but a complex and highly organised set of subsystems linked in functional and interdependent hierarchies '... It is perfectly reasonable to suppose that each functionally differentiated area of the brain has its own chemical signature ...',[50] each with its own biochemical inhibitions and supports. Or is it so reasonable? This reads very much as a statement of scientific hope rather than one of automatic expectation. If it is true, however, the potential for coercion could breed demagoguery of an altogether more irresistible kind; political legitimacy would then be no further away than the nearest municipal reservoir.

Turning finally to their use as weapons of war, it seems that psycho-active drugs have long been considered likely candidates for state armouries. Immediately after the last world war mind-disturbing chemicals came under extensive review and one report notes that a compound which the U.S. military has tested, code-named BZ, caused a guard to forget the password when confronted by an invader, whereupon he 'simply sat down on the ground in an apparent effort to puzzle the situation out'.[51] The same problems mentioned above about the idiosyncratic response by human beings to chemical assault less than lethal in its effects are relevant here, however. There is also the fact that the application of such a chemical, depending upon the dosage, may cause permanent psychological damage which cannot be reversed. Administering dosages within desired limits is thus a further problem, as well as the fact that not all the effects of a drug may be compatible with the military goal – an enemy made depressed might also become more unpredictable, and a national army rendered aggressive might also become inefficient in formulating and carrying out orders or operating the complex machineries of war. All of these problems would apply to domestic, political or police application as well, though one cannot rule out the possibility here of a strategic chemo-assault upon a key decision-maker or set of them. The political bag of 'dirty tricks' could easily include such a strategy.

There is one further attack on the mind I have not mentioned that usually finds a place in biopolitical discussion – the nutritional and disease-produced kind. A pregnant mother who eats insufficient protein can cause the permanent impairment of her unborn baby's mental capacity. A child similarly malnourished in the first eighteen months of life can suffer in the same way and what we see as a biopolitical fact of underdevelopment[52] is a 'devastating assault on the minds of many millions of helpless individuals . . . a great aggregate of human talent now being lost in the urine in the form of unreplaced nitrogen'.[53] Biological damage – nutritional and caused by parasites and illness – will almost certainly slow the process of development in poor states, robbing them of intellectual reserves and of modernising motivation. The north–south division between a developed and a non-developed world might over time become 'biologically based',[54] with non-developed states dominated by self-sustaining elites who have succeeded in stepping outside the crippling sequence of protein deficiency and disease. There is little sign that the assault will end, at least in the foreseeable future, which raises once again questions about the dimensions of the coming eco-crisis and adds a further feature to alternative models of world politics to come.

CHAPTER 8

Biopolitics: Ethology

The second area of biological research to provide substantive findings for students of political behaviour and empirical results of so-called 'bio-political' concern is *ethology.* Ethology, or social biology as it is sometimes called, is the study of the behaviour of animals – how they act towards each other and towards their various environments. The label itself has two obsolete meanings, one being the science of ethics, and the other the 'portrayal of character by mimicry'.[1] It is from the latter usage that the contemporary term seems to have been drawn.

Generally, ethology attempts to construct a 'theoretical framework by which behaviour can be comprehended comparatively in the same way that anatomy is comprehended comparatively'. It is dedicated to the 'accumulation of sufficient behavioural data from all animal phyla, so that theoretical models of the evolution of behaviour may be constructed'.[2] More specifically, however, as a biological or rather zoological science, it has a well-worked Darwinian interrogative that it applies to any particular behavioural repertoire, namely: how does this contribute to the survival of the animal in question?

There are certain causal subsidiaries to this basic enquiry, for example: what makes behaviour happen at any given moment? How does the machinery of behaviour develop as the individual grows up? And how did the behaviour systems of each species evolve until they became what they are now?[3] There is more involved, then, than gathering facts about how animals behave at the moment, either in cages or in the wild. There is the further question of how behaviour has changed over time to become what it is, and how the whole business of natural selection has given rise over many years to characteristic behavioural attributes almost as marked and as readily recognised as physiological ones.

Peter Corning, in a notable article directed specifically at students of world politics, has risen to the ethological challenge and has attempted to cast human behaviour in the perspective explicit above, framing what we do both in terms of the part it plays in our evolution and in terms of its survival consequences. Evolution, he argues, should be used as a 'general theory to explain all human life, including political life'.[4] Thus

> by hypothesising the 'purpose' of society in evolutionary terms we can then proceed to analyse specific social behaviors, institutions, and values in the light of their consequences for the survival of society. . . . The basic question for the social scientist, then, is: How does a particular social phenomenon help (or hinder) the human animal in satisfying his survival needs? And how does it affect the survival and reproductive efficiency of his society as a collectivity?[5]

This is applicable at 'all levels of analysis, from the behavior of individuals to the international system (where we should be able to evaluate the systemic behavior of nations, groups of nations, and various international organisations in terms of its survival consequences for individual societies and for the international system as a whole).'[6]

In the broadest terms, Corning is clearly correct. Whatever else the human species might be, it is also a 'collective survival enterprise', a global system of groups and societies that will continue to succeed, persist in some fragmented or reduced condition, or fail altogether. To do anything else, we must first secure our survival. This particular biopolitical perspective prompts us to ask how the species as a whole might best adapt to its contemporary circumstances, and highlights once again fundamental questions about ecological limits upon present behavioural trends and about our ability to continue not to abuse the technological products of our own, highly flexible, ingenuity.

But is 'survival' in this sense more than just a salutary truism? Much of what we do has direct consequences for our continuance as a species, but does that fact really 'explain human life, including political life'? Survival *is* the indispensable condition for all other human activity, but I would argue that human activity is not always directed to that end, and any *explanation* in such terms will be only a part explanation of human and political life, not the inclusive general proposition that Corning seeks.

This central theme deserves some elaboration. By positing the most fundamental of biological mechanisms, Corning would reduce all explanations of human behaviour to general statements in these terms. The pursuit of survival need not be a *conscious* goal he asserts, but it is necessary to any other end; 'men may acclaim "ultimate" purposes or value preferences *beyond*, or *in addition to* survival. But survival is the *sine qua non*'.[7] The difficulties are clear. Men have often pursued ends and preferences 'beyond' and 'in addition to' survival, and they have also been known to pursue preferences that directly contradict their own survival and perhaps that of their species as a whole. To survive but not to be Christian, Muslim, 'Communist' or 'free', has been variously deemed no survival worth the experience. Corning would explain his desire not to consider these other ends, and the human propensity to pursue them, by emphasising that

> an evolutionary conception of politics does not require that everything governments or political leaders do be functional for the survival of the collectivity. As with any other aspect of social life, it is possible to speak of adaptive and maladaptive behaviors, political leaders or political systems, and part of the task of an evolutionary political science should be to make just such appraisals of political phenomena.[8]

Objective criteria of adaptability or maladaptability in genetic, ecological, economic and political terms will be scarcely more adequate, however, for *explaining* human and political behaviour than the essential condition of survival itself. The fact is that human and political behaviour have often been and will continue to be performed without reference to them. John Burton has elaborated this attribute of adaptability and I discussed the difficulties involved in its use in a previous chapter under the general description of his systemic approach to world politics. How can we predict what will prove adaptive or nonadaptive in the short, middle, or long run, or for anything in between? In evolutionary terms that behavioural repertoire which secures the reproductive efficiency of the breeding population has shown itself to be adaptive for the time being, but the distinct possibility remains that it might be maladaptive in the middle or long term. That which succeeds and survives is adaptive, and that which is adaptive and survives is successful – the circle is closed and there is no way out, no way, that is, to allow for abrupt changes in circumstances and the human ability to respond in kind. We have no way of knowing that what we are doing now will continue to succeed and to enhance our survival, or whether it will jeopardise that success, or how to change if we think we should. Objective criteria of adaptability and maladaptability are oriented to a future of which we know very little indeed.

The biological standard of survival, then, is most readily used to judge and justify human behaviour. To employ it as an explanation is to over-simplify, and will miss the extensive body of motivation that lies beyond the range of survival-oriented performance as such. These additional behavioural sequences will inevitably have survival consequences, however remote, but to contemplate such consequences alone is to do something less than justice to the full extent of behavioural causation in man; it is to offer something less than the full explanation of how behavioural patterns are arrived at and acted upon by the human beings concerned. Furthermore, I seriously doubt Corning's or anyone else's ability to construct criteria of survival success, whether in terms of 'adaptation' or whatever, that will allow us to pierce the future and predict the long-run reproductive efficiency of most of the political behaviour in train today. Evolution judges us, but it offers little to help in our political judgements. Corning himself admits that natural selection 'cannot work to complete a design and cannot plan ahead; it can only produce results of immediate biological advantage . . .'[9] and yet survival, the biological success of the species, is only evident in the long run where we have living proof that the blind alleys have been avoided. His initial and more modest assessment is most telling: 'to say that there are elements of randomness . . . in the evolutionary process is not to say that it has no structure at all. . . . Long-run unpredictability may not rule out short-run regularities and probabilistic, "if–then" projections.'[10] Species are not assessed in such a point-to-point probabilistic way, and the long-run unpredictability that Corning concedes may indeed rule out short-run projections of the evolutionary worth of any particular behavioural repertoire or foreign policy.

Corning's reductionist error stems from his comparative neglect of human attributes at the sociological level of mankind itself, his comparative neglect, that is, of cultural as opposed to biological evolution. Cultural evolution has been and continues to be so rapid in comparison with biological evolution that we 'cannot assume that any culture is in a state of equilibrium either internally or with respect to its environment. Whereas we can reasonably assume that a non-human species exists because it is "adapted", we cannot assume that any culture exists because it is adapted. Cultures are too short-lived. Possibly none of them is adapted.'[11] Corning does point to the bifurcation of biological and cultural evolution, and to the fact that there is no guarantee that mankind will use its transcendent status to enhance its adaptive capacity to reproduce and survive.[12] Having identified the problem, however, he then defines it away, despite the fact that any explanation of human and political behaviour would have to consider as part of our continuing survival kit more than just its biological component. That is only half the question. That it is the whole question in the one sense that we must at least survive to continue to act at all cannot disguise the fact that it is only a fragment of a reply that attempts to understand how and why mankind behaves in the world, if we wish to understand, that is, the fundamental principles that animate human life rather than how these might be assessed.[13]

To the fundamental biological questions – how does an individual and species-characteristic behavioural trait contribute to an organism's survivial, and what use is it in terms of evolutionary success? – any answer for the human group must remain inconclusive. Utilitarian judgements will elude the character of a creature that has transcended utilitarian concerns alone.

The ethological case does not rest only upon the general question of adaptation and survival. There are important and specific corollaries to this question that ethologists advance for separate scrutiny. Whatever the adaptive consequences of behaviour as such, most ethologists would argue, for example, that certain particular components of man's behaviour are biologically, that is, genetically 'determined', or at least predisposed in particular, more or less predictable, ways. It is apparent by now that beneficial behavioural patterns can confer a functional and selective advantage upon their animal bearers as readily as randomly generated structural attributes do. The requisite genetic cause of, or capacity for, such patterns are consequently sustained or even enhanced by natural selection under conditions that favour them, patterns such as pair-bonding and mating, courtship, hunting and the building of social hierarchies. Evolved and adapted behavioural forms can be as characteristic of a species as its physiology. Man's cultural capacity itself must have evolved in this way, and ethologists argue that important contents of any human culture and the *unnatural* selection these can make of the human practitioners who survive, are also 'innate'.

Further, ethologists feel that these 'innate' biological repertoires compare, at least analogously, with 'innate' behavioural traits common to other orders of the animal kingdom.

Let us look first at the initial factor, the biological basis of particular human activities. Corning argues that there is, indeed, growing evidence to support those who would identify an 'intrinsic' basis to how humans behave and how they sustain their societies. The activities he identifies as derived in this pre-programmed way are:

> (subject in all cases to individual variation and environmental molding) the nuclear family (including pair-bonding and parent–sibling affectional bonds) antipathy to strangers, self-motivated learning activities and exploratory behaviour, at least some forms of territoriality, fear, ethical or authority accepting capacities, play, the proclivity for forming peer groups, aggressiveness, individual competitiveness, and the tendency to form fairly stable hierarchies.[14]

Not enough is known to specify these basic human drives in terms of specific neurophysiological structures of the body or brain, or in the hormonal and other chemical processes that occur there, so the concept remains ultimately imprecise. But mankind as a whole does seem to evince certain species-characteristic motivations of this sort that fulfil fundamental needs or requirements as these have evolved over time, both of a physical kind and of a more intangible sort, needs like those of security, love, self-fulfilment, self-esteem, knowledge and power.[15] All can be modified, even negated, by cultural constriction, but the negation in particular can lead to frustration and aberrant effects.

Tiger and Fox talk in a similar vein, using an extended analogy with the construction of language, about a human 'bio-grammar', a set of biological rules that outline the principles upon which our diverse repertoire of behaviour is thought to rest. These rules cannot be used to predict absolutely what one human being will do, but they will indicate how we will probably behave in important areas of human action. Because of these biological rules some behavioural attributes will be developed in the process of aculturation without much difficulty, almost as if there were worn and ready grooves in the infant mind to accommodate the conditioning to come; others will not be so easy to acquire and will run across these seductive channels. Behavioural traits likely to have a biological base, they argue, are those which lead ineluctably to status systems, to rules about incest and how and whom to marry, to rules about property, and to rules about what is taboo and what is to be ritually avoided. To this they add the human propensity to 'defer to the supernatural' and attempts to regulate this realm in some mediatory way, the prevalence of ceremonies of initiation and courtship, the adornment of young females, the male tendency to form all-male associations that exclude women, gambling and tool-and-weapon manufacture. Underpinning any human community there is a diverse substructure of 'myths and legends, dancing, psychosis and neurosis, adultery, homosexuality, homicide, suicide, loyalty, desertion, juvenile delinquents, senile fools, and various ills from which communities and people suffer.'[16] Most fundamentally, they conclude, 'we are wired for hunting for the emotions, the excitements, the curiosities, the regularities, the fears, and the social relationships that were needed to survive in the hunting way of life . . . civilised man is an evolutionary afterthought. We remain . . . fine-honed machines designed for the efficient pursuit of game.'[17] Learning that formulates and encourages the behavioural patterns above is easily acquired; that which suppresses and discourages them is more difficult to inculcate.

This is a comprehensive and highly contentious list to say the least. Tiger and Fox discuss in only the most general terms, however, the mechanism of the patterns they point to, and leave undefined the exact nature of what the biogrammatical base might be. The most they do is to talk in terms of 'wiring' and 'DNA'. For example:

> There is nothing specific in the genetic code about initiation ceremonies for young males. There are no instructions about circumcision whizzing around the bends of the alpha helix. But neither are male initiation ceremonies pure cultural inventions – results of the free activity of the intellect. They occur because we are biologically wired the way we are.[18]

One is clearly justified in asking just what 'wiring' means in this context. Having shied away from the word 'instinct', Tiger and Fox offer an equally imprecise construction in its place.

Konrad Lorenz maintains that 'human behaviour, and particularly human social behaviour, far from being determined by reason and cultural tradition alone, is still subject to all the laws prevailing in all phylogenetically adapted instinctive behaviour. Of these laws we possess a fair amount of knowledge from studying the instincts of animals.'[19] Lorenz, then, would have us discover not just a *human* biogrammar, but a biogrammar for all the animal kingdom. These laws, most accessible to us through the study of the less complex behaviour of other birds and beasts, will constitute an independent body of first principles applicable to human beings. These 'laws' will include, presumably, general observations about aggression, ritual submission, territorial behaviour, the construction of social hierarchies, bonding patterns, group suppression of individual behavioural deviance and group defence of social norms.

Irenaus Eibl-Eibesfeldt, in his text-book on ethology, has listed a number of 'fixed action patterns, internal motivating mechanisms, releasers, and innate learning dispositions'[20] that act in man and determine on the face of it certain behavioural patterns that contribute to the preservation of the human species as a whole. Under *fixed action patterns* he includes the nipple-seeking behaviour of babies, and their grasp, climb, swim, walk, crawl, cry, smile and fixating reflexes. By comparing the behaviour of adults from different cultures for evidence of common expressions and gestures, he also attempts to demonstrate the existence of such fixed and species-characteristic patterns in mature individuals too. Through cunning use of a film camera he is able to present evidence of innate expressive actions which seem to be non-cultural and include the friendly smile, laughter, rage, sadness, flirting, greeting, arrogance and disdain, the alert behaviour of lone eaters, and the way people approach conspicuous landmarks without any special reason. Certain very common gestures, he argues, might also have an innately determined base of this kind – bowing, for example, as a sign of submission, the flung arms of triumph, the open palm of greeting, the erect and forward posture of aggressive display and threat, the frustrated gestures of indignation, the nodding head of approval, the food-sharing of 'contact readiness', and the flinch reaction to loud noise. Most of these have only remote political importance.

Under *release mechanisms* he considers the way in which humans react 'almost automatically to certain releasing stimulus situations in a predictable manner',[21] a reaction quite possibly unlearned. The parental response of care and consideration for the young, for example, is most likely triggered without cultural cause by certain characteristically infantile attributes of a physical and behavioural kind. Our emotional responses often seem automatically related to the stimulus that prompts them. Our standards of sexual desirability, for example, our musical and artistic judgements, even our ethical value judgements, may be to some extent intrinsic and exercised regardless of environmental acquisition. He goes on to consider territorial defence, aggressive behaviour, the readiness to accept authority and subordinate status, and group pressures to conform, as innate dispositions as well. These have much more import for political discussion.

The result of anything like success along this line of research would be extensive. If ethologists could identify with precision those mechanisms and environmental cues that prompt known tendencies to specific actions, then these cues could be used or suppressed to extrinsic ends. If innate action or releasing or learning patterns of fixed or more flexible kinds could be shown to exist, then knowing what they were would enable us consciously to dominate them by cultural means alone. Our room for behavioural manoeuvre would be directly confirmed thereby.

The nub of the matter is the question of *instinct* and 'wiring', of our innate behaviour as against what we acquire from our social environment as we mature, of the 'genetic' as opposed to or in combination with the environmental reasons for why we do what we do. The contemporary approach resists the dualism implied, and generally asserts that: 'it is obvious that genes are determinants of behavior and that environmental factors available as stimuli are also critical. But it is no longer profitable to argue that one of these general classes is more important than another. Both are necessary; each is insufficient alone; and they interact in a complex nonlinear fashion.'[22]

'Instinct' varies enormously from species to species. It is generally manifest in behaviour of an unconscious, stereotypic kind, but differs widely in the closed or open way such behaviour can be modified by external influences. In its most extreme form we have the precise, invariant, firmly fixed behavioural repertoire of insects and other comparatively simple living things. Even here, however, 'learning' behaviour can often be shown to occur. Generally, though, adaptation at such a level depends upon the selective survival of random variants in species members that are best fitted to the changed circumstances, and not upon the learning capacity of individual members as they process the experiences of a lifetime. At the other extreme we have the higher mammals, the primates, and in particular man, where the genetic endowment is so open-ended and unresolved that learning, culture and environment seem to be all. Generally, the ontogenists argue that: 'The notable thing about *human* behaviour is that it is learned . . . that heredity plays a role in some human behaviour can scarcely be doubted; but this is a very different thing from saying that any form of human behaviour is determined by heredity. Given the limits set by his genetic constitution, whatever man is he learns to be.'[23] In this latter view, then, what we describe as 'human nature' and explain or prescribe on those grounds is acquired from other human beings in the process of aculturation, and this is the most conspicuous feature of growing up. Thus the human species is considered as having passed beyond the pre-programmed pre-determined urgings of its phylogenetical inheritance, to a level of self-determination characteristically its own. Those who hold to this approach are also apt to extend their stand to a direct attack upon the very idea of 'instinct' itself. 'The truth is', Montagu adds, 'that the concept of "instinct" has assumed the form of a doctrine, and perhaps represents the outstanding example of reification in the whole realm of science....'[24]

What gives this debate an especial force is the fact that it reflects very closely the philosophical distinction between behavioural determinism and human free will. Those who argue for 'instinct' in terms of innate drives, needs, or even capacities, are much more likely to claim that they can predict certain behaviour patterns, and to deny human beings that voluntaristic control over their actions that many such beings assume they have. On the other hand, those who deny the fixity of 'instincts' in humankind are much more ready to believe that we behave as we do because we have been taught so, that what is learned can be unlearned, or at least programmed ahead in a flexible and self-conscious fashion, that man is born neither bad nor good but potentially either or anywhere in between depending upon environmental and cultural circumstances. This approach cannot explain manifest differences in temperament, but it does explain the adaptive character of the human intellect. It is deterministic in its own way, environment prompting performance in a direct and predictable fashion, but the potential for human intervention is seen as decisive.

What can be made of this debate? Certainly there is a biological evolutionary descent of which man's most recent millennia are only a fragment, and it would be no surprise if fixed behaviour patterns were a part of this inheritance. It is equally certain, however, that the higher up the evolutionary chain we go in terms of complexity, and in terms of the selective value placed in the past upon a capacity for learning and for using daily experience to modify what is done, the less important 'instinct' in terms of genetically determined fixed action or releasing or learning patterns seems to become. In the strict sense, of course, all behaviour is 'genetically determined'. 'If all the behaviour and, indeed, all the characteristics of an animal are influenced by the genes, we must ask what writers are trying to distinguish, when they say that some behaviour is "genetical" and some not. The distinction is . . . in the *development* of behaviour.'[25] By the time we get to man inherited behaviour of a species-characteristic kind seems to be minimal. It depends in fact on where we place the line, though by drawing a line at all we divide an interactive and nonlinear process which is essentially indivisible. The questions stubbornly recur. How much of our behaviour is tied, if tied is not too strong a word, to inherited predispositions that prevail throughout humankind, regardless of whether those predispositions are wide 'open' *capacities* that have to be triggered or somehow completed by environmental cues at particular stages of the individual's development, or whether they are hormonally or physiologically derived and species-preserving *drives* that are encouraged or denied as culture permits, or whether they are inchoate and subtle *needs* difficult to pin to a genetic base but sufficiently pervasive and predictable to suggest that they might be? Or are behaviour patterns of each sort insignificant in man, irretrievably buried beneath a huge outgrowth of culture-constructing attributes and a unique ability to abstract and symbolise?

If we keep in mind that there are nurtured components to practically all behaviour, however intricate and however 'natural' it might seem, and that the lowliest creature can often display an ability to adapt to changed circumstances in its environment that constitutes 'learning', it is hard to grant the case of those who would argue a closed genetic pre-determination to social and hence political behaviour. 'Of course, it is one thing to say that behavior is "determined" by "instincts" and quite another to say that it is "shaped" and "organised" in part by genetic or neurophysiological components as well as by environmental factors.'[26] Though 'shaped' and 'organised' are less than precise concepts in this context, what the ethologists have done is to place such factors beside cultural ones as worthy of our immediate consideration. Their mood is contagious. 'Are we seriously to believe', Robert Ardrey asks, 'that in ten thousand years . . . we have repealed those natural laws that prevailed for the previous one billion, nine hundred and ninety-one million, nine hundred and ninety thousand . . . ?'[27] Further: 'One can no more say that the *kind* of instinct motivating man is qualitatively different from the *kind* of instinct motivating higher animals than one can inspect the fossil record of the gradual human emergence and say: Here, here at this anatomical moment, animals ended and men began.'[28] The contagion must be treated antiseptically, however. What Ardrey does not describe is the way in which modern palaeontological research is bringing to light the nature of that anatomical progression from ape to ape-man to man-ape to man, and is pointing up in the process that which is characteristically, if not uniquely human. By turning the analogy back on itself we may find that ethology, in spelling out much more precisely the sources of and constraints upon behaviour in animals, may thereby explicate what is special to man.

On the one hand, then, any conception of 'instinct' other than that of genetic 'capacity' is likely to prove irrelevant to the study of our species. On the other hand, we may yet find, disguised but recognisable none the less, biological pre-programming of a profound order underlying important things we do. Somewhere in between will lie the detailed description of genetic components that limit how we learn and what we can know. This last question may turn out to be the most interesting and important ever posed by the human intellect; it is the one to which ethological research naturally tends.

The second of the ethological contributions appended above is closely related to this debate about 'instinct' versus 'culture'. Those who argue for 'instinct', for the survival of inherited behavioural predispositions in man, are also apt to compare such predispositions to broadly analogous behaviour in lower animals. The behavioural patterns that are seen to be 'biologically' based in man are usually those, ethologists declare, that are evident in other animals. As primates human beings have much in common anatomically and physiologically with chimpanzees, for example, or gorillas. Since they share physical features with other members of the animal kingdom there is no reason to suppose, most ethologists assume, that they do not also share behavioural features. Despite strictures about emergent properties at the human level, recent studies of the interaction of animals in their natural state are a valuable source, it is felt, of concepts and hypotheses about the interaction of human beings. The one may be a model for the other – a simpler version that, depending upon the purpose of the enquiry, highlights important aspects of the more complex and human traits. What are these 'important areas' that it is felt can be understood best by the study of animals? The list usually includes, though the items overlap, some consideration of the nature of aggression, of territoriality, of imprinting, of social hierarchies of rank and pecking order, and of various social groupings like families and male clubs, as well as parallels drawn from the pathological performance of animals kept in over-crowded or otherwise deprived conditions.

Because of its consequences, *aggression* has drawn the most attention, and Konrad Lorenz, one of ethology's most distinguished figures, has written a well-known book specifically drawing lessons on aggression from animal behaviour that explicate, he would claim, the predicament of man.[29] An act of aggression is an act of unprovoked attack. Though aggression and violence are not synonymous, the concept of aggression assumes assault and an aggressive person is clearly likely to be a violent person. Though aggression between individuals does not automatically spell aggression between states, if it is a species characteristic of mankind as a whole then men are quite likely to go to war. War provides an outlet for aggressive tendencies, and these same tendencies are exploited to garner support for wars already extant. As a cause of war, however, the aggressive tendencies in state populations and individual decision-makers must also be weighed against the role, the societal and the systemic constraints that may lead a government into violent conflict for quite different reasons of calculated risk and interest.

Aggression, Lorenz argues, is an 'instinct', the playing out of an innate and spontaneous neuro-physiological function; in the tortured language of the discipline it is 'an appetite seeking consummation in its expression upon release by an appropriate stimulus presentation'.[30] It needs periodic satiety, and an organism denied such release is apt to find its inhibitory thresholds falling away. It will then exhibit an urge to hunt about seeking a stimulus that will discharge its pent-up potential.

What is aggression for? Under natural conditions it helps any particular animal species to survive just as much as any other adaptively selected attribute might. Lorenz mentions three of its most beneficial functions, though these do not readily apply to man – it results in the balanced distribution of animals of the same species over the available environment, it plays a significant part in the selection of the strongest by rival fights, and it has a useful role in the defence of the young. He also argues, however, that it can be seen subterraneously sustaining a host of behavioural responses that on the face of it have little or nothing to do with aggression at all – territorial behaviour, for example, the building of hierarchies and patterns of leadership, and affection. The last is the least obvious, but Lorenz is prepared to argue that mutation and selection have chosen, 'of all unlikely things, the rough and spiny shoot of intra-specific aggression to bear the blossoms of personal friendship and love'.[31] Animal societies where aggressive behaviour is common are paradoxically those where personal ties seem most marked as well. To fight to the death would be maladaptive and many animal species have developed ritually submissive behavioural signals that inhibit attack once dominance has been established. Ritual submission often involves quite complex patterns of interaction, and it is upon this mechanism of containment that Lorenz builds his affectional case.

In man, however, aggression no longer performs an adaptive function, that is, it no longer serves the survival ends of our species. The growth of human culture, culminating in the advent of thermo-nuclear weapons, has outstripped our capacities for behavioural inhibition. We have morality, and we have the concept of rational responsibility, but we have no 'instinctive' restraints upon our aggressive intra-specific actions because we did not need them, because our intra-specific killer potential was limited until the invention of weapons. There was no selective pressure, it seems, to develop innate constraints, and while moral safeguards and social resistance to the killing of conspecifics have been sufficient to preserve humanity so far, at the same time weapons have become progressively more effective and the distance, both physical, and hence emotional, between attacker and attacked has grown far beyond the range of personal-appeasement mechanisms and often far beyond all but the empathetic realisation of what is being perpetrated, usually from a great height, upon fellow human beings. The aggressive drive builds up regardless, spontaneously servicing a whole range of more desirable attributes, but waiting to be discharged none the less. The consequences of its discharge could now be disastrous, a problem that is further compounded by the fact that in the modern world there are few legitimate outlets for its free expression.

The most dangerous form of human aggression is that which Lorenz calls 'militant enthusiasm', in origin most likely a function of communal defence, but in the present day easily fixed upon symbols and ethical values and absurd causes without count. It is a 'true autonomous instinct' with its 'own appetite behaviour, its own releasing mechanisms and, like the sexual urge or any other strong instinct it engenders a specific feeling of intense satisfaction. The strength of its seductive lure explains why intelligent men may behave as irrationally and immorally in their political as in their sexual lives.'[32] His conclusion is sombre: 'the fate of humanity hangs on the question whether or not responsible morality will be able to cope with its rapidly growing burden. We shall not lighten this burden by overestimating the strength of morality, still less by attributing omnipotence to it.'[33]

What can we do? Five things, according to Lorenz, though one of them – eugenic planning to breed out the aggressive drive – he finds highly inadvisable. Aggression has diverse and often desirable side-effects, he maintains, and any breeding programme would also reduce these. His favoured recommendations include the redirected discharge of aggression upon substitute objects, its sublimation in some cathartic way, the promotion of contact and friendship between individuals of different belief-systems or states, and the channelling of militant enthusiasm into good causes other than war. To implement these alternatives he suggests that we turn to sport, to the pursuit of beauty, truth, and health, and to the human capacity for laughter. Thus: 'laughing men hardly ever shoot.'[34] Perhaps *this* is the way the world ends, not with a bang, but with a satiric chuckle.

Lorenz's analysis has been assailed most often for his concept of aggression as a phylogenetically engendered, compulsive and spontaneous 'instinct', and the debate rehearsed earlier applies here. As far as his suggestions for social engineering are concerned, many difficulties remain. The promotion of interstate contact may breed intolerance as readily as understanding; competitive games might well *cause* war rather than circumvent it; and it is far from clear how one would set about making people laugh in a socially and politically advantageous way.

Lionel Tiger, by contrast, sees aggression not as an autonomous attribute but as a direct function of another unlearned propensity in man, that is *male bonding*. He argues that it is both the product and cause of strong affective ties between men.[35] He and Fox, however, have claimed elsewhere that we are a 'naturally' aggressive species prone to violence, though they are ambivalent as to the 'instinctual' status of this tendency. While they lean away from identifying it as a fundamental drive, they do not see that it can be eliminated by educative means.

Another eminent ethologist, Niko Tinbergen, explicitly accepts the same view that learning will not eliminate the 'internal urge to fight'.[36] He argues, as does Lorenz, that culturally induced evolution has advanced beyond our behavioural capacity to adjust to the consequences. Heightened levels of inter-group contact, cultural sanctions against the adaptive response of flight, our weapon-making capacity, and the impersonal way modern weapons are applied to their targets, all have made man unique in the animal kingdom – a mass murderer. On the whole, however, Tinbergen is much more cautious than Lorenz or Tiger. He points self-consciously to work that is still to be done, and explicitly denounces those who would apply ethological findings uncritically to man. It is more the questions that his discipline prompts us to ask, rather than any substantive results it has to offer, that he sees as the primary contribution of the ethological field.

Aggression is inextricably interwoven with concepts of *territorial defence*, and this is the second most popular of the ethological concepts to be applied to human beings. Lorenz talks of the connection; Tinbergen discusses the motivational conflict between attack behaviour and withdrawal behaviour which defines animal boundaries, and the group territorialism that man still carries with him as part of his 'animal heritage' from the time when he was a hunting primate organised into social groups;[37] but the best-known exponent of this focus is a playwright turned populariser of science, Robert Ardrey, in his book *The Territorial Imperative*. Under normal circumstances one would dismiss such a work out of hand, but this one has enjoyed extensive popular success and deserves at least summary rebuttal here.

Ardrey sets out to demonstrate that man defends territory by 'instinct', a behavioural response that he shares with many beasts and birds.

> We act as we do for reasons of our evolutionary past, not our cultural present, and our behaviour is as much a mark of our species as is the shape of a human thigh bone or the configuration of nerves in a corner of the human brain. If we defend the title to our land or the sovereignty of our country, we do it for reasons no different, no less innate, no less ineradicable than do lower animals.[38]

'Territory' does not cause war as such, but those who would transgress territorial boundaries must weigh thereby the strong possibility that war will occur.

There is a natural biological morality, Ardrey thinks, in the way animals observe territorial limits in the wild, for territorial defence is the 'natural mediating device between the good of the one and the good of all'.[39] Not only this but territory (as well as war) satisfies the three motivating needs of all higher animals including man – the need for identity rather than anonymity, for stimulation rather than boredom and for security rather than anxiety.

By animal example, Ardrey identifies two basic sorts of human society, the *nation* – 'a social group containing at least two mature males which holds as an exclusive possession a continuous area of space, which isolates itself from others of its kind through outward antagonism, and which through joint defense of its social territory achieves leadership, co-operation, and a capacity for concerted action';[40] and the *noyau*, a society like that of the sportive lemurs of Madagascar held together by inward rather than outward antagonism and by the mutual animosity of its members. The Jews, in occupying Israel and defending it against Arab overthrow, became a 'nation'. Italy he says is a 'noyau' and such a country, confronted by an aggressive power, will lose or make deals.[41]

As an ethological formulation Ardrey's argument is loose, unscholarly, and has drawn severe critical assessment. His penchant for the selective use of evidence for example, his disdain for intervening factors such as aculturation, material self-interest and social values, places him at the extreme end of the 'instinct' scale. His definitions have been assailed as flimsy concertina constructs that disintegrate on touch, and his use of the term 'territory' is one of these. The 'need' for 'identity' in man has very little to support it from the evidence of studies of animals not human, and indeed each and all of the tri-fold hierarchy of motivating needs he postulates are readily satisfied in human beings in ways that have nothing to do with property and territorial possession. This would seem to run against the species-characteristic certainty of such an 'instinct'. It is also apparent when we examine the detailed evidence which already exists that man's collateral relatives among the apes are 'singularly lacking in simple territorial behaviour',[42] and indeed

> the behavior of our closest animal relatives varies so greatly, in territoriality . . . as in everything else, that we cannot attribute any animal 'instinct' to man on the basis of its being omnipresent in nature. In observing man himself, one is struck less by a uniform concern for some such aim as territory than by man's astonishing capacity for variation and innovation.[43]

At the level of the human species itself Ardrey's treatment of the anthropological findings on most of mankind, the section of it, that is, which lives outside Western industrial societies, is almost non-existent.

As the basis for a political ideology Ardrey's views are decidedly unpalatable, a fact he notes himself. Any analysis that subscribes to the existence of 'instincts', he points out, is likely to be considered somewhat reactionary and party to potentially fascist ideas; one dedicated to the superordinate status of culture and learning, however, is apt to be seen as progressive and liberal.[44] Nevertheless *The Territorial Imperative* has drawn exactly the sort of response Ardrey might have predicted, and for good reason: 'Who knows whence a "New Right" may gather a cloak of respectability to condone . . . the defence of racial garrisons in the *noyaux* of the near future? The new genre of popular biological exposition neglects the humanity of man.

We would do well to meditate upon the reasons.'[45] The lessons engendered by the Social Darwinists have not been forgotten.

Apart from aggression and territoriality, ethologists have also applied the concept of *imprinting* to human behaviour. Lorenz, for one, uses the example of various animal abilities to lock onto a particular environmental cue at a pre-programmed point in maturation to describe the process of what he calls 'object fixation' in man. Imprinting refers to certain patterns of behaviour that are not learned in the ordinary way, but are triggered once and for all by an external event that occurs at an appropriate age in an organism's development. Just after puberty, Lorenz argues, humans go through such a sensitive period of innately determined change. They tend at this time to examine their childhood allegiances in a highly critical way, and then, perhaps, to cast about for others to take their place: 'If . . . the clever demagogue, well versed in the dangerous art of producing supra-normal stimulus situations, gets hold of young people at a susceptible age, he finds it easy to guide their object-fixation in a direction subservient to his political aims.'[46] Two innate mechanisms are implied, one an 'overpowering urge to espouse a cause', which if unsatisfied is then directed at 'inferior substitutes'; the other an 'instinctive need to be the member of a closely knit group fighting for common ideals'[47] so strong that it seems to be irrelevant what the ideals are or what they are worth in humanistic terms. The process is of great significance. It occurs only once but it is the well-spring of that form of aggression Lorenz identifies as 'militant enthusiasm'. Conditioning at the critical age can determine, he declares, 'neither more nor less than that which a man will live for, struggle for, and under certain circumstances, blindly go to war for'.[48] Again, however, the argument from 'instinct' is by assertion and anecdote. Lorenz is quite unsystematic about the evidence he puts forward, and his ideas are properly suspect because of this. He is scientific in his treatment of animals, but he is impressionistic and unconvincing in the parallels he draws to man. There are no certainties in this particular matter despite the confidence with which Lorenz declaims upon it.

A further ethological finding that is often used to explain human behaviour is that of *rank order*, seen by some as a biological mechanism that operates in many species of animal including the human one. Where animals remain together long enough to form a social unit, within that unit there usually develops a hierarchy of dominance and submission, and man, 'homo hierarchicus' as he is properly named, is clearly prone to a similar trait. Tiger and Fox attribute this fact to the drive to breed. The result, they say, of the reproductive struggle is a social system that is both hierarchical and competitive. In evolutionary terms competition for status and its differential achievement has determined differential access to resources in general and to reproductive resources in particular. Human political systems are essentially hierarchic systems based upon the urge to pre-eminence which is grounded in turn in a desire for self-perpetuation. This equation no longer obtains, if it ever did, in such a crude one-to-one way, and Tiger and Fox indeed point out that while the same motives operate today the ends have been redirected elsewhere. In the development of contemporary Western society they observe: 'Power became divorced from control of the genetic future of the population, and fastened instead onto the control of material goods and the symbolic future. The leaders could not ensure that they controlled the future merely by peopling it with their own offspring; they had to ensure that their offspring controlled the future by having the monopoly on wealth and power.'[49]

It seems a pity to point out the simplistic reductionism of such a clear-cut idea, but in rendering politics as nothing but a linked chain of hierarchy, dominance and breeding, even to emphasise that such factors underpin and inhibit all else, is to do considerably less than justice to the existence of political values, political ideology, and the impact these phenomena have had upon the political behaviour of humankind.

One final example should suffice to demonstrate the way in which the findings of a biology of animal behaviour have been applied to man. Studies of animals other than man suggest that there is a felt need in the individual bird or beast for a species-specific zone of *personal space*. When the group population exceeds a certain level over-crowding results and behavioural patterns become pathological. This usually leads to rapid population decline, and experiments conducted on rats have provided the most dramatic examples of such a mechanism at work.[50]

Physiology and behaviour are closely interwoven in these cases, and it is no accident perhaps that arteriosclerosis is a zoo disease as prevalent in captive animals as in urban industrial man. Tension not diet is implicated by the studies so far performed.[51] 'Personal space' in animals has an analogous application to human beings, since the 'private office, and the secluded country estate, are prerogatives of high social rank in human society',[52] but these factors might just as well or better represent a symbolic domination of scarce resources as some predefined expression of an innate desire for a private spatial domain. As far as world politics is concerned those attempts to correlate population, its growth and density, with the behavioural incidence of war have been inconclusive. The intervening variables are too complex and too uncertain in their effects. As population grows, however, can we expect behavioural pathologies to arise therefrom, or will we simply adjust our culturally acquired expectations of interpersonal distance? We clearly have no innate mechanism for population *control* unless of course it has yet to be triggered, and one critically overcrowded day we will find ourselves, against all our learned constraints, marching into the sea like ripe lemmings.

From the behavioural patterns discussed above it should be apparent that caution is critical at every point of the transfer from animals in general to man in particular. Conclusions about human beings cannot readily be inferred from general principles arrived at by the study of other species, firstly because the use of carefully selected examples can support any principle at all that one wants to apply to humankind, and secondly, because men are indeed animals in the strict evolutionary sense, but they are more than animals in very important ways. Suggestive analogies from our bestial confrères may well apply to us, but *homologies* are much more difficult to establish and it will be insufficient, then, to look for the animal parallel of human behaviour alone. By a singular concern with the common denominator between ourselves and other beasts we may miss most of what is characteristically 'human' about human behaviour, and indeed the most useful study of mankind may yet begin simply with man.

Nevertheless how can we be justified in deciding in advance how far the attributes we share with some or all of the rest of the animal kingdom extend as explanations of social behaviour? This is something we cannot do I think, and our uniqueness with respect to aggression, territoriality, and the rest must be demonstrated, it cannot be simply asserted or assumed. We will have to come to terms not only with ethological concepts and hypotheses, but with the clear chance that certain critical aspects of our political behaviour may be accounted for to some extent in the light of unlearned and 'innate' predeterminations. General statements of this kind that are cast in falsifiable terms must be rigorously scrutinised at the human level. Behaviour that looks the same in other animals and man must be shown to be so, and the prompting mechanisms explicitly identified in 'biological' and cultural terms. Only then will we approach an ethology of all behaviour including that of man. Simplistic examples drawn from observations of what animals do fail to constitute a science, but they cannot be rejected out of hand because of that. Indeed they cannot be verified or rejected 'until such time as there exists systematic propositional inventories recording the consonant and dissonant behavior patterns of men and other species in their full variety and complexity'.[53] In this way the differences may emerge without the similarities being overlooked. 'It is always hazardous to generalise from animal to man, but it is also dangerous not to try always to see man in the perspective of evolutionary development, when one is searching for principles of human behavior, as a corrective for the myopia inherent in regarding him as *sui generis*, quite unrelated to anything that is earlier or lower in the phylogenetic scale.'[54]

Caution is needed not only in comparing one set of results with another but in erecting *criteria of relevance* for the study of world politics itself, and I wish to conclude the chapter on this note. MacFarlane Burnet has said that: 'if we are to understand human behaviour and devise ways of dealing with social problems, *the best starting-point* is in the study of mammalian behaviour in Nature or in artificially contrived situations . . . patterns of behaviour in mice or antelopes, baboons or chimpanzees. . . .'[55] (Emphasis added.) Lorenz has likewise claimed that we must seek to understand our 'animal' nature first before the species meets disaster, and he makes explicit suggestions for our continued survival based upon his understanding of our 'innately' determined selves. This ordering of research priorities has been, as might be expected, trenchantly attacked. 'To be frank', one physical anthropologist has argued,

> such lines of reasoning often seem like . . . conservative forms of evading the central critical issues concerning the human condition. What faces most humans is poverty, starvation, substandard health, exploitation, increasing relative and absolute deprivations, disease, poverty of self-identification and evaluation, and little if any chance for meaningful self-participation in the 'grandeur of human adaptation, civilization'. . . . The real problem facing men is not to better understand lower animals, but to implement drastic social changes throughout the world; to find a way to structure power on a world-wide sharing basis, to prevent the social conditions that lead to violence and war. This problem is a political one, not a biological or psychological one.[56]

Where *should* we begin – with an explication of our diverse 'human natures' or with the socio-eco-political phenomena identified above? The question of relevance is a continuing one. Any answer as confident as this, however, relies upon a prior commitment to where the instrumental causes are seen to lie, something that I would argue cannot be decided in advance. It seems a limp conclusion to come to, but both approaches are important and both must be built into a comprehensive conception of man and his politics. They assail us from different ends to the same purpose, and either one could co-opt our perspectives entirely given the chance. It is no easy task to suspend causal judgement and to arrange their meeting somewhere nearer the middle until we know better where we can, without contradiction, begin. But anything less, I maintain, will beg the very questions we seek to resolve.

CHAPTER 9
Psychopolitics

The transdisciplinary traffic from the study of biology and from the biological end of the psychology discipline is both older and more recent than the parallel attempts to apply socio-psychological findings to contemporary world politics. The distorted laissez-faire biology of the Social Darwinists, Stalin's insistence that biological science bow to an environmental voluntarism that most readily embraced the socio-economic verities of Karl Marx, the racial myths and eugenic proclivities of Hitler's National Socialists, all transferred biological results to the field of political phenomena and predated the inter-disciplinary resurgence of behavioural and post-behavioural concerns, and each served in turn to delay a more objective scrutiny of what biology might contribute to political affairs. Crude and simplistic versions of Darwin's conclusions were used very early as ideological weapons, and other such misrepresented results continued to be employed to support political ideas. This has meant that more moderate observers have tended to eschew any shred of biological evidence in political discussion, a trend that is only just being reversed.

Social psychology has had a much easier time of it, however, largely one suspects because of the more impressionistic and humanistic nature of its results, and the less absolute conviction with which it has been used as a science in support of political positions. In contrast to those who study the structure and function of the brain itself,[1] social psychologists 'black box' the mind and scrutinise the regularities in human performance which the individual feeds out as various social stimuli are fed in. They are not so interested in the precise neurophysiological substrata of either the patterns of behaviour they observe or of the ideas they use to describe, explain and predict such patterns.

They are concerned rather to identify general behaviourally manifested attributes of the mind as a whole, to classify in conceptual terms alone the source of such attributes and the process by which they vary and can be varied, and they turn the field over to the biological end of their discipline to specify how these functions and phenomena work in precise material detail.

There are a number of socio-psychological ideas and findings that have been used in an attempt to understand world politics. On the whole, as I have said, it is seen as a respectable transfer to make, much more so than a bio-political one. There is the same problem of reductionism as in the last two chapters, however, and the variation in the way politics has and has not been reduced to psychology is very wide. The systemic Kaplanesque view, for example, construes the individual psychology of leaders or led as marginal to world political concerns. Here the question of reductionism hardly arises at all, since world politics is seen as explicable, almost exclusively, at the global level of state and trans-state organisations, in terms, that is, of the gross correlations between the attributes of such sub-systems and the global patterns of their interaction; personal behaviour is not given much weight in the list of sub-systemic attributes. There is also the tendency to describe and explain the policies of states and extra-state systems as if they were real people who act upon images, attitudes, emotions and personal variables of their own. Global behaviour is reduced in this view to nothing but the individualised relations of a set of state caricatures which are by turn defensive, aggrandising, forthright, or whatever else the policy output anthropomorphically suggests. In its view of states and non-state organisations as impervious, precisely bounded, and comparatively autonomous, this second predisposition is very close to the primary systemic one. In the way it attributes psychological characteristics to the institutional actors involved, however, it is reductionist in the extreme. It is a simplistic distortion and one that the more careful analyses of global affairs seek to avoid.

The focus of social-psychological research is largely upon individual behaviour, albeit individual behaviour in its social contexts, and upon human behaviour in groups. Ignoring the two extreme positions just mentioned, the more common approach to world affairs is to examine the social-psychological profiles of state leaders and their citizens, and to use these profiles in whole or part explanation of particular policies and policy potentials. Reductionist fallacies are common again. Policy at the global level is the result of a process of aggregation that social psychology tells us little about. What a state does, for example, will not necessarily reflect the attitudes, personal attributes, motives and opinions of its mass publics, or for that matter, of its elites. In the process of interaction what emerges is usually a rather complex and indirect reflection of individual or group characteristics.

The practice of world politics is thick with objective constraints that modify individual performance and modify therefore the usefulness of general statements based solely upon psychological variables. We might learn a good deal about a state's foreign policy, for example, in terms of the personality, the motives, the attitudes, the beliefs, the stereotypes, the emotions and perceptions of its key decision-makers and their advisers, or in terms of the psychological attributes of its people, or at least of those sections of it which the decision-makers take into account, but to explain the particular configuration of a particular policy we will still have to understand something of the roles these people play, the inhibitions and expectations implicit in their office or station, and the continuity such expectations confer, as well as determining the structural imperatives of the global system as a whole and the distribution of the various forms of economic, political, military and ideological power that impinge upon what state leaders can do. The psychological picture is a part picture, more or less informative depending upon the influence of role constraints and the immediacy of systemic imperatives. Psycho-political delusions cannot substitute for human mortality, military vulnerability, industrial weakness, a disadvantageous geographic position, or for a society riven by serious divisions, whatever the deluded leader or led might try. The relevance of social psychology to world politics will therefore be a partial and conditional one.

This is not to say that individuals and groups have not been directly responsible for important initiatives in global affairs, and that psychological explanations might not illuminate these initiatives in striking and fundamental ways.[2] Resolute leaders or social groups may defy all the objective 'realities' of their situation to act in ways only explicable in social-psychological terms. The individual and the constraints that enclose him are in constant interaction, and each will to some extent reorganise the other. Policy decisions are made in the end by human beings, and human beings act upon their *understanding* of reality; they do not apprehend it directly. The 'images' they have of the world and how it works may be accurate and clear, or inappropriate and distorted, and policies based upon the latter preconceptions, while succeeding despite themselves, readily lead to disaster. At very least the 'wise selection of leaders and wise decisions by leaders depend upon an understanding of the ways in which the human mind seeks to comprehend reality'.[3]

Several psychological concepts and findings have been adapted to the study of world politics. 'Images' are mapped for their selective effects upon the perceptions of elites and of the led; personality traits are scrutinised for possible political implications; psychological 'drives' are assessed for their part in producing aggressive behaviour and war or in maintaining the peace; and public opinion, or rather the opinions of diverse publics, are plumbed as contributing causes of one external stance or another.

The psychological attributes of elites may be assumed to work directly upon policy, keeping in the mind the environmental constraints already outlined. When dealing with the social-psychological profiles of all the individuals in a state or other world system, however, how might these be summed? If a character-trait is widely distributed within a state population, does this provide a basis for understanding that state's foreign affairs? If most Chinese are parochial and self-reliant, not favourably disposed towards outsiders, and clearly inclined toward keeping their country's autonomy intact, does this help to explain, for example, China's generally cautious and defensive foreign-policy practices? Some analysts come close to saying so. While well aware that social groups should not be treated as anthropomorphoid beings with attitudes and opinions in their own right, J. D. Singer thinks that for descriptive purposes at least: (1) the statistical aggregation of the modal personality traits of a state's citizens is the key to its *national character*; (2) the sum of personal attitudes represents the mass *ideology*, (though the mass ideology may differ markedly from the operative attitudes and the ideology of the elite, which may vary in turn from the formal and officially-sanctioned ideology of the state organisation the elite inhabits); and (3) the sum of individual opinions on a matter is the *climate* of opinion. 'We can and should', he argues, 'employ the distribution and aggregation of individual attributes in order to measure certain social attributes.'[4] The second sum, that of *attitudes*, he considers the most important for understanding foreign affairs. 'Neither as remote from policy concerns as personality, nor as evanescent as opinion, attitudinal configurations provide the most salient non-material incentives and constraints within which nations decide upon their behavior in world politics.' Its aggregate, *ideology*, is likewise crucial, '. . . not only because it provides the matrix within which the present is interpreted, the past recalled, and the future anticipated but because it provides the boundaries within which the climate or distribution of opinion can range.'[5]

Let us accept Singer's assessment of significance, despite the fact that opinion and personality may well be much more immediate determinants of state response than he admits, and probe the central concept of 'attitude' for its psychopolitical effects upon world affairs.

An 'attitude' is most readily construed as a mode of mental readiness, or as any implicit predisposition which exerts a general but consistent influence upon a large body of evaluation responses.[6] This predisposition, though open to change, is a comparatively enduring one. It is learned, not innate, and can be relearned and revised in various ingenious and experimentally tested ways. It is a *cognitive* phenomenon that underpins what we believe and think we know about an object, person or group; it is an *affective* phenomenon, constructed in terms of what we like and dislike or see as good and bad; and it is a *behavioural* phenomenon, reflected in what we do. A change in what we think or feel can change what we do, and conversely changed behaviour will work its own revisions upon our emotional responses, our values or our beliefs.

The particular attitudes we hold reflect our most fundamental perceptual assumptions, and these in turn are conditioned by what our personality happens to be. Holding personality aside, it seems that our basic ideas are built out of what is the most basic of all psychological processes, the recognition of *pattern* and of *form*. We learn very early to divide the world into similar and dissimilar, like and unlike, and to act upon these conceptual divisions with reinforcing results. The significance we derive in doing so is sufficient to render the universe meaningful and intelligible to us. Out of infantile chaos we derive ordered constructs, and a sense of order itself, which we then re-impose upon events.[7] So strong is this ability that we will impute a pattern where very little information exists or where the information is quite inappropriate to such an activity. We impose suggestive forms upon random blotches of ink; we may assert, when asked, that boulders, for no immediately evident reason, are sad rather than happy;[8] and we extol or denounce another state or system, though all we know of it may be chance or childhood hearsay and miscellaneous scraps of reportage.

We live by organised images of several basic sorts. The human capacity for organising sense data into extensive and complex structures of this kind is our most marked intellectual attribute. Indeed, 'image' in this sense is more or less synonymous with 'mind'. Our 'imagination', then, consists in the private manipulation of these mental forms, one of its functions being our ability to make connections and create new things, another being our tendency to build pathological retreats into which, sometimes with disastrous socio-political consequences, we simply disappear. Wishful or wilful thinking is closely akin to such an attribute – thus poor children exaggerate the size of coins they are shown,[9] fearful people exaggerate the intimidating motives of others they meet, and megalomaniac state leaders make bids for national glory, or succumb to paranoia and retreat (metaphorically) into the trees where they posture obscenely with their nuclear bananas.

Many analysts have drawn our attention to the abstract structures that underpin all our mental processes. We each have, it is claimed, a *spatial* image of how we are physically located in the world; a *temporal* image of the passage of time; a *relational* image of the universe 'as a system of regularities' (this I would see as the primary construct, the recognition of pattern that I have mentioned above as underlying all else), part of which is a *personal* image of ourselves as enmeshed in a web of social interactions; a *value* image with which we scale good and bad, better of worse; an *affectional* image that renders the rest in our own idiosyncratic and socially derived emotional tones; an image of *reality* or *unreality* (where we square what we think we know with its environmental referents), and an image of *public* and *private* as we share what we believe with others or keep it to ourselves. To this list we may add the Freudian dimensions of the conscious, unconscious and subconscious minds.[10]

In general: We now know that what used to be regarded as primary sense data are in fact highly learned interpretations. We see the world the way we see it because it pays us and has paid us to see it that way.'[11] We find what we want to find there and we tend to disregard the rest. Our 'images' and attitudes act to some extent at least as prejudgements, as simplified models of the world, as working hypotheses that make sense of what we perceive but at the cost of complexity. Most important of all they resist change. The psychological urge evident in nearly all human beings to order, to simplify, and to retain their mental orders and simplifications intact, has never been located in neurophysiological detail. The attribute is sufficiently common and pervasive, however, to suggest that it has such a locus, and it certainly seems to be germane to every mode of human experience.

In world politics this fact draws our attention to politically relevant images, 'stereotypes' for example, and the way that individuals and groups of individuals, far from, or close to, or part of decision-making structures, conceive in a particularistic or summative way of their own state or system, of other states or systems, of the world system as a whole, and of the interactions between all these and with themselves. Thus the Japanese, the French, or any other national group comprehend themselves in a direct way, and their image of themselves as individuals and as a nation-state, especially the image of the decision-makers in this regard, will influence what is done in the global arena. They – decision-makers in particular – infer from their present status and experiences, from their past memories and their interpretations of historical events, from their future prospects and expectations, a cognitive construct that works upon the world at large as 'Japan' or 'France'. The image so constituted will carry affectional connotations and this loading for most Japanese or Frenchmen will be a favourable one. It will be detailed and complex, implicitly as much as consciously conceived, and will not readily suffer revision. It will be internally consistent to some degree, though psycho-logic does not necessarily obey the rules of formal logical resolutions. Indeed 'The degree of consistency of images . . . can vary widely; the representation of an object can be coherent and organised even though it contains contradictions and ambiguities.'[12] There is great variety in the human ability to tolerate such contradictions, and we might also conjecture culturally-induced proclivities in this capacity.

The Japanese also apprehend other countries, like their neighbouring state of China, but in a much more indirect way. The widely shared images of China and of the Chinese held by Japanese citizens and Japanese elites will be a much more simple, less refined and detailed construct than the image they hold of themselves. For that reason it will probably be more explicit and perhaps even more resistant to change. It is much less likely to be a favourable view and much more likely to be wrong. Attitudes and opinions will be generated by it, and actions taken in its light will often have unintended effects. Misperception – wilful or unconscious – will distort the most objective-seeming realities, running before the policy-making process and conditioning it at every point. Testing the validity of their images of China will be a more difficult and indirect process than testing their estimation of themselves; erroneous ideas will find it easier to survive a confrontation with externally perceived facts and will tend to prompt, in a self-confirming, self-fulfilling or self-denying fashion, what was perceived in the first place. The circle is easily closed, and in world politics to various and possibly dire effects.

The Japanese – citizens and elites – will also have images, differing in their degree of articulation, of the world system and the way this works as a whole. They may see it, hazily or in defensible detail, as a balance-of-power construct, or as a balance-of-payments one; as an arena of ideological conflict or of economic co-operation; as a place of antagonisms, potential compromises or both, or in one of a vast variety of other ways. Each image will precede action and partly pre-determine it. An understanding of any of the images above, particularly those of the policy-making elites, will contribute a great deal to an understanding of Japanese foreign politics.

Finally, in their dealings with individual members of other states and systems, either as accredited representatives of Japan on state business in another state, or at some world forum like the United Nations, or even in an informal capacity as tourists, we can observe Japanese state relations in progress in its human detail and can learn much about global interactions that we would miss at the more formal levels of international exchange. Here images are tested and perceptual realities reassessed, views of the world are defined and re-defined and particular inter-state relations likewise predisposed.

Testing and changing cognitive systems is a personal business, regardless of the extent to which it is socially derived. Boulding posits a large-scale process that aggregates what revision has occurred with respect to world politics, and concludes that:

> The one possible cause for optimism about the international system is that there exists what might be called a 'macro-learning' process, which seems to be cumulative in much the same way as science. It is only within the last 200 years, for instance, that we have achieved something that could be called a security community or stable peace in segments of the international system. During that period, we can trace something that could be called a progression from stable war into unstable war into unstable peace and finally into stable peace.[13]

To temper Boulding's optimism we might remember that the international system that existed two centuries ago is far from identical to the one we have today, and the change he observes could well be due to a change in systemic parameters rather than any process of 'macro-learning' or the like. It is also far from intuitively evident that there has been such a change, and if anything, over a 200-year time-scale, the global record would suggest more movement the other way.

The process by which our images and the attitudes they predispose are revised and defended is one that social-psychologists have taken special pains to discuss. Faced with seemingly discordant facts, they conclude that we have three basic strategies open to us: (1) to adjust some aspect of the image being assailed or that aspect of the attitudes predisposed by such an image that is at odds with the new information; (2) to ignore altogether or to discredit the environmental *source* of those facts; (3) to ignore, discredit, distort, reinterpret or treat as exceptional the intervening *message* that is rocking the cognitive, affective and behavioural boat. The leaders and the led of powerful states, for example, in their efforts to keep treasured images intact, have been known to attempt to remove the source of the discrepant information altogether. Thus we have witnessed the express desire of certain Americans to liberate Vietnam by largely levelling it, and their substantial attempts to do so. Imposing images and attitudes upon those who choose not to accept them can be a costly affair to all concerned.

The urge to keep images and the attitudes that attend them in some sort of internally ordered repair, as mentioned above, varies considerably from person to person. Different people can withstand diverse degrees of cognitive inconsistency depending upon their personality, as well as upon such factors as the importance to them of the issues involved, the nature of the aims they are pursuing, and their chances thereby of ignoring the discrepancy or of demeaning its source. Nevertheless the urge seems to be species-characteristic in scope.

Leon Festinger's theory of 'cognitive dissonance' has been the most conspicuous attempt to date to clarify and predict its effects. The presence of an inconsistency in a person's images or attitudes, between, for example, the fact that one knows and believes something not to matter, feels that it is good in fact, but acts as if it were bad, leads, he concludes, to 'psychological discomfort'.[14] The resultant drive to re-establish mental ease is primary and powerful, cognitive dissonance giving rise to attempts to reinstate consonance 'just as hunger leads to activity oriented towards hunger reduction'.[15] Human beings seem to prefer their perceptions to make sense,

> to add up to some meaningful and manageable, or at least tolerable, whole. In this desire . . . they suppress or reject items of information that do not fit into their image of the world; or they may seek, consciously or unconsciously, for some simplified image of the world that will seem clear, understandable, and consonant to them, and that will relieve their feelings of disorientation, frustration, alienation and anxiety.[16]

'Dissonance' and 'consonance', in Festinger's language, refer to the relation that exists between pairs of cognitive 'elements', by which he means the 'knowledge' we have of how we see and map ourselves and our environment. This would seem to be synonymous with the use of 'image' above. He talks in familiar terms of 'reality testing' and the gap, where it is relevant, between discordant realities and their cognitive appreciation as a measure of the extent to which dissonance exists. Generally dissonance seems to increase the more important or valuable the 'elements' (images) are to the individual concerned, and the total dissonance between two images will be the sum of all their discrepant relations, minus the sum of their concordant ones, depending again upon the importance and value of the images and interactions involved. Consonance can be achieved by manipulating personal behavioural elements, manipulating the environmental situation or the 'reality' from which the element is derived, or simply by adding new images that reduce the importance of the dissonance itself or reconcile in some way the elements in opposition. Consonance may also be *resisted* for several reasons. If the elements, despite their counter-position, seem to respond closely to the 'reality' of the situation, if the required behavioural compensation involves pain, discomfort or loss, if the present predicament is in fact satisfactory in other respects, or if the change is just not conceivable because of the involuntary, limited or irrevocable nature of the course of action that caused the dissonant state of affairs, it may be actively sustained. Furthermore the discordance may involve many basic images, and consonance may be resisted because it can only be achieved at the cost of generating wide-scale conflict with other cognitive elements in turn.

A dissonance-debilitated individual will not only tend to seek the resolution of his psychological discomfort, but will tend to avoid situations and items of information which might cause the dissonance to grow, depending, that is, upon his own estimate of his ability to deal with them. This leads to the familiar principles of selective attention, selective remembering and forgetting, and distorted perceptions of several kinds, where the individual screens out the information from those areas of the environment that increase his unease. Premeditated apprehension about the dissonant effects of a possible or likely course of action can also lead to apathy and to inaction, or to a tension-breaking admission after the fact that the behavioural sequence performed was in fact a dissonant one.

There are, it is widely admitted, gaps and ambiguities in Festinger's ideas, but they describe a broad and important psychological process in a useful fashion, and little ingenuity is necessary to see examples of each of the mechanisms above at work in world politics. Their very general character prohibits, however, the adequate explanation or prediction of political results in any specific case. An American who has an image of his country as bearing the highest democratic standards to the world, when confronted with an outline of the practice of American foreign policy since the Second World War that emphasises the high-handed and subversive ways in which his policy-makers have denied the democratic expression of opinion in many parts of it, may resolve the discrepancy in several ways. If his idealistic image is important to him he will not ignore the difference, nor is he likely to change his ideas about what the American political project stands for, but it is not clear at this point which of many paths he might take. Each path has its own set of consequences. If he is a policy-maker himself, and the dissonant information issues from Radio Peking, he may simply dismiss the source as one not worth considering under the circumstances. If he is in the right position to issue the orders, however, he may have the transmitters subverted or bombed. If the source is an eminent and respected university professor, on the other hand, he may find it more difficult to dismiss, and so he casts about for new information with which to plug the gap, or finds some way to discredit the man, such as a past record of sympathy for radical movements or a secret reputation for gross moral turpitude. The theory depends for predictive worth upon further information about the precise circumstances and the personality of the individual involved that it does not in itself contain.

Generally, the idea of dissonance underlines the locked-on effect of personal preconceptions. When a state or other system of which one already believes the worst begins acting in generous or responsive ways, an obvious discrepancy is produced that unconsciously urges its own resolution, usually in cynical, image-preserving ways. Once a course of action is decided upon, such as war, tension is resolved. A policy commitment points to the future and helps to prevent the rehearsal of the former dissonance-bearing debates, until, of course, other and equally disturbing consequences become clear.

Else Frenkel-Brunswick's studies of the recognition, or as she calls it, 'the intolerance of ambiguity', are relevant here. Brunswick found that some people were more able to tolerate emotional ambiguities than others, and hypothesised an attitude of intolerance to complex and confusing situations as an important aspect of an 'authoritarian personality'. 'It is apparently the great number of conflicts and confusions present in the prejudiced which leads to their resorting to black–white solutions', she argued. 'It is as if everything would go to pieces once the existing discrepancies were faced. To avoid this catastrophe everything that might abet the uncertainty and opaqueness of life is desperately avoided by a selection of undisturbing, clear-cut, and therefore too general or else too concrete aspects of reality . . . ';[17] 'intolerance of ambiguity is intrinsically equivalent to an over-simplified and thus reality-inadequate approach, characterised by the dominance of crude, relatively unessential aspects, and often combined with glaring omissions of fact'.[18] The reluctance to deal in anything less than certainty, and to embrace at the first instance whatever seems most definite and hence most safe, is one of a syndrome of general attributes that has 'more than an empirical affinity' with 'strength of hostility', 'power-orientation', 'externalisation', and 'rigid stereo-typing'.[19] Those who cannot abide ambivalence and who tend to see the world in black-and-white terms are much more likely to be prejudiced and authoritarian as well. None of this bodes well for an ability to view the world in a 'realistic' fashion.

Festinger himself has restated these ideas in terms of his theory of pattern preservation.[20] Those most intolerant of 'ambiguity' would presumably be those most intolerant of 'dissonance', and would be those most likely to opt for extreme positions where dissonance cannot reside. The converse also applies. Indeed 'it would be plausible to expect that persons with low tolerance would actually have considerably less existing dissonance at any time than comparable persons who have a rather high tolerance. . . . One would expect a person with low tolerance for dissonance to see issues more in terms of "black and white" than would a person . . . able to maintain "grays" in his cognition.'[21] The one can be used to measure the other, since they are in this effect the same. Festinger goes on to point out that those most intolerant of dissonance, who fear it and avoid decisions where they must face that fear, will also tend to be dogmatic, stubborn, and, one might add, 'authoritarian' too. Those at a loss in an ambiguous situation, who find the ambiguity inconsistent with their simplified expectations of the world, will move to alleviate their subsequent unease.

Simplistic thinking of this sort is a particularly dangerous phenomenon in such a complex realm of practice as world politics. The history of the Cold War and the views of those who sustained that confrontation attests to the fact. Stereotyped ethnocentric prejudices, crude biases based upon absolutist ideologies, sharp dogmatic images of any kind and the one-sided opinions and attitudes that flow from them, seriously distort the individual capacity for sophisticated political perception. There is no reason to suppose that foreign-policy decision-makers or diverse state publics are immune from their influence. Indeed they may actively cultivate a vigorous fallacy for tactical reasons of their own. Dare a bold construction upon events, dare to win.[22]

> There are real threats abroad, which must be considered. But there is also a significant possibility that we exaggerate the threat and make matters worse by ill-conceived policies in relation to it. . . . We must be chary of our tendency toward self-delusion and of the notion that we know reality whereas other countries lack our wisdom. In these respects, we need constantly to be aware of the problems of national images and to avoid the extremes of the nation-hero and the nation-villain. . . .[23]

Simplistic thinking leads to simplistic perceptions, to erroneous definitions of aggression or self-defence ('they attacked without provocation') and of commitment or neutrality ('you are either for or against us, there is no middle way'), to the extreme separation of state priorities ('we have only two choices, and one aids and abets the enemy'), and to a general tendency to neglect evidence and seize foreclosed options without further ado. Competing global groups build up and maintain sparse images of the world, and in their dealings with each other tend to suspend the group-specific codes of morality they apply to themselves. Our power to symbolise undermines our meagre resources for empathy, inhibitions are readily abolished, and the most appalling results become common-place. Adversaries are depicted as less than human and as abstract embodiments of feared or hated ideas. Little or no guilt is consequently felt over resorting to violence when state interests are construed as requiring it.

Another pychological feature of the Cold War, it is claimed, was the advent of 'mirror images'. The two major protagonists, Russia and the United States, tended for nationalistic reasons to converge upon a similar and equally simplistic double standard – a 'black' image of each other, different only in ideological detail, and a 'white' image of themselves. Thus Americans tended to see Russians and the Russians tended to see Americans as badly led though basically good people, as imperialistic, exploitative, anti-democratic, dishonest, immoral and materialistic. The images were couched in terms of the shortcomings of communism or of capitalism in the opposing case, but they were surprisingly alike in most aspects and persist to a large extent today. The 'white' image that both held of themselves was the logical obverse of this list, the Americans viewing the United States and the Russians viewing Russia as non-expansionist and non-exploitative, as respecting the sovereignty of other states, and as peace-loving, generous, truly democratic, honest, moral and sincere.[24]

While its self-fulfilling effects are obvious, the theory has certain distorting features of its own. It has in fact given rise to a number of spurious riders, generally because convergence is too easily construed as a form of equidistance or rather of mutual approach upon a central course.[25] The social and political values of the two sides have been seen, mistakenly, as more or less the same; neither side, it is often felt, can properly be considered as aggressor or defender when one or both may be; they are construed as equally right, equally wrong, equally responsible for the tensions of the Cold War; their strategic behaviour can be accounted for in basically the same ways, and rectifying the false views they hold of the world ought to be attained with similar ease on each side, when this may not be the case at all.

The 'mirror-image' notion has an even more insidious side-effect, however. It seems to have been expressly invented by American social-psychologists to help to explain the perceptual character of the Cold War, but it also emerges, at least in part, as a weapon in that conflict. In the end, it is argued,[26] the Russians really do betray a greater tendency toward simplistic imagery, moral self-righteousness, mistrust, displacement of blame away from themselves, perceptual distortion and denial of reality than the Americans. Or has the analyst here fallen prey to his own dispositions?

Finally, the idea of 'image' has been used to draw our attention to a 'little discussed aspect of international politics, the way states can affect the images others have of them and thereby exercise influence without paying the high cost of altering their own major policies'.[27] This was a major function of old-fashioned diplomacy, and the possibility for clever manipulation of a state's image regardless of its more objective standing and its more immediate behaviour in world affairs has led one analyst at least to illuminate strategies of state deception. Jervis draws a distinction between state *signals* ('statements or actions the meanings of which are established by tacit or explicit understandings among the actors'), such as diplomatic notes, military manoeuvres, the extending or breaking of diplomatic relations and the choice of the shape of a negotiating table, and *indices* ('statements or actions that carry some inherent evidence that the image projected is correct'),[28] such as private messages overheard or intercepted, important information that is revealed without the actor's knowledge and major actions that involve high costs. Using these devices, leaders and diplomats can vary their behaviour, and can influence as a result the images others have of the states they represent. They can use 'signals', for example, to indicate a state policy they want others to believe they will pursue; they can use 'indices' to mislead others into drawing inferences from actions they cannot or will not employ; they can 'decouple' signals from their usual meanings and couple them to new ones; and they can influence the interpretations others make about aspects of their behaviour taken to be indices but which are not. Consciously perpetrated fraud is something that those who live in consumer societies ought to be familiar with, since manipulating images is the main task of commercial advertising and has been extended to service the electoral desires of political parties and their candidates as well. It has always had a secure, if academically neglected, place in the conduct of world politics.

Social factors condition and modify the pattern-seeking and the maintenance of mental forms discussed above. The most important social-psychological force of political consequence is that of *conformity*, and the most quoted experiments are those by Solomon Asch[29] in which he displayed to groups of students cards with lines drawn upon them, and asked apparently rather obvious questions about comparative length. All but one member of these groups had agreed beforehand to give the same wrong answer at various points in the experiment. Many of the single 'naïve' subjects, when faced with the contrary judgements of the rest of the group, went against the evidence of their own visual sense and agreed with the majority assessment of the problem, despite its manifest errors. Even those who resisted the pressure usually felt at least the urge to compromise. However, the presence of just one other person instructed to give the correct answer throughout and thus to support the visual perceptions of the 'naive' participant significantly reduced, though it did not eliminate, the pressure to conform. Under these circumstances there was generally 'a less oppressive and tense attitude and the quality of the disturbance was more complacent. . . . The presence of a single voice pointing to the true state of affairs had an unmistakable liberating effect. With one person at their side most subjects were able to face the majority with independence and the weakest were spared the extremes of yielding.' As Asch concludes, 'The finding points to a fundamental difference between the condition of being alone and having some source of human support.'[30]

Experiments by Richard Crutchfield have confirmed the susceptibility of the individual to combined group assertions even under much less immediate experimental conditions. A wide spectrum of conformist and non-conformist behaviour was found to occur over the whole set of 'critical items'[31] which he tested, and these ranged from factual to attitudinal questions, from highly structured to highly ambiguous and from impersonal to personal ones. Indeed 25 to 30 per cent of the subjects later admitted to conforming quite deliberately, without rationalising their anxieties in any way, though the anxieties generated were often acute. Further, on controversial social or political questions the power of conformity upon the expression of opinion was clearly enhanced and was more long-lasting as well.

Personality tests revealed, predictably, the 'independent man' as showing more 'intellectual effectiveness, ego strength, leadership ability and maturity of social relations, together with a conspicuous absence of inferiority feelings, rigid and excessive self-control, and authoritatian attitudes'.[32] The 'overconformist' was pictured as having 'less ego strength, less ability to tolerate [his] own impulses and to tolerate ambiguity, less ability to accept responsibility, less self-insight, less spontaneity and productive originality, and as having more prejudiced and authoritarian attitudes, more idealization of parents, and greater emphasis on external and socially approved values'.[33] It will depend upon the regime which sort of person a state or trans-state body might send to represent its interests at a conference or at some global forum. As a negotiator, however, the former would be clearly preferable to the latter in any conceivable situation of this sort.

Cross-cultural comparisons would be interesting on this question of conformity, and one might also find changes in conformist effect over time, which would constitute a socio-political comment of its own. Certainly group opinions, since they are a significant source of information for many individual citizens, will be pervasive levellers of attitude and generate powerful support for the illusory images of other people. Once established such illusory images will tend to confirm themselves and many a dissident voice will reduce itself to a compromising silence. The process may not, however, be as irrational and deferential as it seems. Crutchfield concludes that the individual may separate out to some extent the nature of his responses and the extent to which in different situations he will rely upon the group or resist it. On matters where there is some objective standard to measure the group against, his tendency to accept the social judgement will be less. On more subjective questions he will still fail automatically to adopt the orthodoxy of his peers. Here the factor of individual 'intelligence' seems to be decisive.[34]

Conformity and *loyalty* go hand in hand, with social-psychological evidence supporting the familiar contention that group majorities are discomfited by dissent and seek to persuade, then to exclude and otherwise penalise, those who espouse images and attitudes that differ from their own. The general effect is to reinforce the boundaries and the cohesiveness of the group, be it family, tribe, race, class, nation or the whole of mankind. Given the pathological effects of this attribute, at the national level in particular, one pressing contemporary need would seem to be the development of human loyalties that transcend the sovereign-seeming restrictions of the state, and the development of ideals that would sustain that goal. The systems perspective has laid the academic foundations for any initiative of the kind. Loyalty to humanity as a whole, however, requires an ability and a willingness to empathise with others that could expose many individuals to a level of dissonance and a degree of ambiguity they would probably prefer not to face. Discovering a sense of personal purpose and significance in the membership of such a large group might also be difficult, but then one assumes on this purely numerical argument that the Chinese share a reasonably widespread concept of loyalty to their state, and a global identity would only need to raise that particular phenomenon by a factor of four.

Returning to the idea of dissonance, the question persists: does it encompass enough? In fact, as Ralph White has pointed out, it does not include the 'most common and familiar form of unpleasantness – frustration . . .',[35] though dissonance itself might be construed as a sub-form of frustration, a blocked need, that is, for consonance in one's images of the world. So broad is the idea of *frustration* that it is no surprise to find it being used by social psychologists to explain another very pervasive feature of human society – *aggression.*

Unlike the ethologists, who deal in biological antecedents and tend to see all behaviour in these terms, social psychologists are generally convinced that aggression is not due to anything intrinsic or predetermined about human nature, and therefore that war is not inevitable in any 'innate' or 'instinctual' sense. Though they emphasise the individual basis of human action ('wars begin in the minds of men . . .'),[36] they tend to emphasise the part played by social learning, experience or education.

Though they look beyond causes of a political, economic or ideological kind to watch for the workings of each 'in and through' human individuals – how they are interpreted in the idiosyncratic case and how interpretations are changed in the course of social interaction[37] – they refuse on the whole* to resort to the explanation of aggression in terms of a deterministic predisposition to it.

The best known of the social-psychological contributions here, the essay by John Dollard *et al.*, is extremely deterministic in its own way. In their book *Frustration and Aggression*, published in 1939, the authors make the basic assumption that 'aggression is always a consequence of frustration'. More specifically, they say, 'the occurrence of aggressive behavior always presupposes the existence of frustration and, contrariwise, . . . the existence of frustration always leads to some form of aggression',[38] and they lump together under this reciprocal relationship a diverse number of social phenomena including war. Frustration on the one hand they define as 'that condition which exists when a goal-response suffers interference'.[39] (James Davies interpolates here a set of politically relevant, organically engendered human needs, which he derives in detail from the work of Abraham Maslow, to explain what instigates an action sequence before it becomes frustrated by the environment and turns nasty. His short list includes physical needs, self-affectional or love needs, self-esteem or dignity needs, self-actualisation and fulfilment needs, and the implemental or procedural need for knowledge, security, and power or control.)[40] Aggression, on the other hand, they define as 'an act whose goal response is injury to an organism (or organism-surrogate)'.[41] The strength of the instigation to the latter varies directly with the amount of the former. Aggression can be covert as well as overt and is more likely to be so as the anticipated punishment to a loved object, or as the anticipated likelihood of failure, is increased. Its inhibition, also, is likely to lead to its displacement upon some substitute body including the self, or its transformation into other but still injurious forms. Its

* Following Freud and his concept of an instinct to aggression which civilisation serves, imperfectly alas, to contain, psycho-analysts subscribed for many years to propositions of the instinctual kind. Freud argued that 'the tendency to aggression is an innate, independent, instinctual disposition in man . . . it constitutes the most powerful obstacle to culture . . .' and his bald assertion still bears a popular, particularly journalistic, appeal. See *Civilisation and its Discontents* (London: Hogarth Press, 1930) p. 102.

discharge leads to catharsis, that is a reduction in all other acts of an aggressive kind.

It is not my intention to review the detailed debate that has arisen over the Dollard hypotheses. Suffice it to say, however, that because of the diverse ways they can be defined, the concepts come very close to being circular, with the adherents of the original idea retreating to a psychological equivalent of the theological defence that 'God moves in mysterious ways'. If, for example, 'frustration' is shown not to have caused a particular aggressive act it is assumed nevertheless to be lurking in a causal corner somewhere. Frustration does *not* always lead to aggression, as one author of the original study quickly went on to point out.[42] It can lead, depending upon personal perceptions and interpretations, to a diverse repertoire of responses – righteous indignation, self-transcendence, heightened devotion to a cause, faith, symbol, leader, or political ideology, apathy, fear, helplessness, day-dreaming, resignation and repression.[43] Conversely, aggression is *not* always and only a consequence of frustration.[44] There is an important class of aggressive actions which are purely instrumental in character, aggression 'coldly and deliberately carried out as a matter of policy . . . oriented toward the attainment of some goal other than doing injury',[45] (though harm may still, of course, be involved in the attempted attainment of the posited end). The sort of disengaged violence characteristic of contemporary war is evidence of this phenomenon. Indeed, the best solution in times of war for the decision-makers of modern developed states may be 'rather, to keep the population *immobilised*, or not much more "mobilised" than they are already. . . .'[46] Organising for war in industrialised countries at least 'is organic to the routine position of the citizenry – which is, ordinarily, fragmented, alienated, bureaucratized, and subject, without noticeable enthusiasm, to civil imperatives . . .'[47] Killing is done under these conditions out of a dissociated attachment to political symbols, by individuals who have become the bearers of social function alone, divorced from any potential for aggression as such or its transcendence.

The frustration–aggression thesis is a static conception and even to the extent that it might apply it does not explain the range of human variation in aggressive response, the widely discrepant levels of toleration that exist between individuals, that is, between cultures, between age-groups and between sexes. Nor does it explain away the effects of an equally powerful human urge to altruism, co-operation and appeasement. This and the nature of instrumental response outlined above leads one to ask to what extent aggressive behaviour is learned:[48] 'like many other learned responses, aggression does not necessarily have identifiable antecedents. An attaching response may occur simply because it has led to a reward in the past and not because it is provoked by an immediate noxious or frustrating situation.'[49]

Not only do individuals differ despite their similar social and hence learning contexts, but human societies as a whole vary widely in their interpretations of who it is they hate or will aggress against.[50] These social differences 'have profound significance for the role of frustration in generating aggressive deeds . . . the social context is essential for analysing both . . . [the individual's] experience of frustration and its consequences for his behaviour'.[51] The fact, for example, that one frustrated society resorts to lynching while another does not, though thwarted in similar ways, is a cultural phenomenon that can only be explained in terms of the canons of group behaviour and the way these are perpetuated or learned.

Nevertheless, the Dollard hypotheses live on in a self-conscious fashion. Human aggressiveness is traced directly to frustration, which in turn is felt to be a necessary and inevitable result of social conditioning. Frustration begins early in life and rendering a child moral and humane cannot be accomplished without thwarting many of its felt needs and wants, and 'an average quantity of aggression is the inheritance of each individual'.[52] An elaborate number of social sub-routines are evolved to alleviate this effect, and where no overt channels exist for its expression underground ones have to be dug. At this point the argument usually descends into the selective use of anthropology. McNeil cites the Hopi and the Salteaux as examples of this sublimation process at work. The latter, for example, are a tribe where war is unknown, or at least unrecorded, but gossip, slander and bad magic abound. The anthropological record is sufficiently rich, however, to provide examples of 'primitive' groups who live without war and without these 'inevitable' side effects either, such as the Eskimos or the Kalahari Bushmen.

A critical factor remains. Whatever its psychological source, man's capacity for aggression does not necessarily lead to war between states or explain the occurrence of world war when it happens. We return again to the problem of levels of analysis. Social psychology employs variables from the level of society (the total composition of a group, its properties and inter-relations for example) in its analysis of phenomena at the individual level where psychological events occur. Indeed, it seeks to integrate these two levels in comprehensive ways. But psychological principles like that of aggression are not sufficient to explain such patterns of world politics as war. There are times, in fact, where they are neither 'significant' nor necessary. World politics consists of the aggregate interactions of many factors of an economic, political and institutional kind. While these factors are apprehended individually and hence in that sense are psychologically induced, they are not explicable in psychological terms alone unless these terms are so expanded that they fail any longer to discriminate in an analytic way. Wars result from a decision-making process that incorporates objective criteria, however subjectively these are perceived. Aggressive statesmen have led reluctant peoples into violent conflict, and persuasive and pacific leaders have sublimated widely shared and popular sentiments for war, but contexts in general cannot be wished away.

Thus the 'frustration–aggression' principle is not one that is automatically transferable from a personal level to that of states and other world systems. While Dollard *et al.* suggest its relevance for studies of international violence and use it to explain the Marxist doctrine of class conflict, the application of the hypotheses to such phenomena must be demonstrated and not simply asserted. If state leaders are frustrated, aggressive and war-like, then their personal predispositions will have considerable effect, (the same applies if large groups of the people they lead are similarly aroused), just how much effect, however, will depend upon constraints that a psychological approach alone does not consider. Thus widespread frustrations can be contained by dedicated minorities with the objective, technological means to do so as, for example, in Rhodesia, South Africa or Guinea Bissau, and this is firstly a political fact.

Social-psychologists have usually felt obliged to conclude their psycho-political works by advancing some positive and tangible suggestions for the more effective construction of foreign policy and the more peaceful pursuit of world politics as a whole. Zimbardo and Ebbesen,[53] for example, in their review of the techniques and strategies developed by psychological research into people's attitudes and how they may be changed, document an extraordinary sales campaign that was conducted in Uruguay to sell standard-sized curtains to housewives who usually buy such items custom made, and in autumn when they mostly purchase them in the spring. The subtle and scientifically documented assault was a success. As they comment themselves: 'today textiles, tomorrow the world'. The psychological findings that were used are applicable to any social or political problem relevant to the individual. They are used in contemporary political campaigns, but their scope for crafting attitudes to world affairs, and engendering policy in turn, has hardly been tapped. In this regard some knowledge of psychology is usually seen to be its own defence. Simply an awareness of the basic principles of the discipline is often felt to contribute to the conduct of world affairs. Familiarity with the idea of the 'image', with the subtle ways in which psychological consonance is maintained, with the debates about aggression and its multi-form effects; all supplement what we know already about the factors involved in policy-making and in particular the diverse cognitive mechanisms at work there.

A common-sense mood of caution is the main result. Policy-makers must continue to act, but their information is always incomplete. The dangers inherent in this situation are avoidable to some extent if we resist reducing complexities to simplicities, resist ruling out alternative sources of information and evaluation and closing off to our scrutiny competing views of reality: 'one of the cruel paradoxes of international politics is that those decisions that require the most serious consideration of alternative interpretations of reality often carry with them the greatest pressures for conformity to stereotyped images'.[54] Decision-makers should be told and should remain aware that they are 'biased', and that they will tend to see what they are disposed to see and to neglect information to the contrary. They should resist any unambiguous interpretation of events, any tendency to hold views supported by logically inconsistent mental arguments, and any over-estimation of a similarity of interests between their own and other states. They should scrutinise their beliefs and assumptions about other state leaders and systems, keeping them as explicit as possible. They should maintain a similar watch upon the theories and images developed by the organisations that support them in their role.[55]

The most extreme of the psychological recommendations is that advanced by B. F. Skinner, whose novel *Walden Two* and discursive essay *Beyond Freedom and Dignity*[56] would have the behaviourist principles of operant conditioning applied in a benevolent but total fashion to human beings. Thus, he declares, we might build a planned society without the 'undesirable' attributes of the accidental constructs we have about us today. Behavioural technology could do 'scientifically' what has been left to a random process of ill-directed socialisation before. Human survival demands nothing less. We must develop a deliberate willingness to design our personalities in advance and to fashion them self-consciously in behaviourist terms. His implicit vision depicts the world's peoples integrated into a benign but comprehensive psycho-despotism, where 'freedom' is preserved only by the proper regard for the nature of social control.

I doubt if in fact we will ever know enough about the stimulus–organism–response chain to implement the sort of utopia Skinner finds attractive. The social shaping he depicts is more likely to come about through genetic engineering, or through the direct methods of intervening in the workings of the brain already described. Even if we could do what he would like, the potential is one for evil as much as good, and any 'ideal' people so deliberately produced would probably be rather dull – safe, perhaps, cheerful even, but dull. Skinner's challenge does point up, nevertheless, in unequivocal terms a potential that psychology might conceivably come to provide. Then the decision will be made, either consciously or in some subterranean way, what to do with it.

More modest proposals are common. After a detailed review of the psychological dimensions of foreign policy, J. de Rivera, for example, suggests a number of concrete improvements in the process of its formulation,[57] namely, that there should be established and recognised officers of the state for collecting and presenting information that contradicts the prevailing policy; a body of 'impractical planners' to expand perspectives upon what is feasible; secret mental-health facilities for government officials;

an agency to advocate the welfare of peoples and not just that of their governments, and to encourage a respect for international law; a group of officials to enhance communications with hostile states and to improve them within the government itself; some means of assessing the intellectual compatibility of a governmental appointee and those with whom he will deal; and public participation in forming the administrative consensus of any particular foreign policy before the administration makes its decision. There are difficulties with several items on Rivera's list, and their consequences might not all be as beneficial as he would seem to assume, but they are worth contemplation and improvement, and they also deserve some partial implementation at least.

'Cognitive dissonance' could well be used in a deliberate way to influence international relations, and one state's leaders, by bringing dissonance to another's stereotyped images of it, might affect their mutual process of interaction for the better (or worse). Charles Osgood devised a programme[58] by which American leaders might carefully create changes in policy stance to improve the conditions between them and their counterparts in the Soviet Union, though there is no evidence that it has ever been used. He pointed up as well the necessity for those involved in world politics to resist the psychological habituation process that leads to the 'meaninglessness of assigns',[59] the process, that is, by which the emotive connotations of language are unpacked and only the most impoverished of its informational values left behind: '"Intercontinental ballistic missiles", "megatons", and "30 million casualties", just simply do not have the emotional gut meanings of words like "blood", "bread", and "mother".'[60]

Much work has also been done to elucidate patterns of small-group behaviour and some of the findings have prescriptive import here. Indeed, empirical studies of the performance of small groups have contributed rigorous, often experimentally derived conclusions, which are relevant to our understanding of foreign policy for at least two reasons. Firstly, the focus of decision upon any state policy is usually to be found in a small body of people who plan, debate, husband and hand through those acts that are eventually endorsed as state directives. This is certainly not to detract, as W. J. M. Mackenzie points out,[61] from the policy effects of a mass meeting or strike, of a state-wide election or referendum and the public debate that goes with it, or of the workings of large houses of assembly and review. It is simply to assert that important conclusions about foreign policy emerge at critical loci from differentiable face-to-face groups of many kinds, both formal and informal. In such a place two to twenty or so advisers, official policy-planners, military and corporate consultants and other personnel, who associate over an extended period of time in some mutually supportive fashion, construct new state moves or seek to justify old ones. A knowledge of the general principles which any and all primary groups exhibit in practice might help us to understand how these groups work, and help us therefore to explain from the nature of their deliberations something of the conclusions they come to. Secondly, any justification of a foreign policy that emerges from such groups is most effectively transmitted to bigger bodies of people, like the citizenry at large, through the primary groups into which they gather in turn. Media presentations are usually perceived in a selective fashion, and what we do not want to know in what we are told by newspapers, radio and television we largely ignore or repress. Primary groups are much better, however, at exerting influence upon individuals and the powerful factor of conformity comes into play.

Generally, then:

> If we are to understand the political process, greater consideration must be given to the role of face-to-face contacts. Primary groups of all sorts mediate political relationships at strategic points in the political process. They are the locus of most political decision-making, they are important transmission points in political communications, and they exercise a major influence on the political beliefs and attitudes of their members.[62]

Considering primary groups helps to close the gap between the analysis of individual political behaviour and the analysis of the way the political system works as a whole. Between the personal level and that of the state or other world system lie a host of small human sets – families, committees, collections of friends, office cliques and purposeful associations of many kinds – with a significant part to play in socialisation, reinforcement, and other diverse and politically relevant human activities.

Laboratory studies have been done on small groups, and though there are difficulties in transferring such results to the wider world, precise if rather culture-bound generalisations have come out of them.

The principles arrived at have a good deal to do with the patterns of group communication – the way the intra-group traffic in messages is organised, the way it influences the structure of the group and is influenced in turn – and the emergence of a leadership with all its associated trappings of influence and power. Thus: 'In most groups, there is a rough ranking of members, implicit or explicit, depending on the extent to which the members represent or realize the norms and values of the group: the more they do, the higher they rank.'[63] 'Given . . . a testing or feeling out period . . . a small group will typically establish working lines of communication which can then be more or less formalized within the group.'[64] And these communications 'are more likely to be directed from equal to equal and from the higher-ranking members to the lower-ranking members than from the lower-ranking to the higher-ranking'.[65] If one seeks to discover that member of a policy-formulating group with most influence over its affairs, then it may be quite misleading to look for formal patterns of ranking such as those that distinguish a president or prime minister from his advisers, his party or his administrative colleagues. Given suitable access to the process of interaction our findings on the direction in which messages flow will indicate who in fact are the first-ranking figures with most effect over setting goals and the way these are achieved, who then it is we should seek to understand, and whose behaviour we should seek to explain and predict. In terms of official status they may be comparatively insignificant to the order of the group, but small-group theories alert us to the unofficial development of policy-formulating structures that vary from those we might normally expect.

Though hardly an unexpected conclusion it also seems that:

The less definite the standards external to the group itself (scientific evidence, objective reality, the mores of the larger

> community, religious revelation, the moral code, etc.), the more control the group itself can exercise – and, if its own standards are clear, the more it will exercise. . . . What is correct is what the group says is correct, especially when it can claim to be in a position to judge.[66]

This would suggest that the formulation of foreign policy, which is performed to a considerable extent in the light of internally generated standards and where objective referents are often ambiguous, tends to become on account of its small-group character an incestuous business of self-sustaining abstractions and incipient control. The perceptual mechanisms of consonance, image-maintenance, and conformity are also relevant here. One way in which the individual tests the reality of his beliefs, attitudes and opinions is to compare them with those of his primary group peers, and when discrepancies arise the preference for agreement and the tendency of small groups to treat a dissenter as a threat to the achievement of its ends or purposes leads, as often as not, to a personal compromise. Conversely, group members usually perceive the consensus of the group as much closer to their own position than it really is.

There are consequences here for decision-making. If the goal is an urgent one, such as formulating an external policy in a time of crisis, this phenomenon will tend to reinforce the closure effect upon perceived alternatives and options, since small-group pressures for conformity and consensus will tend to cause individual members to converge upon the solution least likely to cause conflict, which need not necessarily be the one best fitted to the political task at hand. This effect is 'most evident in those cases in which group membership is highly important to the individual – in traditional groups, for instance, where relations among members are diffuse, deeply affective, and have existed for an extended period'.[67] It will be least evident, presumably, and this must be seen against the argument above, in the councils of modern states where relations among members are often precisely and rigidly defined in bureaucratic terms as well as being impersonal and temporary in nature. Indeed an individual member may actively not conform to the group consensus in an attempt, perhaps, to impress a decision-maker or leader and so enhance his personal prospects for promotion, or because he believes the group consensus to be wrong-headed and is prepared to risk its sanctions to say so because he has sufficiently little to lose. These rational–legal councils, however, usually overlay more informal bodies where decision-makers solicit face-to-face support and advice, and these will tend much more to the model of traditional groups and the effects this model predisposes. The extreme case here is the coterie that exists merely to applaud the opinions of the decision-maker. The more practical leader will attempt to keep as balanced a set of views as possible about the world, actively soliciting small-group contacts over a wide range of attitudes, values and beliefs, and testing the contents of his political ideas upon them. Even without all other things being equal, a foreign-policy formulator who consciously uses several different primary groups to probe and expand his perspectives is preferable to one who does not.

Psycho-politics in general throws considerable light upon state and systemic interactions and upon the potential for political change. Social-psychological analysis prompts us to consider not only the economic, political, institutional and strategic factors a policy-maker or a people has to face, but how these factors are perceived and why some aspects of them are perceived in one way and not in others. We are made aware that events are not inevitable. Things need not go on happening in the way they have done and look like continuing to do. Where there is the psychological will, however engendered, time and time again a political way can be found or constructed to subvert events despite the inevitable appearance of apparent constraints. States face real obstacles to their complex and various concerns, but they face illusory ones as well. It is not usually clear in any particular situation where the truth of the matter lies. But in any event, political leaders and publics, their images, personalities and mental profiles, are factors to be included in any comprehensive equation of the whole.

Objective political, military or economic factors have a diminished significance when viewed in this way. Conflicts in world politics result from distortion, misunderstanding and complex misperception, as well as the collision of incompatible interests. In principle, the resolution of conflict should be in part a matter of *re*-perception, of restructuring the subjective realities of the key combatants. John Burton has written of just such a technique[68] and experimented with it in practice, but the possibilities are limited by the same problems that prevent the reduction of the study of world politics in general to the understanding of psychological processes in particular. And yet, there is much to Burton's exposed stand.

> The international system, although it imposes certain limits and imperatives on the policies of the actors, is largely the outcome of their decisions and operations. The basic trends are often malleable enough to be twisted or even reversed by the main actors' moves. Thus, reality is in considerable part the product of a conflict of wills, of a contest of active perceptions competing for the privilege of defining reality. . . . When the physics of power declines, the psychology of power rises.

We should define world politics today then

> less as a struggle for power than as a contest for the shaping of perceptions. When force loses some of its prominence, power – my exercise of control over you – becomes the art of making you see the world the way I see it, and of making you behave in accordance with that vision. International politics in the past was often an arena of coercion without persuasion; it is tending to become an arena of persuasion, more or less coercive.[69]

The arts of persuasion are first and foremost psychological ones, and their political implications are profound.

CHAPTER 10

Conflict

The previous chapter concludes the summary of other disciplinary ideas which I take to be of relevance to global political affairs. It now remains to consider, in more detail than I could do while discussing these various perspectives, frameworks and substantive findings themselves, how they might apply to the contemporary analytic and quantitative study of two of the most fundamental political processes in the world – 'integration', and 'disintegration', coalescence or conflict, the growth of greater communities as opposed to their descent into war.

Integration is the making up of a whole by the adding together or the consensual combination of separate parts. It represents, on the international level, the centripetal force by which superordinate state constructs are derived from political groupings already extant; it renders the latter in varying aspects and to varying degrees, subordinate. The opposite process, the disintegrative pressures that lead to conflict, overlay these centre-seeking attributes at every point. Much of the diverse and often bizarre character of world politics results from the contradictory turn of political vortices against the centrifugal thrust of human conflict and war.

> Just as the physicists can solve certain problems only by assuming the wave character of light and others, on the contrary, only by assuming a corpuscular or quantum theory, so there are problems of sociology [and of world politics too] which can be adequately attacked only within an integration theory and others which require a conflict theory for a meaningful analysis. . . . While the integration theory likens a society to an ellipse, a rounded entity which encloses all of its elements, conflict theory sees society rather as a hyperbola which, it is

true, has the same foci but is open in many directions and appears as a tension field of the determining forces.[1]

At the beginning of this work I argued that the 'behavioural' revolt had two beneficial effects upon the study of world politics; one was its emphasis upon interdisciplinary research, and the other was the encouragement it gave to those who sought to construct a 'theory' of the subject or at least important aspects of it such as 'foreign policy'. The analytical approaches were bolstered, too, by attempts to quantify theoretical hypotheses and to test them, and to discover and measure with explicit precision the patterns evident in global affairs. I would like to return to these analytic endeavours and their subsidiary quantitative concerns, and to place the transdisciplinary ideas outlined above in the context they provide. The findings I shall outline are widely scattered throughout the contemporary academic literature on the subject, and there is considerable value in assembling and comparing these results directly with respect to some more comprehensive framework.

It is important at the outset to realise that the behavioural reflex prompted analysts to look beyond war as such, beyond social phenomena of this characteristically intense and large-scale kind, to seek a general theory of human conflict of which war between states is only one particular example. As discussed already, this can be seen as a virtue in itself. Concentrating on just the one type of conflict, such as war alone, can lead to the neglect of facts and principles which may in the end prove essential to an adequate understanding of it. Marital conflict, animal, racial, class, religious, economic and interstate conflict, each instance may illuminate the other, and a general theory establish the conditions common to them all. A generalising approach may generate a more comprehensive understanding of the phenomena involved than a piecemeal set of particularistic explanations that are difficult to summarise in any more inclusive way. Furthermore, restricting the study of war to the study of large-group interactions depends upon a prior assumption that questions of cause and consequence can be satisfactorily resolved at the state level alone, which is an assumption behaviouralists are loath to make. And if the study of interstate interactions is not seen as sufficient to encompass the significant variables involved, then a more eclectic transdisciplinary approach becomes imperative, and the analysis will turn as a matter of course to insights about conflict at all levels – between animals, within the individual human psyche, between pairs of people and within groups, within states as well as between them; and from several substantive directions – biological, psychological, anthropological, sociological, and so on.

The case for such an outlook is very strong. The idiographic counter-statement – that the detailed understanding of unique aspects of particular kinds of conflict, aspects likely to be overlooked by any proposition sufficiently general to encompass several sorts or them all, is the best or only possible way to proceed – can be carried to logical and unworkable extremes: 'idiographic arguments would rule out not only general theories of conflict but also special theories of war, of religious conflict, or of any other class of conflict phenomena . . . each instance of conflict would have to be analyzed in its own right from a historical or clinical viewpoint'.[2] This method has its virtues, but 'once one admits the possibility of a special theory of one *class* of conflict phenomena, the entire discussion is shifted into a nomothetic framework, since even the most limited special theory aims to generalise about properties shared by all instances of a given type. In that framework, it becomes difficult to set arbitrary limits on how far one may fruitfully and validly generalise'.[3] Such limits may not be arbitrary however. They are governed by results, by the success of the general theory that is finally proposed in explaining the particular nature of the conflicts it sets out to encompass. Mannheim's paradox – the likelihood that social propositions of an abstract character will contain little useful information – can be resolved by the ability of such propositions to enhance the analyst's explanatory power, none the less. It is worth keeping this criterion in mind when we come to consider the present-day study of conflict in general and war in particular as outlined later in the chapter.

Critics also argue that general theories are realistically built up from below, rather than deduced intact from above. This, however, is not an assault of substance, since theory-building advances on many levels at once, and in fact proceeds best when it is done in a mutually supportive way:

> the gradualist strictures (against generalizing too much, too soon) apply only to the formulation of a complete, fully developed general theory of conflict from which all the special theories can be derived. . . . If the generalist argument is interpreted to mean that special theories will contribute most to scientific advance only when developed in relation to the broader conceptual framework provided by a general theory of conflict, then it is not inconsistent with the gradualist view of scientific progress.[4]

We should recognise that some such reciprocity will inevitably occur since specialist attempts at conflict classification, at empirical research or the construction of *particular* theories, will always be carried on in the light of more general notions about conflict and human nature, its causes and how it is sustained.

We have, finally, the problem which has occurred throughout this work of combining levels of analysis. How can we relate the fact of conflict within the individual psyche itself to conflict between states? How can we combine our findings about the nature of man with what we know about the structural imperatives of his social systems? I have discussed these issues already, but the difficulty persists of plugging the micro-models of individual and small-group behaviour into the macro-circuits of world politics. Certainly this problem is much less acute than it was. Psychologists and anthropologists have studied the individual in his group, institutional, and all-embracing cultural contexts. Political scientists pay increasing attention to the role of individual factors in determining collective behaviour, to the process of political socialisation, to psychological needs, drives and diverse behavioural idiosyncracies. But the gap remains. A description of psychological states will not wholly explain social and political behaviour, and social and political processes alone will not fully account for individual competence. World politics is not completely explained by either. Nevertheless, fusing such dimensions will be the final step in any comprehensive theory of social conflict, and hence in any adequate theory of war.

There is, as one might guess, nothing approaching such a fusion or such a theory at the moment. There are considerable difficulties in clarifying the terms of the debate since the same idea is often given different labels, and the same label is invariably used to encompass a number of ideas. These difficulties reflect the confusions of the field, and no amount of theoretical endeavour has managed to advance systematic propositions conspicuously superior to those of the 'folk' wisdom that preceded the behaviouralist revolt. There is, for example, no accepted or agreed list of the social units by which conflicts might be classified. To talk of conflict in intra-personal, inter-personal, familial, group, class, ethnic, religious, intra-state or interstate terms is to assume, perhaps erroneously, that 'each kind of social unit, having its own range of size, structure, and institutions, will also have its own modes of interaction and thus its own patterns of conflict with other social units'[5] like and unlike itself. Such an assumption merits scrutiny on its own, since, despite the plausibility of some sort of analytical link between the parties to a conflict and the nature of the confrontation that ensues, the link should be demonstrated and not allowed to stand by assertion alone.

There is, furthermore, no agreed classification for conflict itself. Rapoport,[6] for example, talks in terms of an 'ideal' division between fights, games and debates. Bernard[7] outlines three competing approaches – social-psychological, sociological and semanticist – which place their main emphasis in turn upon personal frustrations, mutually incompatible interests, and mutual misunderstanding. There is also the familiar distinction by discipline between biological, economic, political, psychological and social conflict.

An attempt to *define* 'conflict' will help to set some of the guidelines for the subsequent discussion. The broadest construction we can place upon the term includes the putative incompatibilities that precede the collision whatever it may be (the 'dashing together of physical bodies' as one dictionary graphically depicts it) which is the usual sense of the word. Such a definition includes

> any social situation or process in which two or more social entities are linked by at least one form of antagonistic psychological relation or at least one form of antagonistic interaction. This emphasises that while *antagonism* . . . is the common element in all conflicts, there are a number of different kinds of psychological antagonisms (e.g. incompatible

> goals, mutually exclusive interests, emotional hostility, factual or value dissensus, traditional enmities, etc.) and a number of different kinds of antagonistic interaction (ranging from the most direct, violent, and unregulated struggle to the most subtle, indirect, and highly regulated forms of mutual interference), none of which is necessarily present in all instances of conflict.[8]

Interstate war, as one form of social conflict, comes at the overt, violent end of the continuum, but it is only one of several sorts of interstate conflict. Conflict can also be seen as a pervasive or marginal feature of human society, as an objective phenomenon or one that is subjectively derived, as functional or dysfunctional in its effects, and each of these views and combinations of them will predispose certain preferred modes of conflict termination.[9]

Despite my own conviction that a generalising approach is the most sensible way to proceed, because of the attention it gives to transdisciplinary concerns, the question of whether we should think of war as a separate and special kind of antagonistic behaviour or not is still an open one in the discipline. Analysts give it both separate consideration and treat it as one, albeit comparatively organised example, at a particular social level, of a much more pervasive human condition. This analytic dualism has allowed discrepant approaches to proceed regardless of any attempt to work out in principle if and where the substantive continuities and discontinuities come. It is an ambiguity that runs through much of what follows.

War, violent conflict, is the armed contention of the values and interests, habits or impulses, of one human group against another. 'The prime objective, even as in the days of Lagash and Ur, is still to put the enemy to flight or render him *hors de combat* by dissecting nerves, muscles, viscera, and bones through the subcutaneous introduction of pieces of metal into his body.'[10] Chemical and biological assault has played a significant but subsidiary role, and difficulties in controlling the effects of such weapons will hopefully sustain their secondary status. 'Not until the invention of the atomic bomb was a truly novel means hit upon to end enemy resistance by ending enemy existence.'[11] War is not peace, and yet it is often difficult to distinguish from other forms of conflict – thus 'when does a blockade become an act of violence? When does a rebel band take on the character of a political unit?'[12] It is a rare pursuit in the animal kingdom as a whole; an attribute so characteristic of humankind that it might well be listed as one of our distinguishing features.

Attempts have been made to discern macroscopic patterns in the history of war. Using data collected by Lewis Richardson in his study, *Statistics of Deadly Quarrels*, Frank Denton[13] has detected a cyclical recurrence of international conflict for the period 1820–1949, which coincides with the dividing dates given by Rosecrance for six of the nine historical systems he used (the ones that fall within this timespan).[14] In a later study Denton and Warren Phillips[15] tested both the Richardson data, and other statistics compiled by Quincy Wright for the period 480–1900, for evidence of short-term and long-term fluctuations in war and peace. They found a regular upsurge of violence every 25 years on average (about 20 years before 1680, and 30 years after this date), and also a more extended fluctuation every 80–120 years. They have explained the shorter cycle as a 'generational' effect when memories of the last war begin to fade and new decision-makers come to power. They account for the longer cycle in terms of an 'action–reaction' process, a regular alternation between periods of turmoil when philosophers emphasise the virtues of political stability, and times of peace when they grasp the opportunity to exalt change and the achievement of ideals.[16]

J. D. Singer and Melvin Small[17] have analysed international wars for the period 1816–1965 as part of Singer's Correlates of War (COW) project.[18] They conclude that the incidence of it seems to be 'neither waxing nor waning',[19] with only a 'modest increase in the severity and magnitude of war over the entire span'.[20] Their quantitative treatments also suggest a 20–40 year generational cycle in the level of world violence: 'discrete wars do not necessarily come and go with regularity but with some level of interstate violence almost always present; there are distinct and periodic fluctuations in the amount of that violence'.[21] They are cautious about this result, and can find no such recurrence in the case of separate states that took part in a number of the wars of the period, but the combined findings clearly indicate where we might look for a cause.

There might be, further, a seasonal influence on the decision to go to war; 64 of the 93 conflicts counted were initiated in autumn or spring. Major powers seem to be the most war-prone, and do well in such conflicts. To have initiated hostilities is also an advantage, but less so if those assailed are of equivalent strength. It is interesting to note, too, that just over half of the states Singer and Small list never went to war at all over the considerable timespan involved.[22]

The study of social conflict and that of war can be separated into four main fields: I the study of its *causes*; II the study of the *course* of conflict (the dynamics of its procession; III the study of control and *termination* processes; and IV the study of its *effects*.

I shall not consider the last aspect here. Certainly the demographic consequences of war or its social side-effects, on the status of women for example, can be extensive, but they are not a conspicuous feature of the contemporary approach to the subject, and will not be given separate scrutiny.

I CAUSE

The study of *cause* is the most comprehensive of these categories, and questions of conflict termination, for example, will closely depend upon the conclusions one makes about the origins of the antagonistic sequence one is attempting to bring to an end. Nevertheless, in Quincy Wright's compendious two-volume treatment of war there is only one short chapter on its causes, perhaps because, as he states in a monumentlly understated way: 'There is no single cause of war. Peace is an equilibrium among many forces.'[23]

In a common-sense fashion we might distinguish wars of greed and material aggrandisement from those of security – 'long-term or short-term, real or imagined' – and those undertaken out of devotion to a religio-political faith or some such transcendental creed.[24] We might add the case where a continued state of internal national chaos or penury begets an attack upon an ideological opponent or the imperialist preserver of the exploitative status quo or whatever else might be the frustrating force; the case where a belief in the useful function to be served by threatening violence leads itself to war, like driving leads to traffic accidents (if interacting units run risks at high speed, under the best of conditions two of them will eventually collide); and the case of the 'just war' which is prompted by the idea that 'military self-help is necessary to vindicate justice, law, and rights if peaceful negotiation proves ineffective'.[25] We might add other reasons, such as the fact of political lag or the failure of our mechanisms for social change to cope with the results of rapid technological progress and ideological change; the 'inherent' aggressiveness of certain states and state leaders; traditional interstate feuds; the 'bipolarization of power through rival alliances';[26] and most intractable of all, the 'inherent' difficulty of keeping peace: 'Conditions of peace can never be taken for granted. They will have to be continually reconstructed and maintained by human efforts. Peace is artificial: war is natural'[27] as Thomas Hobbes maintained.

There are many provacative points about this last position, the use of the concepts of 'inheritance' and 'nature', for example, to lend a spurious sense of the weight and inevitability of war, and to disguise the host of qualifying statements that might be made. Once we begin to unpack it, however, the question of cause is difficult to contain, even by the rigid use of criteria of relevance or significance of some kind. We need a convenient organising device, and I propose to adopt the most common of these here, the grouping of the origins of international conflict under three analytic levels, that of *man*, the *state*, and the *world system and society*. Between 'man' and 'the state' come a number of other politically relevant levels, particularly that of the small-group kind but also political parties, bureaucracies, military establishments and legislatures. The 'world system and society' also consists of interactions other than the obvious interstate ones that occur there. The three-tier hierarchy, however, has considerable cogency and most contemporary studies can be successfully subsumed under one or another of the categories outlined.

A. MAN

At the primary level of human behaviour as such there are several fields of enquiry. Much work has been done, for example, by assuming that individuals act in a *rational* way, in working out replicable modes of choice, strategy and bargaining. A complex and technical literature on game theory, with its carefully structured runs of 'chicken', its prisoners' dilemmas and the like, now provides models which might help decision-makers to maximise state interests and to minimise the risk of war. Granted that human beings often act irrationally and inconsistently, using means not obviously consonant with their desired ends, hope is still held out that these strategies and others like them might serve as guidelines at least for a 'satisficing' set of decisional responses.[28] Given the small return on these efforts, however, I have not reviewed them here.

At this level, too, the substantive effects of biopolitics become apparent. This is one point where we can locate the transdisciplinary findings in their analytical context. Researchers in this area attempt to understand what is seen as the *irrational* side of our animal selves, in the sense of what is determined, perhaps regardless of our voluntaristic intervention. As discussed above, they seek the 'inherent' source of patterns of behaviour, and particularly those with destructive consequences. The attempt to locate a physiological basis for the 'paranoid streak' in man is clearly part of this attempt, as is the search by ethologists for general principles that might explain animal behaviour, including that of man, in terms of its evolutionary utility. 'In spite of great social changes, man still inherits', it is claimed, 'the biology which adapted him to live in a small society in which many forms of conflict were highly rewarded.'[29] Such a pessimistic result supports the Hobbesian case for the 'right' ordering of society to contain our weakness or substitute for it.

Another major approach here is the *psychopolitical* one, likewise discussed above. Social-psychological studies attempt to discern the sources of conflict in the social or personal profiles of a society's members at large, or more particularly in its decision-makers, and we can clearly fit their findings here. A memorable summary of the latter (mainly American) literature is provided by Michael Haas:

> The prototypic dove decision-maker is seen as a middle-aged Jewish Negress who has received a college education to attain the status of a physician or college professor, who resides outside a big city but not too far from the nation's capital;

> she is non-authoritarian, non-ethnocentric, flexible, achievement-oriented, uncynical, non-alienated, optimistic, and an intellectual with much tolerance of ambiguity; her political views are neither conservative nor nationalist; she participates politically, does not anticipate war, does not expect her country to survive or be victorious in war, and takes few risks.[30]

Presumably, one source of war could be a set of global decision-makers without these compound attributes. Along lines pursued already there has been much work upon perception and the processes by which human judgement is conditioned and political realities misconstrued. Thus, for example, in a general way: 'Peace is more likely to emerge if the prototype decision-maker is in possession of accurate information, advisers are in disagreement over alternatives, while stereotypic decoding of inputs and provocative encoding of outputs is absent; there is concern for long-range implications and longer time for making a decision and drawing up contingency plans.'[31]

B. THE STATE

At the second level, that of *societal structures*, there are at least four key avenues of search, though each converges upon an understanding of the sort of state and citizenry that seems to be most disposed to conflict and war. These are the *imperialist*, the *cybernetic*, the *psycho-cultural* and the *quantitative* approaches, and I shall outline each in turn.

(i) *The Imperialism Approach*

Marxist–Leninist theories about productive forces and the international movements of capital have been used to rework our appreciation of the link between imperialism and war. Hence the recent spate of studies, largely a response to the Vietnam war, that attempt to explain that conflict and much of the Cold War too, in terms of an expansionist American foreign policy, tracing the source of the expansionism in turn to the market needs of monopoly capitalism. Contemporary imperialism has one 'essential feature', Magdoff argues, which is 'the competitive struggle among the industrial nations for dominant positions with respect to the *world* market and raw material sources'.[32] With this in mind the 'reality' of imperialism can be seen to go 'far beyond the immediate interest of this or that investor: the underlying purpose is nothing less than keeping as much as possible of the world open for trade and investment by the giant multinational corporations. . . .'[33] If commercial hegemony or future access is threatened by an intra-state revolution whose aims include the strict regulation of the profits on foreign investment and an end to dependent status as a source of raw materials, as a market for manufactured goods, and as an area for investment opportunities, violent intervention is almost inevitable. Business interests must be protected and commercial access preserved. Where there exist reformist or revolutionary elites, or the countervailing concerns of other industrial states, we have an actual and potential cause of war.

This argument has been met in a number of ways. Most importantly, it is said that the degree of economic and political premeditation necessary to plan and direct such a conscious campaign does not exist. The United States' neo-colonial record is best read as an ideological defence, misconstrued perhaps, certainly clumsy and presumptious, of 'freedom' and 'order'. To talk as Magdoff does about the 'inevitability' of imperialism is to argue the existence of a set of socio-economic forces over which Americans themselves have had little choice or control. The debate continues, and it is an important one. Perhaps the determinism is wilful, rather than blind, voluntaristic in the sense that American policy-makers have preferred not to deny the logic of intervention once set in train. Certainly there is much credence now in the neo-colonialism case.

(ii) *The Cybernetic Approach*

The *cybernetic* approach is most closely associated with the work of Karl Deutsch. It has been discussed above in some detail, and stands here as a possible contribution to the study of the causes of conflict and war. It has been used by John Burton to depict states as self-steering communication nets, whose capacity to learn and adapt may well be insufficient to meet the environmental demands placed upon them. Bureaucratically moribund departments of foreign affairs, such as those which characterise large industrial nations today, may show evidence of a 'dinosaur' effect – extended channels of communication with in-increasingly inefficient reactions to the need for change. Several modes of cybernetic collapse suggest sensible causes of war.

(iii) *The Psycho-Cultural Approach*

The *psycho-cultural* category subsumes those attempts to understand the causes of conflict and war in terms of national character, the summed psychological characteristics of state populations, the propensity of particular societies for aggression or defence, and diffuse predictions made on the basis of 'national moods'. It is the *psychopolitics* approach, pursued at the level of the state as a whole. Thus, for example, it has been argued that the attitudes of the American people and their governors have alternated 'between phases of extroversion (when the nation tends to exert direct pressure, particularly military, ouside its borders) averaging about 27 years in length, and phases of introversion, averaging about 21 years'.[34] As the cause in turn of this psychological periodicity, however, we are offered only vague comment on the effects of 'human nature and historical processes'.[35] Rudolph Rummel[36] has also correlated particular measures of the psychological motivation of a nation's people, based upon David McClelland's indices of achievement desire, desire for affiliation with others, desire for power, and other-directedness, with state foreign-conflict behaviour, but he has found no significant link between quantitative assessment of these attributes and a number of dimensions of external conflict including war.

(iv) *The Quantitative Approach*

The *quantitative* approach is very extensive and many of the studies in this field are recognised as examples of the behavioural method at its correlational best. Three foci are evident here: (A) those works that measure the material, institutional and social features of states against their foreign-conflict behaviour; (B) those that examine the comparative differences and similarities between states, also as an indicator of external conflict (whether, for example, states that espouse the same political ideology are less likely to engage in war than those of divergent beliefs, or whether pairs of rich states go to war more often than those rich states statistically matched with poor ones); and (C) those that seek to explain the cause of conflict and war in terms of a state's relations with others, or in terms of the relationships between pairs of them. The procedure for operationalising the crucial indices usually varies from study to study, as do the statistical treatments used, and the empirical findings are not therefore comparable in a strict way. This presents particular problems when results contradict each other, as happens frequently, though they do point out in a general fashion those areas of search where a study of cause might be most productive.

(A) What results have been adduced from the first of these concerns, from the empirical correlates arrived at by matching state *attributes* with modes of interstate conflict, including war? Let us separate internal attributes into four analytic areas – (1) the extent of domestic strife, (2) the political system, (3) the economy, and (4) factors indicative of 'stress and strain' – and consider in turn how each has been seen as related to a country's external conflict behaviour. Other attribute dimensions exist, but they can be lumped into a residual category of their own.

(A.1) Examining the hypothetical link between *domestic strife and foreign conflict* has been the particular province of the best known of all the quantitative correlational enterprises, the Dimensionality of Nations (DON) project. In 1963 Rudolph Rummel published the first of the DON studies.[37] In it he reported the results of a series of inter-correlations, factor analyses, factor-score calculations and multiple regressions carried out upon twenty-two measures of foreign and domestic conflict behaviour for all the states in the world system (77) for the three years from 1955 to 1957. There were nine measures of 'domestic conflict', which emerged under factor analysis as members of three discrete groups – a *turmoil* dimension (number of spontaneous, comparatively unorganised anti-government demonstrations of more than 100 people, excluding those of a distinctly anti-foreign nature, number of riots of more than 100 people where physical force was used, and number of major government crises), a *revolutionary* dimension of organised, overt response (number of successful or unsuccessful revolutions or regional rebellions, number of people killed in all forms of domestic violence, number of purges of political opponents or dissidents, and number of general strikes of more than 1000 industrial or service workers involving more than one employer and aimed at the government), and a *subversive* dimension of organised covert responses (presence or absence of guerrilla warfare, as carried on by independent or irregular bands dedicated to the overthrow of the ruling regime, and number of politically motivated assassinations of high government officials or politicians).[38] Of these the first two were found to be the more important. There were thirteen measures of 'foreign-conflict' behaviour which likewise varied in three comparatively unconnected ways: a *war* dimension composed of measures of the number killed in all forms of foreign-conflict behaviour, the number of wars (defined here as any military clash of a particular country with another in which more than 0.02 per cent of its population were militarily involved), the number of official diplomatic or government statements of a derogatory kind by one state against another, the number of such statements that could be construed as threats, the number of military actions short of war, the number of official protests, and the number of mobilisation moves; a *diplomatic* dimension, composed of measures of the number of expulsions or recalls of ambassadors or diplomatic officials of lesser rank, and the number of troop movements made; and a *belligerency* dimension composed of measures of the number of countries with which diplomatic relations were severed, the number of boycotts, withdrawals of aid, and like sanctions, brought against another state, and the number of anti-foreign demonstrations or riots by more than 100 people directed at another state or its policies.[39] Of these three, the first was found to be the most important. We should note as well that international conflict is 'not unidimensional – a sort of Guttman scale of behavior, with each act becoming more severe until was is reached – but tridimensional'.[40] *War* may grow out of an intensified form of another foreign-conflict dimension, but generally, Rummel concludes, it occurs independently of these other two sets of events.[41]

The most significant result Rummel found was an apparent and almost complete lack of any regular relationship between domestic- and foreign-conflict behaviour. Thus, contrary to much intuitive wisdom on the subject, 'domestic instability has little relation to a nation's foreign conflict behavior';[42] peace at home does not predispose a passive approach abroad, and vice versa. Thus, as a general rule, an elite facing domestic difficulties will not necessarily wage war against another state to solve its political problems or unify the nation. This does not mean that such a policy has never been used before and will not be again, but the DON statistics suggest that it is decidedly uncommon, and no place to look for an explanation of cause.

There are further consequences of the negative conclusion here. 'The general independence between domestic and foreign conflict behavior indicates that different necessary and sufficient conditions for both must be sought – that rapid industrialisation, or underdevelopment, or dictatorships, or unstable political systems, or technological changes cannot be general conditions of both domestic and foreign conflict behavior.'[43] If they are independent of each other in this way then it is unlikely that they will be caused by the same thing. 'War' occurs independently of the other two dimensions of international conflict, Rummel discerns, and hence any particular conflict situation need not predispose it.

In his second study Rummel[44] introduced the 22 measures of domestic- and foreign-conflict behaviour outlined above as *dependent* variables, as outcome; and levels of technology, state size, demographic patterns, and the contrast in income and external relations, as *independent* ones.[45] Among other things, he found that foreign conflict was inversely related to the existence of internal *subversion* ('assassinations' and 'guerrilla warfare'), which would suggest, for whatever reason we might subsequently discover in the particular case, that where the incidence of guerrilla warfare and political assassination is high, states are less likely to conflict and go to war.

A later study by Raymond Tanter[46] retested the Rummel results, manipulating the same measures for the three years, 1958–60, for a total of 83 states. This replication arrived at the same conclusions; Tanter found no significant relationship for this subsequent time-span between domestic- and foreign-conflict behaviour. However in matching the domestic-conflict factors of the *first* run (1955–7) against the foreign-conflict factors for the *second* (1958–60), al mited order of significance emerged for the 'protest' and 'severance of diplomatic relations' attributes, which is limited evidence for a time-lag effect at work, and a possible link between domestic- and foreign-conflict behaviour after all.

The pattern of the DON results has been corroborated in a general way by Michael Haas,[47] who has run variables that purport to measure the 'warlike behavior' of states against 200 of their societal attributes, and found that, while nearly all types of violent domestic-conflict behaviour relate in a positive way to high levels of national aggression, few of the relationships are significant, with the exception of 'rioting'.[48] Nevertheless, he was sufficiently persuaded by the links that do exist to consider 'political apathy' to be a guarantee of international peace, and in an earlier study[49] he found it opportune to emphasise the connections between internal and external conflict. There he noted the positive correlations that show up in Rummel and Tanter's work and the way these relationships are most evident when the domestic conflict is expressed *anomically* (Rummel's *turmoil* dimension – the occasional riot or demonstration for example), as compared to when it proceeds within 'legitimate' institutional channels or 'illegitimately' outside them by means of a revolution or guerrilla war: 'Anomic reactions evidently constitute pressures which can make a decision to go to war more possible',[50] though the correlations are too low to indicate this link as a sufficient cause or explanation in any way.

A number of studies run counter to the pattern exposed by the DON reports, but most of them are nowhere near as explicit or statistically sophisticated.

Richard Rosecrance[51] concluded after a general examination of nine historical interstate systems that internal instability, and in particular a sense of insecurity on the part of state elites, did cause international instability. Frank Denton found for the time-span 1820–1949 that 'civil instability may be a prelude to international conflict'.[52] Ivo and Rosalind Feierabend have argued too, in a probabilistic fashion, that domestic political instability can be used to predict external aggression. Countries with a permissive political regime, a low rate of change on economic indicators, and a small discrepancy between social wants and satisfactions, tend to be stable and internationally pacific. The converse situation predisposes internal turmoil and international hostility. 'While the impulse to external aggression is less compelling than the impulse to internal instability, aggression is likely to occur if the country is also unstable.'[53]

(A.2) Most important of these contra-indications is Jonathan Wilkenfeld's[54] study of the hypothetical link between the nature of a state's *political system* and its foreign-conflict behaviour, including war. Rummel and Tanter did not differentiate between the states they used, and may have concealed thereby positive connections that run against their results. Working with 74 states, Wilkenfeld divided them into three factored groups[55] – politically *personalist* (Latin American dictatorships for example), *centrist* (socialist and Middle Eastern regimes) and *polyarchic* (economically developed, Western and westernised)[56] – and correlations were then carried out using these groups for all the possible pairs of foreign- and domestic-conflict dimensions that Rummel identified. Correlational tests were made using zero time lags and lags of one year and two. In the *personalist* group internal conflict was accompanied by foreign conflict of the 'diplomatic' sort (diplomatic expulsions and troop movements). Using a two-year time lag a significant association was discernible between the 'turmoil' dimension (demonstrations, riots, government crises) and external 'belligerency'. Most interesting of all, however, was the occurrence of 'war' and the apparent outbreak two years later of the subversive domestic activities of assassination and guerrilla revolt. This link Rummel's 1964 study, in its generalised, perhaps overgeneralised way, explicitly denied. For the *centrist* group domestic 'revolutionary' activity (purges, general strikes, revolutions and numbers killed within the state) was followed in one or two years by all the thirteen types of foreign-conflict behaviour. Wilkenfeld's results here might support the traditional argument that foreign conflict is used by state elites to distract from domestic disorder. Finally, *polyarchic* states experiencing 'turmoil' (anti-government demonstrations, riots, and major government crises) engage in all types of foreign-conflict behaviour, and vice versa. The relationship is a mutually reinforcing one, which likewise supports the traditional view.

We might conclude, then, that there does seem to be a relationship between internal- and external-conflict behaviour, and that this emerges most readily when we consider not the dimensions of conflict themselves, but the types of political system involved, and the possibility of effects that work themselves out over time. This finding about types of political system has been examined elsewhere, however, to conflicting ends. Michael Haas, in his study of societal approaches to war,[57] for example, ran foreign-conflict data compiled by Gregg and Textor (a composite, following Rummel, of diplomatic and military behaviour) against six variables relevant to the degree of a state's internal democracy (constitutional status, number of political parties, competitiveness of party system, freedom of group opposition, representativeness of regime and degree of press freedom). 'The most direct test', he discovered, 'of the nature of a political system as a factor affecting foreign conflict levels is supplied by the categorization of countries in "constitutional", "authoritarian", and "totalitarian" forms.'[58] He found that authoritarian regimes were the most war-prone, constitutional regimes the least and the totalitarian regimes in between, though none of the links were very pronounced. Generally, he concluded, there was a 'slight but consistent tendency for democratic countries to have less foreign conflict than undemocratic political systems',[59] at least for the comparatively placid post-war period the study data encompassed.

Rummel,[60] however, has tested the 'totalitarianism' of a government in terms of the freedom possessed by its opposition, its voting system, and press censorship, and found no significant correlation with foreign-conflict variables, a result that was not affected when intervening influences such as economic development were taken into account. Only three indices were used to measure 'totalitarianism', however, while Haas used six, which might explain some of the discrepancy in these results.

(A.3) The nature or state of a country's *economy* has also been tested for the difference in the way it and foreign-conflict behaviour concur. Rummel[61] finds no correlation between the two, measuring the economic development dimension in terms of telephones per capita, G.N.P. per capita, energy consumption per capita and percentage of the population engaged in agriculture. He cites other studies that corroborate this conclusion. Dina Zinnes, however, in reviewing Rummel's empirical results, notes a set of positive correlations within them that would seem to indicate that the more developed countries (measured by their G.N.P., rate of population increase, number of calories consumed in relation to the number nutritionally required, steel production and electricity generated) engage in more foreign-conflict behaviour, particularly of the protest, expulsion of lesser diplomatic personnel and troop-movement sorts.[62] Haas, too, has found that 'the most and, to a lesser extent, the least developed countries, which one might expect to have a high degree of economic stability, exhibit more significant foreign conflict than do the underdeveloped and intermediate types'.[63] Retesting this result, using U.N. data to estimate national wealth, Haas has confirmed that rich states have more foreign conflict than most developing countries.[64] In a later study, however, he draws the opposite conclusion: 'rural international systems' he says, 'are more peaceful than transitional industrial international systems . . . [but as] industrialization proceeds, war is less necessary for solving internal problems'.[65] Here, however, indices of social 'stress' and 'strain' have intervened.

(A.4) Haas in particular has developed a set of domestic measures in these terms, and looked for foreign-conflict correlations with them. In terms of 'stress', he tested a limited sample of ten countries for the years from 1900 to 1960 and found a positive connection between 'unemployment' and the frequency of war. Rural countries differed markedly from states with large urban populations in this regard, though the sample itself was loaded with industrialised nations.

> Lacking an industrial base for prolonged or total war rural states are much more aggressive in entering war as an immediate escape from sudden stress than are urban countries. Nevertheless, rural nations are so often isolationist . . . that they respond to few of their economic crises in a violent external manner. Urban countries are less immediately aggressive, but many of them find it convenient to eliminate the unemployment problem. And the effect of militarization by several countries has been to feed fears and suspicions of other states, thus triggering fateful arms races.[66]

Another 'stress' factor, 'population pressure', was considered, and war, population density and urbanism were found to be 'highly intercorrelated'.[67] Population density alone was found to vary inversely with the incidence of foreign conflict, more dense countries exhibiting less foreign conflict and vice versa.

But by introducing an urbanisation factor Haas was able to conclude that 'stress within over-crowded cities bears more relation to international conflict than the stresses associated with life in densely settled farmlands'.[68] In support here we might include Rummel's findings[69] that demographic variables (population density, birth rate, infant mortality and rate of population increase) were the most important predictors of conflict within and between states. Singer asserts[70] on the other hand that while population, population change, population density and number of battle-connected deaths do indeed covary, for the European state system at least, the correlation decreases and turns into a negative one when smaller groups of states are examined for smaller periods of time than the total span of 1816 to 1965. The number of people and a propensity for war go together for Continental conflict, but not for wars by European states with those outside their area. As to growth rate or population density, he has found no significant associations, though dyadic differences have not yet been assessed.[71] Choucri and Bennett,[72] and Choucri and North[73] use population figures as part of a more general equation that, they also feel, leads in a general way to foreign conflict and war. In this equation, however, there are at least two important intervening variables – the contemporary demand for resources, and the level of technology. An increase in population must bring about increased demands for resources and a greater level of technological development before 'lateral pressures', competition and crisis are likely to lead to violent conflict.

'Strain', Haas argues, manifests itself in deviant, or nonconformist behaviour, and he classifies evidence of such behaviour under four headings, two along an *active* dimension of social conflict and personal assault (such as homicide) and two along a *passive* dimension of escapism (bureaucratic rigidity and formalism) and self-destructiveness (drug-taking, alcoholism and suicide for example). The social conflict focus has already been discussed separately but, homicide figures were inversely related, Haas found, to foreign conflict, 'contrary to the Marxist view that capitalists' dehumanization of man has made war a more congenial form of state behavior'.[74] Where passive deviance was high, however, as measured by the death-rate due to alcoholism and suicide, a propensity to war became more evident.

Again, the process of urbanisation was also seen to be involved.

In a later and more detailed study based on the above, Haas[75] defined 'stress' in terms of 'unemployment', but also in terms of the 'rate of industrialisation', rather than 'population pressure', which he did not use again. The 'rate of industrialisation' was measured by the yearly increments in per capita kWh production of electricity, which measured in turn the rate of modernisation by the extent of technological change, by the extent of economic and hence social change. His foreign-conflict dimension consisted of a 'violence' variable of participation in war (in terms of frequency of entry into international aggression, and aggressiveness generally), and a 'non-violence' measure of military outlay as a percentage of total government expenditure.

Keeping in mind the limited sample used, Haas argued that high unemployment makes for aggression and that 'using time lagged longitudinal correlations . . . countries with high rates of suicide and fatal alcoholism are much more likely to be participants in arms races. Countries with rising rates of homicide, on the contrary, decrease their financing of military efforts'.[76]

These 'stress' and 'strain' connections are related in turn to the process of industrialisation. 'Ruralism', he concluded,

> is associated with assaultive deviance, low military expenditure levels, and aggressiveness in deciding on war, but there is only a fifty–fifty chance that a rural country beset by stress will go to war. Transitional industrial-urbanism brings more suicides and alcoholism, militarization, and frequent but non-aggressive war participation. As industrialization is more complete, deviance and warlike behavior taper off.[77]

This leads back to the discussion of the effects of a state's economic system, and introduces the idea that such analyses might be more useful if they correlate the interaction of a number of state attributes. Rummel has in fact looked for such an effect,[78] and failed to find it.

(A.5) There is a final, rather untidy and residual category, where we might detail diverse societal attributes that have been tested for their statistical connection with foreign conflict and war, and which do not fit any of the more general groupings outlined above. Rummel, for example, has correlated[79] state 'power' (in terms of physical size, population size, G.N.P., resources, railways, military personnel, total defence expenditures and political centralisation) with foreign-conflict behaviour, and found no significant link, a result both confirmed[80] and denied by J. D. Singer.[81] Various measures of a state's 'values', the number of borders it has, and its military capabilities and armaments, likewise do not predispose a propensity to foreign conflict.[82] The question of number of borders was also examined by Lewis Richardson for the thirty-three states he detailed from 1820 to 1945,[83] and he found a *positive* connection between this number and the number of wars where more than 7000 people were killed. The discrepant results here, Rummel considers, are due to the greater generality of the DON findings, but until the question is further confirmed, he leaves it in doubt. Elsewhere in the same work Richardson looked in a general way for 'bad' states and other groups that consistently cause wars. He did not find any, which suggests that war is a general phenomenon and not just the predilection of particularly recalcitrant peoples. He did find, however, evidence of a desire for revenge as a significant cause of war,[84] though it is not self-evident how we might sum individual propensities to right an old wrong that would produce a societal attribute of this kind. Haas has considered the 'heterogeneity' of a state (in ethnic, linguistic, religious, racial, and national terms) and found it to correlate consistently with frequency of wars, military actions, and foreign-conflict casualties.[85] Voting support in the United Nations, for either the East or West Cold War bloc, is not associated with foreign conflict,[86] though simply the extent of participation in foreign affairs (in terms of bloc prominence, giving or getting aid, and the number of representatives at the United Nations) seems to be correlated in a positive way.

(B) What quantitative research has been done, not on the domestic attributes of states as possible causes of foreign conflict and war, but on the comparative *differences* and *similarities* between them? Rummel has talked in such terms of a 'social field theory'[87] where one measures the distance between nations on attribute dimensions, not just their single standing there, as causes of conflict and war, and the DON project results include the general observation that: 'The more similar two nations are in economic development, political orientation, Catholic culture, and density, the more aligned their voting in the UN and the less conflictful their interaction will be';[88] further: 'the more dissimilar two nations are in economic development and size and the greater their joint technological capability to span geographic distance is, the more overt conflict they have with each other';[89] and finally that: 'Racial distance is the most important characteristic distinguishing between peace and conflict in international systems.'[90]

Richardson, on the other hand, found little relationship between economic inequality and a propensity for war,[91] though the distance between states on the dimensions of language and religion did correlate in particular unambiguous ways.[92]

Finally, Bruce Russett, after a detailed study of interstate integration, concludes that: 'At best, cultural similarity and voting behavior [in the United Nations] make essentially no difference in the probability of conflict. . . . But countries belonging to the same groupings by organisational membership, proximity, or trade are more than *twice* as likely to fight than are nations which belong to different groups, or to none.'[93] Generally, the clustering of states into regions does have significance in terms of the likelihood of war, and conflict and integration are related though in a three-step way: when the states involved are mutually irrelevant, war is not likely to occur; however, it is likely to be quite common when 'capabilities and salience are moderate and narrowly focused'. When capabilities are 'numerous and varied', though, war is unlikely again.[94]

(C) The last of the quantitative approaches to the causes of conflict and war, at the societal level at least, looks at the *relationships* between states. Rummel, again,[95] has attempted to correlate the amount of national co-operation (in terms of membership of international organisations, treaties, aid and diplomatic representation) and the level of a state's international communications or transactions (in terms of mail, economic aid and trade measures) with foreign conflict behaviour, but has found very little connection. 'Alliances' and foreign conflict, have also been examined for covariant effect. Richardson concluded that previous alliance did reduce the likelihood of war between those who had been allied, though with many exceptions.[96] Singer and Small[97] have discovered a strong association between the number of alliance bonds which a nation has and the amount of war it subsequently experiences in the following years. Here the question of integration is pertinent, and though the summary includes *attribute* criteria, we may follow Haas in concluding that: 'States are more likely to settle their differences peacefully if they share compatibility in main values, a distinctive way of life, mutual responsiveness, a joint core area with rising capabilities, expect economic growth, and have an unbroken social communication network with a wide range of transactions.'[98]

What are we to make of this complex list of conflicting results? There is a convincing air about statistical studies that we ought to resist, but not uncritically so. We should ask at each point what intervening variables might have been ignored, and whether, as seems to have happened in more than one case, the conclusions are merely the manufactured products of the analytic techniques employed, research artefacts with a spurious sense of substance. And, after all, we are in fact dealing with correlations, not cause. The covariances noted should indicate where the pursuit of an explanation will be fruitful or not, and no more than that. A general statistical association cannot predict the outbreak of a war or the avenue to peace in any particular case, and until we can explain why war does occur in the particular case our statement of origins must remain incomplete. We should remain aware, as well, that the pursuit of regular correlations of the behavioural sort may serve to obscure the peculiar combination of circumstance and perceptions that may have led to war at any one time or place, and we should allow for this effect too.

C. THE WORLD SYSTEM

The third analytical level at which we might pursue the causes of conflict is the *interstate* one, and researchers have attempted to detail the attributes and the changes in the attributes of the world system as a whole that seem to lead to disintegration and war.

One prominent body of such research has been conducted by

Kaplan, Deutsch, Singer, Rosecrance, Waltz and Haas on the structural power properties of the global system, and this group of results shall be considered first.

Kaplan, as earlier described, has listed six ideal-typical models of the political world (with variants) which differ in their stability and in their implications for conflict, war and peace. The 'unit-veto' model of twenty or so states with a credible nuclear first-strike capacity he finds in principle unstable, though any war that did occur there would tend to be limited and non-nuclear. The 'tight bipolar' one, too, would not be very well integrated. The 'hierarchical' system with its densely interwoven functional connections, and the 'universal' system with its political, probably confederate sub-system, would be the most stable, though the status quo prevailing in each would depend upon access to resources, and upon the level of authority which the political sub-system came to wield over its state members. The 'balance of power' and 'loose bipolar' types would fall in between. The stability of the former would depend upon the number of essential state actors and on a willingness to abide by the rules of the game, and wars would tend to be limited in their objectives there. The second sort, with its supranational organisations and clear separation of systemic roles, would also have limited wars, though even these would be rare.

Of the four variants to these basic six, the 'very loose bipolar system' would be the most unstable, 'and would not be presented at all, except that it has striking resemblances to contemporary international politics'.[99] Stability would depend upon the self-restraint of bloc leaders. The 'unstable bloc system', too, would tend to be a tense one, and big power intervention in other states' affairs, limited by fear of nuclear escalation, would be its most conspicuous feature. The 'incomplete nuclear diffusion' system would suffer more interventions and greater tensions than the 'unstable bloc' type, and the possibility of nuclear escalation would also be greater, but wars would tend to be more limited thereby. Only the 'detente' system would be a relaxed and peaceful one.

From the parallels that Kaplan draws he would seem to see the 'real' world as a compound of a number of these 'ideal-typical' types. He would probably find the 'very loose bipolar system' the closest to the present-day world, and would emphasise its instability. Both issues – the extent of global polarisation, and the conflict consequences of a unipolar, bipolar, tripolar and multipolar world – have been the subject of continuing debate, though most interest has centred on the question of bipolarity versus multipolarity.

No one world system, no one magic number of poles or organisational structures has been able to ensure world peace. Rosecrance, however, has concluded that the multipolar ones are more stable than the bipolar.[100] In a semi-quantitative examination of the consequences of this historical and theoretical conclusion – that as the world system now moves from bipolarity to multipolarity (a change they assume as fact) the frequency and intensity of war should diminish – Deutsch and Singer[101] find this to be so, provided that nuclear proliferation can be controlled. 'In the long run . . . even multipolar systems operating under the rules of balance-of-power policies are shown to be self-destroying, but both in the short and the long run the instability of tight bipolar systems appears to be substantially greater.'[102] Singer, in his later work, has confirmed the statistical ability to predict war, at least in the twentieth century, from the fact of major-power bipolarisation.[103]

In direct contradiction, however, Waltz[104] argues (1) that the period since the Second World War has seen not the dissolution of force in a multipolar way but the 'formation and perpetuation' of a bipolar balance of power, and (2) that this bipolar world has been a highly stable one. In a detailed prescriptive review of the comparative merits and demerits of bipolarity and multipolarity Rosecrance[105] opts for an intermediate two-tier system of bi-multi-polarity, which combines the desirable features of both the others. This hybrid he sees as the most likely model to contain conflict. Haas,[106] finally, from a correlational study of twenty-one interstate sub-systems in Europe, Asia and Hawaii, has come up with a 'Hobson's choice . . . Multipolarity entails more violence, more countries at war, and more casualties; bipolarity brings fewer but longer wars.'[107] The question is, and will remain, unresolved.

Apart from the debate about polarity and stability, some work has also been done, under the auspices of the COW project, on *alliance aggregation* and on the amount of *intergovernmental organisation* in the system.[108] The latter measure, it appears, has no discernible association with the *incidence* of war, though a falling off in the rate of growth of intergovernmental organisations in the world is seen to 'precede (anticipate?)' it.[109] *Alliance* studies have come up with a negative correlation between the aggregate alliance commitments of all nations in the world system and war, for the nineteenth century at least. A stronger and positive connection appears in the twentieth century and this is so 'whether it is nation-months of war or battle-connected deaths, whether the data are for the total system or the central one only . . .'.[110] These results, however, have to be treated with the same caution adduced above. There are important problems which are common to all the statistical work of this kind.

Another prominent contribution to the question of the systemic origins of conflict is the 'rank-disequilibrium theory' proposed by Johan Galtung and developed empirically by Maurice East and Michael Wallace. Galtung[111] sees the world system as consisting primarily of nations, that can be ranked for their comparative status either 'T' (topdog) or ('U' (underdog) along a number of scales – industrialisation, for example, income per capita, military power, educational level and past glory: '. . . an interaction system is a multi-dimensional system of stratification, where those who have and those who have not, those who have more and those who have less, find, are given, or are forced into their positions'.[112] Galtung argues that an interstate system will be unstable if there are high levels of rank-disequilibrium or status discrepancy in it, that is, if too many states are not rank-concordant, but are high on some scales but low on others. Disequilibrium can work two ways, either dampening down conflict between the topdogs and underdogs, or where the alternatives have failed, the degree of system integration is low, mobility channels are blocked, and violence has been used before, giving way to aggression and war. A rank-discordant state will be continually exposed to differential treatment and therefore constantly reminded of its disequilibrial position. It will use the resources of its top-ranking dimensions in a self-righteous way to raise its standing on those dimensions where it has a 'U' score.

Assuming the validity of this device, Galtung argues that economic development is likely to cause more not less rank-disequilibrium, and therefore more not less potential in the world system for conflict and war. Furthermore, the world is neither one world-state nor a pluralistic plethora of them; it is in between and tends to form into sub-systems which can be either 'like' groups that alleviate disequilibrial tension or 'unlike' groups that exacerbate it. The most stable world systems, then, will either be *feudal* (complete topdogs and complete underdogs only), *pluralistic* (a large number and variety of states or of criteria of ranking and achievement) or *unitary* (one state or one dimension of evaluation). For 'aggression to be avoided a necessary condition is multi-dimensional change',[113] a principle which has led Galtung to predict that China – populous, large, historically illustrious and socio-economically mobile – will eventually become aggressive if denied concordant great power political status.[114]

In a later study Galtung[115] maintains that interstate interaction tends to be rank-dependent, with more interaction between topdogs, less between top- and underdogs, and least between underdogs. A global system of this sort he calls *feudal* – pinned together at the top, and held apart at the bottom – and he finds therein 'the seeds of its own destruction, because it permits more exploitation of the underdogs than the underdogs themselves will, in the long run, tolerate . . .',[116] which seems to contradict his earlier conclusion above, though he does not acknowledge, let alone resolve, the anomaly. If the underdogs unite, a cross-cutting *class* system results; if the rankings become mixed, and are no longer completely on one level or the other, the system is mixed too; and if class unit and rank mixing both occur, we have an *egalitarian* system, equally unstable.

If the feudal relationship exists between two blocs or systems, they are effectively polarised and 'stripped for conflict action'.[117] Galtung analyses the NATO alliance and the Warsaw Pact to determine if underdogs and topdogs can be distinguished, and if the pattern of feudal interaction obtains between them. Generally he finds this to be so, for governmental initiatives at least. He concludes that 'international politics (not non-governmental interaction) is big power politics, for good and for bad, between friends and (particularly) enemies . . .',[118] and that 'a system will become more resistant to violent conflict when the general level of positive interaction is higher and less dependent on rank . . .'.[119] An increase in the interaction between small-power underdogs, a sewing together of the split feudal base, would therefore, he argues, make the East–West system less prone to conflict, providing improved inter-bloc communications, cross-cutting loyalties, as well as a model stimulus and testing ground for the big powers. To avoid the risk of a *class* system and the class conflict that could ensue, interaction rates of all kinds need to be kept even.

Empirical studies have been done along these lines, and Singer, for example, has found that the greater the discordant character of state rankings on dimensions of 'capability' and 'diplomatic importance', the greater will be the systemic propensity to war.[120] More detailed work has been done, however, by Wallace and East.

Wallace[121] has calculated the 'achieved' status of a country in terms of its power capability (total population, urban population, iron and steel production, number of armed forces personnel, and military expenditure), and its 'ascribed' status in terms of attributed diplomatic importance (number of diplomatic missions received by a nation). He has determined the status inconsistency scores for each nation for the period 1920–64, aggregated a measure of it for the system as a whole, and tested the relationship between this and the amount of war allowing for five-, ten- and fifteen-year time lags. He has partially verified Galtung's hypothesis, though as he points out, in a strict sense nothing is explained thereby. A significant association was found between status inconsistency in the system and the amount of war that occurred ten to fifteen years later. This would suggest that the international hierarchy of power capabilities is a factor to be considered, but hardly, one would assume, on its own.

East[122] takes a much shorter time-span: 1946–64. He applies Weber's three dimensions of 'class' (economic position, measured by total G.N.P.), 'status' (prestige, measured by number of embassies in the state capital) and 'power' (politico-military force potential, measured by total defence expenditure per year), to determine the extent of status discrepancy in the global system and the congruence in state rankings on these three scales. He tests for a link between rank discrepancy and international violence (variously measured) with one- and two-year time lags, and finds a general and consistent pattern that confirms the connection. Even stronger correlations are produced when the data is lagged and time lapses allowed for; the most peaceful world, he asserts, will be the most status concordant one.

The final approach one might consider here under the systemic causes of war, though it is relevant as well to the question of conflict *dynamics*, is the mathematical modelling by Lewis Richardson of arms races.[123] Arms races are a peculiarly pernicious phenomenon in world politics and plausibly related to the occurrence of war. The more the amount of military capability in the system the higher it would seem is the probability of violent conflict. Not all arms races have resulted in wars, and interstate violence of this kind does not always have an arms race leading up to it, but generally, Richardson assumes, the more military preparedness in the system as a whole the more the likelihood of war. We might also argue that, irrespective of this absolute amount, the *relative* imbalance between states might be associated with such a probability too.

No particular purpose is served by a detailed explanation of Richardson's work in this regard. Suffice it to say that by modelling state interaction processes in terms of 'hostility' and 'friendliness' and finding their points of equilibrium, assessing initial levels of hostility, calculating 'reaction coefficients' with differential equations, determining the rates of change of such coefficients as mutual distrust and fear, compound and reinforce each other, Richardson attempts to understand the arms race phenomenon in general, and its contribution to the causes of the First and Second World Wars in particular. Certainly, the complexities of the 'real' world lead one to view Richardson's abstractions with caution, and the attempts to test them for the post-war period, using the arms race between Russia and America, bear this caution out.[124]

II DYNAMICS

The second dimension of the study of social conflict and war is that of conflict *dynamics*, the course of its procession. Four main groups have researched this dimension – formal mathematical theorists (such as Richardson), strategists, psychologists and historians and political scientists. The work of the first has already been introduced, and the second – with their theories of deterrence, arms control, crises and the like – are so much a part of the mainstream body of the study of world politics that their findings merit no further consideration here. Political scientists on the other hand, have had little to say on the political dynamics of conflict processes and war once it is in train. It is seen as of largely historical interest to spell out the interactive links between, for example, domestic revolution and war. The attention given to the conflict in Vietnam is an exception, readily explained because of its far-reaching effects upon domestic American politics, a country where after all a majority of the professional analysts of world affairs reside. Once a conflict process is under way, however, there is a considerable body of *psychological* findings pertinent to the perception of the events involved. The black and white downgrading of the opponent's good points, and the defendant's bad; the foreclosure effect that operates to narrow the perceived choice of options once a sense of 'being-in-conflict' is aroused; the feeling of threat itself; all become part of the decision-making process and a part of the spiralling feed-backs that not only lead to, but serve to sustain a conflict or war. Here is another important point at which psychopolitical results can be applied.

III TERMINATION

The third and final dimension of conflict I shall mention is that concerned with controlling particular conflicts or wars, or bringing them to an end.[125] The 'end' to a particular conflict is not a state as simply described as might at first appear. What is the nature of such a conclusion? Is it the conflict-less maintenance of a perpetual harmony? Or can we perhaps in 'any given social situation or subsystem . . . postulate an optimum amount or degree of conflict . . .' despite the fact that there is clearly 'no simply operational definition of such an optimum'.[126] Conflicts may be too destructive and there may be too many of them, but we might argue none the less that without social conflict, without war even, human life would be robbed of much of its creative and constructive as well as destructive resolve.

From this point of view conflict is probably inevitable, and in the right amount, is positively desirable as well. It is conceivable that conflict can serve a social, beneficial, unifying function[127] – establishing group identities, strengthening the collective consciousness, and reinforcing boundaries. Conflict is commonly used to discharge feelings of dissent, of deprivation and frustration; it acts to stabilise and integrate antagonistic relationships. No evidence of conflict is, of course, not a necessary indication of a relationship's stability and strength, and not all conflicts are positively functional, regardless of the evaluative standpoint adopted. But generally it enables a measure to be made of relative power, and by struggle groups construct the balancing mechanisms which help to maintain and consolidate them.

Does *war* also serve beneficial economic, political, sociological, ecological, scientific and moral functions that cannot be achieved in any other way? This point has been put by the *Report from Iron Mountain*, and it is interesting how little the arguments above need be exaggerated to make a satire of their consequences. 'War is not', the Report concludes, '. . . primarily an instrument of policy utilized by nations to extend or defend their expressed political values or their economic interests. On the contrary, it is itself the principal basis of organization on which all modern societies are constructed . . . at the root of all ostensible differences of national interest lie the dynamic requirements of the war system itself for periodic armed conflict.'[128] Any substitute for war would need to have all or most of its positive effects – stabilising and controlling national economies, underpinning political authority, ensuring social cohesion, maintaining the ecological balance between human populations and the resources they need to survive, motivating artistic, scientific and technological progress. To this end the Report recommends massive state spending on social welfare and space research, the re-establishment of slavery, the deliberate intensification of environmental pollution and applied eugenics. The prime social value is, naturally, stability, and in this light it is the war system that should prevail since a peace system would be destabilising, however justifiable it might otherwise seem on moral or emotional grounds.

The whole concept of conflict termination is culture bound. Bringing a particular conflict to an end means 'deciding on an issue so that the action system can move on to new issues, which is tantamount to saying that some kind of *change* takes place.

But this is only of value provided change is of value in the culture; if it is not, an everlasting conflict, properly maintained and managed at an adequate cost level, may be seen as functional . . .'[129] Change may be of value, one could add, but may also be construed as this very process of everlasting conflict itself, controlled and encouraged as a beneficial vehicle for ideological renewal. This is the concept of conflict *stimulation*, and is best represented in the conflict literature by Mao Tse-tung's idea of permanent revolution. Whether this concept is appropriate to world politics is another question. A belief in conflict's benign effects sufficiently strong to recommend its cultivation rather than cure may be a fruitful approach to intra-state affairs, but disastrous when applied to relations between them. Then again, such an attitude may be the only one likely to shake the exploitative realities of the contemporary world system to its fundaments. We simply do not know.[130] There is a paucity of evidence upon which to decide such a question; there are different levels at which global conflict can occur; and the multi-dimensional results of world conflict may be dysfunctional for one state but functional for others, dysfunctional in one context or time, but functional in others. Criteria of functionality and dysfunctionality are themselves value-bound concepts possessing few of the objective referents we need if we are to decide between them with any degree of behavioural confidence.

The concept quoted is much closer to that of conflict *management*, that is, the attempt to contain conflict or its consequences within desired limits or bounds; the attempt to cure symptoms rather than confront directly the nature of cause. Again, just what these limits might be and just what alleviating the symptoms involves is a matter of continuous debate, and a cause of conflict in its own right. The most simple form of conflict management is conflict *avoidance*, where the distance between the protagonists is sufficiently enhanced to make the conflict as such mutually irrelevant. The parties involved may 'deliberately cultivate ignorance of each other and avoid overt communications . . .',[131] and international conflict 'may be mitigated by devices like arms control, which, in effect, move the nations farther apart'.[132] This latter device is not self-evidently avoidant in its results, but the principle is clear enough. The policies that result, however, will reflect the value predilections of the state that proposes them, whether they be construed in terms of non-violence or violence, in terms of stability or a radical redistribution of the world's wealth. They will also tend to result in favourable terms to one global quarter or another. Imposing rival conceptions of what avoidance of 'control' might mean can be a critical source of further contention, likely to exacerbate the conflict it seeks to contain.

Conflict *resolution*, on the other hand, implies more than just containment or control, rather an 'end' that ranges from mutual convergence upon one of the opposing points of view to the complete physical victory of one protagonist over the other.[133] To resolve a conflict means 'to decide a. who is the winner and who the loser, b. what the future distribution of value shall be' and to administer that distribution.[134] There are many mechanisms that might be used to arrive at such a decision. Galtung, for example, mentions twelve: those where neither of the opposing groups participates (chance mechanisms and oracles), those where one of the groups participates (ordeals), and those where both groups participate (regulated warfare, fights, private duels, judicial duels, verbal duels, debates, mediation/arbitration, courts and voting).[135] None of them, however, is fully accepted at the global level, and no agency exists there to administer any distribution that might be made.

John Burton[136] has experimented with another device that attempts to reconcile protagonists in a more thorough-going fashion than the coercive or non-coercive use of one of the procedural techniques above, whose findings must then be authoritatively administered. He suggests that conflicts be seen as essentially subjective in character,[137] and that by a face-to-face 'marriage counselling' method the misperceptions of the parties in dispute might be exposed and a non-coercive solution arrived at in a non-zero sum way that enhances the values of each side.

> The underlying assumption is that states are not in themselves a cause of conflict, aggressive, or power motivated, but that they are responding to their environment within the limits of the knowledge they have available about their interests and the responses of others. Given perfect knowledge of responses of others, or tested theories and rules of conduct

> that could act as a substitute for perfect foresight, states would avoid any conflicts that were more costly than alternative means of achieving their goals.[138]

By altering the attitudes of representatives of states in conflict, by persuading decision-makers to re-perceive the nature of the conflict process in general and their own differences in particular through a controlled and carefully crafted confrontation, competing goals might be peacefully reconciled.

Burton has applied his device in a tentative way to on-going conflict situations, but only subordinate government representatives have participated in his experiments, not decision-makers themselves, and the problem of the 're-entry' of re-perceiving officials into their own and 'unenlightened' state environments has not been clarified. Furthermore, we might ask if conflicts are only the result of subjective psychological factors, when so many seem to stem from objective conditions of incompatible interest.

> Imperfect information and misunderstanding are of course frequently influential in international relations. But there is nothing mutually exclusive about the occurrence of genuine conflicts and the importance of imperfect information. Moreover, it is worth noting that imperfect information sometimes serves to reduce the impact of genuine conflicts rather than to create perceived conflicts where none actually exists.[139]

The world still condones power rivalries and ideological competition. Burton's optimistic hopes for voluntary agreements may be unrealistic in the light of the conflicts of interest and the 'objective' perceptions of them that continue to flourish. Reconciliation of this sort is most likely to occur where reconciliation itself is prized higher than conflict, and all the re-perception possible may not be enough to resolve the values at issue in a mutually advantageous way. Nevertheless, conflict-resolution mechanisms do depend to a large degree upon perceptions: 'The resolution mechanism is ultimately anchored in the minds of men; it is rooted in the social framework, but without a solid basis in the culture as internalized in the members of the system, it is lost. Thus, when the belief in a mechanism is shattered, its days are numbered.'[140] Perhaps, and this is what Burton seems to argue, if only the belief in his novel and more effective mechanism or something like it can be created, its day would lie at hand.

Which, then, is the most appropriate approach – conflict management or conflict resolution? Certainly both will have a place, and will in particular cases complement each other, but there are times when either one may be 'inappropriate' to whatever point of view we adopt. To 'manage' a conflict may perpetuate an injustice, for example, while resolving it may mean war and the 'neglect of the feasible'.[141] How can human values be maximised and a stable world sustained at one and the same time? What should those values be and should revolution and not stability be the system's goal? How can we resolve the tensions between order and justice?[142] In any ultimate sense we probably cannot, though these fundamental puzzles are worked and reworked at every point in the political process. We are deep here within the territory of contemporary *peace research*, and I shall conclude by briefly considering the major features of this corollary field.

Peace research arose as part of the behavioural revolt of the 1950s. It was a historically specific response to the Cold War and the threat that conflict contained of nuclear disaster. It shared many of the attributes of the general move in political studies away from more traditional methods, but its practitioners saw it as a separate focus with commitments of its own. If one looks at what people who call themselves 'peace researchers' do, one finds in fact a wide range of theoretical and empirical activities that would seem to bear little over-all resemblance. Any particular peace research study will exhibit at least five features however:[143] it will be *systems-oriented* and not, for example, state-based in its perspectives; it will be *applied* research and not 'pure' (though we should remember that peace research can be an 'easy way out for those who want to be relevant yet do not wish to risk too much of their secure academic life');[144] it will be about the 'conditions for *positive* peace – the creation of systems where violence is unlikely to arise – rather than *negative* peace – the prevention of violence [emphasis added]', and whereas 'negative peace results in the stabilization of the *status quo*, positive peace has much more revolutionary implications';[145] it will be *subjectivist* in its attempts to see social processes from the stand-point of the participants and not that of a removed observer; and it will be frankly *prescriptive* rather than predictive.

The weak link here is the concept of 'positive peace', and only recently have peace researchers begun to come to terms with the implications of this central concept. 'Negative' peace, as Galtung first defined it,[146] is the absence of war and the reduction of violence, and the *narrow* approach to peace research seeks ways in which we might avoid a major world war, in particular a thermo-nuclear one, or at least reduce the probability of such a war. Negative peace at the global level is mostly a question of arms control and crisis management,[147] and is one point where peace research clearly overlaps strategic studies.[148] 'Positive' peace Galtung defined as 'the integration of human society',[149] which in terms of world politics means the integration of the international system. This assumes a *broad* approach to war and peace, one that sees these phenomena as part of more general questions of conflict and conflict control or termination. Adherents to this view would tend to decry the inadequacies of a narrow approach. Galtung, however, has now rejected this definition[150] as too symmetric in its demands, and now extends the positive conception of peace to include even broader notions of 'social justice'.

This has served to admit the force of the *radical* critique that has grown up within peace research in the last few years, a critique of two major kinds. The established radical faction has sought to expose the political nature of peace research itself. It seeks to demonstrate the part that has been played by the great powers and by Western capitalism in setting up and sustaining the world war-system and the global structures of dependency, exploitation and oppression, a part which peace researchers have heretofore played down for ideological reasons of which they are hardly aware; and they attack both the *narrow* and *broad* schools for the way they have, wittingly or unwittingly, supported the decision-makers of the industralised status quo powers in their global assault, identifying with and serving the interests of the major powers in their research: 'as soon as one rejects the assumption that the peoples of the world have basic interests in common with the present international system, it becomes a political and non-neutral act to support this system and to manipulate it in accordance with the needs of the system.'[151] Peace research has on the whole been one more prop for the world system as it stands, helping to provide the expertise that it might remain the way it is. 'Given this situation, change *of* the system can not be advocated by peace research. Structural change would be a threat to the power-holders of the international system. Only adaptive change within the system is possible.'[152]

In a sense such critics seem to have surrendered any notion of peace at all, and put in its place the logic of revolution. They feel that the task of peace research should be to formulate its problems,

> not in terms meaningful to international and supranational institutions, but in terms meaningful to suppressed and exploited groups and nations. It should explain not how manifest conflicts are brought under control, but how latent conflicts are manifested. It should explain not how integration is brought about, but how conflicts are polarized to a degree where the present international system is seriously challenged or even broken down.[153]

They would hold that without revolutionary change and an end to the war-system as it presently exists, peace is finally impossible. This must be the necessary precondition.

Such an attitude accepts a systemic conception of the causes of conflict and war, and supports the idea that it is the structure of the global distribution of power and resources that is the source of dissension, not anything intrinsic to the nature of man or any of his governmental institutions. Though there are inadequacies in this restriction, the radical critique has made peace researchers more aware of the conservative and captive nature of their earlier concerns, and redirected their attention to critical questions about implicit and indirect conflict, rather than its more overt and manifest forms. The definition of *violence* has been considerably expanded thereby to include potential and latent as well as actual kinds.

There are difficulties with this expansion, and with its implications. What are we to make of the notion of 'latency', for example? – 'peace is always latent war, and war always latent peace', which does not advance the argument very far.[154] Nevertheless, it has become clear that violence need not be overt for it to form an important part of a social structure. The systematic deprivation of a class or ethnic group in economic, political, educational or other ways can be construed as violence just as readily as more bloody forms of oppression. It is not the common usage of the concept, but the effects of the process can be every bit as pernicious, and exploitative structures have a *capacity* for direct violence which likewise should not be ignored.

One other radical faction mounts an even more subtle critique, however. It attacks all other forms of peace research – narrow, broad *and* the 'revolutionary' radical school as well – for their explicit glorification of power-as-*dominance,* and their profound neglect of an alternative formulation: power-as-*competence.* The preoccupation with big states and their decision-makers, with nation-states in general and their comparative might, is likely to miss the pervasive competence of the 'powerless', and to ignore the vagaries of an important ingredient of fundamental social change which we will need to understand to bring about a peace system in the long run. 'In brief . . . the prevailing preoccupation with the powerful – with major powers and their elites, with nation-states and their capabilities for war and for imposing their will on others – is unlikely to bring us any closer to peace, since it assumes the perpetuation of the power system which may well be at the root of war.'[155]

Berenice Carroll lists nine such competences: disintegrative power, inertial power, innovative power (norm-creating), legitimising power (integrative, socialising), expressive power, explosive power, power of resistance, collective power (co-operative) and migratory power (population).[156] These amorphous capabilities can have considerable effect and their implications are extensive too. Thus 'dissociative policies may be more suitable peace strategies in some conditions than integrative policies . . . [and] the world's best hope for avoiding thermonuclear war may lie not in world integration, but in the political and technological disintegration of the nuclear superpowers'.[157] Further, the *inertial* power of the world's people seems to be a pacific one on the whole, but peace itself is paradoxically not their urgent demand. No solution to war is likely to be found until we understand this discrepancy and can allow for it with some measure of predictive precision.

CHAPTER 11

Integration

The contemporary study of interstate political integration attempts to explain and predict how countries might come together in more comprehensive communal sub-systems than those of a nation-specific kind. This sort of non-coerced coalescence, the growth of a functional or transactional, usually regional loyalty, to transcend that of the state, as I indicated earlier, is one of the two fundamental dimensions of world politics. Constructing a new nation, for example, out of the more or less arbitrary legacies of an empire in retreat, often involves the deliberate attempt to destroy or at least inhibit the boundary-smudging loyalties that may already exist along tribal, racial or religious lines. Running alongside efforts like these to inculcate a common national consciousness at the expense of a transnational one, are a host of formal interstate interactions that might predispose, if not economic or political unification, then at least a sense of the mutual expectation of peace. In the case of the longer-established countries, like those of Western Europe, we might expect this process to proceed with much less of the negative, nation-building undertow that would threaten to drag such efforts under elsewhere. Concrete examples of such a process are problematic, however, since the increasing evidence of transnational contact, of common market arrangements, and interdependencies of many kinds, has not been followed in any case by the surrender of territorial sovereignty that political integration would seem to imply. Independent room for national manoeuvre becomes more and more restricted, but the 'spill-over' that we might expect to occur has conspicuously failed to come about. The paradox of a rise in global interdependence at the same time as a rise in national preoccupations has led to a complex, complementary as well as competitive interplay, that could lead almost anywhere in general and nowhere in particular.[1]

Unlike the study of conflict, very few transdisciplinary insights have found their way into the literature on integration. This is surprising because many of the behavioural and perceptual issues involved would seem to me to be amenable to the sort of treatment discussed in earlier chapters. The cybernetic/communications approach to the subject is the conspicuous exception here. However, the study of integration provides one of the clearest examples in the discipline of a theory-building imperative at work, and an outline of the most important 'theories' to date should exemplify the second beneficial feature of the behavioural legacy as I have presented this throughout.

The contemporary study of integration has a well-established air. Its intellectual roots, like those of peace research and the quantitative approach to conflict and war, lie in the academic revolution of the 1950s, in the general shift in emphasis from institutional and descriptive concerns to a more systems-oriented, analytic and process-minded approach. 'In the boldest possible summary of trends in the literature, it is possible to say that during the first postwar decade "regionalism and security" was the principal theme; that this was replaced by "integration" in the second decade; and that the period of transition between the two . . . coincided with the shift to "systems thinking". . . .'[2] The political science schools of the United States began to concern themselves with the West European attempt to coalesce in significant administrative ways, a distinctive set of analytic frameworks were evolved to explain this phenomenon, and they have dominated the study of interstate integration ever since.

Any definition must encompass the fundamental distinction between an integrative process imposed from without, and the same engendered from within. The construction of bigger political units from smaller ones by the process of external *addition* is usually achieved in world politics by the use of force. Empire-building in particular is carried on by the coercive efforts of some 'catalytic agent – external colonizing elite, military conqueror, or hegemony-seeking state'.[3] The process of consensual *collusion*, on the other hand, is the one that preoccupies analysts today. The advent of nuclear weaponry has made integration by force a perilous alternative at best, and so the contemporary task is mostly seen now as explaining integration among nations without recourse to historical vehicles like these.

The end-point of the integrative process is usually considered to be some sort of communal construct with over-arching jurisdiction within which socio-economic and political change proceeds by peaceful rather than violent means, at least most of the time. On the global level, such a body would need to possess a discrete and super-ordinate authority over the actions of its constituent units, or rather, their decision-making elites. Analysts have differed, however, in their estimates of how automomous and superordinate this body must be to qualify as the end-point discussed. Karl Deutsch, for example, defines the culmination of the integrative process as the establishment within a given territory of a political 'security-community', that is, a social group as defined by the extent of its transactional boundaries, possessing machineries of legislative enforcement and some popular habits of compliance that have 'eliminated war and the expectation of war' within the boundaries mapped above.[4] He specifically resists a concept of an integrated end-point as the merger of peoples and governmental units into a single unit alone, and opts to talk of such communities as either *amalgamated* (formal submergence of independent units under a common unitary or federal government) or *pluralistic* (security communities where the separate units retain their legal independence and do not officially combine).

Though Deutsch has performed a useful analytic task in identifying as fit for separate scrutiny an important class of interdependencies – the pluralistic ones – where the resort to large-scale physical force is remote but separate sovereignty is retained, I would argue that it misleads the enquiry to posit such a class as constituting examples of integration as this is generally understood. It is not even self-evident that such a class can be construed as an intermediate step between non-integrated conditions and integration proper, though Deutsch says that it is a 'practicable pathway' there. In delineating an area where significant conflicts are peacefully resolved, it seems to me that two quite separate processes are involved. *Amalgamation* is almost synonymous with integration,[5] and conclusive evidence of changed conditions emerges with the establishment of some overarching institution, whether unitary, federal, confederal, or something in between. The growth of *pluralistic* interdependence, however, still leaves unassailed the most important aspect of world politics – the formal status of the state, however 'penetrated' in practice such bodies might be, and however important parallel transnational organisations have nowadays become. There is no conclusive evidence of the change. Integration is equated with co-operation and with interdependence, and loses much of its distinctive analytic focus thereby.

The integrative process itself, as opposed to its institutional consequences, is particularly complex. Joseph Nye[6] has argued that we can avoid much conceptual confusion if we regard it less as a series of successive stages and more as an aggregate of three component sub-types, and I shall follow his recommendation here. Thus he talks of three important sorts of integration – *economic* (the growth of a transnational economy), *social* (the growth of a transnational society) and *political* (the growth of a transnational polity). Development in each dimension may be uneven and a group of states, growing together on one scale, may be falling apart on the others. A state of 'integration', however, is only likely to be reached when all three occur together, though the political aspect is the key one. It remains to be verified empirically what the exact causal relationship between the three component types might be in any particular case.[7]

Nye goes on to subdivide each process further – the economic into a *trade* sector (rise in proportion of intra-regional exports to total exports of the region) and a *service* sector (rise in expenditure on jointly administered services as a percentage of G.N.P.); the societal into *mass* and *elite* sectors, measured here by the increasing level of transnational transactions in mail, telephone calls, and so on; and the political into an *institutional* sector (strength of central institutions – confederative, federal or unitary – measured by growth of bureaucratic budget and staff as a percentage of the total budget and staff of member governments; heightened ability to make binding supranational decisions), a *policy* sector (increasing propensity for a group of states to act as a group in making domestic and foreign policy decisions), an *attitudinal* sector (growth in the extent to which a group of people share a sense of common identity and mutual obligation, though one might add that identity can follow integration as well as succour it) and a *security community* sector (growth in the reliable expectation of non-violent relations). This seems a useful breakdown of the diverse issues involved, though there are many difficulties in trying, as Nye does, to indicate quantifiable indices of them. The list is suggestive, but it is far from conclusive at any point.

One of the key problems in integration 'theory' lies in specifying the exact relationship between the fact of *interdependence* and a feeling of community. The question of interstate interdependence is very important, and after its summary deferral from my earlier discussion of 'linkage', deserves separate scrutiny here.

No state is isolated in the contemporary world system, but only in the most general terms can Costa Rica and Afghanistan, for example, be seen as interconnected, interdependent and hence susceptible to integration. If this is so, then merely asserting heightened interdependences in the world tells us little about what the phenomenon actually involves.

For a start, interdependence is a result of the loss of effective autonomy, and as such is quite distinct from questions about the legal fiction of sovereignty. States' leaders often consider themselves on an equal footing with others, and the elaborate mechanics of diplomatic deference seek to maintain this formality regardless of the relative viability of the countries concerned. However, the true measure of autonomy and independence will lie elsewhere, in the stability and coherence of their decision-making machinery, in their ability, or lack of it, to formulate, execute and remake their own decisions, and not to have these things made or remade for them from the outside.

Secondly, the loss of effective autonomy is a difficult thing to measure in any empirically precise way. Australia and the United States are sovereign entities and interdependent in certain respects, but how can meaningfully concrete measurements be made in political terms of the extent of this interdependence, of the extent to which Australian autonomy is undermined by its self-declared dependence for continued domestic development on economic capital lodged by American investors? How can the reciprocal and far less significant dependence of the United States on Australia be assessed for political effect? What indicators will be relevant, accurate, and beyond dispute? Several have been suggested, but none directly confronts the *quality* of dependence, and there may indeed be none capable of doing so.

Thirdly, the loss of effective autonomy may be a multi-dimensional affair. In other words a state may be more inter-dependent, and variably so, in one or more spheres of its activity than in one or more others. Thus the People's Republic of China has traded with ideologically adverse states, thereby compromising its economic autonomy in a way that it would never contemplate in matters of strategy and defence.

> We want to know what units are interdependent in terms of specified sets of activities (e.g., technology or transportation), geographical or functional areas (e.g., the North Atlantic region or international trade), and in terms of specified state objectives (e.g., security, peace, wealth). To speak of inter-dependence on a general level of abstraction without specifying these matters can result only in fruitless disputation over its empirical existence or its usefulness as a concept.[8]

Similarly, and this too will have to be taken into account, a group of states may be more interdependent on each other than on outside states or in comparison with a group of outside states. That is, regional sub-systems may exhibit differing degrees of interdependence. An historically delineated area such as that of Western Europe not unexpectedly displays greater interdependence in more areas of mutual concern than an area like that of South-east Asia or East Africa.

There is an attendant danger in the ready equation of inter-dependence and levels of economic development. It has sometimes been argued, for example, that interdependence is a direct function of 'modernisation'. The links between foreign and domestic politics, the consideration given to domestic welfare compared to externally oriented security considerations and the ability of a state to control by itself the overall system of inter-dependence, is considered to be of a somewhat lesser order in the case of the more industrialised, bureaucratised, specialised societies of the world. As a result, the list of contemporary advances in communications, weaponry and the like, though applicable to all world states, is not unaturally felt to apply more to the technologically advanced ones.

This line of argument, however, overlooks the fact that the very unchanged character of a technologically primitive society or country may heighten the impact of the introduction of more sophisticated mechanisms into it. The advent of one transistor radio in an Andean Indian village may result in a more significant advance toward intra-state interdependence, and hence interstate interdependence,[9] than the addition of television to an English home that already has radio and newspapers. Such differences, however, are almost impossible to measure in a precise way, involving as they do the comparative quality of a response rather than any more simple quantity such as the number of radios in Peru as opposed to that of television sets in England. Satisfactory and agreed indicators of this more qualitative kind do not exist, but impressionistic reflection certainly indicates a complexity that 'modernisation', however defined, does not explain away.

Further, it is sometimes argued that the advanced states depend more on stable international monetary and commercial arrangements that no one of them alone can decisively regulate. Given their inter-linked character at all levels, this economic interdependence makes the domestic sector of their affairs as vulnerable as their foreign sector, and consequently places certain limits on their freedom of action. However it seems reasonable to suppose that a 'non-modernised' state like Burma depends just as much on a stable world market in rice which it does not unilaterally control and which has extensive domestic effects when it declines, as it did in the 1950s, as any more economically sophisticated country. And advanced states have also evolved advanced methods for cushioning the effects of and bargaining about the ups and downs in their mutually disadvantageous, but also mutually advantageous, areas of overlap. Though no single advanced state can regulate the system alone, they are not as a group at the mercy of capricious and incomprehensible forces that threaten continually to overwhelm them. Thus 'modernisation' or 'non-modernisation' would seem, as far as interdependence is concerned, to produce differences in degree only. The idea of a difference in kind, 'modernised' states being interdependent and 'non-modernised' states not being so, would seem to conceal more than it explains.

The phenomenon of contemporary interstate interdependence

has been elevated by now to the status of a descriptive cliché. Some of its logical components and the difficulties in its use have been indicated, but what is meant more precisely by the term?

To begin with, it is generally agreed that the *absolute* level of interdependence in the global system has risen significantly over the last few years.[10] Though satisfactory empirical indicators of this rise are difficult to come by,[11] a generalised checklist is usually made up from technological advances in communications, transport, weaponry and the like, and from the broadening of human perceptions and expectations, and from the recent appearance of important non-state participants in the world system.[12] These are then cited as having produced this trend, as well as providing convincing evidence of it. Increasingly, it is argued, states have come to depend upon what goes on in their environments, and the level of interdependence has increased if only in the minimal sense that what happens within a state, and what its leaders decide to do, would be difficult if perceived trends, events and policies outside it were also different.

There is less certainty, however, as to the *relative* rise in the level of interdependence – relative, that is, to what Karl Deutsch has called 'national preoccupation'. Here the same evidence, or selective examples of it, have been used to argue two opposite conclusions: on the one hand that the rise in the level of interstate interdependence has been overtaken as it were, and overshadowed by an increase in the attention paid to intra-state affairs,[13] and on the other that innovation has resulted in higher levels of interstate rather than in intra-state interaction, regardless of the absolute change in either. In other words, given an increase in interdependence, 'national preoccupation' is seen as having either outstripped it, or by contrast as having either increased but by not as much, or as having remained the same, or as having fallen off in comparison to some sort of pre-contemporary level, each leaving the predominance of interstate interdependence unassailed.

It is quite conceivable, however, that both the level of interdependence *and* the level of national or state preoccupation have increased, but not in the competitive way envisaged above. The relationship between these two levels is often viewed as a sort of zero-sum conflict, in which gain in interdependence means relative loss of state autonomy and vice versa. But the argument for increasing interdependence is not necessarily an argument for a decrease in state preoccupation, as the protagonists often imply. Indeed:

> Many political continuities still occur solely within the boundaries of a single polity and cannot be understood without reference to the existence and character of boundaries. Transnational politics are a long way from supplanting national polities, and, if anything, the world may well be passing through a paradoxical state in which *both* the linkages [of interdependence] and the boundaries among polities are becoming more central to their daily lives.[14]

Both interdependence *and* national self-consciousness may be increasing as important considerations in the study of states. One may outweigh the other depending on the issue involved or the nature of the regional sub-system, or conceivably they might complement or balance each other off.

Nation-states are still key units in world politics, despite contemporary claims to the contrary. Deutsch has not been remiss to talk of a rise in 'pre-occupation'. Significantly, what John Herz has labelled as global 'universalism' has not replaced the physical, legal and psychological boundaries of 'territoriality'.[15] The nation-state has not been rendered obsolete; indeed it has undergone in many parts of the world something of a resurgence. To talk at all about domestic and foreign politics, or about the internal and external dimensions of state affairs, is to assume a present as well as a historic separability. However much the line between the two is blurred, they have remained in very real terms stubbornly apart.

In the past it was considered almost self-evident that this should be so. Traditional Western concepts of space, sovereignty and state equality under international law, were bolstered by growing governmental predominance in most aspects of sociopolitical life. The increasing reliance of the individual, in old states and new, on central administrative action for his economic well-being; the growing ability of a state to monopolise communications within it and to regulate traffic of all kinds across its borders; attempts to fill out state boundaries, whether discernible or fictional, with a common content of 'nationality'; all these things have reinforced the idea and ideals of statehood, however much in fact autonomy may have been in doubt. The 'end-of-the-nation-state' debate recalls another and similar debate which arose over the 'end of ideology', and there are instructive parallels.

What survives from Herz's original argument is not his prediction, but his analysis of cause, and especially the idea of 'permeability' – the extent to which formal and particularly informal penetration can now be used to reach into another country to exert influence and even control there[16] This phenomenon has been matched by the contemporary upsurge in 'transnational relations', by an upsurge in 'contact, coalitions and interactions across state boundaries that are not controlled by the central foreign policy organs of governments'.[17] One particularly belated analytical attempt to replace the 'state-centric' paradigm with a 'world politics' one, as the systems theorists have been recommending for many years, appeared under this rubric in 1971.[18] Its authors sought to underline the fact that: 'A good deal of intersocietal intercourse with significant political importance takes place without government control. . . . Furthermore, states are by no means the only actors in world politics' and that we must also consider as parties to world politics 'multinational enterprises and revolutionary movements; trade unions and scientific networks; international air transport cartels and communications activities in outer space'.[19] This overdue 'discovery' bears incidental witness to the introversion of the academic main-stream of world political concerns.

Accepting the relevance of transnational affairs, we can probably assume that the effect of an increased traffic in them has been to raise the general level of interstate interdependence.[20] The growth in transnational traffic, accelerating over the century, has been both consequence and cause of the heightened interdependencies characteristic of the contemporary world.

Given the paradoxical increase in transnationalism *and* state-building activity, in interdependence *and* national consolidation, a state of affairs not necessarily manifest in a competitive or zero-sum way, the relationship between interdependence and integration remains ambiguous. Until the implications of the one process become apparent, its implications for the other will also remain unclear. The ultimate predominance of 'national preoccupation' over an interconnected world, the least likely of the projections to date, would probably though not conclusively sustain and enhance the divisive characteristics of the global system. The ultimate predominance of 'interdependence' might or might not lead to integration as there is no predictable function between the two, between heightened reliance and the growth of an overarching sense of community. Some would argue that integration is not necessarily dependent on such a factor at all, and it ought to be evident that an increase in levels of interdependence breeds conflict as readily as co-operation.[21] What the ultimate predominance of both together, related in complex and subtle ways, might portend in terms of world government, regional integration or whatever, is at the moment anybody's guess.

There are four ways that states might logically integrate or be integrated into larger communities at the global level: (1) in some worldwide sectional fashion; (2) in a more limited, regionally defined but still sectional way; (3) in a regionally bounded but much more comprehensive coalescence; (4) a global coalescence of this latter, all-inclusive kind. The last category is difficult to imagine in practice, short of some world empire that contemporary weapons would seem to exclude. The first is also such a totally embracing idea that, despite the world success of co-operative ventures of a 'posts and telegraphs' sort, the chances of a process of integration taking off from what are politically and economically rather marginal concerns is remote. This leaves the two regional categories outlined, the one a sectional–functional affair and the other a more comprehensive amalgamation. A regional rather than a global focus is a major feature of contemporary pre-theories of integration. The distinction drawn here between the *sectional–functional* and *amalgamative–coalescent* models also coincides with the two major attempts to analyse the integrative trends apparent in the post-war world: the 'neo-functionalist' and the 'communications' approaches respectively. In the literature on the subject the neo-functionalists have recently made more of the running, so I shall begin by briefly outlining what they have to say.

'Functionalism' has had extended usage in world politics, both as a descriptive concept, and as an action-oriented prescription for change in world affairs.[22] Ideas of the kind that were current in the 1930s and in the immediate post-war period, associated most notably with David Mitrany, have made something of a return with the 'neo-functionalist' writings of Ernst Haas,[23] Philippe Schmitter and others. A retrospective mood has recently crept across the field, however, and this is a clear symptom that all is not as well there as it might be.

The functionalist/neo-functionalist doctrine rests upon the assumption 'that man will learn from the experience of international co-operation and begin to owe loyalty to those institutions which best satisfy his welfare needs'.[24] Man acts in his own self-interest, and will consistently seek to secure such ends.

> If individuals and groups can make co-operative arrangements across nation-state borders for their mutual benefit, these arrangements will grow first into habits of behavior and later into institutional structures. As the structures become stronger with increasing (and increasingly remunerative) co-operation, they will tend ultimately to undermine the power of state governments, because those who benefit from the co-operative arrangements, both mass and elite, will perceive them as too important to be upset by political differences.[25]

Technical and economic agencies will become so numerous, so important in the end in servicing the needs of earth's people, that it is to these and not the nations we separately inhabit that legitimacy and authority shall accrue.

We have under this rubric, for example, the Haas–Schmitter typology,[26] an attempt to spell out the variables we would need to assess if we want to predict how economic union leads to integration of the political sort. We are given here a check-list of typical conditions and factors, with an abstract attempt to relate these and delineate their implications for regional integration. These factors are listed in three groups, under (1) background conditions (the relative size and power of the interacting states, the initial rate of transactions between them, the extent and the nature of 'pluralism' prevailing within each, and the complementarity of their elites); (2) conditions as they stand at the outset of economic union, including the congruence of intent that the governments concerned display, and the supra-national powers granted by them to the emerging amalgamate; and (3) process conditions, such as the decision-making style that the new union develops as interactions take place, the rate of transactions that develops among the participants, and the adaptability demonstrated by the actors involved as the experiment goes forward and begins to run into strife. All other things being equal (which they never are) we might identify as one highly likely to find its economic relationships growing progressively more politicised, a group of states: (*a*) with a high rate of previous transactions, a high degree of similarity in size and power, a high degree of individual pluralism and marked elite complementarity; (*b*) with identical or converging economic aims, a strong commitment to political union, and an independent body of uninstructed 'regional bureaucrats' with the power to make significant policy and with active state and interest group collaboration; (*c*) who develop over time (generally three years minimum) a way of making decisions which defers to such uninstructed experts, these experts tending to agree on what they are doing and how to do it while working closely with state administrators and the representatives of major private interests; (*d*) exhibiting a rate of intra-regional transactions that grows faster than their rate of transactions with the outside world; and (*e*) meeting the inevitable crises by redefining the means of subsequent action at a higher rather than lower administrative level, where *more* mutual interdependence and *more* delegation of power occurs rather than less.[27]

> Transcendence, in the context of economic decisions, almost always involves entry into neighbouring spheres which were not previously part of the shared aims and the explicit program of the union. The test of transcendence, therefore, is the occurrence of a spillover into new fields, economic at first but increasingly political as the process continues. Crisis is the creative opportunity for realising this potential to redefine aims at a higher level of consensus.[28]

The idea of a *spill-over* is the most important aspect of the neo-functional model. It refers to the fact that interstate policies derived initially to carry out a common, usually economic, task with a grant of power to secure it, can be realised in practice only by the introduction of other task areas and by further state compromises: 'members of an integrated scheme – agreed on some collective goals for a variety of motives but unequally satisfied with their attainment of these goals – attempt to resolve their dissatisfaction either by resorting to collaboration in another, related sector (expanding the *scope* of the mutual commitment) or by intensifying their commitment to the original sector (increasing the *level* of mutual commitment) or both.'[29] The interlinked nature of state affairs means that one issue-area leads to another, a fact that becomes most apparent at a time of crisis. The opportunity then presents itself for decision-makers to level up their supra-national concerns rather than allow the integrative progress made so far to fail. There is nothing automatic about this sequence, however, though Haas and Schmitter have referred to the *automaticity*, or the high probability under the conditions outlined for spill-over to occur without any deliberate decision taken to ratify a centralised political structure. In general, there is an emphasis on the behaviour of state elites, and their ability to meet the integrative challenge with concrete resolve: 'Implicitly contained in the neo-functionalist model . . . is the assumption that integration can be analyzed profitably over shorter periods of time since it involves primarily small elite groups with relatively large learning capacities.'[30]

'Spill-over', then, is accompanied by two complementary processes – that of *externalisation*, or the consequent compulsion under regionalising conditions to evolve collective foreign policies to present to the outside world, and *politicisation*, or the tendency for joint decisions to become more controversial and to implicate more agents in the process; to trigger a redefinition of the common goals and to bring about the development of new loyalties to a new and emergent supra-national body.

Detailed attempts have followed the publication of this typology to make it more specific, so that it can be rather more precisely applied.[31] There are difficulties here, however. Haas himself, because of recent doubts about the foreclosure effects of such a framework and its inability to describe the 'total shape of the outcome',[32] has now rejected it.[33] A 'spill-around' concept has joined the 'spill-over' one in the attempt to accommodate those cases where interdependencies tend to rival each other and thereby to resist political integration. Highly successful functional interdependencies may also fail to enhance the integrative prospects of the group because of a tendency for the organisations concerned, and the attitudes that underwrite them, to become 'encapsulated'.[34]

Trenchant criticisms have also been made by those who would advocate an explanation of integration in terms of the 'inexorable pressures of global international systems, the charisma or guile of heroic leaders, the appeal of pan-regional ideological currents, or the "hiding hand" of economic rationality or market forces'[35] rather than any functionalist or neo-functionalist logic as spelled out above. The scheme furthermore contains no concept of social learning. This last is a feature of the communications process, and it is interesting to find that Haas has now specifically called for such a consideration.[36]

Joseph Nye[37] has drawn attention to several weak points of the kind just mentioned, arguing that 'politicisation' may be a discontinuous rather than a continuous affair; that the concept as it stands 'smacks too much of the functionalist preference for "the administration of things" . . . ',[38] and takes too little account of the historically unique and comparatively accidental *catalysts* in the integrative process; and that it underplays the effects of the external domain of world politics as a whole. Generally the attack has continued to question the extent to which economic union can carry a political union before it.[39] One can attribute the lack of a spill-over effect in post-war Europe to the assertiveness of the separate states[40] – a 'logic of diversity' that has run counter to the integrative progression Haas and Schmitter envisaged – and to the influence of the world system as a whole that has intruded its bipolar proclivities upon the European project. The relevance of the Haas–Schmitter typology is also limited when we come to examine 'spill-over' in underdeveloped countries, where a 'premature overpoliticisation'[41] or 'instant politicisation' effect tends to undermine the original idea of this process as an incremental one punctuated by periods of crisis.

Haas has mounted a rebuttal of most of these points. Implicating extra-regional variables he construes as a sly appeal to a 'deus ex machina capable of reviving a floundering common market in Pago Pago'. 'Nor should we expect', he says, 'a charismatic leader or an ideology with consummatory qualities to ride to the rescue.'[42] He does, however, admit the limitations that are apparent in the use of the 'spill-over' concept, which is a central feature of the original model.[43]

The Haas–Schmitter typology is not the only attempt to list factors pertinent to a process of integration.[44] Karl Deutsch,[45] for example, from a comparative study of historical communities, has listed nine conditions either essential to or at least helpful in the formation of 'amalgamated' security-communities from constituent state units (the discrete sense in which 'integration' is used here). The *essential* factors include a measure of the states' compatibility on major values, the increase in their political and administrative capabilities, the distinctiveness of their joint way of life, the superior rate of economic growth in at least some of them, their expectations of joint economic reward, their range of mutual transactions, the breadth of their elites, the unbroken nature of the links of social communication that define them, and the mobility of persons between them. *Helpful* but not so essential factors include a 'compensation' of transactional flows, a reasonably frequent interchange of group roles, and a considerable mutual predictability of behaviour. A group of states fulfilling all these conditions is more likely than not, Deutsch argues, to integrate.

The Haas–Schmitter paradigm is the most developed such attempt, however, to organise the variables involved. Specifically informed by a functional logic of 'task expansion, increased controversiality, and institutionalisation of decisional capacities',[46] it provides a schedule of events that can be used to predict the likelihood of a political union growing out of an economic one. It is still a matter of debate, though, just when integration has been completed, and the framework falls short, despite the idea of 'politicisation', of explaining why the process occurs as it does.

I shall turn now to the second major post-war approach to the study of integration – the *cybernetic communications* focus identified most closely with the further work of Karl Deutsch.

'Communications theory suggests – it does not assert or prove – that an intensive pattern of communication between national units will result in a closer "community" among the units if loads and capabilities remain in balance.'[47] Unlike the neo-functionalist one, the cybernetic model is concerned with the 'relatively slow processes of social learning which include large numbers of people with comparatively small learning capacities'.[48] It deals in transaction flows, measurements of the traffic in communication, and the outline of expectations of conflict, co-operation and reward.

Deutsch's scheme has long been characterised as a 'socio-causal' approach to political integration, and this concept captures exactly the import of his ideas.[49] Political integration, defined as already discussed in 'pluralistic' as well as 'amalgamative' terms, must be preceded by a process of social coalescence: 'the way to integration, domestic or international, is through the achievement of a sense of community that undergirds institutions . . .', 'consent has to come before compliance if the amalgamation is to have lasting success.'[50] Thu the growth of a regional community necessarily comes before the emergence of supranational institutions with superordinate power. The measure of the one is a measure of the potential to the other, and these measurements are made in terms of the rate of flow of inter-state transactions. We can assess, Deutsch argues, the ' "integration" of individuals in a people by their ability to receive and transmit information on wide ranges of different topics with relatively little delay or loss of relevant detail',[51] and this assessment serves to identify political as well as social integration, at an international as well as a national level.

The integrative process itself Deutsch has described as the 'assembly-line'[52] compilation, in no fixed sequence, of a specified number of necessary elements. Integration usually develops, he says, around nuclear 'cores of strength'[53] that consist of political units 'larger, stronger, more politically, administratively, economically, and educationally advanced' than others. Pay-offs are anticipated of various kinds, though the burdens of co-operation generally have to be timed to come after the rewards.[54] Historically he has found that the issue of political integration usually arises when people demand 'greater capabilities, greater performance, greater responsiveness, and more adequate services of some kind' from the governments by which they are ruled;[55] as a means to anticipated ends rather than as an end in itself. The 'take-off' point is reached when a major group of political institutions commits itself to the cause. The issue is taken up at a later stage by large numbers of people, and enlisting broad popular participation and support has been in the past the best guarantee of amalgamative success.[56] Old habits of allegiance are broken down by the new and emergent way of life, by the expectation of better things to come, by the presence of any external challenge that requires a co-operative response, and by the process of generational change which brings younger, more committed men into the decision-making elites.[57] Political cleavages develop that ignore the old political lines, and coalitions grow across them, provided, that is, that no serious gulfs of a linguistic, religious, ideological, economic or class kind reinforce state divisions irrevocably. Political innovation and invention become decisive, creative solutions provide original avenues of escape, thus preserving a new union that would otherwise collapse, and single-minded pursuit of the integrative goal serves to inhibit alternative propositions that might dissipate the amalgamative resolve.

Much more is involved here than the neo-functional framework attempts to describe. Indeed, as Deutsch concludes: 'Functionalism and functional arrangements . . . have little effect by themselves upon the eventual success or failure of efforts to establish amalgamated security communities. The outcome in each case is most likely to depend on other conditions and processes, particularly on how rewarding or unrewarding were the experiences associated with functional arrangements.'[58] The usefulness of these arrangements lies in the way they foster a sense of community, and habits appropriate to integration of a much more extensive and remunerative sort. The integrative trade here is in trust rather than material interdependencies; social assimilation takes place as people learn habits of mutual confidence which are then translated into co-ordinate perspectives on world affairs and political union.

This socio-causal logic has been the focus for criticism and at least one explicit scrutiny[59] has failed to find an adequate link in it between social assimilation and political integration. It mainly falls down, it has been argued, in its failure to explain how mass attitudes of a communalistic kind give rise to integrative elite behaviour.[60]

Deutsch's general assessment that the rate of regional integration has given way to the multiple advent of national coalescence can also be assailed, and his use of 'iterative transactions',[61] indices of foreign trade, migration, tourist and letter flows, demands on domestic resources, interstate wage interdependencies and so on, often fail to capture the essential characteristics of the processes they purport to describe: 'perhaps, it is not trade or other kinds of transactions that are crucial in our judgement so much as the *perception* of present and future benefits in the minds of the actors. In that case this type of data is not a good indicator unless it is reinterpreted in terms of actor perceptions'.[62] There is clearly room here to apply some of the psycho-political findings already discussed. As yet no study of integration has met its obligations in this regard. Can the 'communications' and 'neo-functional' approaches be combined into a more comprehensive framework with which we might analyse integration? Their fundamental predispositions tend to point in different directions, one to the value of whole systems and the other to the performance of individual participants, but in other ways they do seem to be complementary, and much might be gained in the attempt.

Apart from these two general approaches, the contemporary analysis of integration is mainly preoccupied with particular examples of interstate unification or non-unification as the case may be and as the analyst is disposed to see it – most notably debates about the state of European economic union and its political concomitants.[63] Bruce Russett is a prominent exception, however, and his book, *International Regions and the International System*,[64] is a broadly conceived and strictly executed attempt to discover regional groupings in the world and to assess in an operational way key integrative factors like cultural compatibility, economic interdependence, geographical contiguity and institutional 'spill-over', for their congruence and the durability of their effects. Regions, he argues, might be defined in terms of social and cultural homogeneity (identified by internal attributes of several kinds), political attitudes or external behaviour (identified by the voting positions of the national governments in the United Nations), supra-national or intergovernmental political institutions, economic interdependence (identified by intra-regional trade as a proportion of national income), and geographical proximity. The analysis of world politics abounds with intuitive judgements about sub-systemic regions in such terms, with labels for groups of states like Western Europe, Eastern Europe, South-East Asia and Latin America. Russett attempts to be somewhat more specific and rigorous in his judgements, however, manipulating large amounts of quantitative information to see how it lumps together, and how the indices which he constructs point to the way states themselves clump in turn: 'we should be able', he says,

> to identify certain areas of the world where the potential for further integration is high, and perhaps point out other areas where, despite present or projected institutions, some apparent conditions seem weak or absent. . . . We cannot, of course, say whether the degree of similarity or interdependence that we find is sufficient to support a given level of integration, but we can point out areas of more and less, and note important discontinuities.[65]

What he concludes, predictably, is that only the traditional nation-state fits the same aggregate boundaries on all five scales: socio-cultural similarity, political orientation, institutional membership, transactional interdependence and geographical proximity. By implication, then, this study would suggest that no great potential exists for integrative processes between them. Rather than general propositions about the relationship, for example, between membership of international organisations and trade, he is forced to admit that causal questions like this 'are more complex and less regular' than he had supposed.[66]

Russett's study has been criticised[67] for its lack of an underlying theoretical framework. Data-processing in this random fashion, uninformed by a systematic set of basic propositions, is felt to contribute very little to debates about regionalism and integration. Russett has indicated himself how necessary a 'careful theory'[68] is, if we are to arrive at causal conclusions of any kind, but the general argument that he fails to develop such a framework is rather silly. He has replied by turning the critique on its head.[69] His study makes one important contribution, he claims. Many analysts have elaborated descriptions and theories of the world system and its sub-systems without recourse to any rigorous *empirical* foundation. On the basis of his work, he feels, no-one can legitimately do so again. Geographically derived assertions about 'Africa' for example, or some particular 'Latin American' nation, can now be given comparatively precise referents, providing of course we accept Russett's five criteria and his modes of measurement as adequate to the task.

What is the present status of integration theory? What can it offer in the way of general empirical propositions of more than contingent worth?[70]

In *global* terms, studies of integration have verified the fact that a rise in the rate of inter-state transactions is perceived by the participants as interdependence, evaluated favourably if equal benefits accrue to them, and negatively if they do not. They verify the fact that the relative size of participant states is no indicator of the likelihood of their integrative success; that a growth in organisational links in a region leads to greater interdependence, a development that may or may not be viewed in favourable terms; and that a 'critical mass composed of integrative activities in a number of issue areas likely to result in a culminination of de facto or de jure political union is difficult to identify and hazardous to predict',[71] though of 'all issues and policy areas the commitment to create a common market is the most conducive to rapid regional integration.'[72]

In *regional* terms there are many more, and more specific, conclusions to be found, and Haas has outlined these under three headings – those pertaining to socialist groupings, those pertaining to industrialised–pluralistic nations, and those pertaining to late-developing states. For socialist countries, for example, we find that 'mutual interdependence and dependence on the regional "core area" is a disintegrative force because the smaller nations resent it with varying degrees of intensity and consistency'.[73] European economic union, built though it is upon a tissue of mutual expectations of governmental and private group advantage, still cannot rely upon such interests remaining the same, and not being reversed should expectations change. As far as the late-developing states are concerned, it seems that African integration has been largely symbolic and not along European lines at all, a situation that obtains for Latin America too except that economic integration there does have something at least in common with the European case.

If we take account of the effects of extra-regional factors upon regional integration processes we have a concluding set of propositions. For example, 'perceptions of being victimized by the global system tend to spur integration as a way of "getting out from under" ', though 'perceptions of dependence on a larger system may be so pervasive as to be a disincentive' to any regional efforts at all.[74] Further, a single extra-regional state may either subvert or support integrative tendencies among a group of states, while an endogenous counter-union can give clear if short-lived support to the subversive ones as well.

The list is not long, and is distinguished largely by its lack of precision and lack of explanatory power. Analytically derived predictions of regional integration have an indeterminate air about them, while the chances of multi-bloc or global integration seem even more remote. Nevertheless the long view does reveal a macro-communalistic process at work. From an historical perspective, kingdoms, tribal areas and city-states have been known to coalesce or have been caused to coalesce into countries, and they continue to do so in large parts of the post-war world. There is sparse evidence at the moment, however, of two contemporary states merging to manufacture a third and superordinate one, and there is absolutely 'no basic' as yet 'for projecting uncritically this trend to the stage of a world state'.[75] Despite such a conclusion, the only certainty about the present state of affairs is that it will not last, and it is a brave man who predicts what the predominant world actor of the next century might be, and a foolhardy one who would assert the same for the century after that.

CHAPTER 12

Conclusion

It remains to draw together the somewhat disparate threads traced above into a more coherent pattern. This is a formidable task, since the study proceeds to separate topics that range over the whole spectrum of the possible levels of contemporary analysis. The character of their coherence is a tenuous one – Spengler and Toynbee, systems theory, and studies of the human brain, to take just three examples, do not lie down easily together along the same analytic loom – but there is an order to these topics and I would like in conclusion to make that order clear.

The work began by tracing the history of the study of world politics, dwelling in particular upon the behavioural and post-behavioural periods and their chief methodological concerns. Etymologically there seems little justification for it, but in my opinion 'behaviouralism' sought essentially a *science* of world affairs, and it did this in several ways: (1) it attempted to build comprehensive 'theories' from the same mould that had produced the authoritative cumulative statements of chemistry, for example, or physics; (2) it applied the substantive findings of several diverse sciences to the subject matter of world politics, on the one hand that global affairs might be placed more precisely in the context of the human enterprise as a whole, and on the other that we might better understand individual and group behaviour; (3) it sought to employ particular conceptual frameworks that occur in the natural sciences in the hope that their apparent success in ordering natural phenomena would also apply to social concerns; and (4) it used several of the experimental and quantitative techniques common in the natural sciences in the hope that the precise treatment of social phenomena would yield the reliable and comprehensive results so ardently desired.

The 'theory-building' enterprise was exemplified initially by an examination of some recent studies of 'foreign policy'. This is one of the most important foci of international relations research. It is also one field in which academics have felt hopeful of breaking through to that system of generalised, logically developed and consistent propositions, from which one might deduce explanatory or predictive statements amenable to disproof, that is 'theory' in its strict and most scientific sense. This end has so far proved elusive and promises to remain so.

The substantive perspectives of several distinct branches of modern knowledge – cosmology, cosmogony, palaeontology, biology, anthropology, ecology and social philosophy – were used to locate the subject matter of global politics as one part, albeit an important and determining part, of the human project as a whole. I argued, as Teilhard de Chardin has urged us to do, that we should view humankind not as the static centre of the world but as the axis and leading shoot of evolution, a process whose path we must consciously define ourselves.

These perspectives were treated in the most summary fashion. They provide the basis, however, for a set of 'radical' values in the world community, in the original sense of the word. The qualities which these values affirm are common to most human beings, and are inherent in us by reason of the evolutionary descent of humankind as a whole and by reason of the cultural conditions under which we have been reared. To understand what we are and what we might aspire to be we must come to terms at some point with the natural parameters that define us and with the cultural and philosophical parameters as well. These limits and conditioning factors apply to all human behaviour, and to the practice of world politics as one component thereof. Grant a random distribution of hydrogen molecules in space, for instance, with a given amount of angular momentum, and we can sketch an explanation of all that follows, up to and including ourselves, in terms of natural process and not miracle. We have assumed the level of consciousness which such a sketch implies, and would know the meaning of it too. Having taken up such a task it would be a pity if it were lost, or if we failed to carry it to a fitting conclusion.

Whether these root values will emerge or not as a force in the world political system will depend, I suppose, on the conviction with which they can be conveyed in the face of more immediate questions about individual moral or bodily well-being. Furthermore their utopian import can take both pernicious or humanitarian forms. The National Socialists firmly ratified the significance of the human project in cosmic terms and the desirability of furthering that project as a value in itself, but they construed this as direct support for the conquest of the world by the Germans. Hitler's use of science was highly selective, however, and there is no basis in biological thought for asserting the innate 'superiority' of the Aryan 'race', or any other human group for that matter. Even if there were, there is no necessary connection between whatever the nature of that superiority might be and a right to global rule.

However, there does seem to be an impelling logic, for example, in the fact that one-half of the intellectual and moral capacity of the human race is located in women, regardless of state or nation, and when we consider the fact in terms of the human enterprise as a whole, their historical and contemporary subjugation and the gross wastage of human potential which this subjugation involves takes on a greater sense of significance than it might otherwise do. The same applies to the biopolitics of underdevelopment, the nutritional assault upon half the world's population, male and female, which has already been discussed.

The concepts and the conclusions of several other distinct branches of knowledge – cybernetics, theoretical and social biology, neurophysiology and social psychology – were then used, firstly, to reinterpret old issues in novel frameworks, generating new insights and information along the way, and, secondly, to relate the impact of science in its various comprehensive and more exact forms to the basic issues of world politics. They are relevant to these issues in varying degrees – some more directly than others – and I have tried to make their implications clear in each case.

Finally, I discussed two of the most important substantive questions that confront the analyst of world affairs – the character of conflict and war, and the nature and likelihood of interstate integration. I suggested where transdisciplinary material might cast light upon each subject, or has already done so, and traced the patterns apparent in the contemporary studies of each respective concern.

Two key threads are apparent throughout. One is the generalised quest for 'theory' or theory-like structures of deductive import that allow of explanation, prediction and control. The other is the pursuit of detailed information, specific facts that might enable us to better understand on several analytic levels at once why particular global events come to pass as they do, and what general patterns they might display.

On the whole, the conclusions arrived at are negative ones. The 'theories' have proved to be rather insubstantial affairs, their explanatory range is small, and the substantive findings too are often incomplete with only the suggestion of an answer to go on. This is no cause for despair, however, and before I finish I would like to look once again at these two essential ingredients in what lies above. The study of integration led back to the theory-building enterprise discussed at the outset, and the first case can be confirmed with a final example from the literature on 'foreign policy' with which I began.

James Rosenau has outlined a framework which illustrates, he claims, the 'possible contours' of a 'viable linkage theory'[1] for the East Asian state system. The national societies of China, Japan, the United States and the Soviet Union are assumed to have one primary goal each in their policies toward the region, and these single policy goals are presumed measurable in turn on a five-point scale of intensity. China, for example, seeks the maintenance of its sovereignty over a five-strength gradient from 'vigorous' to 'half-hearted'; Japan seeks to secure markets and resources over the same range; the United States seeks to maintain the balance of power in the region; and the U.S.S.R. seeks to defend its eastern borders. Each national society can also be depicted, again in a five-point fashion, on a single domestic dimension of a structural sort which is related to the foreign-policy goals just given. China and the Soviet Union, for example, are ranked on a *leadership* scale, the former from centralised to decentralised, and the latter from singular to collective; Japan is ranked by *economy* from growth to stagnation, and the United States is placed in an *interventionist/isolationist* dimension.

In this way, Rosenau argues, the degree of stability of the East Asian system can be seen to act directly upon a state's domestic affairs, and, alternatively, placing a state on its particular domestic scale can be related to the way it pursues its political aspirations in the region as a whole.

> Given five-point scales, the possible permutations and combinations in this regard are too numerous to record here. They can readily be calculated with the aid of a computer, however, so that the only obstacle to viable linkage theory is the obvious inadequacy of the assumption that societal goals and structures can be reduced to single dimensions. Leaving this inadequacy aside, the example is pervaded with linkages.[2]

Rosenau gives the game away with one hand, and then snatches it back with the other, which is hardly a very admirable or honest ploy. The crucial 'inadequacy', he states, cannot be cast aside in this fashion, and while linkages between domestic and foreign affairs may well abound, the complex and multi-dimensional character of 'societal goals and structures' is likely to militate against their precise specification in strict deductive terms. Instead of one generalised analytic order to events that otherwise lack meaning or coherence, we are left with the detailed discussion of a plethora of particular orders, the diverse patterns and the various meanings we might extract from the separate political systems and the foreign options they pursue. This is not to say that these political systems or policy options have nothing in common at all, but rather that the differences will probably be more important than the similarities when it comes to explaining East Asian affairs in terms of domestic state structures, or domestic state structures in terms of East Asian affairs.

The point is also made by a related work.[3] Rosenau has built a huge inverted pyramid of ideas and principles pertaining to foreign policy that totter away upon the slender apex of 'adaptation', a notion familiar from General Systems 'Theory' and from the language of cybernetics. All nations, he says, can be viewed as adapting entities with similar problems that arise out of the need to cope with their environments. 'What is the order of this similarity?' we might enquire. 'What do such generalised principles look like?' Adaptive foreign-policy behaviour, Rosenau maintains, 'copes with or stimulates changes in the external environment of the society that contribute to keeping the essential structures of the society within acceptable limits.'[14] What the 'essential' structures and 'acceptable' limits might be are empirical questions, we are told, to be measured in some way and not just asserted as values in advance.

I sincerely doubt that anybody will arrive at a reliable estimate of 'essence' and 'acceptability' in terms both sufficiently precise and broadly applicable to be of use. To a large extent a number of simple ideas have been rephrased by Rosenau in a plausible and elaborate way to no apparent analytic advantage. As pointed out earlier, we do not have the predictive ability to know what changes will prove adaptive in the *long* run where adaptability really counts. The subject could well be spared such extravagant attempts to pre-empt our ignorance with ephemera.

The critiques just rehearsed have a retrospective flavour since the major methodological battle between the behaviouralists, and their critics has passed. The war continues, however, in a guerrilla fashion, and it is likely to do so for some time, since literature of this sort is still being produced in prodigious quantities. As an end-place, most of it is a disappointment, if not positively misleading. There is something to recommend it, though, as a point of departure.

Where does this leave the subject? Where do we go from here? Should we encourage more of the same, and what further work would appear most fruitful at this stage if we do?

I have conveyed some sense, I hope, despite the pessimism evinced above, of the import of contemporary behavioural concerns, partial though these may be. I have conveyed too, I hope, some sense of my own conviction that the transdisciplinary enterprise in particular ought to continue. The idea of a 'scientific' study of world politics carries us in different directions. The chances for theory in the strict sense are slim, though this observation will not deter those who seek theory-like explanations in terms, for example, of world economics and the structural dependencies that penetrate politics at every point. The potential usefulness of the findings of several, sometimes quite remote disciplines, however, and of some of the methods of the natural sciences, is great indeed, and it is the transdisciplinary ingredient which I wish to underline at the end.

We can be carried only so far by scientific concerns. True

science, as Claude Bernard observed, teaches us to doubt, and in ignorance to refrain. The first injunction is all to the good but the second in practical political terms is impossible. The political realm is one of action, not immobility, and what we do not know does not deter us, indeed, it may serve to spur us on. All political decisions are taken on incomplete information and it is difficult to conceive that it could be otherwise. But 'so far' appears to me to be quite a long way. Much more time should be spent by the discipline in attempting to connect the conclusions that emerge at different levels of analysis from that of the individual to systems as a whole. The study of world politics should set itself to synthesise the concepts, the substantive findings and the methodological insights of the sorts of fields mapped out above in a more self-conscious fashion than has been done heretofore, that these findings may more readily be brought to bear upon the core issues of integration and conflict. This is easy to say, but in each case proves very difficult to do. The material is organised only through the problems it purports to illuminate and explain. The cybernetic model of decision-making systems, Toynbee's or Spengler's notion of civilisation in decline, the biopolitics of the human brain and the psychopolitics of individual patterns of perception and image maintenance, for example, are linked only by virtue of their common applicability to the political behaviour of states and the political behaviour of the elites and the masses these states contain. The definition of politics itself, the definition of what is *political* behaviour as opposed to other sorts of behaviour, becomes problematic in the extreme.

To Morgenthau, the main signpost to the subject was 'the concept of interest defined in terms of power';[5] the 'power' of a state should be its predominant concerns, he argued, and affect all else it might do. This sets politics as an autonomous sphere of prudential action apart from economics, morality or law. Without such a concept, he maintained, it would be impossible to achieve a measure of order in the field, or to discriminate between politics and anything else; it is the essential 'truth', he argued, that the study of world affairs variously strives to 'disguise, distort, belittle, . . . embellish'[6] and to explain away.

This definition, this notion of a human currency that the global polity serves to exchange analogous to its exchange of money in the economy, is too narrow, it seems to me, and we must run the risk of losing the clarity of our focus to include the breadth of concerns that politics really contains. It is a spurious clarity anyway. 'Power' and 'interest', so narrowly conceived, are important considerations in world affairs since, all other things being equal, might is more likely to prevail and to convey the sense of right that animates its cause. 'Power goes far to create the morality convenient to itself, and coercion is a fruitful source of consent.'[7] When we consider power as a *relational* phenomenon, however, and not so much a material one, the dichotomy between power and morality becomes difficult to sustain and the focus upon 'power' alone becomes quite inadequate.[8] Moral imperatives have an equivalent political status of their own and we find that the evolutionary, historical, cybernetic, biopolitical and psychopolitical phenomena discussed above bear directly upon any analysis of either 'morality' or 'power' or the international politics they predispose.

We cannot expect transdisciplinary reasearch to solve such problems of world politics as integration and war, but we can place these considerations beside any other as worthy of our concern. There are many partial theories that can be applied and since conventional propositions about world politics and conventional specifications as to root causes are proving insufficient to explain and predict the patterns that appear there we must simply look somewhere else for the information we require. When we do, however, we find that most of our journey lies ahead. How little distance it is that we have come since the narrator of *Tono-Bungay*, gazing out from the Thames, could summarise our condition in terms yet to be revealed: 'We make and pass,' he said, 'We are all things that make and pass, striving upon a hidden mission out to the open sea.'[9]

Notes

CHAPTER 1

1. E. H. Carr, *The Twenty Years' Crisis* (London: Macmillan, 1962) p. 1.
2. I use the familiar appellation, despite its Europocentric inadequacies, because it is the one still most common in the literature on the subject. I much prefer, however, Peter Lyons's usage: 'the First World War' becomes the First Atlantic War – the penultimate major European war - and 'the Second World War' becomes the First World War – the second Atlantic War and the First War of the Pacific. P. Lyons, *War and Peace in South-East Asia* (Oxford University Press, 1969) p. 6.
3. F. Neal and B. Hamlett, 'The Never-Never Land of International Relations', *International Studies Quarterly*, vol. 13, no. 3 (Sep 1969) p. 283.
4. Carr, *The Twenty Years' Crisis*, ch. 4.
5. Ibid. p. vii.
6. H. J. Morgenthau, *Politics Among Nations*, 3rd ed. (New York: A. Knopf, 1966).
7. R. Dahl, 'The Behavioral Approach in Political Science: Epitaph for a Movement to a Successful Protest', *American Political Science Review*, vol. 55, no. 4 (Dec 1961) pp. 763–72.
8. H. Bull, 'International Theory: the Case for a Classical Approach', *World Politics*, vol. 18, no. 3 (Apr 1966) pp. 361–77.
9. M. Banks, 'Two Meanings of Theory in the Study of International Relations', *Yearbook of World Affairs* (London: Stevens & Sons, 1966).
10. D. Easton, 'The New Revolution in Political Science', *American Political Science Review*, vol. 63, no. 4 (Dec 1969) pp. 1051–61.
11. Dahl, 'The Behavioral Approach', p. 766.
12. Ibid. p. 767.
13. See further, H. Arendt, *The Human Condition* (New York: Doubleday Anchor, 1959) p. 253: 'the test of theory became a "practical" one – whether or not it will work. Theory became hypothesis, and the success of the hypothesis became truth. . . . The criterion of success is inherent in the very essence and progress of modern science quite apart from its applicability. Success here is not at all the empty idol to which it degenerated in bourgeois society; it was, and in the sciences has been ever since, a veritable triumph of human ingenuity against overwhelming odds.'
14. Cf. K. Boulding, *The Meaning of the Twentieth Century* (London: Allen & Unwin, 1964) p. 55: 'The crucial date in the birth of science is the point in time at which its fundamental theoretical structure is first formulated; a theoretical structure which is then capable of successive refinement and modification in the light of further evidence.'

15. T. Kuhn, *The Structure of Scientific Revolution*, 2nd ed. (University of Chicago Press, 1970) p. 166.
16. J. Watkins, 'Against "Normal Science"', K. Popper, 'Normal Science and its Dangers', I. Lakatos, 'Falsification and the Methodology of Scientific Research Programmes', in *Criticism and the Growth of Knowledge*, ed. I. Lakatos and A. Musgrave (London: Cambridge University Press, 1970).
17. P. Feyerabend, 'Consolations for the Specialist', in Lakatos and Musgrave, ibid. p. 209.
18. Ibid. p. 210.
19. Masterman, 'The Nature of a Paradigm', in *Criticism and the Growth of Knowledge*, ed. Lakatos and Musgrave, p. 74.
20. See H. Stretton, *The Political Sciences* (London: Routledge & Kegan Paul, 1969) pp. 261–3, chs 13, 14.
21. Q. Wright, *The Study of International Relations* (New York: Appleton-Century-Crofts, 1955) p. 116.
22. E. J. Meehan, *The Theory and Method of Political Analysis* (Illinois: Dorsey Press, 1965) pp. 231–2.
23. M. Landau, 'Due Process of Enquiry', *The American Behavioral Scientist*, vol. 9, no. 2 (Oct 1965) p. 9.
24. Bull, 'International Theory'.
25. K. Knorr and J. Rosenau (eds), *Contending Approaches to International Politics* (New Jersey: Princeton University Press, 1969).
26. J. Rosenau, *The Scientific Study of Foreign Policy* (New York: The Free Press, 1971) p. 31.
27. Banks, 'Two Meanings of Theory', p. 226.
28. Ibid.
29. Dahl, 'The Behavioral Approach', p. 768.
30. Masterman, 'The Nature of a Paradigm', p. 75.
31. Wright, *The Study of International Relations*, p. 118.
32. The behavioural school of 'peace research' is a notable exception here, however.
33. R. Jenkins, *Exploitation* (London: Paladin, 1971) p. 20.
34. D. Horowitz, 'Billion Dollar Brains', *Ramparts* (May 1969) p. 42.
35. Ibid.
36. D. Horowitz, 'Sinews of Empire', *Ramparts* (Oct 1969) p. 42.
37. Wright, *The Study of International Relations*, p. 119.

CHAPTER 2

1. K. Waltz, *Man, the State and War* (New York: Columbia University Press, 1959).
2. Ibid. p. 47.
3. P. Baran and P. Sweezy, *Monopoly Capital* (Harmondsworth: Penguin, 1968); A. G. Frank, *Capitalism and Underdevelopment in Latin America* (Harmondsworth: Penguin, 1971) and *Latin America: Underdevelopment or Revolution* (New York: Monthly Review Press, 1969); H.

Magdoff, *The Age of Imperialism* (New York: Monthly Review Press, 1969); P. Jalee, *The Pillage of the Third World* (New York: Monthly Review Press, 1968) and *The Third World in the World Economy* (New York: Monthly Review Press, 1969).

4. A. Huxley, 'Human Potentialities', in *Man and Civilisation: Control of the Mind*, ed. S. Farber and R. Wilson (New York: McGraw-Hill, 1961) p. 63: '. . . human oversimplification may be described as the original sin of the intellect . . . politics are not enough, law is not enough, science is not enough, religion is not enough, in fact, nothing short of everything is enough.'
5. J. Rosenau, 'Compatibility, Consensus, and an Emerging Political Science of Adaptation', *American Political Science Review*, vol. 61, no. 4 (Dec 1967) p. 983.
6. See P. Feyerabend, 'Against Method', in *Analyses of Theories and Methods of Physics and Psychology*, ed. M. Radner and S. Winokur, Minnesota Studies in the Philosophy of Science, vol. 4 (Minneapolis: University of Minnesota Press, 1970).
7. 'A theory of international politics normally cannot be expected to predict individual actions, beeause the interaction problem is too complex and because there are too many free variables. It can be expected, however, to predict characteristic or modal behavior within a particular kind of international system. Moreover the theory should be able to predict the conditions under which the system will remain stable, the conditions under which it will be transformed, and the kinds of transformations that may be expected to take place.' M. Kaplan, 'Some Problems of International Systems Research', in *Readings on the International Political System*, ed. N. Rosenbaum (New Jersey: Prentice-Hall, 1970) p. 419.
8. M. Levy Jr, in *Contending Approaches to International Politics*, ed. K. Knorr and J. Rosenau (New Jersey: Princeton University Press, 1969) p. 93.
9. E. Meehan, *The Theory and Method of Political Analysis* (Illinois: Dorsey Press, 1965) p. 145.
10. J. Rosenau, 'Pre-Theories and Theories of Foreign Policy', in *Approaches to Comparative and International Politics*, ed. R. Barry Farrell (Evanston: North Western University Press, 1966).
11. A. Kaplan, *The Conduct of Inquiry* (San Francisco: Chandler, 1964) pp. 264–5.
12. M. Black, *Models and Metaphors* (Ithaca, N.Y.: Cornell University Press, 1962) p. 241.
13. R. Snyder, H. Bruck, B. Sapin (eds), *Foreign Policy Decision-making* (New York: Free Press, 1962).
14. Ibid. p. 212.
15. O. Holsti, R. North, R. Brody, 'Perception and Action in the 1914 Crisis', in *Quantitative International Politics*, ed. J. D. Singer (New York: Free Press, 1968) p. 127.
16. Snyder *et al.*, *Foreign Policy Decision-making*, p. 72.
17. R. Snyder and G. Paige, 'The United States' Decision to Resist

Aggression in Korea: the Application of an Analytical Scheme' in *Foreign Policy Decision-making*, ed. Snyder *et al.*; see also G. Paige, *The Korean Decision: June 24–30* (New York: Free Press, 1968) and *1950: Truman's Decision: the United States Enters the Korean War* (New York: Chelsea House, 1970).

18. Snyder *et al.*, *Foreign Policy Decision-making*, p. 212.
19. Ibid.
20. Ibid.
21. Ibid. p. 137.
22. Snyder and Paige, 'The United States' Decision', p. 246.
23. H. McCloskey, 'Strategies for a Science of International Politics', in *Foreign Policy Decision-Making*, ed. Snyder *et al.*, p. 196.
24. J. Rosenau, 'The Premises and Promises of Decision-making Analysis', in *Contemporary Political Analysis*, ed. J. Charlesworth (New York: Free Press, 1967) p. 209.
25. Snyder and Paige, 'The United States' Decision', p. 208.
26. Ibid. See his n. 13, which outlines five general values that overrode uncertainties at the time. All are strategic values; there is no mention of ideological commitments, perceived images of the enemy, or the nature of the change in such values over time.
27. R. Jones, *Analysing Foreign Policy* (London: Routledge & Kegan Paul, 1970) p. 37.
28. M. Pilisuk, 'The Guts of Foreign-policy Decision-making', in *Inter national Conflict and Social Policy* (New Jersey: Prentice-Hall, 1972) p. 74.
29. G. Allison and M. Halperin, 'Bureaucratic Politics: a Paradigm and Some Policy Implications', in *Theory and Policy in International Relations*, ed. R. Tanter and R. Ullman (New Jersey: Princeton University Press, 1972) p. 41.
30. G. Allison, 'Conceptual Models and the Cuban Missile Crisis', *American Political Science Review*, vol. 63, no. 3 (Sep 1969) p. 698.
31. Allison and Halperin, 'Bureaucratic Politics', pp. 49–50, 53–4, 60–6, 70–9.
32. Allison, 'Conceptual Models', p. 718. See also *Essence of Decision: Explaining the Cuban Missile Crisis* (Boston: Little, Brown, 1971).
33. Allison and Halperin, 'Bureaucratic Politics', p. 54.
34. Ibid. p. 60.
35. See the discussion of 'meta-theory' in D. Bobrow, 'The Relevance Potential of Different Products', in *Theory and Policy in International Relations*, ed. Tanter and Ullman, pp. 206–7.
36. E. Kedourie, *England and the Middle East* (London: Bowes & Bowes, 1956) p. 9.
37. J. Rosenau (ed.), *Linkage Politics* (New York: Free Press, 1969) p. 44.
38. Empirical conclusions do not always support this generalised view. For example, see I. W. Zartman, *International Relations in the New Africa* (New Jersey: Prentice-Hall, 1966) p. 53. 'Although there may be some relation between domestic and foreign politics . . . for the most part, intra-African foreign policy has little to do with domestic needs and

purposes. Instead it is often an exercise in pure politics . . . and at times has no other criterion than whim, emotion or accident.'

39. J. Rosenau, 'Introduction: Political Science in a Shrinking World', in *Linkage Politics*, ed. Rosenau, p. 4.
40. J. Rosenau, 'Compatibility, Consensus and an Emerging Political Science of Adaptation', *American Political Science Review*, vol. 61, no. 4 (Dec 1967) p. 985.
41. See, for example, E. Morse, 'The Transformation of Foreign Policies: Modernisation, Interdependence, and Externalisation', *World Politics*, vol. 22 (Apr 1970) pp. 379–83, and 'Crisis Diplomacy, Interdependence, and the Politics of Internation Economic Relations', in *Theory and Policy in International Relations*, ed. Tanter and Ullman.
42. Rosenau, 'Introduction: Political Science', p. 2.
43. A point further developed by A. Scott, *The Revolution in Statecraft* (New York: Random House, 1965), and *The Functioning of the International Political System* (London: Collier-Macmillan, 1967) ch. 13.
44. W. Hanrieder, 'International and Comparative Politics: Toward a Synthesis', *World Politics*, vol. 20, no. 3 (Apr 1968) p. 481.
45. J. Galtung, 'The Social Sciences', in *Contending Approaches to International Politics*, ed. Knorr and Rosenau, p. 274 and n. 24.
46. J. Rosenau, 'Toward the Study of National–International Linkages', in *Linkage Politics*, ed. Rosenau, p. 51.
47. Ibid. p. 46.
48. Ibid. p. 51.
49. *The Concise Oxford Dictionary* (Oxford University Press, 1964) p. 751.
50. Rosenau, 'Toward the Study', p. 60.
51. Ibid. p. 49.
52. See his new linkage framework in J. Rosenau, 'Theorizing Across Systems: Linkage Politics Revisited', in *Conflict Behavior and Linkage Politics*, ed. J. Wilkenfeld (New York: David McKay, 1973) pp. 53–6.
53. K. Deutsch, 'External Influences on the Internal Behavior of States', in *Approaches to Comparative and International Politics*, ed. R. B. Farrell (Evanston: North Western University Press, 1966).
54. D. A. Chalmers, 'Developing on the Periphery: External Factors in Latin American Politics', in *Linkage Politics*, ed. Rosenau. Cf. N. D. Palmer, 'Foreign Policy and Political Development: International and Comparative Dimensions', *The Indian Journal of Political Science*, vol. 33, no. 3 (July–Sep 1972) pp. 253–69.
55. Chalmers, 'Developing on the Periphery', p. 68.
56. M. Meadows, 'Theories of External–Internal Political Relationships: a Case Study of Indonesia and the Philippines', *Asian Studies*, vol. 6, no. 3 (Dec 1968) pp. 297–324.
57. Deutsch, 'External Influences', p. 18.
58. Meadows, 'Theories', p. 315.
59. Ibid. p. 314.
60. R. Macridis (ed.), *Foreign Policy in World Politics* (New Jersey: Prentice-Hall, 1962).

61. Rosenau, 'Pre-Theories and Theories of Foreign Policy', in *Approaches to Comparative and International Politics*, ed. Farrell, p. 31.
62. Ibid. p. 52.
63. Ibid. p. 65.
64. Ibid. pp. 89, 90–1.
65. Ibid. p. 47.

Suffice it to note that the potency of a systemic variable is considered to vary inversely with the size of the country (there being greater resources available to larger countries and thus lesser dependence on the international system than is the case with smaller countries), that the potency of an idiosyncratic factor is assumed to be greater in less developed economies (there being fewer of the restraints which bureaucracy and large-scale organisation impose in more developed economies), that for the same reason a role variable is accorded greater potency in more developed economies, that a societal variable is considered to be more potent in open polities than in closed ones (there being a lesser need for officials in the latter to heed non-governmental demands than in the former), and that for the same reason governmental variables are more potent than societal variables in closed polities than in open ones.

Despite Rosenau's covering note to the effect that given the present undeveloped state of the field, rankings like these can be neither proved nor disproved, their impressionistic and question-begging character should be self-evident.

66. Ibid. p. 44, n. 44.
67. Ibid. p. 49.
68. Jones, *Analysing Foreign Policy*, pp. 115–16.
69. Rosenau, 'Pre-Theories and Theories of Foreign Policy', pp. 51–2.
70. Ibid. pp. 89–92.
71. Ibid. p. 47.
72. Ibid. p. 47.
73. J. Rosenau, 'Foreign Policy as an Issue-area', in *Domestic Sources of Foreign Policy*, ed. Rosenau (New York: Free Press, 1967).
74. Ibid. p. 46.
75. Ibid. p. 49.
76. Ibid. p. 22.
77. Rosenau, 'Pre-Theories and Theories of Foreign Policy', pp. 71–88.
78. Ibid. pp. 71–2, and T. Lowi, 'American Business, Public Policy, Case-studies, and Political Theory', *World Politics*, vol. 16, no. 4 (July 1964) pp. 677–715.
79. W. Hanrieder, *West German Foreign Policy, 1949–1963* (California: Stanford University Press, 1967) p. 230.
80. Rosenau, 'Toward the Study', p. 46.
81. See W. Hanrieder, 'Compatibility and Consensus: a Proposal for the Conceptual Linkage of External and Internal Dimensions of Foreign Policy', *American Political Science Reivew*, vol. 61, no. 4 (Dec 1967); and J. Rosenau, 'Compatibility, Consensus and an Emerging Political

Science of Adaptation', *American Political Science Review*, vol. 61, no. 4 (Dec 1967) pp. 983 and 984; also Hanrieder, 'Communications', *American Political Science Review*, vol. 61, no. 4 (Dec 1967) p. 1097.

82. However, see the attempt by Charles Hermann to organise information provided in books by K. Waltz (*Foreign Policy and Democratic Politics: the American and British Experience* [Boston: Little, Brown, 1967]), and Z. Brzezinski and S. Huntington (*Political Power: USA/USSR* [New York: Viking Press, 1967]) under the factor-group headings Rosenau provides, in 'The Comparative Study of Foreign Policy', *World Politics*, vol. 20, no. 3 (Apr 1968) pp. 521–34.
83. By Rosenau's criteria 'status' resources cannot be photographed by a camera and money cannot buy them (intangible end and means), while 'territorial' resources can be photographed, but again cannot be bought (tangible end and intangible means). See matrix in Meadows, 'Theories of External–Internal Political Relationships', p. 318.
84. Ibid.
85. Ibid.
86. Ibid. p. 319 n.
87. Ibid. p. 322 n.
88. Ibid. p. 324.
89. G. Modelski, *A Theory of Foreign Policy* (New York: Praeger, 1962).
90. Ibid. p. 39
91. Jones, *Analysing Foreign Policy*, p. 98.
92. Modelski, *A Theory of Foreign Policy*, p. 126.
93. Ibid. p. 129.
94. Ibid. pp. 1–2.

CHAPTER 3

1. P. Handler (ed.), *Biology and the Future of Man* (Oxford University Press, 1970) p. 165.
2. F. Rhodes, *The Evolution of Life* (Harmondsworth: Penguin, 1962) p. 18.
3. E. Barghoorn, 'The Oldest Fossils', *Scientific American*, vol. 224, no. 5 (May 1971) p. 32.
4. M. Gardner, *The Ambidextrous Universe* (Harmondsworth: Penguin, 1970) p. 151.
5. T. Dobzhansky, *The Biology of Ultimate Concern* (London: Rapp & Whiting, 1967) pp. 53–5.
6. T. Thorson, *Biopolitics* (New York: Holt, Rinehart & Winston, 1970) p. 178.
7. Dobzhansky, *The Biology of Ultimate Concern*, p. 57.
8. P. Teilhard de Chardin, *The Phenomenon of Man* (London: Fontana, 1969) p. 243.
9. W. Sullivan, *We Are Not Alone*, revised ed. (New York: McGraw-Hill, 1966) p. 290.
10. Dobzhansky, *The Biology of Ultimate Concern*, p. 45.

11. Thorson, *Biopolitics*, pp. 179–80.
12. Teilhard de Chardin, *The Phenomenon of Man*, p. 307.
13. C. Geertz, 'The Impact of the Concept of Culture' in *New Views on the Nature of Man*, ed. J. Platt (University of Chicago Press, 1965) pp. 112–13.
14. G. Vickers, *Value Systems and Social Process* (London: Tavistock, 1968) p. 61.
15. A. Alland, *Evolution and Human Behavior* (New York: Natural History Press, 1967).
16. 'Coming of Age', *Scientific American*, vol. 226, no. 2 (Feb 1972) p. 41.
17. I. Asimov, *The Universe* (Harmondsworth: Penguin, 1971) p. 334.
18. A. Wallenquist, *The Penguin Dictionary of Astronomy* (Harmondsworth: Penguin, 1968) p. 101.
19. Sullivan, *We Are Not Alone*, ch. 19.
20. J. Platt, *The Step to Man* (New York: Wiley, 1966) p. 151.
21. See H. Stretton, *The Political Sciences* (London: Routledge & Kegan Paul, 1969) part 2 and chs 13, 14.
22. Thorson, *Biopolitics*.
23. J. Monod, *Chance and Necessity* (London: Collins, 1972) pp. 48–9.
24. These are, respectively, the diachronic and synchronic approaches. See J. Galtung, 'The Social Sciences', in *Contending Approaches to International Politics*, ed. Knorr and Rosenau, pp. 249–59.
25. K. Holsti, *International Politics: a Framework for Analysis*, 2nd ed. (New Jersey: Prentice-Hall, 1972) ch. 2.
26. R. Rummel, 'Some Empirical Findings on Nations and their Behavior', *World Politics*, vol. 21, no. 2 (1969) p. 226.
27. W. J. M. Mackenzie, *Politics and Social Science* (Harmondsworth: Penguin, 1967) pp. 33–4.
28. K. Boulding, *The Meaning of the Twentieth Century* (London: Allen & Unwin, 1965) p. 71.
29. Ibid. pp. 69–71.
30. Mackenzie, *Politics and Social Science*, p. 34.
31. F. Schuman, *International Politics*, 6th ed. (New York: McGraw-Hill, 1958) pp. 6–7.
32. G. Modelski, *Principles of World Politics* (New York: Free Press, 1972).
33. Mackenzie, *Politics and Social Science*, pp. 35–6.
34. Modelski, *Principles of World Politics*, p. 10.
35. Ibid. p. 11.
36. Ibid. p. 26.
37. Ibid. p. 11.
38. Ibid. p. 25.
39. Ibid. p. 27.
40. Ibid.
41. Ibid. pp. 33–4.
42. Ibid. p. 39.
43. J. Burton, *Systems, States, Diplomacy and Rules* (Cambridge University Press, 1968) ch. 10 (1).
44. Modelski, *Principles of World Politics*, pp. 53–4.

45. Ibid. p. 55.
46. Ibid. pp. 55–6.
47. Ibid. p. 34.
48. G. Daniel, *The First Civilisations: the Archaeology of Their Origins* (Harmondsworth: Penguin, 1971) p. 79.
49. See, however, C. Gordon, *Before Columbus* (New York: Crown, 1971).
50. Daniel, *The First Civilisations*, p. 177.
51. O. Spengler, *The Decline of the West* (New York: Knopf, 1961) vols 1 and 2.
52. A. Toynbee, *A Study of History*, Somervell abridgement (Oxford University Press, 1946 and 1957) p. 248.
53. Ibid. p. 11.
54. Ibid. pp. 242–3.
55. Ibid. p. 547.
56. Ibid. p. 328.
57. Spengler, *The Decline of the West*, preface to rev. ed., p. xiv.
58. Ibid. vol. I, table I.
59. Ibid. vol. I, table II.
60. Ibid. vol. I, table III.
61. Ibid. vol. II, p. 500.
62. Ibid. vol. II, p. 503.
63. Ibid. vol. II, p. 501.
64. Ibid. vol. II, p. 503.
65. Ibid.
66. Ibid. vol. II, pp. 503–4.
67. Ibid. p. 504.
68. See L. White, *The Evolution of Culture* (New York: McGraw-Hill, 1954) pp. 19–28.

CHAPTER 4

1. H. Marcuse, *One-Dimensional Man* (London: Sphere, 1968) p. 10.
2. R. Hailbroner, *The Future as History* (New York: Grove Press, 1961) p. 193.
3. F. Engels, *Herr Eugen Dühring's Revolution in Science* (Anti-Dühring), trans. Emile Burns, ed. C. P. Dutt (London: Lawrence & Wishart, 1934) pp. 307, 311–12.
4. See F. Fanon, *The Wretched of the Earth* (New York: Grove Press, 1965).
5. H. Arendt, *The Human Condition* (New York: Doubleday Anchor, 1959) p. 225.
6. Ibid. p. 246.
7. Ibid. p. 296.
8. Monod, *Chance and Necessity*, p. 50.
9. M. Seeman, 'Alienation: a Map', *Psychology Today*, vol. 5, no. 3 (Aug 1971) pp. 83–4.
10. R. Laing, *The Politics of Experience* (Harmondsworth: Penguin, 1967) pp. 11, 12.

11. Ibid. p. 24.
12. Ibid. p. 137.
13. V. Frankl, *Man's Search for Meaning* (London: Hodder & Stoughton, 1964) and 'Reductionism and Nihilism' in *Beyond Reductionism*, ed. A. Koestler and J. Smythies (New York: Macmillan, 1970).
14. Marcuse, *One-Dimensional Man*, p. 26.
15. Ibid. p. 20.
16. Ibid. p. 21.
17. E. Fromm, *The Sane Society* (New York: Holt, Rinehart & Winston, 1962) p. 69.
18. Ibid. p. 72.
19. Ibid. p. 124.
20. See E. Fromm, *The Art of Loving* (London: Allen & Unwin, 1961) ch. 2, 'The Theory of Love'.
21. Fromm, *The Sane Society*, p. 196.
22. K. Walker, *Diagnosis of Man* (Harmondsworth: Penguin, 1962) p. 106.
23. Frankl, *Man's Search for Meaning*, p. 120.
24. L. Mumford, *The Conduct of Life* (London: Secker & Warburg, 1952) p. 7.
25. Ibid. p. 55.
26. Ibid. p. 57.
27. Ibid. pp. 35–6.
28. G. Steiner, *In Bluebeard's Castle* (London: Faber & Faber, 1971) p. 98.
29. Ibid. p. 103.
30. Ibid. p. 104.
31. B. Murchland, *The Age of Alienation* (New York: Random House, 1971).

CHAPTER 5

1. B. de Jouvenal, 'Political Science and Prevision', *American Political Science Review*, vol. 59, no. 1 (Mar 1965) p. 29.
2. B. Akzin, 'On Conjecture in Political Science', *Political Studies*, vol. 14, no. 1 (Feb 1966) pp. 4–5.
3. de Jouvenal, 'Political Science', p. 35.
4. Ibid. p. 36.
5. P. Goodman, 'Can Technology be Humane?', *New York Review of Books* (20 Nov 1969) p. 30.
6. Akzin, 'On Conjecture', pp. 10–11.
7. H. Kahn and A. Wiener, *The Year 2000* (New York: Macmillan, 1970), and H. Kahn and B. Bruce-Briggs, *Things to Come* (New York: Macmillan, 1972). See also H. Kahn, 'The Alternative World Futures Approach', in *New Approaches to International Relations*, ed. M. Kaplan (New York: St. Martin's Press, 1968). A brief but interesting comparison might be made with Harold Lasswell's 'The Political Science of Science: An Inquiry into the Possible Reconciliation of

Mastery and Freedom', *American Political Science Review*, vol. 50, no. 4 (Dec 1965) pp. 961–79.

8. M. Levy, 'Our Ever and Future Jungle', *World Politics*, vol. 22, no. 1 (Oct 1969) p. 307.
9. Ibid. p. 315.
10. Ibid. p. 317.
11. Ibid. pp. 317–19.
12. Ibid. pp. 325–7.
13. Kahn and Bruce-Briggs, *Things to Come*, p. 231.
14. Ibid. p. 116.
15. These maxims range from the general statement that: 'The friend of an enemy is often an enemy', to the unsinkable fact that: 'A hostile but submerged and suppressed emotion may easily emerge when conditions allow it to', in *New Approaches*, ed. Kaplan, p. 90.
16. Ibid. p. 83.
17. Ibid. pp. 108–18.
18. I. de Sola Pool, 'The International System in the Next Half Century', *Daedalus*, vol. 96, no. 3 (Summer 1967) p. 932.
19. J. Galtung, 'On the Future of the International System', in *Mankind 2000*, ed. R. Jungk and J. Galtung (Oslo: Universitets-forlaget, 1969) p. 36, n. 1.
20. Ibid. p. 25.
21. Ibid. p. 26.
22. J. Galtung, 'On the Future of Human Society', *Futures*, vol. 2 (June 1970) pp. 132–42.
23. B. Russett, 'The Ecology of Future International Politics', in *International Politics and Foreign Policy*, ed. J. Rosenau, rev. ed. (New York: The Free Press, 1969).
24. R. May, 'A Survey of the Crisis', *Australian Left Review*, no. 36 (July 1972) p. 4.
25. J. Maddox, *The Doomsday Syndrome* (London: Macmillan, 1972) p. 37.
26. D. Meadows *et al.*, *The Limits to Growth* (London: Earth Island, 1972); D. Meadows, 'The Predicament of Mankind', *The Futurist* (Aug 1972).
27. Meadows, 'The Predicament of Mankind', p. 138.
28. D. Meadows and J. Randers, 'Adding the Time Dimension to Environmental Policy', *International Organization*, vol. 26 (1972) pp. 213–14.
29. Meadows, 'The Predicament of Mankind', p. 144.
30. Ibid.
31. Meadows, *The Limits to Growth*, p. 142.
32. W. Beckerman, 'Economists, Scientists and Environmental Catastrophe', *Oxford Economic Papers* (New Series) vol. 24, no. 3 (Nov 1972) pp. 332–3.
33. Ibid. p. 335.
34. See chs 1–14 as published in *Futures*, vol. 5, nos 1 and 2 (Feb and Apr 1973).
35. C. Freeman, 'Malthus With a Computer', *Futures*, vol. 5, no. 1 (Feb 1973) p. 10.

36. K. Pavitt, 'Malthus and Other Economists', *Futures*, vol. 5, no. 2 (Apr 1973) p. 173.
37. T. Sinclair, 'Environmentalism', *Futures*, vol. 5, no. 2 (Apr 1973) p. 201.
38. See for example, J. Galtung, ' "The Limits to Growth" and "Class Politics" ', *Journal of Peace Research*, vol. 10 (1973) pp. 101–14.
39. D. Meadows *et al.*, 'A Response to Sussex', *Futures*, vol. 5, no. 1 (Feb 1973) p. 135.
40. Ibid. p. 138.
41. Ibid. p. 143.
42. Beckerman, 'Economists, Scientists and Environmental Catastrophe', p. 327.
43. Meadows, *The Limits to Growth*, p. 46.
44. P. and A. Ehrlich, *Population, Resources and Environment* (San Francisco: Freeman, 1970) p. 1.
45. P. Ehrlich, 'The Population Explosion: Facts and Fiction', *Sierra Club Bulletin* (Oct 1968).
46. M. Caldwell, 'The Politics of Ecology', *Australian Left Review*, no. 36 (July 1972) p. 28.
47. S. Weissman, 'Why the Population Bomb is a Rockefeller Baby', *Ramparts* (May 1970) p. 43.
48. Ibid. p. 47.
49. R. C. North, 'The International Political System: the Future', in *Toward Century 21*, ed. C. S. Wallia (New York: Basic Books, 1970) p. 169.
50. N. Choucri and R. C. North, 'Dynamics of International Conflict: Some Policy Implications of Population, Resources and Technology', *World Politics*, Supplement, vol. 24 (Spring 1972) p. 86.
51. N. Choucri and J. Bennett, 'Population, Resources and Technology: Political Implications of the Environmental Crisis', *International Organization*, vol. 26, no. 1 (1972) pp. 183–4.
52. Ibid. p. 184. The Correlates of War Project (J. D. Singer) and the Studies in International Conflict and Integration Project (R. C. North).
53. Ibid. pp. 198–9.
54. E. Woodhouse, 'Revisioning the Future of the Third World: an Ecological Perspective on Development', *World Politics*, vol. 25, no. 1 (Oct 1972) pp. 29–30.

CHAPTER 6

1. M. Banks, 'Systems Analysis and the Study of Regions', *International Studies Quarterly*, vol. 13, no. 4 (Dec 1969) p. 346.
2. G. Modelski, *Principles of World Politics* (New York: Free Press, 1972) pp. 6–7.
3. Banks, 'Systems Analysis', p. 347.
4. J. G. Miller, 'Living Systems: Cross-level Hypotheses', *Behavioral Science*, vol. 10, no. 4 (Oct 1965) pp. 380–411.

5. J. G. Miller, 'Living Systems: Basic Concepts', *Behavioral Science*, vol. 10, no. 3 (July 1965) p. 203.
6. Miller, 'Living Systems: Cross-level Hypotheses', p. 381.
7. By analogy: 'A formation of troops in which the successive divisions are placed parallel to one another, but no two on the same alignment.' *Shorter Oxford English Dictionary*.
8. Miller, 'Living Systems: Cross-level Hypotheses', p. 383.
9. Ibid. p. 407.
10. Miller, 'Living Systems: Basic Concepts', p. 204.
11. Miller, 'Living Systems: Cross-level Hypotheses', p. 402, Hypotheses 5, 3–9.
12. Ibid. p. 402.
13. Ibid. p. 403, Hypotheses 5, 3–15.
14. Mao Tse-tung, Speech at Supreme State Conference, 28 January 1968 in Mao Chu-hsi tui Peng, Huang, Chang, Chou fan-tang chi-t'uan ti p'i-pan [Chairman Mao's Criticism of the P'eng-Huang-Chang-Chou Antiparty Clique], *Chinese Law and Government*, vol. 1, no. 4 (1969) pp. 10–14.
15. See the work of Ralph Gerard discussed by Jerome Stephens, 'Some Questions About a More Biologically Oriented Political Science' *Midwest Journal of Political Science*, vol. 14 (1970) esp. pp. 688–701.
16. Modelski, *Principles*, p. 7.
17. G. Almond and J. Coleman, *The Politics of the Developing Areas* (New Jersey: Princeton University Press, 1960).
18. C. Alger, 'Comparison of Intra-national and International Politics', *American Political Science Review*, vol. 57 (June 1963) pp. 406–19.
19. For example see Kingsley Davis, 'The Myth of Functional Analysis as a Special Method in Sociology and Anthropology', *The American Sociological Review*, vol. 24, no. 6 (Dec 1969) pp. 757–72.
20. D. Easton, *A Systems Analysis of Political Life* (New York: Wiley, 1965); *A Framework for Political Analysis* (New Jersey: Prentice-Hall, 1965).
21. M. B. Nicholson and P. A. Reynolds, 'General Systems, the International System, and the Eastonian Analysis', *Political Studies*, vol. 15, no. 1 (1967) pp. 12–31.
22. For a good short summary see R. Scott, 'Systems Analysis Without Tears: Easton and Almond', *Politics* (Australian Political Science Association) vol. 7, no. 1 (May 1972) pp. 74–81.
23. D. V. Edwards, *International Political Analysis* (New York: Holt, Rinehart & Winston, 1969) pp. 265–6.
24. K. Deutsch and J. Singer, 'Multipolar Power Systems and International Stability', *World Politics*, vol. 16 (Apr 1964) pp. 390–406; K. Waltz, 'International Structure, National Force, and the Balance of World Power', *Journal of International Affairs*, vol. 21, no. 2 (1967) pp. 215–31; R. Rosecrance, 'Bipolarity, Multipolarity and the Future', *Journal of Conflict Resolution*, vol. 10 (Sep 1966) pp. 314–27.
25. J. Burton, *Systems, States, Diplomacy and Rules* (Cambridge University Press, 1968) p. 27.
26. Ibid. p. 10.

27. Ibid. p. 8. Also J. Burton, *World Society* (Cambridge University Press, 1972) pp. 35–45.
28. W. J. M. Mackenzie, *Politics and Social Science* (Harmondsworth: Penguin, 1967) p. 340.
29. M. Kaplan, *System and Process in International Politics* (New York: Wiley, 1957).
30. M. Kaplan, 'The New Great Debate: Traditionalism vs. Science in International Relations', *World Politics*, vol. 19. no. 1 (Oct 1966) p. 8. See also Kaplan's four variations to his basic six – the very loose bipolar system, the detente system, the unstable bloc system, and the incomplete nuclear diffusion system, in his article 'Some Problems of International Systems Research', in *International Political Communities* (New York: Doubleday, 1966).
31. Kaplan, *System and Process*, p. 25.
32. J. Dougherty and R. Pfaltzgraff, *Contending Theories of International Relations* (New York: Lippincott, 1971) p. 130.
33. R. Rosecrance, *Action and Reaction in World Politics: Systems in Perspective* (Boston: Little, Brown, 1963).
34. Burton, *Systems, States, Diplomacy and Rules*.
35. J. Burton in *Conflict in Society*, ed. A. de Reuck and G. Knight (London: Churchill, 1966) p. 399.
36. Burton, *Systems, States, Diplomacy and Rules*, p. 36.
37. M. Povolny, review of *Systems, States, Diplomacy and Rules*, in *American Political Science Review*, vol. 63 (1969) p. 980.
38. J. D. Singer, 'The Global System and its Subsystems: a Developmental View', in *Linkage Politics*, ed. J. Rosenau (New York: Free Press, 1969) p. 41.
39. See here J. Rosenau, 'Foreign Policy as Adaptive Behavior', *Comparative Politics*, vol. 2 (1970) pp. 365–87, for another attempt to outline how a state copes with or stimulates changes in the external environment that might serve to keep the essential structures of the society within acceptable limits. It is open to exactly the same critique.
40. Burton, in *Conflict in Society*, ed. de Reuck and Knight, p. 400.
41. Burton, *Systems, States, Diplomacy and Rules*, ch. 10 (1).
42. Ludwig von Bertalanffy, *General System Theory* (New York: Braziller, 1968) p. 17.
43. K. Deutsch, 'Toward a Cybernetic Model of Man and Society', in *Modern Systems Research for the Behavioral Scientist*, ed. W. Buckley (Chicago: Aldine, 1968) p. 390.
44. K. Deutsch, *The Nerves of Government* (New York: Free Press, 1963) pp. 77–8.
45. W. R. Ashby, *An Introduction to Cybernetics* (New York: Wiley, 1956) p. 211.
46. Deutsch, *The Nerves of Government*, p. 95.
47. G. Vickers, *Value Systems and Social Process* (London: Tavistock, 1968) p. 167.
48. Ibid. p. 166.

49. C. McClelland, *Theory and the International System* (New York: Macmillan, 1966) p. 134.
50. K. Deutsch, *Nationalism and Social Communication* (Cambridge, Mass.: M.I.T., 1953) p. 73.

CHAPTER 7

1. First used, it seems, by L. Caldwell in 'Biopolitics: Science, Ethics and Public Policy', *The Yale Review*, vol. 51 (1964) pp. 1–16. The noxious legacy of Social Darwinism largely prevented the development of such a subject until the advent of more recent findings.
2. P. Corning, 'The Biological Bases of Behavior and Some Implications for Political Science', *World Politics*, vol. 23, no. 2 (Apr 1971) p. 321.
3. See the beginning of Chapter 2.
4. K. Waltz, *Man, The State and War* (New York: Columbia University Press, 1959).
5. J. D. Singer, 'The Levels of Analysis Problem in International Relations', in *The International System: Theoretical Essays*, ed. K. Knorr and S. Verba (Princeton University Press, 1961).
6. Roger Sperry, 'Mind, Brain and Humanist Values', in *New Views of the Nature of Man*, ed. J. Platt (University of Chicago Press, 1965) pp. 74–80. Compare here the interesting argument by S. Rose about translating statements between levels of hierarchy in *The Conscious Brain* (London: Weidenfeld & Nicolson, 1973) ch. 13.
7. P. Handler (ed.), *Biology and the Future of Man* (Oxford University Press, 1970) p. 402.
8. J. Rosenau (ed.), *International Politics and Foreign Policy*, 2nd ed. (New York: Free Press, 1969).
9. P. Maclean, 'The Paranoid Streak in Man', in *Beyond Reductionism*, ed. A. Koestler and J. Smythies (New York: Macmillan, 1970) pp. 263–4.
10. Ibid. p. 265.
11. Ibid. p. 275.
12. Ibid. pp. 266–7.
13. Ibid. p. 272. Assuming, that is, the neocortex communicates in 'verbal' terms, whatever Maclean means by this idea.
14. Smythies in Koestler and Smythies, *Beyond Reductionism*, p. 276.
15. Maclean, 'The Paranoid Streak in Man', p. 275.
16. A. Koestler, *The Ghost in the Machine* (London: Pan, 1967) chs 16 and 17.
17. Ibid. p. 276.
18. Ibid. p. 326.
19. Maclean, 'The Paranoid Streak in Man', p. 264.
20. Koestler, *The Ghost in the Machine*, p. 340.
21. Ibid. p. 311.
22. See S. Kety, 'New Perspectives in Psychopharmacology', in *Beyond Reductionism*, ed. Koestler and Smythies, p. 347; and J. Cole, 'Drugs

and Control of the Mind' in *Man and Civilisation: Control of the Mind*, ed. S. Farber and R. Wilson (New York: McGraw-Hill, 1961) p. 112.

23. N. Calder, *The Mind of Man* (London: B.B.C., 1970) pp. 176–278. See also J. Davies, 'Violence and Aggression: Innate or Not?', *Western Political Quarterly*, vol. 23 (1970) pp. 621–2: 'The knowledge thus far is altogether inadequate for any such conclusions. . . . Koestler may be right and he may be wrong, but the great leap forward – the inference he makes as to the fragility of reason in its efforts to control passion – is no more demonstrable now than it was when Freud said substantially the same thing. . . . Or when Hobbes emphasised the need for an omnipresent monarch to control man's passions.'
24. Ibid. p. 277.
25. D. Woolridge, *The Machinery of the Brain* (New York: McGraw-Hill, 1963) p. 147.
26. S. Barnett, *'Instinct' and 'Intelligence'* (Harmondsworth: Penguin, 1970) p. 177.
27. Maclean, 'The Paranoid Streak in Man', p. 272.
28. W. Penfield, 'The Mind and its Integration' in *Man and Civilisation*, ed. Farber and Wilson, p. 11. Penfield is presumably referring here to the corpus callosum.
29. Ibid. p. 10; and see also Barnett, *'Instinct' and 'Intelligence'*, pp. 173–5.
30. Penfield, 'The Mind and its Integration', p. 11.
31. Maclean, 'The Paranoid Streak in Man', p. 272.
32. This concept is far from satisfactory as a description of neural communication, but Maclean is no more specific than this.
33. Calder, *The Mind of Man*, p. 278.
34. H. Kahn and B. Bruce-Briggs, *Things to Come* (New York: Macmillan, 1972) p. 209.
35. J. Delgado, *Physical Control of the Mind* (New York: Harper & Row, 1969) p. 142.
36. R. Boelkins and J. Heiser, 'Biological Bases of Aggression', in *Violence and the Struggle for Existence*, ed. D. Daniels, M. Gilula and F. Ochberg (Boston: Little, Brown, 1970) p. 26.
37. J. Delgado, 'Electrical Stimulation of the Brain', *Psychology Today*, vol. 3 (1969) p. 53.
38. See, for example, J. Delgado, 'Aggression and Defense under Cerebral Radio Control', in *Aggression and Defense*, ed. C. Clemente and D. Lindsley (University of California Press, 1967).
39. G. Quarton, 'Deliberate Efforts to Control Human Behavior and Modify Personality', *Daedalus*, vol. 96, no. 3 (Summer 1967) p. 837.
40. Except of course for the micropipette and coated needle techniques already mentioned.
41. The phenothiazines and Rauwolfia alkaloids are commonly cited in this regard.
42. Cole, 'Drugs and Control of the Mind', p. 115.
43. D. Krech, 'Horizons of Psychopharmacology', in *Man and Civilisation*, ed. Farber and Wilson, p. 121.
44. P. London, *Behavior Control* (New York: Harper & Row, 1969) p. 128.

45. H. Hyden, 'The Mind and its Integration', in *Man and Civilisation*, ed. Farber and Wilson, p. 39.
46. Ibid.
47. Ibid.
48. D. Jaros, 'Biochemical Desocialisation: Depressants and Political Behavior', *Midwest Journal of Political Science* (Feb 1972) pp. 1–28.
49. Ibid. p. 11.
50. D. Krech, 'Brain Research', in *Toward Century 21*, ed. C. S. Wallia (New York: Basic Books, 1970), p. 27.
51. R. Clarke, *We All Fall Down* (Harmondsworth: Penguin, 1968) p. 44.
52. R. Stauffer, 'The Biopolitics of Underdevelopment', *Comparative Political Studies*, vol. 2 (1969–70) pp. 361–87.
53. Calder, *The Mind of Man*, p. 241.
54. Stauffer, 'The Biopolitics of Underdevelopment', p. 379.

CHAPTER 8

1. *Shorter Oxford English Dictionary.*
2. J. Bleibtreu, *The Parable of the Beast* (London: Paladin, 1970) pp. 33–4.
3. N. Tinbergen, 'On War and Peace – Animals and Man', in *Man and Animal*, ed. H. Friedrich (London: Paladin, 1971) p. 121.
4. P. Corning, 'The Biological Bases of Behavior and some Implications for Political Science', *World Politics*, vol. 23, no. 3 (Apr 1971) p. 366. Corning has been careful to avoid the ideological non-science of the first of the biopoliticians – the Social Darwinists.
5. Ibid. pp. 361–2.
6. Ibid. p. 363.
7. Ibid. p. 358.
8. Ibid. pp. 368–9.
9. Ibid. p. 355.
10. Ibid.
11. A. Rapoport, 'Is War-making a Characteristic of Human Beings or of Culture?', *Scientific American* (Oct 1965) p. 116.
12. Corning, 'The Biological Bases of Behavior', p. 333.
13. Ibid. p. 321.
14. Ibid. p. 342.
15. J. Davies, 'Violence and Aggression: Innate or Not?', *The Western Political Quarterly*, vol. 23 (1970) pp. 617–18.
16. L. Tiger and R. Fox, *The Imperial Animal* (New York: Holt, Rinehart & Winston, 1971) p. 15.
17. Ibid. pp. 21–2.
18. Ibid. p. 16.
19. K. Lorenz, *On Aggression* (London: Methuen, 1966) p. 204.
20. I. Eibl-Eibesfeldt, *Ethology* (New York: Holt, Rinehart & Winston, 1970) p. 398. See ch. 18.
21. Ibid. p. 431.
22. G. Quarton, 'Deliberate Efforts to Control Human Behavior and

Modify Personality', *Daedalus* (1967) p. 839. See also D. Freeman, 'Human Nature and Culture', in *Man and the New Biology*, ed. R. O. Slatyer (Canberra: Australian National University Press, 1970).

23. M. F. A. Montagu (ed.), *Man and Aggression* (Oxford University Press, 1968) pp. xii–xiii, 15.
24. Ibid. p. xi.
25. Barnett, *'Instinct' and 'Intelligence'*, p. 211.
26. Corning, 'The Biological Bases of Behavior', p. 323.
27. R. Ardrey, *The Territorial Imperative* (London: Fontana, 1969) p. 47.
28. Ibid. p. 42.
29. Lorenz, *On Aggression*. See also his 'Ritualized Fighting', in *The Natural History of Aggression*, ed. J. Carthy and F. Ebling (New York: Academic Press, 1964).
30. J. Crook, 'The Nature of Territorial Aggression', in *Man and Aggression*, ed. Montagu, p. 146.
31. Lorenz, *On Aggression*, p. 39.
32. Ibid. p. 234.
33. Ibid. pp. 218–19.
34. Ibid. pp. 254–5.
35. L. Tiger, *Men in Groups* (London: Nelson, 1969) ch. 7.
36. Tinbergen, 'On War and Peace', p. 139.
37. Ibid. p. 127.
38. Ardrey, *The Territorial Imperative*, p. 16.
39. Ibid. p. 94.
40. Ibid. p. 210.
41. Ibid. p. 206.
42. Crook, 'The Nature of Territorial Aggression', p. 173.
43. A. Elms, 'Horoscopes and Ardrey', *Psychology Today*, vol. 605 (Oct 1972) p. 127.
44. Ardrey, *The Territorial Imperative*, p. 30.
45. Crook, 'The Nature of Territorial Aggression', p. 30.
46. Lorenz, *On Aggression*, p. 230.
47. Ibid.
48. Ibid. p. 231.
49. Tiger and Fox, *The Imperial Animal*, p. 37.
50. L. Calhoun, 'Population Density and Social Pathology', *Scientific American*, vol. 206, no. 12 (Feb 1962) pp. 139–48.
51. Bleibtreu, *The Parable of the Beast*, p. 189.
52. Ibid. p. 187.
53. M. Bressler, 'Sociology, Biology and Ideology', in *Genetics*, ed. D. Glass (New York: Rockefeller University Press, 1968) p. 189.
54. D. Hebb, 'The Mind and Its Integration', in *Man and Civilisation*, ed. Farber and Wilson, p. 48.
55. MacF. Burnet, *The Dominant Mammal* (Melbourne: Heinemann, 1970) p. 5.
56. R. Holloway Jr, 'Human Aggression: the Need for a Species-specific Framework', in *War: the Anthropology of Armed Conflict and Aggression*, ed. M. Fried (New York: Natural History Press, 1968) pp. 30–1.

CHAPTER 9

1. See Chapter 7.
2. See for example Ole Holsti, 'Cognitive Dynamics and Images of the Enemy', in *Image and Reality*, ed. J. Farrell and A. Smith (New York: Columbia University Press, 1967).
3. R. Stagner, *Psychological Aspects of International Conflict* (California: Brooks/Cole, 1967) p. 16.
4. J. D. Singer, 'Man and World Politics: the Psycho-cultural Interface', *Journal of Social Issues*, vol. 24, no. 3 (July 1968) p. 149.
5. Ibid. pp. 145–6.
6. P. Zimbardo and E. Ebbesen, *Influencing Attitudes and Changing Behavior* (Reading: Addison-Wesley, 1969) p. 6. See also M. Rokeach, *Beliefs, Attitudes and Values* (San Francisco: Jossey-Bass, 1968) ch. 5 and p. 134.
7. This process has been elaborated in detail by Piaget. See J. Piaget, *The Origin of Intelligence in the Child* (London: Routledge & Kegan Paul, 1966).
8. C. Osgood, G. Suci and P. Tannenbaum, *The Measurement of Meaning* (Urbana: University of Illinois Press, 1957) ch. 1, 'The Logic of Semantic Differentiation'; and Osgood's article, 'The Nature and Measurement of Meaning', *Psychological Bulletin*, vol. 49, no. 3 (May 1952) pp. 197–237.
9. B. Berelson and G. Steiner (eds), *Human Behavior: an Inventory of Scientific Findings* (New York: Harcourt, Brace & World, 1964) p. 117.
10. K. Boulding, *The Image* (University of Michigan Press, 1956) ch. 4.
11. Ibid. p. 50.
12. H. Kelman (ed.), *International Behavior: a Social-psychological Analysis* (New York: Holt, Rinehart & Winston, 1965) p. 25.
13. K. Boulding, 'The Learning and Reality-Testing Process in the International System', in *Image and Reality*, ed. Farrell and Smith, p. 14.
14. L. Festinger, *A Theory of Cognitive Dissonance* (London: Tavistock, 1957) p. 2. See also Rokeach, *Beliefs, Attitudes and Values*, ch. 4, 'The Principle of Belief Congruence and the Congruity Principle', and N. Feather, 'Organisation and Discrepancy in Cognitive Structures', *Psychological Review*, vol. 78, no. 5 (1971) pp. 355–79.
15. Festinger, *A Theory of Cognitive Dissonance*, p. 3.
16. K. Deutsch, *The Analysis of International Relations* (New Jersey: Prentice-Hall, 1968) p. 51.
17. E. Frenkel-Brunswick, 'Intolerance of Ambiguity as an Emotional and Perceptual Personality Variable', *Journal of Personality*. vol. 18 (1949) p. 134. See also T. Millon, 'Authoritarianism, Intolerance of Ambiguity, and Rigidity under Ego- and Task-involving Conditions', *Journal of Abnormal and Social Psychology*, vol. 55, no. 1 (July 1957) pp. 29–33.
18. Frenkel-Brunswick, ibid.
19. Ibid. p. 141.

20. Festinger, *A Theory of Cognitive Dissonance*, pp. 266–71.
21. Ibid. p. 267.
22. I do not wish to suggest by this paraphrase that Mao is susceptible to black and white thinking, though Mao Tse-tung Thought has not been immune from it.
23. Stagner, *Psychological Aspects*, p. 50.
24. R. White, 'Images in the Context of International Conflict: Soviet Perceptions of the US and the USSR', in *International Behavior*, ed. Kelman; and for his application of the same idea to the American-Vietnam War, *Nobody Wanted War* (New York: Doubleday, 1970). Also U. Bronfenbrenner, 'The Mirror Image in Soviet-American Relations', *Journal of Social Issues*, vol. 17 (1969), and 'Allowing for Soviet Perceptions', in *International Conflict and Behavioral Science*, ed. R. Fisher (New York: Basic Books, 1964).
25. J. Dougherty and R. Pfaltzgraff, *Contending Approaches to International Relations* (New York: Lippincott, 1971) p. 226.
26. U. Bronfenbrenner, 'Allowing for Soviet Perceptions', in *International Conflict*, ed. Fisher.
27. R. Jervis, *The Logic of Images in International Relations* (Princeton University Press, 1970) p. 3.
28. Ibid. p. 18.
29. S. Asch, *Social Psychology* (New Jersey: Prentice-Hall, 1952) ch. 16. Of related interest are S. Milgram's studies of obedience. See 'Some Conditions of Obedience and Disobedience to Authority', in *Current Studies in Social Psychology*, ed. I. Steiner and M. Fishbein (New York: Holt, Rinehart & Winston, 1965), and 'Liberating Effects of Group Pressure', *Journal of Personality and Social Psychology*, vol. 1 (1965) pp. 127–34.
30. Asch, *Social Psychology*, pp. 478–9.
31. R. Crutchfield, 'Conformity and Character', *American Psychologist*, vol. 10, no. 5 (May 1955) p. 193.
32. Ibid. p. 194.
33. Ibid. p. 196.
34. Ibid.
35. White, *Nobody Wanted War*, p. 291.
36. UNESCO: Preamble to the Constitution.
37. O. Klineberg, *The Human Dimension in International Relations* (New York: Holt, Rinehart & Winston, 1964) p. 6.
38. J. Dollard *et al.*, *Frustration and Aggression* (New Haven: Yale University Press, 1939) p. 1.
39. Ibid. p. 11.
40. J. Davies, 'Violence and Aggression: Innate or Not?', *The Western Political Quarterly*, vol. 23 (1970) pp. 617–18.
41. Dollard *et al.*, *Frustration and Aggression*, p. 11.
42. N. Miller, 'The Frustration–Aggression Hypothesis', *Psychological Review*, vol. 48 (1941) p. 338.
43. L. Berkowitz, *Aggression: a Social-psychological Analysis* (New York: McGraw-Hill, 1962) pp. 36–46.

44. Ibid. pp. 29–36.
45. Ibid. p. 31.
46. S. Diamond, 'War and the Dissociated Personality', in *War: the Anthropology of Armed Conflict and Aggression*, ed. M. Fried *et al.* (New York: Natural History Press, 1968) p. 183.
47. Ibid. pp. 183–4.
48. See A. Bandura and R. Walters, *Social Learning and Personality Development* (New York: Holt, Rinehart & Winston, 1963).
49. A. Buss, *The Psychology of Aggression* (New York: Wiley, 1961) p. 28.
50. M. Sherif and C. Sherif, 'Motivation and Intergroup Aggression', in *Development and Evolution of Behavior*, ed. L. Aronson *et al.* (San Francisco: W. H. Freeman, 1970) p. 575.
51. Ibid.
52. E. B. McNeil (ed.), *The Nature of Human Conflict* (New Jersey: Prentice-Hall, 1965) p. 36.
53. Zimbardo and Ebbeson, *Influencing Attitudes*, pp. 114–21.
54. Holsti, 'Cognitive Dynamics', p. 39.
55. R. Jervis, 'Hypotheses on Misperception' in *International Politics and Foreign Policy*, ed. Rosenau, pp. 244–6.
56. B. F. Skinner, *Walden Two* (New York: Macmillan, 1967) and *Beyond Freedom and Dignity* (London: Jonathan Cape, 1962) ch. 8.
57. J. de Rivera, *The Psychological Dimension of Foreign Policy* (Ohio: Merrill, 1968) p. 434.
58. C. Osgood, *An Alternative to War or Surrender* (Urbana: University of Illinois Press, 1962).
59. C. Osgood, 'Toward International Behavior Appropriate to a Nuclear Age', in *Psychology and International Affairs*, ed. G. Nielsen (Copenhagen: Munksgaard, 1962).
60. Ibid. p. 112.
61. Mackenzie, *Politics and Social Science*, p. 169.
62. S. Verba, *Small Groups and Political Behavior* (New Jersey: Princeton University Press, 1961) p. 24. Small-group interactions have also been studied in reference to game theory and in various simulation situations of a process or crisis kind. On the whole the results explain little about world politics and I have not reviewed them here.
63. Berelson and Steiner (eds), *Human Behavior*, ch. 8, no. C.1, p. 339.
64. Ibid. no. C8.1, p. 348.
65. Ibid. no. C8.4, p. 348.
66. Ibid. p. 334.
67. Verba, *Small Groups*, p. 27.
68. J. Burton, *Conflict and Communication* (London: Macmillan, 1969).
69. S. Hoffmann, 'Perceptions, Reality, and the Franco-American Conflict' in *Image and Reality*, ed. Farrell and Smith, pp. 57–9.

CHAPTER 10

1. R. Dahrendorf, 'Toward a Theory of Social Conflict', *Journal of Conflict Resolution*, vol. 2, no. 2 (1958) p. 175.
2. C. Fink, 'Some Conceptual Difficulties in the Theory of Social Conflict', *Journal of Conflict Resolution*, vol. 12, no. 4 (Dec 1968) p. 414.
3. Ibid.
4. Ibid. p. 416.
5. Ibid. p. 417.
6. A. Rapoport, *Fights, Games and Debates* (Ann Arbor: University of Michigan Press, 1960).
7. Fink, 'Some Conceptual Difficulties', table, p. 426.
8. Ibid. p. 456.
9. O. Young, *Tne Intellectual Bases of 'Conflict Management'*, paper presented to the 12th Bailey Conference on International Relations, London School of Economics and Political Science (Jan 1970) pp. 3–7.
10. F. Schuman, *International Politics*, 6th ed. (New York: McGraw-Hill, 1958) p. 293.
11. Ibid.
12. H. Bull, 'War and International Order', in *The Bases of International Order*, ed. A. James (Oxford University Press, 1973) p. 177.
13. F. Denton, 'Some Regularities in International Conflict, 1820–1949', *Background*, vol. 9, no. 4 (Feb 1966) pp. 283–96.
14. R. Rosecrance, *Action and Reaction in World Politics* (Boston: Little, Brown, 1963). See ch. 6.
15. F. Denton and W. Phillips, 'Some Patterns in the History of Violence', *Journal of Conflict Resolution*, vol. 12, no. 2 (June 1968) pp. 182–95.
16. Ibid. pp. 193–4.
17. J. D. Singer and M. Small, 'Patterns in International Warfare, 1816–1965', *The Annals of the American Academy of Political and Social Science* (Sep 1970) pp. 145–55.
18. For a summary of the research design and some results, see J. D. Singer, 'The "Correlates of War" Project: Interim Report and Rationale', *World Politics*, vol. 24, no. 2 (Jan 1972) pp. 243–70.
19. Singer and Small, 'Patterns in International Warfare', p. 147.
20. Singer, 'The "Correlates of War" Project', p. 265.
21. Singer and Small, 'Patterns in International Warfare', pp. 147–9.
22. Ibid. *passim*.
23. Q. Wright, *A Study of War*, 2nd ed. (University of Chicago Press, 1965) p. 1284.
24. Bull, 'War and International Order', pp. 126–7.
25. Wright, *A Study of War*, p. 1512.
26. Ibid. p. 1515.
27. Ibid. p. 1518.
28. J. March and H. Simon, *Organisations* (New York: Wiley, 1963) pp. 140–1.

29. S. Washburn, 'Conflict in Primate Society', in *Conflict in Society*, ed. A. de Reuck and J. Knight (London: J. & A. Churchill, 1966) p. 13.
30. M. Haas, 'Sources of International Conflict', in *The Analysis of International Politics*, ed. J. Rosenau, V. Davis and M. East (New York: Free Press, 1972) p. 271. Also M. Haas, *International Conflict* (New York: Bobbs-Merrill, 1974). For an interesting sidelight on American psycho-socialisation processes, see H. Targ, 'Children's Developing Orientations to International Politics', *Journal of Peace Research*, vol. 7 (1970) pp. 79–97, which documents the acceptance of a traditional Morgenthauist cold war ideology among 244 American schoolchildren and bears limited witness to the assumptions they imbibe. See the note on this by D. Krieger in *Journal of Peace Research*, vol. 8 (1971) pp. 305–6.
31. Haas, 'Sources of International Conflict', p. 271.
32. H. Magdoff, *The Age of Imperialism* (New York: Modern Reader Paperbacks, 1969) p. 15.
33. Ibid. p. 14.
34. F. Klingberg, 'Historical Periods, Trends and Cycles in International Relations', *Journal of Conflict Resolution*, vol. 14, no. 4 (1970) p. 506.
35. Ibid.
36. R. Rummel, 'The Relationship Between National Attributes and Foreign Conflict Behavior', in *Quantitative International Relations*, ed. J. D. Singer (New York: Free Press, 1968) pp. 210–11.
37. Rummel, 'Dimensions of Conflict Behavior Within and Between Nations', *General Systems Yearbook*, vol. 8 (1963) pp. 1–50.
38. Ibid. p. 5.
39. Ibid. See also Appendix I, 'Definitions of Conflict Behavior Measures', pp. 25–7.
40. Ibid. p. 23.
41. This observation would serve to refute the attempt by Dina Zinnes to arrange the foreign conflict variables along just such a scale of graduated response from the initial accusations and protests to more severe responses like troop movements and war. Her observation, for example, that the less severe forms of foreign conflict then correlate with environmental factors, is suspect as a result. D. Zinnes, 'Some Evidence Relevant to the Man–Milieu Hypotheses', in *The Analysis of International Politics*, ed. Rosenau *et al.*
42. Rummel, 'The Relationship Between National Attributes and Foreign Conflict Behavior', p. 208.
43. Rummel, 'Dimensions of Conflict Behavior', p. 22.
44. Rummel, 'Testing Some Possible Predictors of Conflict Behavior Within and Between Nations', *Peace Research Society Papers*, vol. 1 (1964) pp. 79–111.
45. The independent variables he derived from a factor analysis of domestic variables by Brian Berry.
46. R. Tanter, 'Dimensions of Conflict Behavior Within and Between Nations, 1957–1960', *Journal of Conflict Resolution*, vol. 10, no. 1 (1966) pp. 41–64.
47. Haas, 'Sources of International Conflict', p. 264.

48. Ibid. p. 264.
49. M. Haas, 'Societal Approaches to the Study of War', *Journal of Peace Research*, vol. 2 (1965) pp. 307–24.
50. Ibid. p. 318.
51. Rosecrance, *Action and Reaction in World Politics.*
52. Denton, 'Some Regularities in International Conflict, 1820–1949', p. 294.
52. I. and R. Feierabend, 'Conflict, Crisis and Collusion: a Study of International Stability', *Psychology Today*, vol. 1, no. 12 (May 1968) p. 70.
54. J. Wilkenfeld, 'Domestic and Foreign Conflict Behavior of Nations', *Journal of Peace Research*, vol. 5 (1968) pp. 56–69. See also J. Wilkenfeld, 'Some Further Findings Regarding the Domestic and Foreign Conflict Behavior of Nations', *Journal of Peace Research*, vol. 6 (1969) pp. 147–56. Wilkenfeld develops his viewpoint in the introduction to *Conflict Behavior and Linkage Politics* (New York: David McKay, 1973).
55. The original study from which Wilkenfeld derived his groupings gave four such classes–polyarchic, elitist, centrist and personalist. Countries in each group possess similar political attributes. To keep the state base of the studies consistent, he collapsed these categories into three. See A. Banks and P. Gregg, 'Grouping Political Systems', *The American Behavioral Scientist*, vol. 9 (Nov 1965) pp. 3–6.
56. Wilkenfeld, 'Domestic and Foreign Conflict Behavior', table 2, p. 59.
57. Haas, 'Societal Approaches to the Study of War'.
58. Ibid. p. 312.
59. Ibid. p. 313. Compare the Zinnes interpretation of the Haas results, 'Some Evidence Relevant to the Man–Milieu Hypotheses', pp. 233–4.
60. Rummel, 'The Relationship Between National Attributes and Foreign Conflict Behavior', p. 207.
61. Ibid. pp. 204–5.
62. Zinnes, 'Some Evidence Relevant to the Man–Milieu Hypotheses', p. 231.
63. Haas, 'Societal Approaches to the Study of War', p. 313.
64. Ibid. p. 314.
65. M. Haas, 'Social Change and National Aggressiveness, 1900–1960', in *Quantitative International Politics*, ed. J. Singer (New York: Free Press, 1968) p. 244. For a discussion of development strategies as such and their conflict consequences see M. Haas, 'Societal Development and International Conflict', in *Conflict Behavior and Linkage Politics*, ed. J. Wilkenfeld (New York: David McKay, 1973).
66. Haas, 'Societal Approaches to the Study of War', p. 314.
67. Ibid. p. 315.
68. Ibid.
69. Rummel, 'Testing Some Possible Predictors of Conflict Behavior Within and Between Nations'.
70. Singer, 'The "Correlates of War" Project'.
71. Ibid. p. 267.

72. N. Choucri and J. Bennett, 'Population, Resources and Technology', *International Organization*, vol. 26 (1972) pp. 175–212.
73. N. Choucri and R. North, 'Dynamics of International Conflict', *World Politics*, vol. 24 (Spring 1972) pp. 80–122.
74. Haas, 'Societal Approaches to the Study of War', p. 319.
75. Haas, 'Social Change and National Aggressiveness, 1900–1960'.
76. Haas, 'Sources of International Conflict', p. 264.
77. Haas, 'Social Change and National Aggressiveness, 1900–1960', p. 243.
78. Rummel, 'The Relationship Between National Attributes and Foreign Conflict Behavior', pp. 212–13.
79. Ibid. p. 208.
80. Singer, 'The "Correlates of War" Project', p. 267.
81. Singer and Small,' Patterns in International Warfare, 1816–1965', p. 151.
82. Rummel, 'The Relationship Between National Attributes and Foreign Conflict Behavior', pp. 210–11, 211–12, 209–10.
83. L. Richardson, *Statistics of Deadly Quarrels* (Pittsburgh: Boxwood Press, 1960) p. 176. Corroborated by J. Wesley, 'Frequency of Wars and Geographical Opportunity', in *Theory and Research on the Causes of War*, ed. D. Pruitt and R. Snyder (New Jersey: Prentice-Hall, 1969).
84. Richardson, ibid. pp. 176, 198.
85. Haas, 'Sources of International Conflict', p. 264.
86. Ibid. pp. 264–5.
87. Rummel, 'The Relationship Between National Attributes and Foreign Conflict Behavior', p. 214.
88. Rummel, 'Some Empirical Findings on Nations and Their Behavior', *World Politics*, vol. 21, no. 2 (Jan 1969) p. 238.
89. Ibid.
90. Ibid. p. 239.
91. Richardson, *Statistics of Deadly Quarrels*, p. 206.
92. Ibid. 'There were more wars between Christians and Moslems than would be expected from their populations, if religious differences had not tended to instigate quarrels between them', p. 245; and '. . . the associates of Chinese were on the whole pacificatory, and the associates of Spanish were on the whole bellicose, during the years A.D. 1820 to 1929', p. 230.
93. B. Russett, *International Regions and the International System* (Chicago: Rand McNally, 1967) pp. 198–9.
94. Ibid. p. 202.
95. Rummel, 'The Relationship Between National Attributes and Foreign Conflict Behavior', pp. 206–7, 205–6.
96. Richardson, *Statistics of Deadly Quarrels*, pp. 194–7.
97. J. D. Singer and M. Small, 'Alliance Aggregation and the Onset of War, 1815–1945', in *Quantitative International Politics*, ed. J. D. Singer, (New York: Free Press, 1968).
98. Haas, 'Sources of International Conflict', p. 272.

99. M. Kaplan, 'Variants on Six Models of the International System', in *International Politics and Foreign Policy*, ed. Rosenau, p. 300.
100. Rosecrance, *Action and Reaction in World Politics*.
101. K. Deutsch and J. D. Singer, 'Multipolar Power Systems and International Stability', in *International Politics and Foreign Policy*, ed. Rosenau.
102. Ibid. p. 324.
103. J. Singer and M. Small, 'Alliance Aggregation and the Onset of War, 1815–1945', in *Quantitative International Politics*, ed. Singer, p. 283.
104. K. Waltz, 'International Structure, National Force, and the Balance of World Power', in *International Politics and Foreign Policy*, ed. Rosenau.
105. R. Rosecrance, 'Bipolarity, Multipolarity, and the Future', in *International Politics and Foreign Policy*, ed. Rosenau.
106. M. Haas, 'International Subsystems: Stability and Polarity', *American Political Science Review*, vol. 64, no. 1 (Mar 1970) pp. 98–123.
107. Ibid. p. 121.
108. J. Singer and M. Wallace, 'Inter-governmental Organisation and the Preservation of Peace, 1816–1965: Some Bivariate Relationships', *International Organization*, vol. 24 (1970) pp. 520–47; and the critique by S. Bleicher, 'Intergovernmental Organisation and the Preservation of Peace', *International Organization*, vol. 25 (1971) pp. 298–305.
109. Singer, 'The "Correlates of War" Project', p. 266.
110. Singer and Small, 'Alliance Aggregation and the Onset of War, 1815–1945', in *Quantitative International Politics*, ed. Singer, p. 283.
111. J. Galtung, 'A Structural Theory of Aggression', *Journal of Peace Research*, vol. 1 (1964) pp. 95–119.
112. Ibid. p. 96.
113. Ibid. p. 113.
114. This is the Lowenthal thesis. See R. Lowenthal, 'Communist China's Foreign Policy', in *China in Crisis*, ed. Ping-ti Ho and Tang Tsou, vol. 2 (University of Chicago Press, 1968) p. 1. Presumably China's eventual admission to the United Nations defused such a potentially conflictful status, though there is no evidence before it, despite Galtung's general argument, of tensions in Peking of the sort he predicts.
115. J. Galtung, 'East–West Interaction Patterns', *Journal of Peace Research*, vol. 3 (1966) pp. 146–77.
116. Ibid. p. 146.
117. Ibid. p. 149.
118. Ibid. p. 168.
119. Ibid. p. 172.
120. Singer, 'The "Correlates of War" Project', p. 267.
121. M. Wallace, 'Power, Status and International War', *Journal of Peace Research*, vol. 8 (1971) pp. 23–35.
122. M. East, 'Status Discrepancy and Violence in the International System', in *The Analysis of International Politics*, ed. Rosenau *et al.*
123. L. Richardson, *Arms and Insecurity* (Pittsburgh: Boxwood Press, 1960). See also A. Rapoport, 'Lewis F. Richardson's Mathematical Theory of War', *Journal of Conflict Resolution*, vol. 1, no. 3 (1957) pp. 249–99; and

K. Boulding, *Conflict and Defense* (New York: Harper Torchbooks, 1963) ch.2.

124. P. Smoker, 'A Mathematical Study of the Present Arms Race', and 'A Pilot Study of the Present Arms Race', *General Systems Yearbook*, no. 8 (1963) pp. 51–9 and 61–75. See also N. Alcock and K. Lowe, 'The Vietnam War as a Richardson Process', *Journal of Peace Research*, vol. 6 (1969) pp. 105–11.
125. A useful introductory statement is given by B. Carroll, 'War Termination and Conflict Theory: Value Premises, Theories, and Policies', *The Annals of the American Academy of Political and Social Science*, no. 392 (1970) pp. 14–29; and 'How Wars End: an Analysis of Some Current Hypotheses', *Journal of Peace Research*, vol. 6 (1969) pp. 295–321.
126. K. Boulding, *Conflict and Defense* (New York: Harper & Row, 1963) p. 305.
127. L. Coser, *The Functions of Social Conflict* (London: Routledge & Kegan Paul, 1956).
128. *Report from Iron Mountain on the Possibility and Desirability of Peace* (Harmondsworth: Penguin, 1968) p. 111.
129. J. Galtung, 'Institutionalised Conflict Resolution', *Journal of Peace Research*, vol. 2 (1965) p. 350.
130. Young, *The Intellectual Bases of Conflict Management*, p. 7.
131. Boulding, *Conflict and Defense*, p. 309.
132. Ibid. p. 308.
133. Galtung, 'Institutionalised Conflict Resolution', p. 351.
134. Ibid. pp. 353–4.
135. Ibid. pp. 358–60.
136. J. Burton, *Conflict and Communication* (London: Macmillan, 1969).
137. This notion is elaborated by C. Mitchell, 'Conflict Resolution and Controlled Communication: some Further Comments', *Journal of Peace Research*, vol. 10 (1973) pp. 128–9.
138. Ibid. p. 223.
139. Young, *The Intellectual Bases of Conflict Management*, n. 19, p. 11. See also R. Yalem 'Controlled Communication and Conflict Resolution', *Journal of Peace Research*, vol. 8 (1971) pp. 263–72.
140. Galtung, 'Institutionalised Conflict Resolution', p. 381.
141. Young, *The Intellectual Bases of Conflict Management*, p. 14.
142. For one traditional and conservative answer, see H. Bull, 'Order vs. Justice in International Society', *Political Studies*, vol. 19, no. 3 (1971) pp. 269–83.
143. R. Jenkins, 'Peace Research: a Perspective', *Political Studies*, vol. 17, no. 3 (1969) pp. 348–56.
144. M. Stohl and M. Chamberlain, 'Alternative Futures for Peace Research', *Journal of Conflict Resolution*, vol. 16, no. 4 (Dec 1972) p. 526.
145. Jenkins, 'Peace Research', p. 353.
146. J. Galtung, 'Editorial', *Journal of Peace Research*, vol. 1 (1964) p. 2.
147. See on this last question, C. Bell, *The Conventions of Crisis* (Oxford University Press, 1971).
148. Jenkins, 'Peace Research', p. 353.

149. Galtung, 'Editorial', p. 2.
150. J. Galtung, 'Violence, Peace and Peace Research', *Journal of Peace Research*, vol. 6 (1968) pp. 189–90, n. 31.
151. H. Schmid, 'Peace Research and Politics', *Journal of Peace Research*, vol. 5 (1968) p. 221.
152. Ibid. p. 229.
153. Ibid. p. 219.
154. Jean-Pierre Derriennic, 'Theory and Ideologies of Violence', *Journal of Peace Research*, vol. 9 (1972) p. 363.
155. B. Carroll, 'Peace Research: the Cult of Power', *Journal of Conflict Resolution*, vol. 16, no. 4 (Dec 1972) p. 614.
156. Ibid. pp. 608–14.
157. Ibid. p. 609.

CHAPTER 11

1. Cf. for example, the conclusion of J. Galtung's 'A Structural Theory of Integration', *Journal of Peace Research*, vol. 5 (1968) pp. 375–95.
2. M. Banks, 'Systems Analysis and the Study of Regions', *International Studies Quarterly*, vol. 13, no. 4 (Dec 1969) p. 337.
3. E. Haas, 'The Study of Regional Integration: Reflections on the Joy and Anguish of Pre-theorising', *International Organization*, vol. 24 (1970) p. 608.
4. K. Deutsch *et al.*, *Political Community and the North Atlantic Area* (New Jersey: Princeton University Press, 1968) p. 5.
5. For the area of difference, see ibid. p. 7.
6. J. Nye, 'Comparative Regional Integration: Concept and Measurement', *International Organization*, vol. 22 (1968) pp. 855–80.
7. Haas comments critically on this attempt at conceptual disaggregation in 'The Study of Regional Integration', p. 632, n. 31. See also L. Lindberg, 'Political Integration as a Multi-dimensional Phenomenon Requiring Multi-variate Measurement', *International Organization*, vol. 24 (1970) pp. 649–732.
8. E. Morse, 'Transnational Economic Processes', *International Organization*, vol. 25 (1971) p. 382.
9. The direct function whereby intra-state interdependence leads to interstate interdependence is part of the general argument that the same international activity will have increasingly important implications as domestic society becomes more integrated. This sensitivity is observed in the economic sphere where the same amount of foreign trade, for example, has more significant consequences for internal tax, welfare, and employment policies where the state concerned is more amalgamated. The effect is not too obvious socially, culturally, or politically, but it is probably there none the less. See E. Morse, 'The Transformation of Foreign Policies: Modernisation, Interdependence and Externalisation', *World Politics*, vol. 22, no. 3 (Apr 1970) p. 389.

10. Karl Deutsch has taken a somewhat isolated stand on this issue, but even he does not argue that there has been an absolute *fall* in interdependence. See his: 'The Impact of Communications upon International Relations Theory' in *Theory of International Relations*, ed. A. Said (New Jersey: Prentice-Hall, 1968) ch. 5. Also R. Rosecrance and M. Stein 'Interdependence: Myth or Reality?' *World Politics*, vol. 26, no. 1 (Oct 1973) pp. 1–27.
11. See O. Young, 'Interdependencies in World Politics', *International Journal*, vol. 24, no. 4 (Autumn 1969) pp. 730–4, for his convincing critique of Deutsch's empirical efforts to this end.
12. For a typical list see ibid. pp. 734–40.
13. 'In short, interdependence among countries is spectacularly lower than interdependence within countries.' Deutsch, 'The Impact of Communications', in *Theory of International Relations*, ed. Said, p. 89.
14. Rosenau, *Linkage Politics*, p. 47.
15. J. Herz, 'The Territorial State Revisited: Reflections on the Future of the Nation-state' in *International Politics and Foreign Policy*, ed. Rosenau. Also R. Gilpin, 'The Politics of Transnational Economic Relations', *International Organization*, vol. 25 (1971) pp. 398–419.
16. A point developed by A. Scott in *The Revolution in Statecraft* (New York: Random House, 1965), and *The Functioning of the International Political System* (London: Collier-Macmillan, 1967) ch. 13.
17. J. Nye and R. Keohane, 'Transnational Relations and World Politics: an Introduction', *International Organization*, vol. 25 (1971) p. 331.
18. The special issue of *International Organization* in which the Nye and Keohane article above appeared. Also K. Kaiser, 'Transnational Politics: Toward a Theory of Multi-national Politics', *International Organization*, vol. 25 (1971) pp. 790–817, though this author suffers from skewed perspectives of a Cold War–Defence of Democracy kind.
19. Nye and Keohane, 'Transnational Politics', pp. 330–1.
20. Morse, 'Transnational Economic Processes', p. 380.
21. K. Waltz, 'The Myth of National Interdependence', in *The International Corporation: a Symposium*, ed. C. Kindleberger (Cambridge, Mass.: M.I.T. Press, 1970).
22. P. Taylor, 'The Functionalist Approach to the Problem of International order: a Defense', *Political Studies*, vol. 16, no. 3 (1968) pp. 395–6, 401.
23. Particularly E. Haas, *The Uniting of Europe* (Stanford University Press, 1968).
24. Taylor, 'The Functionalist Approach', p. 408.
25. Banks, 'Systems Analysis and the Study of Regions', p. 344.
26. E. Haas and P. Schmitter, 'Economics and Differential Patterns of Political Integration: Projections About Unity in Latin America', *International Organization*, vol. 18 (1964) pp. 705–37.
27. Haas and Schmitter, 'Economics and Differential Patterns', pp. 711–16. See also M. Barrera and E. Haas, 'The Operationalisation of Some Variables Related to Regional Integration', *International Organization*, vol. 23 (1969) p. 151. Cf. E. Haas 'International Integration: The

European and the Universal Process', in *International Political Communities* (New York: Doubleday, 1966).

28. Haas and Schmitter, 'Economics and Differential Patterns', p. 716.
29. P. Schmitter, 'Three Neo-functional Hypotheses about International Integration', *International Organization*, vol. 23 (1969) p. 162.
30. P. Katzenstein, 'Hare and Tortoise: The Race Toward Integration', *International Organization*, vol. 25 (1971) p. 291.
31. Barrera and Haas, 'The Operationalisation of Some Variables'; P. Schmitter, 'Further Notes on Operationalizing Some Variables Related to Regional Integration', *International Organization*, vol. 23 (1969) pp. 327–36; K. Harmon, 'The Schmitter Operationalisation of the Size–Power Variable', *International Organization*, vol. 26 (1972) pp. 136–42.
32. Haas, 'The Study of Regional Integration', p. 632.
33. Ibid. p. 638, n. 34.
34. Ibid. p. 615.
35. Schmitter, 'Three Non-Functional Hypotheses', p. 162.
36. Haas, 'The Study of Regional Integration', p. 643.
37. J. Nye, 'Patterns and Catalysts in Regional Integration', *International Organization*, vol. 19 (1965) pp. 870–84.
38. Ibid. p. 881.
39. R. Hansen, 'Regional Integration: Reflections on a Decade of Theoretical Efforts', *World Politics*, vol. 21, no. 2 (Jan 1969) pp. 242–71.
40. S. Hoffmann, 'Obstinate or Obsolete? – The Fate of the Nation-state and the Case of Western Europe', *Daedalus*, vol. 95, no. 3 (Summer 1966) pp. 862–915.
41. Nye, 'Patterns and Catalysts in Regional Integration', p. 872.
42. Haas, 'The Study of Regional Integration', pp. 641–2.
43. Ibid. p. 619, n. 18.
44. C. Ake, *A Theory of Political Integration* (Illinois: Dorsey Press, 1967) pp. 8–11; and P. Jacob and J. Toscano (eds), *The Integration of Political Communities* (Philadelphia: Lippincott, 1964) pp. 16–44.
45. Deutsch *et al.*, *Political Community*, p. 58, also pp. 123–54.
46. Schmitter, 'Three Neo-functional Hypotheses', p. 161.
47. Haas, 'The Study of Regional Integration', p. 626.
48. Katzenstein, 'Hare and Tortoise', p. 291.
49. W. Fisher, 'An Analysis of the Deutsch Socio-causal Paradigm of Political Integration', *International Organization*, vol. 23 (1969) pp. 254–90.
50. Deutsch *et al.*, *Political Community*, pp. 7–8, 71.
51. K. Deutsch, *The Nerves of Government* (New York: Free Press, 1966) p. 150.
52. Deutsch *et al.*, *Political Community*, ch. 3: 'The Integrative Process'. Also K. Deutsch, *The Analysis of International Relations* (New Jersey: Prentice-Hall, 1969) p. 196.
53. Deutsch *et al.*, *Political Community*, pp. 38, 72.
54. Ibid. p. 71.

55. Ibid. p. 87.
56. Deutsch, *The Analysis of International Relations*, p. 200.
57. Deutsch *et al.*, *Political Community*, pp. 85–6.
58. Deutsch, *The Analysis of International Relations*, p. 198.
59. Fisher, 'An Analysis of the Deutsch Socio-causal Paradigm'.
60. Ibid. pp. 288–9. See, however, the reservations about Fisher's results expressed by J. Caporaso, 'Fisher's Test of Deutsch's Socio-causal Paradigm of Political Integration', *International Organization*, vol. 25 (1971) pp. 120–31.
61. Young, 'Interdependencies in World Politics', pp. 731, 733.
62. Haas, 'The Study of Regional Integration', p. 627.
63. Numerous studies by A. Etzioni, while a conspicuous analytic and empirical contribution to the integration literature, contain very little that is not implicit in the two dominant approaches already outlined. I have not given them separate treatment here, but see his articles in *International Political Communities* and also 'The Epigenesis of Political Communities at the International Level', in *International Politics and Foreign Policy*, ed. Rosenau.
64. B. Russett, *International Regions and the International System* (Chicago: Rand McNally, 1967).
65. Ibid. p. 11.
66. Ibid. p. 206.
67. O. Young, 'Professor Russett: Industrious Tailor to a Naked Emperor', *World Politics*, vol. 21, no. 3 (Apr 1969) pp. 486–511.
68. Russett, *International Regions*, p. 206.
69. B. Russett, 'The Young Science of International Politics', *World Politics*, vol. 22, no. 1 (Oct 1969) pp. 87–94.
70. See Haas, 'The Study of Regional Integration', pp. 613–21.
71. Ibid. p. 615.
72. Ibid. p. 616.
73. Ibid. pp. 616–17.
74. Ibid. p. 620.
75. Russett, *International Regions*, p. 221.

CHAPTER 12

1. J. Rosenau, 'Theorizing Across Systems: Linkage Politics Revisited', in *Conflict Behavior and Linkage Politics*, ed. J. Wilkenfeld (New York: McKay, 1973) p. 53.
2. Ibid. p. 55.
3. In particular, J. Rosenau, *The Adaptation of National Societies: a Theory of Political System Behavior and Transformation* (New York: McCaleb-Seiler, 1970).
4. J. Rosenau, 'Foreign Policy as Adaptive Behavior', *Comparative Politics*, vol. 2, no. 3 (Apr 1970) p. 367.
5. H. Morgenthau, *Politics Among Nations*, 3rd ed. (New York: Knopf, 1966) p. 5.

6. Ibid. p. 15.
7. E. H. Carr, *The Twenty Years' Crisis* (London: Macmillan, 1962) p. 236.
8. C. McClelland, *Theory and the International System* (New York: Macmillan, 1966) p. 84.
9. H. G. Wells, *Tono-Bungay* (London: Macmillan, 1909) p. 493.

Index